Urban Workers
and
Labor Unions in Chile
1902-1927

During the first quarter of the twentieth century, there originated in Chile a labor movement which was to prove both important and unique. Peter DeShazo sets out here to furnish a detailed case study of that movement. By challenging previously held and often politically motivated conceptions of the Chilean unions, and by examining such hitherto unexplored sources as government documents and labor newspapers, he is able to illuminate the origins and development of an often successful and surprisingly autonomous labor campaign. Students and scholars of Latin America, labor history, comparative social movements, and political science will find the resultant pathbreaking study of the Chilean working class and its progressive mobilization valuable reading.

Urban Workers
and
Labor Unions in Chile
1902-1927

Peter DeShazo

THE UNIVERSITY OF WISCONSIN PRESS

Published 1983

The University of Wisconsin Press
114 North Murray Street
Madison, Wisconsin 53715

The University of Wisconsin Press, Ltd.
1 Gower Street
London WC1E 6HA, England

First printing

Printed in the United States of America

For LC CIP information see the colophon

ISBN 0-229-09220-8

For my Mother and to the memory of my Father

Contents

Illustrations

Tables

Acknowledgments

I am deeply grateful to the many people who helped me with this study and wish to thank them.

Field research was carried out in the Netherlands, England, and Chile during 1974 and 1975 thanks to a grant from the Fulbright-Hayes Commission. Thea Duijker of the Internationaal Instituut voor Sociale Geschiedenis was generous with her time during my stay in Amsterdam. I am especially indebted to my friends María Saavedra, director of the Archive of the Dirección General del Trabajo, and Francisco Benimelli, head of the periodicals section of the Biblioteca Nacional in Santiago. The late Patricio Estellé extended me valuable privileges when he directed the Archivo Nacional de Chile. I would also like to thank the staffs of the above-mentioned institutions, as well as those of the Public Record Office, London, the Library of the Instituto Nacional de Estadísticas and Sociedad de Fomento Fabril, Santiago, the Library of Congress in Washington, and the Memorial Library of the University of Wisconsin–Madison.

Thomas E. Skidmore gave me very valuable and appreciated assistance at every stage of the study: planning, funding, research, writing, and preparation of the manuscript for publication. Peter H. Smith, Richard U. Miller, Paul W. Drake, and Richard J. Walter all made insightful comments which improved the study.

Others contributed their help, including: Clotario Blest, Priscilla Grand, Bob Halstead, Luis Heredia, Gonzalo Izquierdo, Félix López, Luis Miranda, Augustín Pepay, Olga Pérez, Daniel Schweitzer, Larry Stickell, and Nene Vega.

All conclusions drawn in this history are my responsibility, as are the blemishes and shortcomings it contains.

Most of all, I am grateful to my wife, Mary Zahradnik, for her moral and intellectual support during many years of research and writing. Whatever may be useful and positive in this study owes much to her.

Medellín, Colombia
December, 1981

Glossary of Spanish Terms

albergue: a hostel used to house unemployed workers during periods of unemployment.

bajo pueblo: the "lowest class" in the urban population.

carabinero: a national policeman recruited from the ranks of ex-soldiers and generally stationed in rural areas.

caudillo: a personalistic leader or political boss.

cohecho: the system of buying and selling votes prevalent during the Parliamentary Republic in Chile.

comuna: an urban precinct or ward.

concejo: a "council," the basic organizational unit of the Chilean Workers' Federation (FOCh).

conventillo: a tenement house.

empleado: a white collar worker or "employee".

fochista: a member of the Chilean Workers' Federation (FOCh).

gañan: an unskilled, often itinerant laborer.

golpe: a blow; a coup d'etat.

gremio: a craft union or professional society.

jornalero: a day laborer.

lancha-lanchero: a lighter; a lighterman.

maestranza: a workshop; mentioned in this study in connection with the metal trades or the State Railways.

mancomunal: a labor "brotherhood," an important form of working class organization in Chile between 1900 and 1907.

obrero: a blue collar worker.

oficina: a nitrate mining operation.

pampa: the interior desert of the Great North in Chile where the nitrate fields were located.

patrón: an employer or boss.

peón: an unskilled worker or laborer.

porteño: a resident of Valparaíso, the "port" city.

pueblo: the people, the working class.

redondilla: a "turn" system of labor recruitment and use prevalent among maritime workers in the early 1920s.

roto: an unskilled, uneducated rural worker or recent migrant to the city or mine.

salitre: nitrates; saltpeter.

santiaguino: a resident of Santiago.

sindicato: a labor union.

socio: a "member," in this case of a labor union or mutual aid society.

sociedad de resistencia: a "resistance society" labor union, normally of Anarcho-Syndicalist orientation.

socorro mutuo: a mutual aid society.

trabajador: a blue collar worker.

Wobbly: a member of the Industrial Workers of the World (IWW). An English term also used in Chile at the time.

Abbreviations

AOAN	Asamblea Obrera de Alimentación Nacional
CSAV	Compañía Sud Americana de Vapores
DGT	Dirección General del Trabajo
FECh	Federación de Estudiantes de Chile
FOCh	Federación Obrera de Chile
FOI(Ch)	Federación de Obreros de Imprenta (de Chile)
FOOC	Federación de Obreros y Obreras en Calzado (also called FZA, UIC)
FORCh	Federación Obrera Regional Chilena
FTCh	Federación de Trabajadores en Chile
FZA	Federación de Zapateros y Aparadoras (also called FOOC, UIC)
IWMA	International Working Men's Association
IWW	Industrial Workers of the World
OT	Oficina del Trabajo
PC	Partido Comunista de Chile
PD	Partido Demócrata
POS	Partido Obrero Socialista
PSNC	Pacific Steam Navigation Company
RILU	Red International of Labor Unions
SOFOFA	Sociedad de Fomento Fabril
UECh	Unión de Empleados de Chile
UIC	Unión Industrial del Cuero (also called FZA, FOOC)
USP	Unión Sindical de Panaderos
USRACh	Unión Social Republicana de Asalariados de Chile

Introduction

THIS IS A STUDY of working people in the cities of Santiago and Valparaíso and the labor unions they created. It begins with the first recorded strike of a "resistance society" (*sociedad de resistencia*) in 1902 and ends with the repression of the organized labor movement by Carlos Ibáñez in 1927.

Chile underwent fundamental and far-reaching changes during the quarter-century in question. Economic life was dominated by the nitrate industry during the entire period, so that major fluctuations in the production and export of that mineral resulted in a series of boom and bust cycles after 1914. Domestic manufacturing, coal extraction, the extension of transportation facilities, and construction and public works projects all depended to a significant degree on the ability of the nitrate industry to generate income for the national government through a tax on mineral exports, employ a large labor force, and maintain a high capacity to import needed capital goods. Crises in the nitrate industry caused by the sudden loss of foreign markets rebounded through the economy in 1914, 1919, and 1921, causing widespread unemployment and privation for the Chilean middle and working classes. Price inflation was a built-in factor of the Chilean economy during the 1902–27 period, adding to the woes of the wage earner. By 1927, the era of the nitrate economy had almost ended. The industry would experience its last spurt of prosperity in 1928–29 and then fall victim to the Great Depression of 1930.

Economic growth in the early twentieth century stimulated increased migration by rural people to the cities of Santiago, Valparaíso, and the North, where new jobs opened up in occupations paying many times the salary offered to farm laborers. The percentage of Chileans living in towns and cities therefore rose rapidly, and Santiago took its place as an important urban center. Migrants from the countryside and small towns quickly adapted to life in the Capital as they formed the basis of a new urban working class.

Contortions of the economy and urbanization put pressure on the "Parliamentary Republic," Chile's political system established in 1891 after a bloody civil war. An oligarchy of large landowners, financiers, mine owners, and big businessmen controlled political life through their traditional parties, of which the two most important were the Conservative and Liberal. Under the Parliamentary Republic, Congress exercised effective power and the President of the Republic enjoyed very limited influence. Control of Congress, often achieved by joining together the large and small parties and their splinter groups into coalitions, was the key to success. Legislation limited the suffrage to literate adult males, thereby disenfranchising the mass of rural workers and part of the urban working class. The oligarchic parties frequently bought the votes of eligible workers in a process called the *cohecho,* converting presidential and parliamentary elections into carnivals of corruption.

The system functioned more or less smoothly until menaced by middle class frustration and growing labor unrest after 1917. Desire for socioeconomic change far outstripped the ability of Chilean elites to reform the system or even to repress those who threatened it. A military coup saved the Parliamentary Republic from self-destruction in September, 1924, and the new constitution of 1925, drafted in a climate of extreme social tension, cut deeply into the traditional influence of the oligarchic parties by endowing the Presidency with great power at the expense of Congress.

The years 1902–27 witnessed a dramatic change in the power and influence of the Chilean working class. Organized labor rose from near insignificance at the beginning of the period to become a challenger for economic and political power. Heated conflict between employers and workers forged a laissez-faire system of industrial relations during these years, one which stimulated the growth of independent, radicalized labor unions capable of unleashing waves of strikes and disrupting the established order. Elites finally moved to limit labor's independence in 1924 with a series of laws intended to subjugate unions to employers and the state. These labor laws, the first of their kind in Latin America, laid the basis for a system of industrial relations during the 1930s in which electoral politics and association with left-wing political parties, rather than collective bargaining with employers, became major labor union interests.

This study focuses attention on workers and unions in the central cities for several reasons. Santiago and Valparaíso were interdependent financially and economically during the period. The port of Valparaíso was the way station for goods and persons entering Santiago or leaving for abroad or for the nitrate zone in the North. Communication between the two cities was good by the standards of the day. Together, Santiago and Valparaíso contained a majority of Chile's industrial workers and manufacturing establishments during the first quarter of the twentieth century, and the most successful labor unions took root there. Workers in the central cities led the nation in strikes and most effectively shook the socioeconomic foundations of oligarchic society. The urban environment of Santiago and Valparaíso also nurtured an Anarcho-Syndicalist movement which proved to be the most dynamic force in organizing Chilean workers throughout the country.

Urban workers and working class organizations exercised greater influence over elite behavior than did those in the North or South because of the demonstration effect. Chilean political leaders lived in Santiago and could personally witness labor rallies, May 1 demonstrations, and riots, and could measure the effect of strikes. Major outbursts of violence and strikes in Valparaíso sent immediate shock waves to Santiago as well, due to the proximity of the Port to the Capital and their economic interdependence. All but the most prolonged, violent, and important strikes in other parts of the country would go comparatively unnoticed. Elites often got word of the gravity of disorder in the North and South only after bloodshed had occurred and the situation had been "normalized" by repression. Labor's efforts in Santiago and Valparaíso therefore had greater impact. This was borne out on numerous occasions. The Valparaíso riot of 1903 led to the immediate introduction of "Sunday rest" legislation in Congress, which was not passed until just after the June, 1907 general strike in Santiago. Suspension of an unpopular tax on imported Argentine beef came on the eve of a major protest rally in Santiago in December, 1907. The Subercaseaux Residence Law designed to curb "subversion" in the labor movement was introduced in Congress in July, 1912, immediately following successful May 1 demonstrations and a terrorist incident in Santiago and a general strike in Valparaíso in June. The Jaramillo Residence Law reached Congress during the 1917 general strike in Valparaíso and was passed in November, 1918, following a massive labor rally in Santiago. The list of such cause and effect relationships is long, and clearly demonstrates that elites introduced and passed legislation regarding the working class in reaction to events taking place in the central cities.

Readers familiar with the historiography of the Chilean labor movement will find that the conclusions reached in this study run counter to most previous interpretations. A compilation of the literature would produce the following standard description of labor history in the early twentieth century.[1] Nitrates fueled the Chilean economy from the 1880s on, and the labor movement accordingly developed in the nitrate zone of the Great North. Nitrate workers, radicalized by harsh working conditions and exploitation in an industry controlled to a large degree by British capital, placed themselves in the vanguard of the labor movement by organizing combative unions. In the first decade of the twentieth century, workers in the nitrate fields and northern ports founded the influential labor "brotherhoods," or *mancomunales,* the most important labor unions in Chile to date. These brotherhoods

xxiii

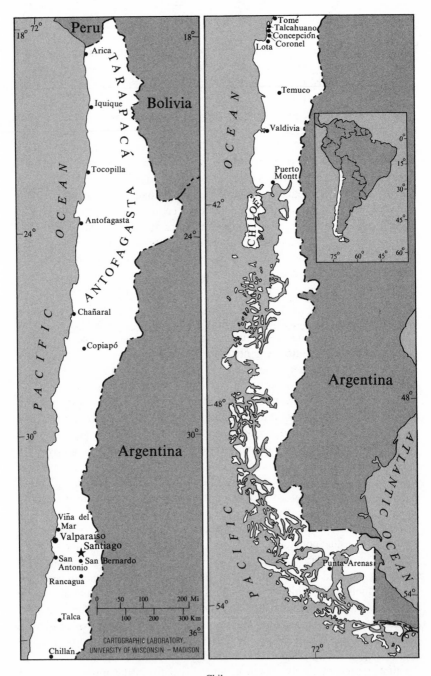

Chile

led a series of strikes in the North which were repressed by the government with great force. In 1909, conservative workers founded the *Gran Federación Obrera de Chile* (FOCh), an organization which would become the labor federation of supreme importance in Chile between 1917 and 1927. Three years later, Socialists dissatisfied with reformist politics took a giant step by forming the Socialist Workers' Party (POS) in Iquique. Under the direction of Luis Emilio Recabarren, who controlled both the POS and the nitrate workers, the FOCh was taken over by Socialist elements and led a great revival of the organized labor movement from 1917 to 1921. This process of radicalization was completed when the POS became the Communist Party of Chile (PC) in January, 1922, and the FOCh joined the Red International of Labor Unions.

According to the standard description, other labor unions existed outside the FOCh. These were generally small trade unions of artisans or skilled workers led by Anarcho-Syndicalists. Their influence was miniscule compared to that of the FOCh and limited only to Santiago and Valparaíso. Immigrant artisans from Europe founded and staffed the Chilean Anarcho-Syndicalist movement, which after 1921 lost even the small influence it once had. By that time, the FOCh contained nearly a hundred thousand members and was continuing to grow, reaching its peak in 1924–25. Recabarren's suicide in December, 1924 deprived the labor movement of its great leader, but the PC continued to expand its role as spokesman for the working class, gaining six seats in the congressional elections of 1925. The labor movement was repressed by Carlos Ibáñez in 1927, but the FOCh and the PC, the key working class forces of the 1920s, were resurrected soon after the dictator fell in 1931, and continued their militant tradition of the earlier decade.

This study reaches conclusions basically different from the above interpretation. It contends that urban workers, especially those of Santiago and Valparaíso, were the driving force of the organized labor movement in early twentieth-century Chile, and that the role of nitrate miners was small by comparison. Despite the predominance of the nitrate industry in the Chilean economy, workers at the production end of the export cycle did not form the vanguard of the working class, but, by all appearances, were better paid in real terms and less inclined to organize labor unions and strike than were their fellow workers in the cities. Other factors, such as the large distances between nitrate oficinas and strict control over the workforce by employers, weakened the labor movement on the nitrate pampa and held down the number of strikes. Labor unions in the cities of the nitrate zone enjoyed far more power and stability than did those formed by miners.

Anarcho-Syndicalists proved to be the most dynamic and successful element in the working class from 1902 to 1927. They led the most strikes, extracted significant concessions from employers, built the most durable labor organizations, and, in historical perspective, pioneered the rise of the labor union movement in Chile. They were the first to organize unions of workers in the leather, baking, construction, coal mining, tramway, metal, maritime, furniture, textile, printing, garment, and tobacco industries. The only significant groups of workers they never organized were those in railroads, communications, metal mining, glass, and beverages. Nor did Chilean Anarchists fit the description painted by many historians. Almost none were foreigners, either at the leadership level or among the rank and file. Chilean Anarchists were workers, not the "artisans," "semiproletarians," or "neobourgeois" types many accused them of being. Some, such as electricians, gas fitters, plasterers, tailors, and printers, had important skills which guaranteed them higher than average wages, while maritime workers, construction laborers, bakers, and shoe factory workers were totally unskilled. The fact that many labor union leaders during the early 1900s came from the skilled trades did not make them any less workers. The impression that the majority of Chilean manufacturing workers toiled in small scale establishments is also false. Most labor union members were engaged in comparatively large-scale production or employed in major transport and construction activities.

The Anarcho-Syndicalist movement in Chile does not merit its consignation to the dust heap of history. As Paul Drake shows in his excellent study of Chilean politics from 1932 to 1952, many Anarchist labor leaders played an important role in forming the Socialist Party in 1933.[2] The presence of an active Anarcho-Syndicalist movement in Chile up to 1927 kept alive antiauthoritarian, anti-Communist, and revolutionary spirit, thereby reserving a place on the left which the Socialist Party would later occupy.

Chilean workers were not dominated by a handful of labor leaders, nor did politicians or other non–working class groups hold leadership positions in the unions during the period. While Recabarren played a major part in establishing the Communist Party and fomenting the spread of Marxist ideology in Chile, his reputation as a union leader is inflated. It cannot be claimed that he organized the FOCh or any other major labor union after 1904. Organized labor in Chile was not manipulated by a few *caudillos* (bosses) before 1927. Just as the labor movement was highly decentralized and regional, so did leadership patterns reflect high rates of turnover and the predominance of leaders whose influence extended no further than one union or one city.

Neither does the FOCh merit its renown as the majority or single national labor union of Chile before 1927. This study will show that the FOCh was regionally, not nationally, based, that Federation membership figures cited in other studies are gross exaggerations, that the organization lost its dynamism as it became more closely linked with the Communist Party, and that the Anarcho-Syndicalists outdistanced the FOCh in effectiveness and zeal.

Politics had lesser bearing on the course of working class history than has been held. The Democratic Party (PD) gave a sizable boost to the organization of the working class before 1907 but after that date lost much of its influence among workers. Most urban workers showed very little interest in either traditional or working class politics until 1925, and membership in the PC remained very small throughout the 1920s. Political action served the working class poorly during the Parliamentary Republic. Traditional parties overwhelmed labor candidates, quickly co-opted reformist parties such as the PD once they demonstrated a significant capacity to attract votes, and showed themselves to be highly unresponsive to labor's demands for socioeconomic change.

These conclusions indicate that the development of the organized labor movement in Chile differed in many ways from that of other Latin American countries in the early twentieth century. Economic growth permitted an industrial working class to take shape in Chile at approximately the same time as in Argentina and Brazil, with the result that workers in these three countries were the first to organize labor unions. Labor organizations of lesser impact also were founded in Mexico, Cuba, and Uruguay in the first decade of the century, while unionization in other Latin American countries did not take place until after World War One or even later.

Anarcho-Syndicalism was the driving force behind the organization of labor in Argentina, Brazil, and Chile from 1900 to 1920.[3] But while the roots of Argentine and Brazilian Anarchism lay in heavy European immigration, especially from countries having significant domestic Anarchist groups, such as Spain and Italy, the growth of Anarchism and labor unions in Chile owed almost nothing to immigrants. The presence in large numbers of immigrant Anarchists gave early impetus to the unionization of Argentine and Brazilian workers but later severely limited organized labor's possibilities for success. While foreigners may have provided unions with effective leadership in the early stages, their extreme antipatriotism and occasional subversive activities invited repression by the state. Chilean Anarchists were more measured in their behavior and did not waste energy on fruitless struggles such as the protest of the Argentine Workers' Federation against the Centennial Celebration in 1910 or the pathetic "revolt" of Anarchists in Rio de Janeiro in November, 1918. Ideology never motivated creole Anarchists in Chile as strongly as it did the foreigners who led the Anarchist federations in Argentina and Brazil. Some Anarchist tactics, such as organizational decentralization, refusal to bargain with the state in labor disputes or submit them to outside arbitration, and boycotting elections, were normally practiced, but Chilean libertarians in general pursued bread-and-butter goals. They did not set themselves up for repression as willingly as did the foreign Anarchists elsewhere in Latin America. Residence laws which permitted the jailing and

xxvii

deportation of "subversive" foreigners were of no service to Chilean elites in stifling organized labor, while in Argentina and especially Brazil, the state used these laws to decapitate major unions. Since Chilean workers spoke the same language, shared the same customs and history, and came from basically the same racial and ethnic stock, employers could not drive a wedge between them as in other countries by playing foreigners against nationals or blacks against whites.

Consequently, the home-grown and more practical nature of Anarcho-Syndicalism in Chile allowed it to maintain its strength until being purged along with all labor unions by Carlos Ibáñez in 1927. Alien-led Anarchist unions in Argentina were played out by 1919, and repression put an end to Anarchist influence in Brazil two years later. Chilean Anarchists, rather than disappearing from the labor scene altogether or becoming Communists as in Brazil, Argentina, and Cuba during the 1920s, remained effective for some years. The survival of Anarcho-Syndicalism in Chile was significant because it forced elites to adopt a formal system of industrial relations, kept alive a spirit of non-Communist yet revolutionary zeal, and provided the Socialist Party of the early 1930s with experienced leaders and labor union militants.

Workers in Chile kept Anarcho-Syndicalism alive as an ideology or tactic longer than did workers in Argentina and Brazil for other reasons as well. The possibility of establishing a working class party capable of effective political action on behalf of labor seemed remote to most Chilean workers, at least before the presidential election of 1925. With the suffrage limited and traditional parties using the cohecho to manipulate working class voters, no labor party could hope to crack the system. Furthermore, the elitist parties approved bits of "social legislation" not in recognition of lobbying efforts by reformist politicians but in response to pressure from the working class in the form of strikes and riots. When it became clear to workers that they could win a shorter workday, lower rents, Sunday rest, and other benefits by directly dealing with employers or landlords rather than seeking legislation, they followed the Anarcho-Syndicalists. It was not until the system for registering voters was reformed in 1924 and major changes in Chilean politics resulted in a clear-cut choice between an oligarch and a bona fide prolabor candidate in the presidential election of 1925 that politics offered anything to Chilean workers. These changes came precisely at the moment when middle class elements sought a common front with workers and the labor laws of 1924 threatened the independence of unions. Many Anarchists may at this time have reconsidered their traditional condemnation of political action.

Argentine workers enjoyed more political options at an earlier date, a fact which in part put the Anarchist movement in that country on a downward trend. The Sáenz Peña Law of 1912, which established universal male suffrage, enfranchised the native working class. This paved the way to limited political success by the reformist Socialist Party of Argentina and, of course, the domination of Argentine politics by the Radical Party in 1916. The opening up of the Argentine political system to the middle classes and workers between 1912 and 1916 had no parallel in Chile and Brazil. Elites in Brazil solved the labor problem not by co-optation but through deportations and repression. Chilean labor unions survived employer opposition and periodic repression by the government to become more committed to revolutionary ideology after 1921.

While the Chilean government on occasion used far greater force to repress strikes and worker protests than was normally employed in Argentina or Brazil, such repression proved to be less effective in the long run because of the structure and tactics of Chilean labor organizations. The extremely decentralized and regionally based Chilean unions could not be eliminated by purging a single institution or party. Because leadership was also decentralized, the state found it difficult to weaken the unions with a few arrests. Furthermore, Chilean elites showed no singleness of mind or will in repressing labor. They toyed with the idea of a residence law for fifteen years before passing one, made halfhearted attempts at enforcing social legislation, and sporadically used brute force to crush strikes but then eased up on the pressure almost immediately. With all parties seeking working class votes in a political system based on tenuous coalitions and alliances subject to frequent change, no political group exercised enough power to bring about the global repression of labor. Violence directed against workers proved embarrassing and politically harmful to those who unleashed it. Laws to preserve freedom of speech and of the press protected working class orators and newspapers, and an independent judicial system made the jailing of union leaders on trumped-up or real charges more difficult than elsewhere in Latin America.

The nature of the labor union movement and the Chilean political system in the early twentieth century assured that workers would play a different role in Chilean than in Argentine and Brazilian society in later years. Political strong men espousing corporatist or populist ideas did not rally labor to their causes in Chile or mobilize the labor movement as an appendage of the state. Ibáñez attempted to create a state-sponsored labor union movement after smashing the independent federations in 1927 but failed to generate any significant following. Authoritarian politicians such as Getulio Vargas in Brazil and Juan Domingo Perón in Argentina, however, based their power to a large degree on labor unions they mobilized for political action and controlled. The number of organized workers did expand dramatically in Chile during the 1930s, but with the leftist political parties, not military men or populist caudillos, leading the way. Labor remained independent of state domination, although the application of the labor laws of 1924 eventually limited the role of labor unions as economic entities. By the late 1930s the leftist political connections of most Chilean unions became well established, and they would remain basically unshaken up to the fall of Salvador Allende's Popular Unity government in 1973.

In other ways, the early development of the labor movement in Chile was similar to that in Argentina and Brazil. All three, as we have already seen, had strong Anarcho-Syndicalist leanings during the first two decades of the century. Unions of transport, maritime, construction, and manufacturing workers in major cities were strongest in all three Latin American countries. Organized labor in Argentina was concentrated in Buenos Aires and (to a lesser degree) Rosario, while Rio, São Paulo, and Santos were centers of working class strength in Brazil. Santiago, Valparaíso, Iquique, Antofagasta, and Concepción had the greatest concentration of labor unions in Chile. In none of these cases did workers engaged in the production of a key export product (nitrates, coffee, meat) form labor unions of great influence. To a certain extent, workers in the nitrate ports of Chile lived and labored in an export enclave environment, but the majority of organized workers in all three countries were not exculsively involved in handling an export product.

Labor union activity came in spurts in Chile, Argentina, and Brazil. Unions rose in membership and carried out strike waves during 1905–7 and 1917–20, as the export-based economies of all three countries marched in lockstep to fluctuations in world demand for primary products. Internal inflation followed similar patterns, spurring workers on to form unions and go on strike. Repression by the state and the establishment of employer associations paralleled labor mobilization and strike activity in all three cases.

Unlike past histories of working class organizations in Chile and most work done on labor in Latin America, this study in intended to provide a "bottom-up" view of industrial relations in Chile by focusing attention on workers and their unions rather than on politics. It is, accordingly, divided into two parts, the first dealing with work and working class conditions in the central cities and the second a chronological discussion of labor unions and other worker organizations from 1902 to 1927. Part 1 will show how the nature of industrialization in Chile, the distribution of the workforce by industry and sex, job skills, inflation, housing, alcoholism, and many other factors influenced working class behavior and the growth of labor unions. The second part breaks down labor union development into five periods set apart by major fluctuations in the Chilean economy and trends in the intensity of working class activity rather than by single events. The decentralized Chilean labor movement before 1927 requires a study based less on institutions than on masses of workers—more on working class action than on the ideological proclamations of labor unions and political parties.

A statistical analysis of the 380 strikes which took place in Valparaíso and Santiago in 1902–8, 1917–21, and 1925, periods which encompassed the three major strike waves of the quarter century, is an important part of this study. Since strikes were the principal form of economic action taken by the organized working class, a detailed account of how they began, were carried out, and were brought to an end tells much about workers and their unions. This evaluation of the course of strikes conveys a broader impression of the laissez-faire system of industrial relations which existed in Chile before 1927.

A definition of terms is in order. "Urban" refers to the cities of Santiago and Valparaíso unless otherwise stated. When references are made to the larger departments and provinces of Santiago and Valparaíso, the difference is noted. The term "labor union" in this study describes an organization of workers whose primary purpose is that of bargaining collectively with employers. No industrial boundaries are placed on the term, since some Chilean workers were organized by craft and others were not. In the case of Chile before 1927, *sociedades de resistencia, sindicatos, mancomunales, uniones, gremios,* FOCh *concejos, uniones locales* of the IWW, and *federaciones industriales* were the names given to organizations which this study labels as "labor unions."

A "worker" is a man, woman, or child who performs predominantly manual labor, whose rate of pay is calculated by the day, week, month, or piece rate, and whose work requires little or no worker-supplied capital. The Spanish terms *obrero, peón, gañan, jornalero,* and *trabajador* come under this definition.

An "Anarchist" in this study is a person who has expressed by work or deed a commitment to any of the various strains of libertarian thought.[4] "Anarcho-Syndicalists" are, broadly, persons participating in the labor movement and holding the conviction that labor unions are the driving force of social revolution and the basis for a new society. "Libertarians" and "libertarianism" are freely interchanged and synonymous with "Anarchists" and "Anarchism." The term "Socialist" in this study is normally attached to persons or groups as a result of self-identification. People who called themselves "Socialists" in early twentieth-century Chile generally espoused little more than a vaguely held desire to socialize the means of production and did not accept an Anarchist's view of the state. A "Communist" is, of course, a member of the Communist Party of Chile. A "mutualist" is a member of a mutual aid society; as an adjective, the term describes persons or organizations adhering to the reformist philosophy of the mutual aid societies.

Urban Workers
and
Labor Unions in Chile
1902-1927

1

Urbanization and Industrialization

CHILEAN SOCIETY CHANGED RAPIDLY during the decades following the country's victory in the War of the Pacific (1879–84). The acquisition of the nitrate-rich provinces of Tarapacá and Antofagasta and a seemingly insatiable world market for *salitre* kindled an export boom which in turn stimulated the growth of manufacturing, transportation, and public works throughout Chile. The country remained in a state of great demographic flux for the next fifty years, as agricultural workers of the Central Valley gravitated to the mining camps and ports of the North and to the fast-growing cities of Santiago and Valparaíso. An organized labor movement also began to take on significant dimensions during this period of change. More and more working class societies came into being as the number of industrial establishments increased and much of the rural workforce migrated to the cities.

This chapter will outline the salient features of urbanization and industrialization in Santiago and Valparaíso between 1902 and 1927 and will examine the possible effects of such developments on the growth of organized labor in those cities. Labor unions during this period were an urban phenomenon. The strength of working class organizations in the North was centered in port cities, not in the nitrate camps of the interior *pampa*. Only in the Province of Santiago and the Territory of Magallanes did rural workers form labor unions of any significance during the 1920s. The labor movement which emerged in Chile between 1902 and 1927 was, therefore, much more a product of urban than of rural or mining enclave experiences.

URBANIZATION

The urban population of Chile (defined in the national censuses as those residing in towns of 1,000 or more) expanded rapidly after the War of the Pacific. Between 1885 and 1930, the urban percentage climbed from 34 to

3

Table 1.1
Population and Mean Yearly Population Growth Rate
of Chile, Comuna of Santiago,
and Comuna of Valparaíso, 1885–1930

Selected Years	Population		
	Chile	Santiago	Valparaíso
1885	2,507,380	177,271	109,581
1895	2,695,911	249,893	127,271
1907	3,321,496	322,238	164,689
1920	3,731,573	427,658	184,430
1930	4,287,445	542,432	196,025

	Mean Yearly Population Growth Rate (percentage)		
	Chile	Santiago	Valparaíso
1885–95	.75	4.09	1.61
1895–1907	1.65	2.41	2.45
1907–20	1.19	2.51	.91
1920–30	1.48	2.68	.62

Source: Chile, *Censo de 1930*, vol. 1, pp. 42, 45.

49 percent of the total population.[1] In 1930, nearly a quarter of Chile's total population resided in the four cities which boasted 50,000 or more inhabitants: Santiago, Valparaíso, Concepción, and Antofagasta.[2]

Santiago grew at a much faster rate than Valparaíso and far outstripped Chile's overall population growth. Between the Censuses of 1885 and 1930, the population of the Municipality of Santiago rose 205 percent, while that of municipal Valparaíso and Chile grew 79 and 71 percent respectively.[3] By 1907, Santiago had become Chile's dominant metropolitan center, and in the following decades it grew to even greater predominance. The figures in table 1.1 demonstrate the rapid and continuous rise in urban Santiago's population as compared to the population growth in Chile as a whole and in the city of Valparaíso.

Santiago's rapid growth apparently occurred mainly as a result of migration within Chile rather than natural population increase or immigration from abroad. Official figures compiled by the Hygiene Institute of Santiago show the number of births and deaths in the Capital to have been nearly equal during the first decade of the twentieth century.[4] Although as many as 13 percent of births in Chile went unrecorded in the early twentieth century, civil records for Santiago were certainly more reliable than those for the provinces.[5] As the infant mortality rate in Santiago began to fall during the 1920s, natural population increase became a more important factor in the Capital's growth.

4

While the arrival of Peruvian and Bolivian workers contributed to the rapid rate of population growth in the North after 1885, few immigrants came to central Chile. European workers found the low salaries and high cost of living characteristic of Chilean industrial and agricultural employment to be most unattractive, especially when compared to the Argentine Republic. Consequently, while more than two million immigrants poured into Argentina between 1889 and 1914, a mere 55,000 found their way to Chile.[6] In 1907, foreigner's comprised only 5.7 percent of the total population in the Province of Valparaíso and 3.8 percent in Santiago.[7]

Even before Chile's acquisition of the nitrate provinces, a sizable number of people had already migrated from the agricultural zone of the Central Valley to work on railroad construction and public works projects in the Santiago-Valparaíso area. The seasonal and labor-intensive nature of Chilean agricultural production maintained a further army of semi-employed workers in reserve.[8] Many agricultural workers before the War of the Pacific comprised a "floating population" which tramped from harvest to harvest, working on a part-time basis with long spells of unemployment. This sector of the rural workforce was to form the basis of the *peón-gañán* segment of the Chilean urban working class when migrations to the cities and the North increased after 1884.[9] A *peón* was generally considered an unskilled manual laborer whose services were normally contracted by the day or week. The term *gañán* in Chile implies mobility; it identifies a person able to work in many jobs, either agricultural or urban, but rarely remaining very long in any one situation. Thus, when Chilean wheat producer-exporters were edged out by foreign competition after the mid 1870s and new, higher-paying work opened up in the North and in urban areas, scores of peón-gañanes took to the road. They built port facilities in Iquique and Antofagasta, extracted salitre from the barren pampa, laid the railroad tracks which linked port to mine, moved freight in the busy harbor of Valparaíso, worked as day laborers on Santiago's many construction projects, and dug coal in the mines near Concepción. A peón-gañán could move quickly from one task to another, from city to harvest to mine and back again. As time passed, many took up more permanent work, although fluctuations in the international nitrate market and the resulting economic disruptions within Chile condemned many workers to continue their transient ways.

Santiago and Valparaíso were key attractions for seasonally employed agricultural workers who had no firm ties to the countryside. As money derived from the export tax on nitrates flowed into the national treasury, the size of government expanded and Santiago with it. Legions of new posts in the bureaucracy were created, most of them requiring residence in Santiago. Public works projects and construction of both government and private buildings increased tremendously during the "nitrate boom." New transportation facilities were built to move an expanding quantity of nationally produced goods and the increasing number of people who traveled to another part of town or to a faraway province. Santiago became the hub of Chile's ever-lengthening State Railway system. The main rail yards and shops (*maestranzas*) were located in the nearby town of San Bernardo and in Santiago itself. The Capital became Chile's main center of manufacturing as the number of industrial establishments increased rapidly in the 1880s. Finally, thousands of new jobs in the service sector were created as the city grew.

Increased maritime activity in the port of Valparaíso after 1879 resulted in a greater demand for labor. Imports to Chile rose nearly 300 percent between 1879 and 1887, measured in gold at a fixed rate of exchange, and more than doubled again by 1912.[10] Valparaíso benefitted from this rapid rise because most foreign goods bound for central Chile first passed through her port and customs house. Manufactured products and some agricultural goods were in turn shipped to the northern provinces through Valparaíso. Net registered tonnage in Chilean ports doubled between 1879 and 1887 and quadrupled during the period 1888-1912.[11] In 1911, Valparaíso handled 11 percent of all tonnage registered in Chilean ports, which placed it second only to the nitrate port of Antofagasta in that category.[12]

Demand for manual labor to move cargo within the city of Valparaíso increased as activities in the port expanded. Railroad yards and shops servicing the important Valparaíso-Santiago railroad offered further employment, as did the drydocks, factories, and construction projects which sprang up in and around the city. As in the case of Santiago, many rural workers found service jobs as cooks, domestic servants, washerwomen, seamstresses, and gardeners.

Santiago on the eve of the War of the Pacific was little more than an oversized colonial town of some 150,000 people. None of the city's streets had been paved until the energetic mayorship of Benjamín Vicuña MacKenna in the mid-1870s, and few homes enjoyed basic services such as running water.[13] Vicuña MacKenna's many reforms and public works projects, however, began to transform Santiago into a city more worthy of being called a national capital. Gas lights were installed in 1873, and ten years later were replaced by electricity. An urban railway went into operation in 1882 to ease the pressure put on the city's horse-drawn tram system.[14] In September, 1900, the British firm of Parish Brothers introduced the first electric trams in Santiago, and within a few years service was extended to cover the entire urban zone of the city.[15]

As population grew, the city limits of Santiago spread rapidly to the north, west, and south from the colonial core area between the Quinta Normal, Alameda, and Mapocho River. Orchards, fields, and vineyards gave way to an ever-advancing urban zone. (See map 1.1.) Expansion towards the foothills of the Andes in the east made rapid progress during the first quarter of the twentieth century, so that by 1929, the suburban *comunas* of Nuñoa, Las Condes, and Providencia contained a total population of more than 85,000.[16] Working class settlements to the west and south pushed the city limits to beyond the Quinta Normal and the Zanjón de la Aguada by 1929. To the north, the city spread from the nineteenth-century *barrio* of Ultra-Mapocho to a point several kilometers north and west.

Public works and services could not keep pace with the sprawling Capital. A November, 1903 law provided for the paving in asphalt, concrete, or macadam of Santiago's major thoroughfares and all of the streets in the well-to-do central part of the city.[17] As in the case of other public and private services, working class neighborhoods, generally located on the peripheries of the urban zone, were the last to receive attention. In 1905, work on the first plumbing lines was begun by a French contractor, but by 1914 only 7,800 buildings in Santiago contained proper plumbing facilities.[18]

Gradually, Santiago became a full-fledged metropolis. Its universities, opera house, theatres, and libraries made it the cultural leader of Chile and one of Latin America's most respected centers of learning and the arts. New parks, plazas, and tree-lined boulevards, combined with the French-inspired palaces of Chile's "aristocracy," lent Santiago a Parisian air of social legitimacy. By 1930 it was indeed "la gran capital," the place where nearly every upper class person was obliged to maintain a residence and where most other Chileans aspired to live. As a center of government, industry, finance, education, culture, and nearly everything else, Santiago increasingly dominated Chilean affairs during the 1902–27 period.

Valparaíso remained Chile's second city in terms of both population and importance from the time of the War of the Pacific to the 1930s. As a major international port, the city became a center of banking, commerce, trade, and transportation, but did not achieve the same rate of population growth and therefore physical growth as Santiago—partly because of its situation between a rugged range of steep hills and the ocean.

In many respects, Valparaíso was as modern a city as Santiago. It boasted Latin America's first gas lights in 1856, and by 1910 enjoyed the benefits of electrically lit streets.[19] The city contracted the services of a British-German company to install electric trams in 1902. Potable water lines and paved streets crisscrossed most of the level portion of the city and a few of the upper class *cerros* (hills) by 1910.[20]

Early twentieth-century Valparaíso was divided into four sectors: the Port, Centro, Almendral, and Cerros.[21] (See map 1.2.) The Port, extending from the Plaza Wheelwright to the Plaza Pinto, contained many of the harbor's most important docks, as well as banks, naval facilities, the customshouse (*Aduana*), government buildings, and a railroad station. Few people lived in

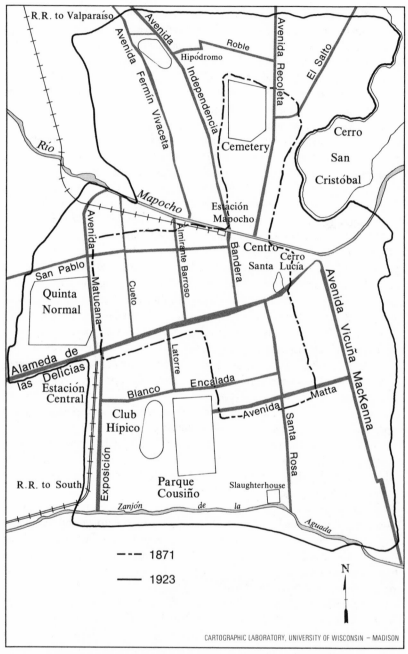

Map 1.1. Urban limits of Santiago, 1871 and 1923. Sources: Plano Tipográfico de la Ciudad de Santiago de Chile, 1871; Guía "Veritas" de la Ciudad de Santiago, 1923.

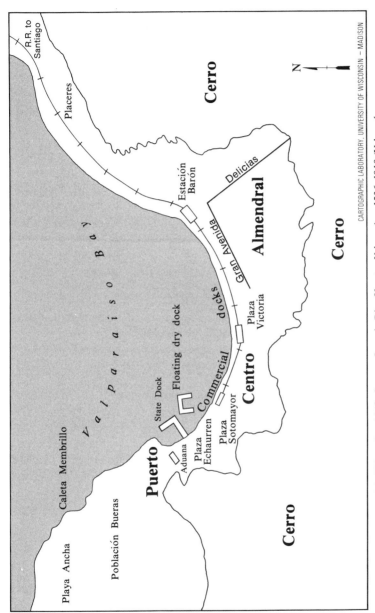

Map 1.2. Valparaíso, 1910. Source: Juan de Dios Ugarte, *Valparaíso, 1536–1910* (Valparaíso, 1910).

the Port, but its narrow streets were always filled with workers. South of the Port lay the commercial Centro, an area of elegant stores and some well-to-do residences. Valparaíso's largest district, the Almendral, extended from the Plaza Victoria to the Alameda de las Delicias (today the Avenida Argentina). The Almendral's residents included wealthy foreigners and Chileans, small-scale merchants, and wretched gañanes who inhabited the many tenements (*conventillos*) which dotted the zone. The fourth district of Valparaíso was composed of the many hills on which thousands of *porteños* (residents of Valparaíso) made their homes. Except for the well-to-do foreign colonies on the Cerros Alegre and Reina Victoria near the Plaza Sotomayor, most cerro residences were inhabited by the working class.[22]

Valparaíso's port extended along the entire harbor, from the fishing cove of the Caleta Membrillo to the Barón Train Station. Most of the actual moving of cargo, however, took place in the Puerto and Centro sections, where the State Docks, the passenger docks, the floating drydocks, the customshouse, and the Puerto and Bellavista train stations were located.

Further physical extension of the city was limited to areas farther up and down the coast and to the side of the cerros facing the ocean. As the 1902–27 period wore on, areas such as Playa Ancha, the Población Bueras, and Placeres received many new inhabitants. The nearby port resort of Viña del Mar grew rapidly during the early twentieth century as important industries and upper class vacationers settled there.

INDUSTRIALIZATION

Several scholars have studied the industrial development of Chile before the Great Depression of the 1930s.[23] Their efforts to quantify the growth of industrial output, the size of the workforce, and the number of manufacturing establishments have, however, been hindered by a lack of comparable and reliable statistics, especially for the pre-1914 period. Nevertheless, a clear enough pattern emerges of periodic growth and recession in the industrialization of Santiago and Valparaíso.

Chile's economy before the War of the Pacific was mainly centered around the exportation of unprocessed agricultural and mineral products. By cutting the country off from foreign sources of imported manufactured goods, depreciating the value of the Chilean peso, and greatly inceasing demand for many secondary products, the war itseif provided impetus to industrial growth.[24] The rapid and continuous expansion of the State Railway system from the late 1870s to 1913 not only fulfilled an infrastructural precondition for industrial development, but also stimulated manufacturing by providing an important market for local foundries.[25] Athough Chilean wheat producers could no longer complete in the world market after the War of the Pacific, the cattle and wine industries grew rapidly during the last quarter of the nineteenth century, thus stimulating production in the food processing, leather, metal, and glass industries.

The tremendous expansion of nitrate exports from the North after 1880 also played a major role in increasing Chilean industrial production. Henry Kirsch, in his study of Chilean industrialization between 1880 and 1930, asserts that a direct relationship existed between the two variables, so that increased exportation of salitre resulted in greater industrial production.[26] The exportation of nitrates increased the buying power of the Chilean government and local capitalists, allowing them to import more capital goods and raw materials necessary for manufacturing. Mining operations required more machinery and better transport facilities in order to expand, further stimulating national industry. Thousands of new consumers of national and imported products were created when peón-gañanes migrated to the nitrate camps, railroad construction sites, and urban factories. Bloated with wealth from an export tax on nitrates which accounted for more than three-quarters of its total revenue, and ever-willing to depreciate the peso with new currency issues, the national government steadily pumped money into the economy during most of the pre-1914 period. Many important national industries also benefitted from the mild protection afforded them by the ad valorem tariff of 1897 and its adjustment in 1912.

The pace of industrialization in Chile before World War One appears to have been unsteady, but it is clear that the trend in industrial output was continuously upward, at least until 1910. The Industrial Census of 1895 compiled by the Sociedad de Fomento Fabril (SOFOFA), a national society of Chilean industrialists whose aim was to foster the growth of manufacturing, noted a great increase in the number of industrial establishments in Chile after 1880 and the predominance of Santiago and Valparaíso as manufacturing centers.

Industrial growth slowed considerably during the depression of 1895–99, increased slightly to 1905, and then expanded rapidly as the nitrate industry boomed. Interest rates fell, investments in manufacturing enterprises ballooned, and industrial output soared until 1910. Marcelo Carmagnani estimated the growth of industrial output to have averaged 7.5 percent per year between 1895 and 1910.[27] Kirsch's time study of industrial production demonstrates a near doubling of output between 1880 and 1910, with especially rapid growth from 1885 to 1890 and 1905 to 1910.[28]

The most reliable calculations available for industrial output, based on production figures gathered from government statistics, nitrate exports, the importation of raw and intermediate materials destined for industrial use, and tariff policy, indicate a drastic decline in 1914, slow recovery until the prewar level was regained in 1917, slow growth to the depression of 1919, a

Table 1.2
Founding Dates of Factories
Listed in the 1895 SOFOFA Industrial Census[a]

	Chile		Santiago and Valparaíso		
					Percentage
		Percentage		Percentage	of Total
Period	Number	of Total	Number	of Total	for Chile
Before 1870	241	9.8	136	9.3	56.4
1870–79	336	13.7	188	12.8	55.9
1880–89	846	34.6	546	37.2	64.5
1890–95	1,026	41.9	596	40.7	58.0
TOTAL	2,449	100.0	1,466	100.0	

Source: Cited in Kirsch, "Industrialization," p. 38. Also in Carmagnani, *Sviluppo,* p. 21.
[a]Artisan work was not included in the study. The geographical range was Petorca to Ancud.

drop in production to 1922, accelerated growth until 1925, and a recession in 1926 and 1927. Industrial production both before and after 1913 paralleled general trends in nitrate production and exports. Vigorous expansion of nitrate exports between 1885 and 1890 was accompanied by rapid industrial growth. Industrial output rose very slowly from 1890 to 1904, a period of decline and then sluggish growth in nitrate production and exports, and then expanded rapidly along with the nitrate industry from 1905 to 1910. Graph 1.1 shows the disastrous effects of the 1914–15 depression in the nitrate industry on industrial output; although nitrate exports by 1916 had already surpassed 1913 levels, industrial output would not again reach prewar levels until 1917. As the nitrate industry boomed during the last three war years, industrial output also grew rapidly. The catastrophic drop in nitrate production in 1919 was, strangely, not paralleled by a similar decline in industry, but the stagnation of the nitrate industry from 1920 to 1922 did correspond to a period of lower industrial production. The boom years in nitrates from 1923 to 1925 and lowered production in 1926 and 1927 were paralleled by similar trends in industrial output.

Table 1.3 clearly demonstrates that, contrary to popular historical opinion, the vast majority of manufacturing workers in Chile during the early twentieth century toiled not in artisan shops but in industrial establishments. A closer look at the manufacturing sector shows that the workforce was concentrated in the larger establishments: roughly 15 percent of all manufacturing establishments in Chile employed 75 percent of the total labor force in that sector.

Small-scale production predominated within the category of industrial

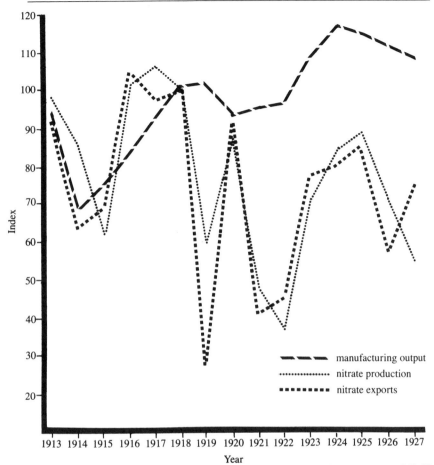

Fig. 1.1. Chilean manufacturing output, nitrate production, and nitrate exports, 1913–27 (index: 1918 = 100). Sources: Manufacturing figures calculated from Kirsch, "Industrialization," pp. 49, 271; nitrate figures calculated from figures in Stickell, "Migration and Mining," pp. 340–41.

establishments, although many more workers were employed by the numerically fewer medium and large-scale industries (see table 1.4).

Just as the large-scale industries contained most of the workforce, so they monopolized production. The first quarter of the twentieth century witnessed the increasing domination of a few large-scale industries in Chilean manufacturing. By the end of the period, one or two major firms had established near or complete control in the production of cigarettes, cement, paper products, shoemaking machinery, beer, cookies, candy, glass products, refined sugar, chemicals, cloth, and matches.[29] In other industries, many medium and

13

Table 1.3
Industrial[a] and Small-Scale Manufacturing
Establishments in Chile, 1921–25

Year	Industrial Establishments	Workers Employed	Small Establishments	Workers Employed
1921	2,984	71,879	5,197	10,112
1922	3,042	76,042	5,402	10,480
1923	3,196	82,118	4,945	7,357
1924	3,254	85,067	4,427	5,574
1925	3,221	83,779	3,847	5,499

Source: *AE*, 1925, vol. 9, p. 2.
[a]Four or more workers.

Table 1.4
Distribution of Industrial Establishments
and Workers in Chile by Firm Size, 1918

Size of Firm (Number of Workers)	Percentage of Total Industrial Establishments	Percentage of All Industrial Workers
6–10	61.8	14.8
11–100	34.9	42.0
101+	3.3	43.2
	100.0	100.0

Source: Kirsch, "Industrialization," p. 176.

large-scale establishments shared the market, especially in printing, shoe-making, tanning, construction, metallurgy, furniture-making, and textiles. Small-scale shops employing few workers characterized baking and locksmithing operations in Chile.

The interindustrial distribution of production and the workforce changed very little between 1910 and 1927. Nondurable consumer industries continued to lead in both output and employment during those years. For example, the food, beverage, tobacco, clothing, and footware industries accounted for 72.9 percent of total industrial production in 1917 and 69.9 percent in 1927.[30] Those same industries employed approximately 48 percent of the industrial workforce in 1910, 51 percent in 1921, and 46 percent in 1925.[31] The sectoral breakdown of industrial production in table 1.5 more clearly demonstrates the nature of Chilean manufacturing.

Not surprisingly, the food, clothing, and footware industries absorbed the greatest amount of capital invested in manufacturing during the first quarter of the twentieth century.[32] On a per establishment basis, the textile, gas, electricity, and tobacco industries were the most highly capitalized in 1925,

Table 1.5
Distribution of Chilean Industrial Production by Sector, 1917–27

Sector	Percentage of Total Production, 1917	Rank, 1917	Percentage of Total Production, 1927	Rank, 1927
food	44.3	1	43.6	1
clothing and footwear	18.7	2	17.1	2
wood and wood products	6.5	3	5.4	5
beverages	5.2	4	4.7	6
tobacco	4.8	5	4.6	7
leather and rubber	4.8	5	4.3	8
textiles	4.7	7	6.3	4
metallic products	3.8	8	7.7	3
paper and printing	2.9	9	2.3	10
chemicals	2.4	10	2.7	9
nonmetal minerals and construction materials	1.9	11	1.3	11
	100.0		100.0	

Source: Adapted from Kirsch, "Industrialization," p. 88.

followed in order by chemicals, printing, beverages, shoes, food products, and metallurgy.[33] Furniture-making, transportation (excluding maritime and electric trams), tailoring, and dressmaking involved far less capital per establishment.

Another salient feature of Chilean industrialization was the high degree of foreign participation in the economy. Between 1914 and 1925, the percentage of industrial establishments (factories employing four or more workers) owned by foreigners ranged between a high of 50 (1914) to a low of 44 (1920).[34] Chilean industry also depended heavily on imported raw materials and technical expertise. Kirsch claims that 75 percent of Chilean enterprises obtained the bulk of their primary materials from outside the country during the early twentieth century and that nearly 50 percent of the technical personnel in these firms were foreigners.[35]

As indicated earlier, the Provinces of Santiago and Valparaíso dominated manufacturing between 1902 and 1927. Statistics show some 58 percent of total manufacturing establishments in Chile to have been located in Santiago and Valparaíso in 1895 and 50 percent in 1925.[36] Similarly, the Port and Capital contained 40 to 50 percent of all industrial workers between 1910 and 1925.[37] Industrial establishments in the two cities had also by 1925 attracted 70 percent of total industrial capital and 67 percent of all machines used for industrial production.[38] Santiago's industrial power was at all times greater than that of Valparaíso, reaching a three-to-one advantage in the number of factories by 1925.

15

Table 1.6
Number of Industrial Establishments and Workers
in Santiago and Valparaíso, 1895–1925
P = Province   D = Department   M = Municipality

Year	Establishments, Santiago	Establishments, Valparaíso	Workers, Santiago	Workers, Valparaíso
1895 (D)[a]	1,052	417	17,567	12,616
1905 (M)[b]	954	—	16,505	—
1906 (D)[c]	1,051	—	24,295	—
1906 (P)[d]	1,086	—	25,183	—
1910 (P)[e]	1,172	638	26,046	12,324
1912 (P)[f]	1,232	658	28,511	13,336
1925 (P)[g]	1,147	453	34,486	13,486

[a]Source: Aurelio Montenegro, *Estudio general de la industria fabril de Chile* (Santiago, 1947), p. 66.
[b]Source: *BSOFOFA*, September, 1906, pp. 347–50.
[c]Source: Adolfo Ortúzar, *Chile of To-Day* (New York, 1907), pp. 348–51.
[d]Source: SOFOFA, *Resumenes generales de la estadística industrial* (Santiago, 1908), p. 10.
[e]Source: *BOT* 3, 1911, p. 106.
[f]Source: *BOT* 8, 1914, pp. 284–85.
[g]Source: *AE*, 1925, vol. 9, p. 4.

Figures for the number of industrial establishments and the size of the workforce in Santiago and Valparaíso between 1902 and 1927 cannot be compared over time with much certainty. The Sociedad de Fomento Fabril collected all industrial statistics before 1910 and the Oficina Central de Estadísticas afterward. These statistics were obtained by sending questionnaires dealing with size, capital, number of workers, and mechanization to owners of manufacturing establishments, who were counted on to voluntarily furnish accurate information concerning their plants. Some employers feared increased property taxes based on their answers and therefore did not reply or falsified their information.[39] It is likely that industrial statistics became more reliable during the 1920s, although government figures for both the number of establishments and the number of workers are certainly understated.

A comparison of SOFOFA and government statistics indicates almost no growth in the Valparaíso manufacturing workforce between 1895 and 1925 and a moderate rise in Santiago figures after 1912.[40]

THE WORKFORCE

As of 1920, many more workers in Chile were employed in agricultural labor than in any other economic pursuit, despite the fact that the percentage of agricultural workers in the labor force had fallen during the preceding

Table 1.7
Size of Chilean Workforce by Sector, 1920

Sector	Number Employed	Percentage of Total Active Population (Rounded)
agriculture	487,852	36.5
manufacturing	137,843	10.3
domestic service	132,923	9.9
other service[a]	124,179	9.3
commerce	119,012	8.9
various occupations[b]	77,259	5.4
transportation	64,636	4.8
construction	64,202	4.8
mining	56,092	4.2
police and armed forces	27,413	2.0
liberal professions and fine arts	18,464	1.4
education	12,426	.9
public service	10,942	.8
hunting and fishing	4,525	.3
TOTAL WORKFORCE	1,337,768	99.5
TOTAL NON-ACTIVE	2,416,031	
TOTAL POPULATION	3,753,799	

Source: Adapted from Chile, *Censo de 1920*, pp. 405–8.

[a]Includes jewelers, watchmakers, barbers, butchers, tailors, dressmakers, seamstresses, embroiderers, bootblacks, midwives, washerwomen.

[b]For the most part classified as "unspecified employees" or "day laborers" (*jornaleros*).

decades as a result of steady migration to urban areas. Table 1.7 demonstrates that the tertiary sector of the economy provided jobs for large numbers of people, many more than could mining and manufacturing.

A disproportionately high percentage of the total workforce of Santiago and Valparaíso was involved in manufacturing, commerce, construction, and transportation. Recent arrivals to the city from the countryside found work performing the many unskilled tasks available in these sectors, or took positions as domestic servants. Table 1.8 shows the sectoral breakdown of the active population of Santiago and Valparaíso according to the Census of 1920.[41] I have classified the occupations listed in the first part of the table as "working class" because they meet all of the following requirements:

1. Workers performing these tasks were paid a wage calculated by the day, week, month, or piece rate.
2. Neither a superior (high school) education nor a primary school degree was needed for entry into or performance of these occupations.

17

Table 1.8

Employment by Economic Sector in the Departments of Santiago and Valparaíso, 1920

	Number of Workers	
	Santiago	Valparaíso
Working class		
manufacturing	32,541	14,490
domestic service	29,923	9,915
other service[a]	16,737	5,055
agriculture and fishing	15,464	2,125
construction[b]	14,000	6,828
transportation	10,089	7,667
various unskilled[c]	4,708	3,781
mining	1,678	297
WORKING CLASS TOTAL	125,140	50,158
Non-working class		
jewelers and watchmakers	555	124
telephone and telegraph	2,283	566
commercial employees	24,261	14,040
medical profession	2,769	701
fine arts	993	486
schoolteachers	3,193	901
public service employees	3,599	1,700
police, armed forces	6,183	2,273
Various professions	2,887	5,790
NON-WORKING CLASS TOTAL	46,723	26,581
TOTAL ACTIVE POPULATION	171,863	76,739
TOTAL NON-ACTIVE POPULATION[d]	377,504	146,981
TOTAL POPULATION	549,367	223,720

Source: Adapted from Chile, *Censo de 1920*, pp. 459–67.

[a]Includes embroiderers, newsboys, barbers, midwives, bootblacks, butchers, tailors, washerwomen, and seamstresses.

[b]Only half of the "constructores" category included to account for contractors.

[c]Includes unskilled day laborers.

[d]Includes priests, nuns, students, landlords, and those performing no work.

3. Little or no worker-supplied capital was involved in carrying out these tasks.

Many of the people placed in the "non–working class" category could hardly be considered of middle class status, since they often earned nearly the same wages as many proletarians. The 36,000 "commercial" employees, for example, were often transient peddlars who scratched out a meagre living on a sales commission. Workers and peasants in uniform constituted the bulk

18

Table 1.9
Distribution of Employment within the Manufacturing and Transportation Sectors,
Santiago and Valparaíso, 1920

| | Number of Workers | |
Sector	Santiago	Valparaíso
shoes, tanning, leather	6,994	1,168
textiles	6,843	4,729
metal	2,779	1,300
printing	2,662	785
food products	2,173	1,247
wood products	1,674	352
glass	992	38
tobacco	594	280
brewing	197	83
obrero	3,426	1,319
jornalero	4,127	3,159
marine transport	12	4,553
railway transport[a]	1,927	917
tramways[b]	1,682	311
other transport[c]	5,797	1,712

Source: Chile, *Censo de 1920*, pp. 459–67.

[a]Includes only those personnel who rode and operated trains. Does not include metal and yard workers.

[b]Includes drivers and conductors only. Does not include shop (*maestranza*) workers.

[c]Includes car, bus, cart, truck, and taxi operators.

of the armed forces, and other proletarians were doubtless concealed behind the title of "unspecified employees" in the "various professions" category. To interpret the high percentage of "non–working class" pursuits as an indication of a large middle class would, therefore, be misleading.

Census information also provides a reasonably clear picture of the intersectoral distribution of the working class in 1920. The *jornaleros* and *obreros* recorded in large numbers by census takers were distributed among the various manufacturing, transportation, and construction jobs which required unskilled labor. One might therefore expect figures for the food, brewing, textile, metal, and "other transport" industries to be higher than those given in table 1.9.

The large number of service and domestic workers in the urban workforce demonstrates both the inability of the manufacturing sector to provide more jobs and the attraction that the city held for landless rural workers of the Central Valley. Approximately 80 percent of these service workers were

19

Table 1.10
Women in the Urban Workforce, Santiago and Valparaíso, 1920

Sector	Santiago Women Workers	Percentage of Total Santiago Workers	Valparaíso Women Workers	Percentage of Total Valparaíso Workers
manufacturing	7,890	24.24	5,302	35.48
domestic service	19,990	66.80	8,063	81.32
other service[a]	14,409	86.09	4,469	88.40
agriculture	673	4.30	94	4.42
transportation	508	5.00	71	.92
various unskilled	27	.50	89	2.35
construction	5	.03	0	0.00
mining	0	0.00	0	0.00
TOTAL/PERCENTAGE	43,502	34.68	18,088	35.67

Source: Adapted from Chile, *Censo de 1920*, pp. 459–67.
[a]Includes washerwomen, embroiderers, midwives, and seamstresses.

women, among them a large number of girls. The breakdown of working class occupation by sex in table 1.10 more precisely defines the position of women in the workforce.

Within the manufacturing sector of Santiago, female labor was concentrated in such industries as textiles (5,957), cigarette-making (448), shoes (418), hats (361), glass (219), candy (116), and baking (106). Women tram conductors, 482 strong, accounted for more than one-third of all nonmaintenance personnel in that enterprise. Among nondomestic service workers, the Census lists 4,572 female dressmakers and tailors and 8,714 laundresses.

Many women filled "non–working class" jobs. These included telephone and telegraph operators, salesgirls, nurses, schoolteachers, and druggists. Patterns of female labor in Valparaíso faithfully mirrored those in the Capital. The higher percentage of women in the Valparaíso manufacturing sector was due to the predominance of the textile industry in Valparaíso–Viña del Mar.

Children of less than sixteen years of age comprised a significant portion of the workforce in only a few of the industries in Santiago and Valparaíso. As in the case of the size of the industrial establishment, figures given by available sources for the total number of children at work in the manufacturing sector were certainly understated, since they were compiled by means of a voluntary poll. Furthermore, the Censuses of 1907 and 1920 did not classify workers according to age. We can, however, gain an idea of the occurrence of child labor in those factories surveyed by SOFOFA and the Statistics Office and compare these results over time. In 1906, the Sociedad de Fomento Fabril found that 7.8 percent of all manufacturing workers listed in the Department of Santiago were children.[42] This figure changed very little

20

Table 1.11
Child Labor in Manufacturing Industries,
Department of Santiago, 1906, and Chile, 1925

| | Child Labor as Percentage of Total Workforce | |
Industry	Department of Santiago, 1906	Chile, 1925
glass and ceramics	29.0	34.1
paper and printing	18.0	6.9
metals	16.5	5.6
beverages	15.3	6.3
textile materials	14.8	2.0
wood products	13.1	8.8
furniture	10.3	18.3
food products	7.9	6.9
chemicals	7.9	5.0
various industries	6.5	7.3
tobacco	4.6	14.5
transport equipment	3.6	2.4
construction materials	2.8	4.4
leather and shoes	2.7	5.5
clothing	1.9	1.0
gas and electricity	1.0	.2

Sources: Ortuzar, *Chile of To-Day*, pp. 349–51; *AE*, 1925, vol. 9, p. 25.

over the next twenty years, according to SOFOFA statistics for Chile in 1910 (7.8 percent) and a government survey for Chile in 1925 (6.4 percent).[43] The lower figure resulted in part from the effects of the Obligatory Primary Education Law of 1920, which limited the work of children who had not attended school for a stipulated period of time.

SOFOFA and government figures for 1906 and 1925 show the highest concentration of child labor in the glass, furniture, wood, tobacco, and printing industries, although significant changes in these percentages did take place over time (see table 1.11). Fluctuations between 1906 and 1925 occurred for several reasons. The most notable increases in child labor, as well as the highest 1925 rates, were registered in the tobacco, glass, and furniture industries. In the first two cases, a single company won a monopoly of production by the early 1920s. Both industries were based almost entirely in Santiago and Valparaíso and successfully resisted the unionization of their plants. Workers therefore exercised little control over the ability of their employers to use increasing amounts of child labor. The augmented use of children in furniture manufacture occurred as a result of developments in the provinces, since most Santiago furniture workers had become unionized by the early 1920s. Decreasing child labor in textiles and metals appears to have been caused by stronger labor unions and, at least in the case of the important

21

foundries of the State Railway system, by the enforcement of the 1920 Obligatory Primary Education Law. Developments in the printing industry are quite clear: the powerful Printers' Federation (FOI) effectively barred the use of apprentices who had not completed their primary education as stipulated by the 1920 law.

Child labor never became a factor in other industries, such as transportation, copper and nitrate mining, and construction, because most children were physically unable to perform the backbreaking work involved in those operations. Minors certainly did swell the ranks of the service and commercial sector workers, however, most often in the capacity of domestic servants, peddlars, newsboys, bootblacks, and errand boys. (Child labor will be examined more closely in chapter 2.)

Unlike the workforces of other Latin American countries, such as Argentina, Brazil, Cuba, and Uruguay, the Chilean urban proletariat contained very few foreigners. According to the 1920 Census, foreigners occupied only 5.1 percent of "working class" jobs in Valparaíso and 3.5 percent in Santiago.[44] Only among merchant seamen living in Valparaíso did the non-Chilean element reach significant proportions, in this case some 33 percent of total sailors.

Santiago between 1902 and 1927 contained no single industrial area or neighborhood. The growth of the present-day industrial belts in suburban areas to the north, west, and south of the city did not begin until the late 1930s. Instead, most industrial establishments in Santiago were located within the urban limits of the city but were not concentrated in any particular zone. Factory listings in 1907 and 1912 show the "aristocratic" Third Precinct, the well-to-do neighborhood along the first blocks south of the Alameda in the Sixth, and the residential Fifth Precinct to be almost free of industrial plants (see map 3.1, p. 58).[45] The commercial Centro (First Precinct) was headquarters for clothing manufacturers and many small-scale shoe shops, while the Second, Fourth, Sixth, and Seventh Precincts also contained many factories. Small-scale producers and bakeries were scattered throughout the city. Few factories were located across the Mapocho River in the Ninth and Tenth Precincts, notable exceptions being the Andrés Ebner Brewery (later the Compañía Cervecerías Unidas) and the "El Salto" textile factory. Working class residence patterns paralleled the geographical distribution of industrial establishments with the exception of the Centro, which did not contain many proletarian dwellings, and the Ninth and Tenth Precincts, which did.

Manufacturing establishments in Valparaíso were concentrated in the level portion of the city and in the outlying areas of Caleta Abarca and Playa Ancha. Important textile factories (Gratry, Caupolicán) and Chile's principal sugar refinery operated in nearby Viña del Mar.

22

2

Work in the Cities

THIS CHAPTER WILL EXPLORE the relationship between work and working conditions in Santiago and Valparaíso and the nature of labor unions in those cities from 1902 to 1927. Factors such as industrial skills, pay, hours of work, job security, and employer ideology widely influenced the formation and success of working class organizations. The much-discussed concept of an "aristocracy of labor" will also be applied to the case of the Chilean urban proletariat to determine if a lower middle class of elite workers existed and, if so, whether this group had any effect on the growth of an organized labor movement.

LABOR RECRUITMENT

Employers and organized labor struggled continuously between 1902 and 1927 for control over the hiring and firing of workers. In general, a "free market" system of labor recruitment prevailed, whereby a worker independently sold his labor power to an employer for a money wage. Labor recruiters, called *contratistas* or *enganchadores,* served as middlemen who found jobs for workers in the printing, construction, and maritime industries before being eliminated in most cases by union activity during the 1917–20 strike wave. The power of the enganchadores (literally "hookers") was never as strong in Santiago and Valparaíso as it was in the nitrate and copper industries, where they exercised nearly total control over labor recruitment.[1] Many women and children were mustered into the workforce by their husbands and parents.

The national government first began to regulate labor recruitment during the depression of 1914–15. As the nitrate *oficinas* shut down operations, thousands of laid-off workers were shipped south at government expense and resettled in the Santiago/Valparaíso area. The Oficina del Trabajo then acted as a labor clearinghouse by attempting to find work for these people, either on public works projects or in private industry. Between August, 1914, and April, 1915, the Labor Office managed to find work for some 11,000 people, perhaps a quarter of the total number of the unemployed.[2] This placement service was resurrected in 1919 to deal with the widespread unemployment caused by the depression of that year, and continued operating during the economic crises of the 1920s.

Aside from the activities of its placement service, the government's role in labor recruitment before 1926 was restricted to the marine transport industry. Maritime workers in Chilean ports were required by law to register with the naval authorities who governed each maritime territory. Before 1917, this regulation appears to have been a mere formality for all but merchant sailors. A government attempt in that year to enforce previous regulations and introduce a mandatory photo-identification card for all maritime workers who desired work triggered a strike which had to be broken by force.[3] Marine workers regarded the identification card as a government attempt to break a recently formed Anarcho-Syndicalist labor organization by blacklisting its members. Successful union activity in the port of Valparaíso depended on free access of union men to jobs, an impossibility as long as the government controlled the hiring process and exercised an anti-union bias.

Two years later, the unions turned the situation around. Widespread unemployment in the maritime industry, coupled with increased militancy and efficiency on the part of the labor unions, caused the government in September, 1919, to begin establishing the "rotation" or *redondilla* system of labor recruitment in the principal ports of the North and South.[4] Under the terms of the redondilla, available work was divided equally among all marine workers so that none would be laid off for long periods of time. Labor unions greatly benefitted from the redondilla system because employers were prevented from exploiting a glutted labor market and, more significantly, because the redondilla granted the maritime unions a de facto union shop by assigning them the responsibility of nominating workers for the daily shifts.[5] Valparaíso marine workers during the same period won much control over labor recruitment through a series of strikes. By July, 1921, the sailors' union (Federación de Gente de Mar) had gained the right to a 70 percent union shop on all merchant ships and the Anarcho-Syndicalist Industrial Workers of the World (IWW) controlled the employment of dockers.[6]

Under great pressure from the shipping companies in the form of a nationwide lockout which paralyzed the country in August, 1921, the government finally abolished the redondilla.[7] No further decrees or legislation seriously affected labor recruitment until Law 4053 and its corollaries took effect in March–May, 1926. These laws regulated work contracts and were designed to end the many abuses of the enganche system of labor recruitment for the mines.

24

Several unions in Santiago and Valparaíso won significant control over the hiring and firing of workers in their industries as a result of successful strikes between 1917 and 1925. Some, like the Union of Foundrymen, were called upon by employers to provide them with workers, but only because membership in the union was restricted to master craftsmen and top journeymen.[8] Industrially organized unions of both skilled and unskilled workers faced greater difficulty in winning job control, but nevertheless often managed to do so. Santiago's Federation of Printing Workers won a closed shop in its industry-wide contract of November, 1918, and by 1919, the Shoeworkers' Federation (FZA) provided workers for the many Santiago factories which signed its contract.[9] Other workers, including painters, bakers, and electricians in Santiago and bakers in Valparaíso, won closed or partially union shops through union activity.[10] Most urban workers, however, received their jobs during the 1920s by going directly to employers rather than through labor union membership.

Job Skills and Work Performed

Different jobs in Chilean industries demanded very different levels of skill. Highly skilled workers were generally better paid than the unskilled. Labor organizations formed by skilled workers usually enjoyed a more favorable bargaining position *vis-à-vis* their employers and thus won better pay and working conditions. In order to understand why some urban workers organized labor unions earlier and more successfully than others, it is necessary to examine the skills involved in their jobs.

Printing workers were the best-organized and most highly skilled element in the urban workforce from 1902 to 1927. This industry in both Santiago and Valparaíso appears to have suffered less than others from periodic fluctuations in the economy, and therefore guaranteed greater job security to its workforce. Most of the country's books, government documents, magazines, and newspapers were published in those cities. Yet, the nature of their work rather than the economic position of their industry made possible the success of the printing workers in organizing unions.

The bulk of the workforce in the printing industry was divided into four classifications: typesetters, pressmen, linotype-linograph operators, and binders. Aside from these skilled workers, the industry employed men and boys as peones to run the hand-operated presses of the early twentieth century and to do other unskilled work.[11] Generally, however, the tasks involved in printing required much skill and on-the-job training. A semiformalized guild system governed the recruitment and promotion of printing workers as late as 1927. Apprentices were introduced to their career either by labor contractors, who supplied the printing houses with qualified workmen, or by a master tradesman. Prerequisites for entry included total literacy, a knowledge of arithmetic and fractions, and a good memory. Few working class boys in early twentieth-century Chile could meet those requirements. Once hired, a boy began learning the trade while assisting his master. Promotions resulted from increased skill and length of service. Eventually, the apprentice began to operate independently and assumed the title of "journeyman" (*oficial*) or simply "typesetter," depending on his trade.

The gradual introduction of linograph, linotype, and, finally, offset machines by Chilean printing houses proved only a mild challenge to job security for printers. Santiago employers attempted to break a 1902 strike by threatening their workers with future purchases of modern linotype machines which could be run by women. Well aware of the unwillingness of most printing houses to invest heavily in machinery, the strikers called their bosses' bluff and won a resounding victory.[12] Several Santiago printing establishments nevertheless purchased linotype machines during the second decade of the century, but widespread displacement of typesetters and pressmen was avoided by contracts which stipulated minimum man-to-machine ratios.[13]

Because they were extremely difficult to replace, printing workers enjoyed an excellent bargaining position and formed durable, effective labor unions in both Santiago and Valparaíso. These unions gained significant control over working conditions and the relationship between patrón and obrero. An industry-wide strike of the Federation of Printing Workers (FOI) in Santiago in November, 1918, won a union shop in thirty-four establishments as well as high pay increases.[14] Future contracts, negotiated on an industrial, annual basis, continued to yield benefits. The 1918 contract required apprentices to be at least fourteen years of age, while that of 1925 limited the entry of new apprentices to one per five tradesman with the minimum age raised to sixteen years.[15] By the early 1920s, the FOI in both Valparaíso and Santiago exercised the greatest job control of any labor organization in Chile.

Skills required in the leather industry changed greatly between 1902 and 1927. The majority of leather workers in Santiago and Valparaíso were employed by either tanneries or shoe factories. Tanning operations in those two cities produced for the domestic shoe industry, while other important tanneries in the South exported their leathers to Germany.[16] During the second decade of the century, the important Santiago tanneries, such as Magnere, Duhalde, Etchepare, Ilharreborde, and the American Shoe Company, set up mechanized factories to process their own leathers. Although small-scale production predominated earlier, by 1914–17 the large shoe companies had taken most of the market away from booteries and shops.

While the semiskilled nature of work in the tanneries appears to have changed little during the consolidation of the large shoe factories, skills involved in shoemaking did. Until the mass production stage of the World War One era, most shoes in Valparaíso and Santiago were handmade by shoemakers employed by a multitude of small booteries. A one to two-year apprenticeship normally equipped an aspirant with sufficient training to make a fine pair of shoes.[17] The apprentice served virtually without pay during the learning process, but at the end was generally qualified as a master himself. Shoemakers owned their own tools, usually a simple and inexpensive set of wooden implements. They worked at home, under commission from a bootery owner who advanced the leather and other materials and bought the semifinished product. Women assemblers, called *aparadoras,* stitched the final product by hand. Normally the only machine involved was that which sewed on the sole.

The advent of the factory system greatly eroded demand for the shoemaker's skills. Labor in the major factories was divided into twenty highly mechanized operations.[18] Trolleys bearing two dozen pairs of shoes passed from worker to worker as each performed his brief task. The shop floor was arranged into long corridors of men sitting at their machines, with the assemblers in pairs facing each other across back-to-back stitching machines. Mass production eliminated the apprentice system and reduced to a matter of days the time necessary to learn a single operation. In spite of the unskilled nature of work in shoe factories, the industrially organized Shoeworkers' Federation enjoyed great stability after 1917, due mainly to its cohesiveness and skill in bargaining with employers.

The construction industry required both skilled and unskilled labor. Workers within each of the building trades were paid according to their level of performance, but some trades took longer to learn. Electricians were the "aristocrats" of the construction industry.[19] Young men entering the trade first served as "helpers" to master electricians for four years before being assigned to a master's job. The few tools required were provided by employers. Electricians had to be completely literate in order to read work orders and blueprints, as did master carpenters, plasterers, and bricklayers. Salaries paid to electricians rose steadily between 1902 and 1927, stimulated in part by the growing use of electrical wiring in all aspects of construction.

Stucco plasterers invested as much time as electricians in developing their skills and required the same level of formal education. Architectural design on both the exteriors and interiors of urban buildings during the first quarter of the twentieth century required much ornate plastering, including the shaping of statues, busts, and intricate facades. Only a few master plasterers were able to perform such work, but even less "artistic" jobs demanded a high level of skill.

Gas pipe installers and tinsmiths were often one and the same at the level of master. Tinsmithing could be learned in two years, but much additional training was necessary to become a pipe installer, especially for central heating jobs. In terms both of pay and training, pipe installers ranked just below electricians and plasterers.

Bricklayers normally received lower pay than electricians or plasterers because their work involved less on-the-job training. All competent masons were, however, required to read blueprints. Carpentry work varied in complexity from simple building construction tasks to making doors, windows, and furniture. Pay therefore fluctuated according to the type of work performed, the industry involved, and the individual ability of the carpenter. The work of painters before 1927 was much more complex than it is today. Paints had to be hand-mixed, and therefore a qualified painter had to know about color combinations and be something of a chemist.

Below the tradesman category in the construction industry were the helpers who hoped some day to reach the rank of plasterer, bricklayer, etc., and the laborers who never would. Although their skills did not begin to approach those of the tradesmen, construction laborers received relatively good wages, mainly because they belonged to the same unions as the craftsmen (after about 1920) and participated with them in the collective bargaining process.

Other industries which employed both skilled and unskilled workers included baking, metallurgy, and woodworking. In each case, workers varied greatly in skills and pay scale. Highly competent foundrymen, boilermakers, furniture craftsmen, and master ovenmen were in great demand and received substantially higher pay than their fellow workers. The quality of the product manufactured also determined the skills needed by the workforce. According to the Sociedad de Fomento Fabril, many companies in Chile preferred to turn out a second-rate product with lower-paid, unskilled labor rather than to improve quality by hiring highly skilled, better-paid workers.[20] From contract settlements after strikes, it is clear that the wide range of skills which existed within the baking, metallurgy, and woodworking industries hampered organizational activity until the formation of industrial rather than craft unions.

Other manufacturing establishments, such as breweries and glass, tobacco, and textile factories, employed mainly unskilled labor. In each case, a small percentage of skilled male workers (malters, glassblowers, and dyers, for example) labored alongside large numbers of women and other males who performed the unskilled tasks involved in production, packaging, and transport.

Tram conductors and drivers possessed skills which could be taught in a relatively short time. Unfortunately for employers, the training period was too long to avoid disruption of service. Police and privately recruited strikebreakers often steered their trams into buildings, off the track, or into each other during their first few days on duty. Within weeks, however, the Valparaíso and Santiago tram companies could re-establish complete service even after having fired much of their former workforce, indicating that the skills necessary to drive trams were minimal. In the case of the State Railways, however, the situation was very different. Train engineers of all grades worked their way up from machine cleaner and the lowest of the many firemen rankings. After ten years of satisfactory service, workers became contractual employees of the government, entitling them to greater benefits and job security. The strict seniority system which prevailed among line workers on the State Railways greatly affected union activity. Engineers and firemen between 1913 and 1927 belonged to the Federación Santiago Watt, their own mutual aid society. Brakemen, conductors, and lesser-skilled workers formed other organizations.

Work in the marine transport industry of Valparaíso was labor intensive and largely unskilled. Lack of docks and mooring facilities in the port forced most ocean-going vessels to anchor in the harbor and unload their cargoes onto lighters (*lanchas*) for transfer to shore.[21] Except for the twenty-two revolving portal cranes installed after 1912, loading and unloading was done by hand. Strong backs and stamina to last through a ten to twelve-hour workday earned the lightermen, stevedores, and cargo handlers their daily bread. On board the steamers, work ranged from that of the boilermen, machinists, and cooks to the totally unskilled jobs of stoker and cabin boy. The success of strikes in the maritime industry depended on widespread solidarity and cooperation among the trades. Lightermen, stevedores, customs workers, or sailors could by themselves disrupt the handling of goods for a week or longer, but the unskilled nature of their work doomed unsupported strikes to failure if employers were willing to prolong the conflict and recruit strikebreakers.

WAGES

Between 1902 and 1927, several important changes occurred in the manner in which wages were determined and paid to workers in Santiago and Valparaíso. Before the organizational and strike wave of 1917–20, which greatly strengthened the power of labor unions, most of the manufacturing workforce was paid monthly or biweekly and had its wage determined according to a piece rate. Persistent efforts by workers and their unions established a daily wage paid every week for many industries by the 1920s.[22] Weekly pay calculated by the hour or day insured the worker of money to spend, gave him more practical leverage for demanding and obtaining overtime rates, and limited the number of work hours per day. The unions' campaign for a shorter work week was often linked to the weekly pay issue, as greater numbers of workers won a forty-four-hour week (with an English Saturday) with payment being made before the stores closed on Saturday afternoon.

Before 1917, the pay of many workers was set at a piece rate. Among these were shoemakers, bakers, printers, lightermen, textile workers, cigarette makers, washerwomen, ironesses, tailors, cargo movers, and most others whose work involved the handling of a countable or measurable item. State Railway workers received a wage calculated by the year, month, or day. Construction workers, stevedores, metal workers, and others were paid according to a day rate. By the 1920s, the day rate had become the norm for most urban workers[23]—the most significant exceptions being women employed in laundering, packaging, and textile and cigarette production, who continued to receive a piece rate wage. These changes came about mainly as a result of union activity aimed at fixing pay at a daily rate, lowering the length of the workday, and establishing a time-and-a-half or double rate for overtime work.

Urban workers received the bulk of their pay in cash. The payment of wages in tokens (*fichas*), as in the case of nitrate and coal miners, and the multitude of abuses associated with such an arrangement (the company store, discounts for cash conversion, etc.), did not occur in Valparaíso and Santiago.[24] Some urban workers, however, did receive a small portion of their wages, or a bonus, in kind. Bakers normally took home one to two kilos of bread each day as a supplement to their income, while occasionally other workers were given a sack of coal per week or some other basic item of consumption.

Wages in Santiago and Valparaíso were on the average higher than those in other parts of Chile except the nitrate provinces of Tarapacá and Antofagasta and the faraway Territory of Magallanes.[25] The harshness of life in those regions, their high cost of living, and lack of a resident labor force combined to push wages higher than those in the Santiago/Valparaíso areas. Real wages paid to nitrate workers appear to have been higher as well.[26]

The money wage paid to urban workers varied widely between and within industries. Pay scales were determined by several factors, the most important being the skill needed to perform the task, the size of the available labor pool, the sex and age of the worker, the overall economic condition of the industry, and the strength and effectiveness of labor unions among workers in the industry. Perhaps the most easily identifiable of these factors are sex and age. Women and children normally worked in industries requiring large amounts of unskilled labor, and thus faced widespread competition for jobs. Consequently, their wages on the average ranged from one-half to one-quarter of those paid to men.

Skill was not the only factor that kept female wages low, however. Within the same industries, women and children performing tasks similar to those of men received less pay. Unskilled workers in a Santiago brewery earned $3.00

Table 2.1
Manufacturing Wages Paid to Men, Women, and Children in Urban Santiago and in Chile,
1905–26

| Year | Mean Daily[a] Wages, Current Pesos | | |
	Men	Women	Children
Santiago			
1905	3.17	1.50	.78
1910	4.72	2.38	—
1921	8.26	4.47	3.01
Chile			
1926	10.80	4.95	2.88

Sources: Calculated from SOFOFA, *Boletín*, September, 1906, pp. 562–66; ODT, *Boletín* 1,
1911, pp. 90–99; ibid., no. 18, 1922, pp. 175–99; ibid., no. 24, 1926, p. 141.
[a]The standard workday was generally two hours shorter in 1926 than in 1905.

per day in 1910, while their female counterparts made $1.50.* Similarly,
unskilled men working in laundries made three pesos per day while laundresses earned only $1.85.[27] Even in those shoe factories where both men
and women belonged to the same union (in this case the Federación de
Zapateros y Aparadoras), female workers received considerably less money
for the same type of work.[28]

In most cases, job skills and competition from other workers played a
crucial role in determining wages. Exceptionally skilled workers might take
home up to five times higher pay than unskilled laborers in the same establishment. From the large body of wage statistics for the 1905–27 period, it is
possible to rank workers according to the money wages they received as
follows:[29]

1. Highest-paid workers (more than thirteen pesos per day, 1925 current
   pesos):

> master typesetters
> master pressmen
> master binders
> master linotype operators
> master electricians
> master stucco plasterers
> master gas fitters
> master foundrymen
> master boilermakers
> master furniture makers

*All money figures are current pesos unless otherwise stated.

31

master ovenmen (bakeries)
master mechanics
highest-paid bricklayers
highest-paid carpenters
highest-paid glass makers
highest-paid State Railway engineers

2. Moderate–high pay (nine to thirteen pesos per day, 1925 current pesos):

lesser-skilled metal tradesmen
lesser-skilled printing tradesmen
lesser-skilled construction tradesmen
middle-ranking State Railway workers
highest-paid marine transport workers
most woodworkers
most blacksmiths
most bricklayers
most carpenters
most baking workers
most shoe factory workers (male)
painters
merchant sailors
skilled tannery workers
wagon and truck body assemblers
tailors (male)

3. Moderate–low pay (five to nine pesos per day, 1925 current pesos):

tram drivers
tram conductors
tailors (female)
shoe factory workers (female)
unskilled tannery workers
construction laborers
land transport workers (teamsters)
lowest-ranking metal workers
lowest-ranking wood workers
highest-paid textile workers
most brewery workers
lowest-paid marine workers
lowest-ranking State Railway workers

4. Lowest-paid workers (less than five pesos per day, 1925 current pesos):

ironesses
laundresses
domestic servants

packagers (female)
most female factory labor
child factory labor
lowest-paid male factory labor
most textile factory workers
lowest-paid food industry workers

In cases such as shoe factory and marine transport workers, wages did not correspond to levels of skill. Shoeworkers won their relatively high wages through militant union activity in a competitive, expanding, and highly capitalized industry. The high daily wage paid to maritime labor in Valparaíso reflected the strenuous and irregular nature of their work. The maritime unions claimed in 1903 that the bulk of their members (stevedores, lightermen, cargo handlers) worked on the average only 180 full days per year, while in 1917 the Labor Office estimated the figure to be 180–200 workdays.[30] Marine workers in Valparaíso therefore depended on a high wage with overtime pay to help them through long periods of unemployment, especially during the winter months (June–August), when prevailing winds shift to make anchorage in Valparaíso's harbor difficult.

A key issue in this discussion of the history of the working class in Chile is that of real wages. Part of the total assessment of the effectiveness of labor unions involves their ability to maintain and improve the worker's standard of living. Rising or falling real wages might also be linked with increased strike activity, political participation, crime and urban violence, rent strikes, and the spread of "revolutionary" ideology. Although available statistical information regarding money wages does not lend itself to a precise analysis of changes in real wages, general trends in wage fluctuations between 1902 and 1927 are evident. Both the SOFOFA and the Labor Office recorded money wages in their periodic industrial surveys, and the latter on various occasions attempted to trace real wage patterns over time, although these calculations appear to be skewed in favor of higher wages and lower cost of living figures.[31]

From the more reliable calculations of food prices and cost of living indexes presented in graph 3.1 (chapter 3), a pattern of alternating and sometimes drastic losses and gains in real wages emerges for the 1902–27 period. Chilean urban workers were assaulted by terrible inflation during the quarter-century and doubtless saw their standard of living substantially reduced on several occasions. They responded by going on strike; the strike waves of 1905–7, 1917–20, and 1924–25 corresponded closely to periods of heavy inflation. Workers suffered big real wage losses at the start of these inflationary periods, gradually recovered ground as the strike movements forced wages up, and may have experienced brief gains in real wages when the cost of living declined, especially during the years 1909–1912 and 1921–23.

While real wage losses were most significant at the start of every inflationary period, the most precipitous drop occurred during the depression of 1914–15, when *money* wages fell at a time of heavy inflation. The outbreak of war in Europe in 1914 cut Chile off from her important German market and forced the nitrate industry to curtail production by more than half. By 1915, tens of thousands of Chilean workers were unemployed, and prices had risen by more than 33 percent. These developments alone would have meant drastic losses in real wages, but they were accompanied by wage cuts in several industries. State Railway workers were handed successive 10 percent salary cuts in late 1914 and 1915, while shoeworkers, foundrymen, blacksmiths, brick and tile makers, cargo handlers in the Valparaíso Customshouse, and many others had their wages lowered by 10–30 percent.[32] Money wages among other workers stagnated between 1913 and 1917 or even 1918, indicating a tremendous loss in real wages. From work contracts in several industries, we can readily see this loss of earning power. Wages for tram drivers and conductors in Santiago, for example, were cut from $4.00 and $3.50 per day respectively in 1912 to $3.50 and $3.00 in 1915, and remained at that level until a successful strike in April, 1918, raised them to 1912 levels again.[33] The piece rate for most printers also remained constant between 1913 and the successful strike of the Printers' Federation in November, 1918.[34] Metal workers' wages in most trades either held constant or were cut between 1914 and 1917.[35] In sum, the years 1914–17 proved disastrous to the great majority of workers in Santiago and Valparaíso.

As industrial production began to recover after 1916, employment rose and several major unions were either re-established or founded. Well aware of the sacrifices they had made since the onslaught of the depression of 1914 and the obvious recovery of production, urban workers unleashed the strike wave of 1917–20. A comparison of wages for 1917 in several industries with those of 1920–21 demonstrates rapid gains in money wages. Santiago tram workers won salary increases from $3.50 and $3.00 per day for drivers and conductors in 1917 to approximately $5.50 and $4.75 in 1919, and made further gains in 1921. These increases probably kept pace with inflation, although it appears that wages paid to tram workers were cut again in 1923. Printers in Santiago won pay raises of 40 percent or more by means of the industry-wide strikes of November, 1918, and August and November, 1919. Yearly contract negotiations resulted in successively higher wages for printers in both Valparaíso and Santiago after 1919, and it is therefore certain that their real wages also rose, except during the early phase of the rapid inflation of 1924–25. Labor Office statistics for the metal industry show the wages of master boilermakers, mechanics, and foundrymen to have risen faster than inflation between 1917 and 1921, while those of lesser-skilled workers and journeymen appear to have been outdistanced by cost of living increases.[36]

Although workers in some industries may have suffered wage cuts during the lockout movement initiated by new, aggressive employers' associations between 1921 and 1923, real wages probably remained steady or rose in Santiago and Valparaíso due to the declining cost of living. Labor unions with superior organizational strength, normally those in industries less affected by the depression of 1921, such as printing and construction, continued to win wage increases from 1921 to 1924.[37] Union activity quickened as the cost of living rose sharply during 1924 and 1925. The wave of strikes which resulted once again forced wages up. While the cost of living rose by approximately 23 percent between 1923 and 1925, many workers obtained pay increases of 20 to 30 percent as a result of union pressure in 1925.[38] It is likely, therefore, that real wages fell during the first part of the inflationary period and then rebounded when the strikes of 1925 produced pay increases.

Without actual pay books, it is difficult to say with certainty if the mass of urban workers were better off materially in 1902 than in 1927. It is clear that all workers, regardless of industry, experienced periodic losses and gains in real wages during these years, and it is probable that workers in most industries won wage increases which kept pace with inflation only on a time-delayed basis. Inflation's constant assault on the workingman's pocketbook between 1902 and 1927 was a major factor in the formation of labor unions and their propensity to strike.

The Work Schedule

The length of the workday in Santiago and Valparaíso shrank noticeably between 1902 and 1927. According to the 1905 SOFOFA industrial census of urban Santiago, the average workday for factory labor was approximately ten and a half hours, not including time off for lunch.[39] By 1911, the nine or nine and a half–hour day was more commonplace, while eight to nine hours of work became the norm in many industries during the 1920s.[40] Bakers, marine transport workers, brewery workers, tram drivers and conductors, and gas workers put in more hours than the average, especially before 1907, when twelve or even fourteen-hour shifts were not uncommon. Factory work normally began earlier in the morning during the summer than in the winter, when there was less light. The normal midday lunch break lasted two hours.

Changes in the length of the workday came about as a result of aggressive union activity. As early as 1902, workers in the shops of the State Railway in Santiago won a full day's pay for a halfday's work on Saturday, a much sought-after goal of other labor unions.[41] An analysis of strikes between 1902 and 1908 (see chapter 4) demonstrates widespread preoccupation with shortening the workday without cutting pay. Sunday as a day of rest became the main target of overworked laborers in tram, textile, and baking operations, while bakers also fought furiously (and largely unsuccessfully) to end night work.

Many Santiago painters won the eight-hour day in 1906, but it was not until the 1917–20 strike wave that demands by labor for an eight-hour workday became widespread. Construction workers appear to have been the first to win a standard eight-hour day (1917), followed by wood, tram, printing, textile, and other workers. Legislation taking effect in December, 1917, established a standard eight-hour day for all workers of the State Railway system. By 1925, the eight-hour day, often with a half-day on Saturday and a full day's rest on Sunday, became commonplace. Demands for shorter hours often met tough resistance from employers, and often more than one strike proved necessary to win them.

The length and nature of the workday in Chile was first regulated by law in August, 1907, with the "Sunday Rest Law" (Ley de Descanso Dominical). This piece of legislation, according to critics, merely recognized the fact that most industrial workers already received a holiday on Sunday, while sanctioning Sunday work in most nonmanufacturing enterprises where it was widespread.[42] The law itself did not regulate anything, since its authors riddled it with loopholes which permitted employers in nearly any industry to order work performed on Sunday if they so wished.[43] Neither did the law guarantee Sunday rest for women or children. Workers complained that police officials and judges refused to enforce the law when it was broken, although strike petitions after 1907 in Santiago and Valparaíso did not demonstrate much concern on the part of labor for Sunday rest.

Bakers conducted a strenuous campaign in the face of determined opposition from their employers to eliminate night work in bakeries. Night shifts led to innumerable abuses from the worker's point of view, the most important being the unnatural and degrading way of life that most bakers were forced to lead, sleeping in the bakeries and returning home for only a few hours each day. In 1924, after twenty years of agitation by the unions, Congress finally passed a law prohibiting work in bakeries before 5 A.M., allowing Chilean bakers "to be able to sleep in our own beds."[44] Victory proved short-lived, however. Employers continued to demand nocturnal labor from their workers at the threat of lockout, resisted attempts by police and Labor Office officials to inspect their operations, and eventually won a court ruling which totally precluded enforcement of the law.[45]

In August, 1913, a congressman from Valparaíso introduced a bill into the Chamber which called for a standard eight-hour workday and a fixed minimum wage for most workers.[46] This legislation did not attract much support in Congress, nor did similar proposals in 1917 and 1919.[47] The length of the workday and the number of days worked per week therefore remained issues to be settled entirely by collective bargaining between workers and their employers until 1925. On May 12 of that year, the enforcement acts of Law 4053 (passed September 8, 1924) established a standard eight-hour workday for all but domestic and agricultural workers. In many instances, the legally established eight-hour day merely recognized a de facto condition brought about through union-won gains.

Most workers received days off without pay for the many civic and religious holidays which dotted the calendar. The longest break occurred during the celebration of Chile's independence on and around September 18, when work stopped for five days. Paid vacations for Chilean workers were unheard of before 1927, except in the case of Santiago and Valparaíso printers, who enjoyed a week's paid vacation every year.[48]

Employers, labor unions, and Labor Office officials all claimed that alcoholism among Chilean urban workers caused widespread absenteeism.[49] The Labor Office estimated in 1924 that 40 percent of workers lost one or two days of work per week as a result of drinking.[50] While this figure was derived from pure guesswork and is probably too high, alcohol-caused absenteeism was by all accounts a real problem for both workers and employers. Monday appears to have been the workday most often lost by drunken or hung-over workers, so much so that the phenomenon of Monday absenteeism was (and still is) referred to in Chile as "Holy Monday" (*San Lunes*). Workers began drinking early Sunday and continued far into the night. Sunday and holiday arrests, the majority of which were for violations of the Alcohol Law of 1902 (see chapter 3), amounted to approximately one-third of total arrests in Santiago between 1900 and 1909, further proof of Sunday's role as a prelude to the observance of San Lunes.[51] Absenteeism on Monday seriously lowered the weekly income of the drinking worker, led to longer hours and Saturday work to make up for lost time, and undercut the economic base and effectiveness of labor unions in the cities.

CONDITIONS IN THE WORKPLACE

Urban workers in Chile regarded their working conditions as little importance compared to issues such as pay, hours worked, the right to belong to a union, the presence of job delegates, and the size of production quotas. The following condemnation by SOFOFA official Pedro Luis González of the 1924 legislation regulating work conditions in industrial establishments proved ironically perceptive:[52]

> The objective of the drafters of the Law (of Hygiene and Industrial Security) is most commendable: they wish to transform at a stroke of the pen the social

37

conditions of our working classes, creating within the factory and shop the kind of *comfortable* atmosphere which these people lack in their homes or in the tavern.

Strike figures for the years 1902–25 demonstrate the low priority workers gave to improvements in work hygiene and safety when compared to questions of hours, wages, discipline, and union activity. Between 1902 and 1907, only two groups of strikers put forward demands for better working conditions. Similar demands were voiced only eighteen times during the 300 strikes recorded between 1917 and 1925. Bourgeois journalists, politicians, and social reformers looked with horror on the filthy, often dangerous conditions of industrial establishments in the cities, just as they expressed frequent shock at the wretchedness of working class dwellings. As in the case of the housing situation, however, workers focused their attention on improving the practical, economic aspects of their industrial environment rather than complaining about discomforts which they had learned to live with and considered of secondary importance.

The behavior of bakers is an interesting case. Strikes in the baking industry were aimed at raising wages, controlling hours worked (with the particular object of eliminating night work), lowering the daily production quota, and institutionalizing the power of the union. While labor inspectors and the "respectable" press bemoaned unsanitary working conditions in the bakeries, the workers themselves did not really care.[53] When the time came to strike, however, labor's interest in their filthy shops suddenly grew. The unions realized that strikes could be settled more rapidly and favorably once public opinion turned against the bakery owners as a result of worker "confessions" of unsanitary procedures and the inferior quality of bread sold at a higher price during the shutdown.[54] To insure widespread displeasure with nonunion bread, the wildly aggressive bakers infiltrated the strikebreakers with loyal union men to lace the dough with kerosene.[55] At the bargaining table, however, sanitary conditions in the shop were rarely discussed.

According to Labor Office inspectors, working conditions in most factories in Santiago and Valparaíso varied with the nature of the buildings in use.[56] Large, newly established operations housed in buildings constructed specifically for industrial production offered the best hygiene.[57] A 1921 survey of manufacturing establishments in Santiago noted that 70 percent rented their plant buildings, which for the most part were not originally constructed as factories.[58] Most small-scale manufacturers operated in these buildings, many of which contained underground shops, crumbling walls, no heat, little or no artificial light, and few hygienic facilities. In 1922, another inspection of 100 Santiago factories revealed that washing facilities in forty-eight of them consisted of a single wall faucet. Six contained no bathrooms at all, seventy-four had no fire extinguishers, and sixty-six had no first aid equipment of any kind.[59] One textile factory inspected in 1921 housed twenty-one girls in a 5 x 5 x 4-meter workroom.[60] Conditions in most manufacturing establishments were undoubtedly poor, but the "dark, satanic mills" of the English Industrial Revolution do not appear to have reproduced themselves in Chile, except perhaps for the small factories which employed a low percentage of the total workforce.

Industrial accidents claimed many lives and prematurely terminated the productive careers of thousands of urban workers. Railroad employees were those most frequently victimized by work-related accidents. In 1910, for example, the accident rate on the State Railways was 41.5 per 1,000 workers, with ninety-two deaths. The Labor Office grimly compared those figures with the accident rate of 1.58 per 1,000 for German State Railway workers in 1891.[61] Other Labor Office statistics show that railroad workers (line personnel) usually accounted for a hundred or more work-related deaths per year, about a third of the total work-related deaths for the entire country. Aside from railwaymen, most other deaths and accidents in Santiago and Valparaíso were caused by machines or by falls from a height.[62]

Work accidents stemmed mainly from lack of precautionary measures by employers to prevent them. A 1917 SOFOFA editorial in favor of the new Work Accident Law claimed that accidents in the past had been numerous "because employers in Chile, who have not been subject to any regulation whatsoever, have not taken all the necessary steps to prevent them or to pay indemnities."[63] While unprotected machines, faulty scaffolding, and crowding on the shop floor caused many accidents, the inexperience, youth, and drunken state of many workers added to the problem.[64]

Although organized workers expressed little interest in improving the hygiene and safety standards of their jobs, they were concerned about the economic consequences of industrial sickness or accidents. Before the early 1920s, one of the principal functions of Chilean working class organizations was to provide funds to members in the event of sickness, work accidents, death, and other calamities. Organized labor may have convinced some employers to pay indemnities for work-related accidents before the 1916 law which made such payments mandatory, but few included work accidents among the points of discussion for collective bargaining. Printers attempted to cushion the effects of their main industrial hazard, lead dust poisoning, by forcing employers to accept the retirement with pensions of workers after twenty-five years of service.[65]

Laws regulating working conditions, like other labor legislation, can be divided into two categories according to date of passage: the 1924 labor laws with their subsequent enforcement acts, and pre-1924 legislation. Perhaps the earliest pieces of legislation dealing with work conditions were the 1891

Municipal Labor Regulations of Santiago and an 1892 law regulating the work of women and children.[66] Typically, these laws went unobserved by employers and unenforced by authorities. On December 26, 1901, Democratic Party Deputy Malaquías Concha introduced a labor regulation act in Congress to guarantee Sunday rest, safe and clean shops, a ten-hour workday, and special work rules for women and children. Congress voted down the measure, which industrialists considered to have gone "too far."[67]

Working conditions were next "regulated" by the ineffective Sunday Rest Law of 1907. Another law obliging employers to provide a chair for each clerical worker passed Congress in November, 1914. On January 8, 1917, the Day Nursery Law (Ley de Salas Cunas) took effect, requiring all factories employing twenty or more women over eighteen years of age to install a nursery to care for their infants. This law was followed by a Workmen's Compensation Law effective June 30, 1917, and a new Sunday Rest Law at the end of the year. The Compensation act, the first legislation of its kind in Chile, provided medical aid, hospitalization payments, death and disability payments, and a guaranteed free burial for the victims of industrial accidents in all operations employing ten or more workers.[68]

The terms of these laws were rarely carried out. Labor unions claimed that the Day Nursery Law existed on paper only, and a 1921 Labor Office study of Santiago factories showed that only twelve of the largest establishments maintained free day care for infants.[69] Other employers refused to comply with the regulation, and when pressured by the Labor Office, simply fired their women workers down to the minimum age limit and hired girls of less than eighteen years of age to replace them. The Workmen's Compensation Law achieved a slightly greater effect, but was by no means strictly enforced. Under its terms, individual workers had to prove in a civil process that their injury resulted from involuntary and work-related circumstances. The use of a lawyer to pursue the complaint of nonpayment through Chile's labyrinthine court system involved great expense which only well-founded labor unions could meet.[70] In 1921, no indemnization whatsoever was paid to 49 percent of workers involved in work accidents.[71] Police and Labor Office inspectors proved unable to break the widespread resistance of employers to such social legislation. Perhaps the low point of law enforcement was reached in 1925–26, when bakery owners refused to open their doors to legally empowered police inspectors searching for violations of the Night Work in Bakeries Law.[72]

Labor unions in Chile generally did not attempt to pressure political elites into passing "social legislation," but rather struggled to win better working conditions directly from their employers. Workers did demand specific reforms on occasion, such as the lowering of food or rent costs, but organized labor lacked a permanent lobby to represent its interests before Congress. The "social legislation" passed prior to 1924 resulted in part from the desire of political elites to placate the working class with "humane" or "Christian" reforms, although significant class fear was also involved.[73] The unions had no formal role in the drafting or enactment of the laws.

A wide range of labor legislation was introduced in Congress by members of the Conservative Party in June, 1919. In 1921, the Alessandri Liberals presented the Chamber with a similar measure.[74] Political rivalry prevented the passage of either series of legislation until the military junta forced Congress to pass seven labor laws based on the two proposals in September, 1924. The 1924 laws, if applied, would have seriously altered the laissez-faire nature of the prevailing industrial relations system in Chile. Under their terms, work contracts, the settlement of strikes, the legal incorporation and activities of unions, child and female labor, working conditions, hours of work, industrial accidents, and social security insurance all came under government regulation.

The effect of these laws was, however, minimal by the time of the Ibáñez coup in February, 1927. Only after the passage of a series of regulatory acts in 1925 and 1926 did they acquire any legal teeth, and widespread opposition by workers and employers further prevented their enforcement. Unions generally opposed the labor laws of 1924 because their enforcement would have resulted in the demise of independent labor organizations by subjecting them to the will of employers and the state. Even the Obligatory Health Insurance Law (4054), ostensibly designed to protect the well-being of workers, was bitterly attacked as a mechanism by which the state planned to rob people of 2 percent of their wages. Labor Office inspectors found that during 1925–26, very few employers in Chile complied with the labor laws of 1924, in spite of the Office's active campaign in their favor.[75] Only a handful of legal craft and industrial unions came into being between 1925 and 1927.[76]

It is therefore clear that legislation regulating work conditions in Chile had little effect before 1927. The inability or unwillingness of authorities to enforce the statutes passed by Congress left matters in the hands of capital and labor. In several instances, unions forced the application of these laws by dealing directly with their employers. On other occasions, regulatory legislation was passed only after labor had already established the reformed condition in many industries. The eight-hour-day law of 1924 and the 1923 law setting the maximum weight to be carried per man in the marine transport industry are excellent examples of the latter phenomenon.[77]

Workers fought a hard campaign in many industries to break the disciplinary hold of employers over the workforce and introduce labor unions as a counter-influence. This struggle involved both the issue of job control and the nature of working conditions themselves. In some instances, such as the battle against fines, unionization was not at stake, but rather the workers' desire for greater take-home pay. Other demands, including the hiring of workers and the dismissal of unfriendly bosses or foremen, often accompanied attempts to have a union delegate or shop steward recognized. From the employer's point of view, however, any challenge to managerial prerogatives in dealing with labor was considered a threat to the very foundation of the industrial relations system.

Workers listed fines as a point of grievance in twenty-five of the nearly 400 strikes recorded between 1902 and 1927. Most of these cases took place in urban tramway, shoe factory, and textile establishments. Of these workers, tram drivers and conductors were most often affected. In an effort to tightly regulate their workforces, assure attendance during long shifts and weekend work, and protect company property, the Santiago and Valparaíso tram companies instituted a system of fines and bonuses which a quarter-century's effort on the part of labor could not entirely dismantle. Fines ranged from one-third to one-half of a day's pay for reporting late to work, refusing to work at night, arriving ahead or behind time at a station, and for calling in sick, even with good cause.[78] The take-home pay of workers remained at the mercy of overseers and bosses, who could apply a fine virtually at will. Bosses further exercised their rigid control over labor by requiring drivers to pay a large ($100) deposit to the company to insure care of their machines.[79] It was not until the middle 1920s that most of these strict regulations were abolished through militant union activity.

Shoe, textile, and metal workers also received fines for not showing up for work or for late arrival. After 1919, however, only four strike petitions contained any mention of fines, indicating that the earlier agitation by workers largely eliminated fining as a disciplinary measure.

Countless other work-related issues were resolved through collective bargaining. Workers demanded and often received longer lunch hours, greater freedom of movement within the factory, more favorable rules for commencing and ending the workday, free work clothes, and other benefits. Petitions to employers and strikes proved necessary to win these reforms in some establishments, but employers began to regard them as the norm when they became more widely practiced.

The unionization drives among urban workers in 1905–7 and 1917–20 triggered demands by labor in manufacturing industries to have unfriendly foremen, masters, and workers dismissed. Such demands were voiced in at least thirty-four of the strikes studied, concentrated in the printing (pre-1908), shoe, textile, and metal industries. In most cases, demands for the dismissal of a foreman heralded the attempt of a union to penetrate the establishment or more firmly entrench itself. Employers responded with lockouts, dismissals, and other union-breaking tactics in what normally constituted the bitterest of industrial struggles in Chile, those involving the labor union challenge to managerial authority.

THE LABOR POOL AND UNEMPLOYMENT

Periodic unemployment plagued many urban workers in Chile during the first quarter of the twentieth century. Boom and bust cycles in the nitrate industry, as we have already seen, greatly affected industrial production, government spending, private investment, and the number of available jobs. Nitrate workers were the first to suffer the adverse effects of economic fluctuations, and their plight generally received the most attention from the government and press. The economic ripple effect of lowered nitrate production which caused the unemployment of many urban workers proved less noteworthy, however, because such layoffs could not be easily measured and failed to match the spectacle of tens of thousands being shipped across thousands of miles. Unemployment in the city was more of a day-to-day occurrence. During "good" times, laid-off or fired workers eventually found other jobs. When unemployment peaked, the jobless urban worker became lost in the crowd of nitrate miners resettled in Valparaíso and Santiago. Although they faced no thousand-mile migration and relocation, urban workers in many ways suffered as severely from unemployment as did their more highly publicized fellow workers from the North.

Before 1914, a great question was voiced throughout managerial, government, and labor circles: "Is there a labor shortage in Chile?" Employers normally argued that there was, and blamed the situation on several factors. A 1903 SOFOFA editorial summed up the position of the industrialists regarding the supposed scarcity of labor:[80]

> Life here is relatively easy because the necessities of the working class are greatly reduced by its lack of culture, because wages are high due to the scarcity of good workers, and because the lower classes work whenever they feel like it, generally four or five days a week. The employer therefore has to struggle desperately to meet his responsibilities because of the informality of his workers.

The conclusion that Chile did experience a labor shortage before 1914 appears to have been true, although not necessarily for the reasons listed in the SOFOFA editorial. Immigration to Chile remained insignificant because wages paid to workers were low and the cost of living high as compared to Argentina. Native workers in fact left Chile in search of higher-paying jobs elsewhere.[81] While the SOFOFA, the Radical Party newspaper La Lei, the Conservative daily El Diario Ilustrado, and many leading Chilean intellectuals called for a government-subsidized program to stimulate European immigration, no meaningful steps were ever taken.[82] A 1913 poll of Chilean

43

and foreign idustrialists by the Ministry of Finance and the SOFOFA in fact contradicted the SOFOFA's view that "all" employers favored European immigration.[83] Many claimed that labor scarcities occurred among unskilled workers only during peak production periods, such as the harvest and canning season in the food industry. A large number did not favor European immigration because they thought it would force them to pay higher wages and feared an influx of "anarchists" and "subversives."[84] Disdain for "yellow" immigration was frequently expressed by employers, who argued that the introduction of Asiatic workers would have an adverse effect on "the race."[85] Employers who required a dependable workforce used fines, punitive layoffs, and higher than normal pay to insure efficient operation of their establishments. The fact that wages for unskilled labor were very low and that employers often resorted to firings during strikes indicates that the labor shortage argument may have been overstated, at least in the urban center.

By most indications, demand for skilled workers in Santiago and Valparaíso before 1913 remained more or less constant while the need for unskilled labor rose and fell. There are few accounts of widespread layoffs, unemployment rallies, protest meetings, or labor demands for fuller employment during those years. One unemployment protest meeting did take place in Valparaíso in March of 1903, with a reported 3,000 people participating.[86] Remarkably, when an industry-wide port strike broke out two weeks later, employers proved unable to recruit strikebreakers in Valparaíso until early May, indicating that unemployment was relatively low.

In 1906, the labor shortage reached its peak.[87] Rapid growth in manufacturing, nitrate exports, and construction offered new employment possibilities, and wages began to rise during the strike wave unleashed by organized labor in Santiago and Valparaíso. The disastrous earthquake of August 16, 1906, which killed over a thousand people and leveled much of Valparaíso, increased the demand for labor as the city began to rebuild itself. Wages rose as a result of the labor shortage and rapid increases in the cost of living after the earthquake. Employment in urban Chile does not appear to have dropped significantly as a result of the financial panic of 1907, and it is likely that unemployment remained minimal until the depression of 1914–15.

The pre-1913 labor scarcity was permanently laid to rest by a series of nitrate-related depressions. As the price of nitrates on the world market dropped during the recession year 1913, production was also cut back and small-scale layoffs began.[88] In spite of severe bank credit restrictions and lack of capital investment during 1913 and early 1914, the Chilean economy remained at even keel until the outbreak of the European war in August ushered in the depression. As the nitrate oficinas closed down their operations, production between August, 1914, and January, 1915, fell by more then half, and some 48,000 people were forced to migrate from the Great

North.[89] Employers in many urban industries subsequently lost their lucrative markets among nitrate workers and began to drastically cut back production. A Labor Office survey of 203 factories in Santiago found that of 8,651 workers employed in September, 1914, 44 percent had been laid off by October.[90] Unemployment among manufacturing workers in Valparaíso was estimated to be approximately 35 percent during the latter months of 1914.[91] Workers claimed that unemployment was also high among construction and transport workers, although the Labor Office released no figures for those sectors.[92]

Forced to take action by this unprecedented crisis, the government empowered the Labor Office to open its placement service in August, 1914, and began shipping unemployed nitrate workers from the pampa. At least 10,000 Bolivian and Peruvian laborers were repatriated, while 30,000 or more Chileans (men, women, and children) crowded into steamers to be sent south at government expense.[93] Most of these people only passed through Valparaíso on their way to Santiago, where they boarded trains for the south-central agricultural zone. About 11,000, or one-third of the unemployed Chilean nitrate workers, received a job from the Labor Office placement service by early 1915.[94]

Large-scale unemployment in both mining and urban zones undoubtedly provoked fear on the part of government and employers that social disturbances would result if immediate action were not taken. British nitrate producers in the North desperately petitioned their Foreign Office to pressure Chilean authorities into removing the unemployed from the oficinas as quickly as possible to prevent widespread violence.[95] Workers claimed that the relocated nitrate workers were not allowed to remain in Santiago of Valparaíso because the government feared social unrest.[96] There were, however, no jobs for these people in the cities, and the government did not possess either the desire or the resources to maintain them as it was to do in 1921. The policy of dispersing the unemployed throughout the country proved a wise one, as events would later demonstrate.

The worst of the depression had passed by late 1915, and both mining and industrial production began to recuperate. Ironically, it was the Armistice in Europe which produced the next economic and employment crisis. Wartime demand by the Entente for Chilean nitrates bolstered production and exportation between 1915 and 1918, but at the end of hostilities, both the United States and Britain held more nitrates than they could possibly dispose of. As orders for salitre slowed to a halt, production fell by 30 percent in 1919 and exports dropped to one-sixth of 1918 levels.[97] Layoffs of nitrate workers began in December, 1918, and by July of 1919, some 12,000 people had once again been moved south by the government.[98] Throughout Chile, over 30,000 workers registered with the Labor Office's placement service and some 20,000 received public service, industrial, or agricultural jobs.[99] Aside from a glutted labor market in the marine transport industry both in the North and in Valparaíso, urban workers do not appear to have been greatly affected by the crisis. Strikes peaked in Santiago and Valparaíso in 1919 and workers gained significant wage increases, unlikely happenings at a time of high unemployment. Furthermore, the Workers' Assembly of National Nutrition (*Asamblea Obrera de Alimentación Nacional*), the most formidable popular front organization yet formed by labor, failed to mention unemployment as a problem facing the working class in the petitions it drafted for the massive protest rallies of February and August, 1919.[100]

Nitrate production recovered during 1920 and fell catastrophically again as a result of the worldwide depression of 1921. Once more, the nitrate worker and his family abandoned the pampa for the northern cities and possible relocation in the Center-South. With unemployment spreading throughout the country, the newly inaugurated Alessandri government faced a far more serious problem than that of 1919. At least 55,000 people were without work at the height of the crisis in 1921. The Labor Office could find work for only 11,000;[101] the rest received free food and shelter in government hostels (*albergues*) set up in the northern cities (16,000 persons), Valparaíso (12,000 at peak), and Santiago (20,000 at peak).[102]

Workers, government inspectors, and the daily press all vigorously condemned the miserable condition of life in the hostels. Each resident received a ration of food pegged at a mere $1.30 per day and slept under tin-roofed structures which provided very little shelter against the wind and rain of the Chilean winter. Rightly fearful of the presence of these unemployed workers in the cities, the government attempted to maintain strict control over their movements. In spite of police vigilance and the use of undercover agents, the government failed to prevent the albergue residents from serving as shock troops for labor union rallies and protest marches in Santiago.[103] Furthermore, the Alessandri regime suffered great embarrassment and possible political damage when it was discovered that police and government officials had been embezzling funds intended for the hostels.[104]

Labor Office functionaries paid less attention to the plight of unemployed urban workers than to nitrate miners. It is difficult to say how many of the former lacked work, but judging by the numerous and successful lockouts in 1921–23 and the low number of strikes in Santiago and Valparaíso, it is likely that joblessness and the fear of unemployment weighed heavily upon workers. The Labor Office reported widespread unemployment in the marine transport industry of Valparaíso as a result of the depression and the 1921 law (*Ley de Cabotaje*) which granted Chilean vessels a monopoly of domestic coastal traffic.[105] Manufacturing workers also experienced high rates of unemployment until the depression began to wane during the second half of 1922.

Further fluctuations in employment occurred between 1924 and 1927. Construction workers in Santiago complained that joblessness was high during the latter months of 1924. The Labor Office noted 7,200 unemployed workers in Santiago in 1926, a few thousand of them nitrate miners inhabiting the reopened hostels and the rest residents of the city.[106] Government authorities do not appear to have been greatly concerned about unemployment in 1926, nor did labor, caught up in politics and anti–labor law agitation, pay much attention to the issue.

Employment patterns thus differed greatly before and after 1914. Workers during the earlier period enjoyed reasonably full employment, while after 1914 the periodic threat of joblessness became a fact of life. Urban workers do not appear to have been as dramatically affected as nitrate miners by economic fluctuation, especially in 1919, but thousands did lose their jobs in 1914 and 1921. Lack of reliable statistics makes any numerical analysis of urban unemployment tentative at best. We know when it occurred, but have little information concerning the numbers of the unemployed within each industry.

Workers victimized by layoffs faced great economic privation. Unorganized workers whose incomes were cut off had no recourse but to pawn their personal belongings, seek a loan from friends and relatives, or throw themselves and their families at the mercy of a charitable institution. Some labor unions provided short-term cash payments to unemployed members and others set up soup kitchens to feed the hungry. Employers were under no legal obligation whatsoever to give the worker advance notice before laying him off or firing him, let alone to pay him a severance allowance. Nowhere is there any indication that the urban unemployed sought work as farm laborers. Like the nitrate miners, they may have been unwilling to take the low pay offered for rural work.[107] Most labor unions proved unable to win severance or layoff pay from their employers and received little aid from the embattled and inefficient government bureaucracy. It was the worker, therefore, who suffered most directly from economic crisis, a situation over which he exercised little or no control.

EMPLOYERS AND THEIR IDEOLOGY

The so-called "social question" in Chile captured the attention of early twentieth-century intellectuals of nearly every political and religious persuasion. As labor unions appeared on the urban scene, strikes increased in number and intensity, and the "lower classes" periodically went on a rampage of destruction, the problem appeared all the more pressing to these elites. "What are we going to do about the working class?" became the question of the day, an issue to be discussed in books, on the floor of Congress, in university classrooms, and in the parlor of many an aristocratic residence.

Modern historians have also been attracted by the "social question" as dealt with by Chilean elite groups.[108] Their studies trace the formation of labor legislation through the various stages of elite perception of the social issue, the action of intellectuals within the political parties to which they belonged, and the ultimate passage of such legislation. Intellectuals, however, had little practical effect on the nature of industrial relations in Chile before the enforcement of the 1924 labor laws, and it must be remembered that those laws reflected elite fear of organized labor as well as concern for the well-being of workers. We have already seen that social legislation enacted before 1924 was not enforced and that the labor laws of that year had neither the time nor the necessary support from government to take effect by 1927. Industrial relations before 1927 was the realm of capital and labor, with the government intervening periodically whenever prolonged conflict threatened to greatly affect the economic or political life of the country. Such intervention solved short-term problems, as by settling a strike, breaking a labor union, forcing a lockout to be called off, or suppressing a riot or demonstration. When the government acted, it was rarely intellectuals or Labor Office officials who dictated policy, but rather politicians and military and police authorities. Neither did the intellectuals of the upper and middle classes greatly influence the behavior of employers. As we shall see in later chapters, employers and workers normally turned to third parties only as a last resort, when they could no longer bargain on an equal footing with their adversary.

The nature, outlook, and tactics of employers in Chile thus constituted a crucial aspect of the pre-1927 industrial relations system. Labor and employer behavior were in many ways so entwined that the actions of one group widely influenced the other. Although the outlook of individual employers obviously differed in many respects and for many reasons, certain general characteristics of urban employers do emerge from their pronouncements and behavior during strikes. Most appear to have maintained a laissez-faire attitude toward industrial relations, hence opposing social legislation, government interference, and labor unions. These qualities contributed to what came to be on various occasions a state of industrial war between labor and capital.

Perhaps the most notable characteristic of Chilean urban employers was the high percentage of foreigners among them. During the 1920s, approximately half of the owners, managers, and technical personnel of industrial enterprises in Chile were foreigners.[109] Foreign ownership probably amounted to more than 50 percent of industrial establishments in Santiago and Valparaíso, including many of the largest factories and transportation companies. The international background of Chilean employers does not, however, appear to have greatly affected their patterns of behavior. Very little evidence of rivalry between foreign and domestic capitalists exists, except in the marine transport industry over the issue of the legal monopoly of cargo handling by Chilean ships.

Just as the foreign capitalist appears to have operated in Chile on a more or less equal footing with his domestic counterpart, so was he perceived by workers and public in general as being little different from other bosses. Anti-"imperialist" articles frequently crept into the working class press, but the day-to-day behavior of the labor unions reflects very little bias against foreign employers. Outbursts of xenophobic hysteria in Santiago and Valparaíso usually singled out Peruvians as the target, with a strong side current of anti-"subversive foreigner" sentiment among elites. Workers did not systematically criticize their bosses for being of foreign origin, an exception being the baking industry, where the concentration of Spanish patrones was so great and their tenacity in fighting unions so notable that the foreign issue often came into view.[110] Public opinion became mildly xenophobic when the British-owned tram companies of Valparaíso and Santiago attempted to raise fares or allowed their service to deteriorate.[111]

The opinion of the Chilean worker held by foreign bosses appears to have been virtually the same as that of native capitalists. Most agreed that he was inferior to his European counterpart, lazy, unclean, unskilled, and inclined to drunkenness, absenteeism, and crime.[112] Racist interpretations of working class behavior abounded among both intellectuals and employers. Some extolled the virtues of the noble *roto* (the "broken-down," totally unskilled worker in either mining, agricultural, or urban jobs), while others lamented what they considered the inherently degenerate state of *la raza* ("the race," i.e., the Chilean mestizo) or *el pueblo* (the lower classes).[113] Employers generally voiced the latter perception of the Chilean worker. A 1919 report of the new general manager of the British-owned Chilean Electric Tramway Company of Santiago reflected on management's impression of labor: "It has been assumed that all the members of the lower grade staff, i.e. conductors, conductresses, drivers, car cleaners, and workshop employees, are thieves, drunkards, and evilly disposed towards the company."[114] British diplomats, normally instructed in local economic and industrial affairs by native and foreign capitalists, formed these opinions of the Chilean worker:[115]

"The national (lower class) characteristics are, I fear, cruelty, an utter disregard for human life, laziness, and a strong propensity for drink and theft."

"Their" (unskilled workers') "instincts are largely those of savages," (and in a crowd they) "become wild beasts."

(Coal miners are) "the weak spot in the Chilean coal industry."

(Marine transport workers are) "the scum of the country."

Statements by Chilean employers normally pictured the Chilean worker in the same light, although the daily press in Santiago and Valparaíso often drew a distinction between what they called the "lowest class" and the industrial worker.

Employers in Chile before 1927 clung to the idea that production and industrial relations should be left in their own hands. Interference by either the state or organized labor in the operation of their enterprises was unwelcome, although patrones appear to have resisted state encroachment even more vehemently than they fought the influence of labor unions. Most Chilean bosses vigorously defended what they considered to be their managerial prerogatives against the onslaught of working class organizations. Attempts by workers to eliminate fines, shorten the length of the workday, or remove an unpopular foreman were treated by employers as a direct attack on their inherent right to command and discipline the workforce.[116] The Santiago daily *El Chileno* echoed the opinion of most industrialists during the strike wave of 1905–7 when it labeled as "hateful" all strike demands not relating to wages.[117] Consequently, the first concessions made to labor normally included higher pay and changes in the work schedule or rules which did not affect employer control over workers.

As expected, worker demands for the recognition of their labor unions, the introduction of a job delegate, a checkoff system of collecting union dues, and the closed or union shop were those which employers resisted most forcefully. The strike waves of 1905–7 and 1917–20 stimulated patrones in Santiago and Valparaíso to form a united front against labor by organizing employers' associations in several industries. Baking, shoe, and cigarette industry employers demonstrated an early spirit of cooperation with one another because the small-scale and competitive nature of their operations left them at a disadvantage when bargaining with labor unions formed by workers of many establishments. During the period of rapid mobilization of labor between 1917 and 1920, employers generally proved unable to organize themselves on an industrial basis to effectively counter the unions. Early attempts at lockouts or other forms of coordinated action by employers' associations in the wood, printing, and shoe industries failed to halt the spread of labor organizations.

50

The intensity of the labor-management struggle grew with each strike and the formation of new labor unions and federations. The state usually took no part in the conflict until a decree of Minister of the Interior Eliodoro Yáñez in December, 1917, established steps which the governor (intendente) of each province should take to mediate or arbitrate strikes.[118] On September 20, 1919, another executive decree established a Permanent Conciliation and Arbitration Committee for the Province of Santiago in an effort to settle the large number of strikes taking place in the Capital.[119] Both labor and management generally resisted government interference in work disputes, although the patrones proved more adamant in their desire to maintain a free hand in dealing with workers.[120] Until 1920, their threats, antiunion propaganda, and lockouts failed to stop the advance of the labor unions. Some bosses became so incensed at the sight of picketing strikers that they personally shot at or beat them. The pre-1907 tradition in several industries of arming white collar employees and recruiting private guards for strikes took place less frequently during the 1920s, however, since police protection had become more efficient.[121]

In October, 1921, a national employers' association called the Asociación Nacional del Trabajo was formed in Santiago with some of the largest companies in the country as its charter members.[122] The underlying purpose of the Asociación was to fight the spread of labor unions and, if possible, to roll back those already established. The major tactic for achieving this goal was to strike at the organizational base of labor unions through blacklists and lockouts while at the same time branding efficient or powerful unions as "subversive," "Bolshevik," or "Anarchist." Association propagandists echoed the traditional "big lie" of Chilean capitalists that strikes resulted from the nefarious activities of immigrant labor leaders who came to Chile to foment violence and class hatred. The following recruitment leaflets and official statements reflect the basic outlook of the Asociación del Trabajo toward independent and active labor unions:[123]

Our country has been for some time now experiencing the grave consequences caused by systematic progaganda against capital and order fomented by certain elements affiliated with the resistance societies [labor unions] of the principal cities of the Republic. (1921)

No sir, we're talking now about an organization [the Chilean Federation of Labor—FOCh] which is built upon precise and categorical principles: we're talking about a *declared war against property and capital,* which represent the effort, labor, savings, and privations of *honorable* and *intelligent* men . . .

Don't go on fooling yourself, sir. Join the *Asociación del Trabajo* and help us prepare the defense of your property and interests. (1922)

Every employer ought to sign a tacit agreement to hire for work in his shops only those workers who are sober, reliable, and not associated with the disturbing action of seditious groups [read labor unions]. (1925)

It has been proved that 90 percent of strikes which have occurred in Chile as well as Argentina (we have statistical information right here) is due to the indirect or direct action of foreigners. (1926)

Such statements appealed to Chilean employers, and the Asociación del Trabajo grew rapidly from seventy-eight member firms in 1922 to 1,594 establishments employing over 130,000 workers in 1926.[124] Aside from antiunion activities, the Association spent much energy combating the social legislation of 1924, which it referred to as "a most heavy punishment for national industrial production."[125]

The intense laissez-faire attitude of Chilean bosses served to intensify the struggle between labor and capital between 1902 and 1927 by forcing workers to fight for every benefit they hoped to achieve. Government stepped in occasionally to aid one side or the other and eventually attempted to control industrial relations through the labor laws of 1924. Before 1927, however, the pattern of strike to settlement to lockout to strike to layoff to strike continued with little outside interference, and became especially pronounced during periods of unionization drives and the reaction of employers which invariably followed. Employer ideology therefore appears to have changed very little during the first quarter of the twentieth century.

CONCLUSION

A close relationship existed between the nature of work performed in urban Chile and the growth of labor unions between 1902 and 1927. We have seen that skilled workers generally received more pay than unskilled laborers. Higher-paid workers organized the first labor unions to bargain successfully for wages and material benefits, just as they had formed the majority of mutual aid societies in the nineteenth century. Labor organizations established by skilled, well-paid workers also enjoyed longer life, greater cohesiveness, and more success in winning strikes than those of semiskilled or unskilled workers.

Unions achieving the least organizational success were, conversely, those formed in industries employing large numbers of female, child, and unskilled workers. Nor did mutual aid societies penetrate the ranks of lower-paid workers as frequently as among craftsmen. Other industrial groups, especially shoemakers, formed durable, effective labor federations in Valparaíso and Santiago in spite of the semiskilled nature and moderate pay of their work.

Workers employed by the State Railway system enjoyed many job-related benefits before other urban workers had achieved them. Engineers and firemen under contract with the government (after ten years' service) occupied a unique position within the workforce because they possessed greater job security and could not, being government contractual employees, legally go on strike. Other railroad personnel, both in the shops and on line duty, benefitted from a pension and retirement plan set up for them in 1911 and reorganized in their favor in 1918. These and other benefits, such as generous death and disability payments, sick pay, and an eight-hour workday, were not extended to many other workers either legally or in reality during the remainder of the 1920s. As a result of optimal working conditions, a strict seniority system which governed promotions, and the contract status of veteran engineers and firemen, unions formed by railway personnel tended to be more conservative and less cohesive than those of similarly skilled workers in the private sector. As we will see in chapter 4, the dividing point between aggressive and generally passive behavior on the part of railroad workers came after 1907, when their wages were set at a fixed rate in gold.

Working conditions and the nature of employers also partially determined the organizational structure and tactics that labor unions would assume. Strikes in bakeries and the tramway operations often resulted in violence, arrests, and bloodshed, because the frequent use of strikebreakers and the tyrannical practices of employers in those establishments drove the worker to the point of desperation. Strikes of semiskilled labor or among the unskilled also generated more hatred and violence than those of skilled workers, who enjoyed greater leverage at the bargaining table.

A final consideration remains that of the possible presence of a "labor aristocracy" among Chilean urban workers. Eric J. Hobsbawm, in his study of English workers in the second half of the nineteenth century, offers six basic criteria for determining the existence of an "aristocracy of labor."[126] These include wage level, prospects for social security, work conditions, relations with lower and upper social groups, living conditions, and the possibility for future advancement. The English "labor aristocracy," according to Hobsbawm, began to disappear after 1890, when large-scale industrial production gradually sharpened the distinction between workers and managers.

In terms of wages alone, some Chilean workers definitely qualified for "aristocratic" status. An electrician, printer, or master foundryman might earn a wage five or six times that paid to a factory peón. These wage differentials remained unchanged during the 1902–27 period and, in fact, the gap between the highly paid and the poorly paid may have widened.

In other respects, nearly all workers shared the same situation. Prospects for social security remained very poor for workers in most industries. Future advancement for even highly skilled building tradesmen, metal workers, and printers was limited by the boundaries of craft and industrial establishment. A master carpenter could earn successively higher pay or perhaps become a foreman, but his chances of becoming a manager or contractor were slim. Union leadership and politics provided the means of upward socioeconomic mobility for only a handful of workers before 1927. Chilean society in the first quarter of the twentieth century accepted the upward mobility of new wealth, but financial success normally resulted from capital investment, mercantile activity, or personal connections in the government. Wage earners had none of these means at their disposal. Furthermore, education and the nature of work performed readily identified a person as being of upper, middle, or working class extraction. The social difference between a university professor and a primary school teacher was great, and the latter position was more prestigious than that of a plumber or tram driver. The fact that skilled tradesmen earned more money than schoolteachers, telegraph operators, or lower-ranking *empleados* did not cloud the social differences between them or differences in the prestige given their work.

Another key factor is the attitude toward people in upper or lower social strata. A "labor aristocracy" should by definition consider itself as a distinct social group, a "lower middle class" recognized as such by people above and below it in the social hierarchy. Much evidence exists to support the claim that highly paid urban workers often did receive more respectful treatment from the daily press and considered themselves to be better off than the so-called "lowest classes." Printers attained a high level of education, lived reasonably well, and enjoyed the support of a powerful union, while the unskilled peón, often a recent arrival from the countryside, was submerged in poverty and ignorance. A considerable socioeconomic difference existed between long-term urban residents and migrants to the city. Unskilled gañanes from the countryside obtained the worst housing, filled the lowest-paying jobs, and suffered most from unemployment. Skilled workers were not immune to layoffs, sickness, poverty, alcoholism, and inflation, but they generally had more means at their disposal to combat these problems.

In terms of social solidarity, highly skilled union men acted as members of an industrial proletariat rather than aspirants to middle class stature. Identification with the "working class" remained strong in union documents and pronouncements during the entire period. Highly paid workers generally demonstrated great concern for the success of other labor unions and helped to organize workers in industries having no previous union experience. Revolutionary ideology most frequently penetrated unions composed of highly skilled, well-paid, and well-educated workers, which in turn spread Anarchist and Marxist ideas to the *bajo pueblo*. Although economically fortunate workers did enjoy more prestige in upper and middle class circles, the social and cultural gap between the classes remained too great to be bridged by increased wages. Neither were the "labor aristocrats" of the Chilean working class inclined to identify themselves with middle class culture, which basically reflected elitist attitudes. The so-called "labor aristocracy" in Chilean cities therefore existed in an economic sense, but by no means constituted an upwardly mobile subclass instilled with bourgeois values.

3

The Condition
of the Urban Working Class

THE LIVING CONDITIONS of the working classes of Santiago and Valparaíso influenced the development and nature of their labor unions. Several studies of European workers in the early twentieth century have postulated that housing, diet, education, and many other factors at least partially conditioned the responses of the working classes towards unions and collective action.[1] The concept of a "labor aristocracy" has already been discussed with regard to economic and industrial factors. This chapter will investigate the social conditions of urban working people to determine why some workers were able to organize themselves and others were not.

Unorganized workers generally receive little attention in labor histories, either because they are considered to be of little significance or because information about them is difficult to obtain. Nevertheless, it was from this seemingly faceless mass that the unions and their leaders emerged in early twentieth-century Chile. One of the purposes of this study is the reverse the pattern of "top-down" historical investigation relating to the working classes of Latin America. Here is Chilean urban society at the bottom.

HOUSING

Working people generally lived on the peripheries of urban Santiago and Valparaíso in 1902–27. Neither city contained a single working class neighborhood, but rather a series of them, some extensive, others small and isolated. The vast majority of workers lived within the urban limits of both cities, although one working class suburban *comuna* of Santiago, Quinta Normal, did grow to a population of 40,000 by 1930.[2] Before 1927, however, the trend of the rapid extension of working class suburbs to the north and west of Santiago and middle/upper class districts to the east and south had barely begun.

56

The precise location of working class neighborhoods can be determined by several means. In interviews, four important figures in the labor movement of the 1920s all named the same neighborhoods as being most typically working class in nature.[3] These were popularly called San Pablo, Estación Central, Ultra Mapocho, Matadero, and Avenida Matta. Contemporary sources seldom mentioned the location of working class neighborhoods, but did on many occasions provide the address of a *conventillo, cité,* or *pasaje,* the three major types of working class housing. Locations of random 453 such dwellings obtained from twenty or more different sources indicates a heavy concentration of working class homes in precisely those neighborhoods named in the interviews.[4] (See map 3.1.) Although the 453 buildings in question represent only a small percentage of total proletarian homes in Santiago, they do indicate that the working class was concentrated on the periphery of the city's urban area.

Most well-to-do Chileans lived in the heart of the city, either near the commercial center (Centro) or in the Third Precinct just to the west of it. The first two or three blocks south of Santiago's grand boulevard, the Alameda de las Delicias (today the Alameda Bernardo O'Higgins), was considered a solidly middle and upper class neighborhood. The southern half of the Fifth Precinct also contained a high proportion of elite homes. The closer one moved to the Alameda, at least from the Fifth and Sixth Precincts east, the better the neighborhood became. A map showing the Santiago residences of 114 of Chile's 127 senators and deputies in 1909 demonstrates the trend of upper class concentration in the Centro. (See map 3.1)

In Valparaíso, workers tended to live in the hills which ring the city, although sizable working class neighborhoods existed in the so-called Barrio Barón near the Barón train station, and along the Avenida de las Delicias (today the Avenida Argentina). Wealthy residents of Valparaíso lived either in the level portion of the city, mainly in the Almendral, or on certain hills, such as the German colony of Cerro Alegre and the British settlement, Cerro Reina Victoria.[5]

The most typical working class dwelling in both Santiago and Valparaíso was the *conventillo,* or "tenement." In 1906, sanitary inspectors of the National Institute of Hygiene estimated that 2,000 conventillos existed in Santiago.[6] The average number of people per Santiago conventillo was measured by the Labor Office at 65.4 in 1911, so roughly 130,000 *santiaguinos,* or 40 percent of the city's total population, probably lived in this type of dwelling during the first decade of the century.[7] Although some 700 conventillos were demolished between 1906 and 1915, many buildings were remodeled, and new ones were constructed to take the place of the old, so that the Labor Office estimated that 2,022 conventillos still existed in 1916.[8] Demo-

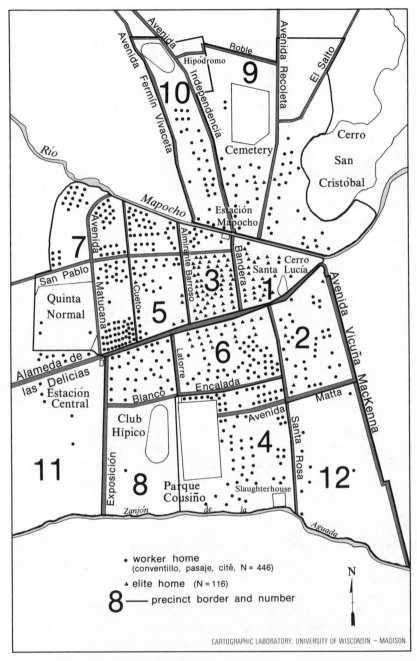

Map 3.1. Elite and worker housing in Santiago, c. 1910. Sources: elite addresses from Policía de Santiago, *Guía de informaciones policiales*; for conventillo addresses, see note 4.

58

lition continued during the 1920s, but the percentage of santiaguinos living in conventillos did not change drastically.[9]

Conventillos were generally one or two-story buildings of colonial/nineteenth-century design, with a single door on the street opening into a square courtyard. Unlike Buenos Aires working class dwellings, conventillos in Santiago during the first quarter of the twentieth century do not appear to have been created from the former homes of elites.[10] Semirural nineteenth-century buildings may well, however, have been transformed into conventillos as the urban limits of the city grew. The traditional extended family dwelling of the nineteenth century was easily converted into a conventillo by merely dividing the rooms up into smaller compartments and opening new doorways onto the central couryard.

The typical working class family occupied a single room. The foundation of the structure was built of brick, the walls of adobe. Wood and tile were normally used to build the roofs, although flattened tin cans also gained popularity as roofing materials. Floors were composed of mud and straw, sometimes of tile. Conventillo rooms facing the interior courtyard had no windows, so that light and air entered only when the door was open. Rooms on the street commanded a significantly higher rent because they had a window. The vast majority of rooms lacked running water and electricity. A 1907 survey of thirty-five conventillo rooms conducted by the Labor Office found the average room size to be 19.64 square meters.[11] The construction of conventillo rooms was so shoddy that roofs and walls frequently caved in during winter storms and earthquakes.[12]

The number of people housed in each conventillo room varied widely according to the size and income of the occupant family. Some couples rented a bed in their room to a single person as a means of further income. Workingmen without families frequently crowded together in one room in order to lower their rent expenditures. Beds were often used around the clock, warmed during the day by night shift workers, then left for those returning in the evening. Investigators from the Labor Office and the High Council on Worker Housing reported instances of ten or more people living in a single conventillo room. In cases of extreme crowding, asphyxiation sometimes occurred when people slept with the door shut.[13] A weary night shift hand returned to his room early one morning and mistakenly threw himself into the wrong bed, crushing a sleeping infant to death.[14]

Figures from the Labor Office indicate that conventillo dwellers were increasingly crowded together during the years 1906–25. According to samplings of Santiago conventillos taken in eight different years, the housing situation for many workers did not improve, but in fact worsened during this period. (See table 3.1.)

59

Table 3.1
Mean Occupancy of Conventillo Rooms in Santiago, 1906–25

Year(s)	Mean Number of Persons Per Room
1906–12	2.48
1911	2.94
1916	2.83
1918	2.99
1919	3.00
1922	3.96
1923	3.98
1924	3.97
1925	3.32

Sources: *AE*, 1915, vol. 2, p. 180; *BOT* 12, 1919, pp. 10, 20, 26; no. 21, 1923, p. 150; no. 24, 1926, anexos 46, 49.

Causes of the notable rise in the number of people per room are not entirely clear. Population growth, coupled with the continued demolition of conventillos pronounced "unsanitary," certainly stimulated greater crowding. How many new conventillos were opened is not known, although it appears certain that landlords stood to profit by outfitting new tenement buildings, and probably did so. The rise in rent costs from 1920 to 1925 may also have caused workers to move in with others rather than rent places of their own. (See graph 3.1.) Crowded conditions, as well as increased rents in 1924, undoubtedly prodded many workers into active participation in the rent strike movement of 1925, which resulted in a drop in both rent costs and residency per room.

The conventillo comprised a tiny community. Its residents drew their potable water from a single faucet in the central courtyard and shared one or two toilets. During the day, women washed and hung up their laundry in the courtyard, while children and domestic animals entertained themselves in the dust or mud. Landlords rarely provided shower or bath facilities, nor were there kitchens in most conventillos. Each family cooked on a brasier placed by the doorstep of its home, filling the rooms and courtyard with thick smoke. Garbage was tossed into the open sewer running through the courtyard and under the toilets. During a heavy rainstorm, the sewer overflowed and its contents eventually seeped into the residences, many of which lay below ground level.

Contemporary sources unanimously agreed that conventillos were unsanitary and often unfit for human habitation. Upper class visitors to conventillos reacted strongly to the foul smells, filth, overcrowding, and unhealthiness of such places, while working class critics of tenement housing generally focused their attack on the high rent paid for each room.[15] The attitude of workers reflected the gradual realization that housing conditions were not

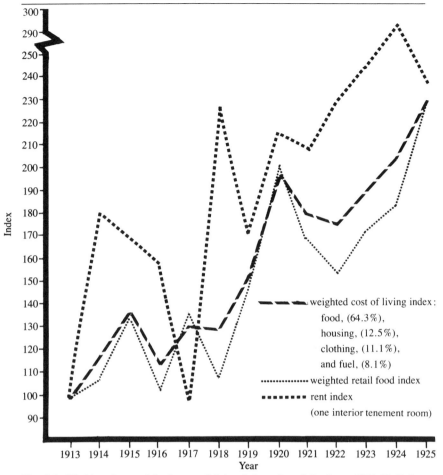

Fig. 3.1. Working class weighted cost of living index, city of Santiago, 1913–25 (index: 1913 = 100). Source: Raw figures from Labor Office statistics as reported in yearly *BOT*. For method of weighting, see note 40, this chapter.

getting better and probably would not improve. Labor organizations knew full well that the conventillo helped fuel Chile's astounding infant mortality rate, that disease spread like wildfire from hovel to hovel, and that alcoholism and prostitution were rife and within sight of small children. They also knew that it was easier to win a reduction in rent than to have the conventillos remodeled and made sanitary.

Ownership of a conventillo was a profitable business. Suitable buildings in working class neighborhoods could be acquired at a very low price, property taxes were minimal, and regulations concerning sanitation facilities went unobserved.[16] To increase one's profit, rooms could be cheaply subdivided by adding new adobe walls. Further gains were made by operating a pawnshop in the manager's room, where the conventillo residents might exchange their scant belongings for a fraction of their real value. One observer claimed that landlords were able to double their original investment within a year.[17] Santiago conventillo owners appear to have been persons of limited means trying to squeeze a living out of their nest egg, although cases were reported of slumlording by wealthy and prominent people, such as the wife of President Ramón Barros Luco and even the director of the High Council on Worker Housing.[18] A study of fifty conventillo owners in 1903 showed that forty-one owned only one building, seven owned two, and only two people owned three or more.[19] During the 1925 rent strikes, landlords fought with workers and police to protect their source of income.

Many workers dreamed of leaving the conventillo for more spacious and healthy surroundings. A select group managed to do so. Several types of housing existed for workers who could afford more than a single room in a conventillo, but these were often in short supply and commanded a much higher price. The cité, termed a "decent conventillo" by one 1920s labor leader, was a collection of small two or three-room brick apartments which opened onto a small corridor leading to a single street entrance.[20] Cité apartments normally contained a private bathroom and a place to cook. Another type of working class dwelling was the pasaje, or "passageway," of a design similar to that of the cité except its central corridor cut completely through the block to another street.

Some cités and pasajes contained only one-room homes and thus were similar, if not inferior, to two-room conventillo apartments. Demolition of "unsanitary" cités also took place on various occasions. Generally, however, a cité or a pasaje could be considered a "step up" from the conventillo. Few workers could afford to take this step, however, because a two-room cité apartment normally rented for three times as much as one room in a conventillo.[21] The cheapest two-room cité apartment in Santiago as surveyed by the Labor Office in 1911 cost $16.50 a month, while the median cost of the sample cités was $30.00. Three-room apartments rented for a minimum of $30.00, with a median price of $58.00.[22] Such rents lay far beyond the purchasing power of the typical workman's wage of two to four pesos per day.

Rent payments normally followed food costs as the most important expenditure in the working class budget. Studies of eighty-nine working class families in Santiago, Valparaíso, and Iquique conducted between 1911 and 1925 by the Labor Office showed that they spent an average of 12.5 percent of income on rent, while devoting 64.3 percent to food, 11 percent to clothing, and 10 percent to fuel.[23] The percentage spent on housing in Santiago and Valparaíso alone was probably closer to 15 percent. Payment was normally made every month, and a month's rent was held as a security deposit.[24]

Housing costs fluctuated wildly in Valparaíso and Santiago between 1911 and 1925, according to Labor Office figures. The general trend of rent prices was upward, however, as seen in graph 3.1. Rent for one interior room in a conventillo rose by nearly 300 percent between 1907–8 and 1920–25. Housing in Valparaíso remained more costly than in Santiago until 1917, perhaps as a lingering result of the 1906 earthquake which destroyed much of the city.

The disgraceful condition of most working class homes in Chile during the first quarter of the twentieth century was not caused by lack of regulatory legislation. In December, 1901, the Municipality of Santiago passed an ordinance making running potable water, flowing sewers, separate showers for men and women, and kitchens mandatory for each conventillo. Another municipal regulation of April, 1905, stipulated that each room in a conventillo should have running water, a toilet, and a window. The "Law of Workmen's Dwellings" passed by Congress in February, 1906, incorporated Santiago's municipal provision as well as calling for the demolition of unsanitary structures, guaranteed loans to private companies to build sanitary, low-cost housing, and the creation of departmental councils to see that the law was enforced.[25]

None of the regulations of either the national 1906 law or the municipal acts were ever systematically enforced. Conventillos declared unhygienic sometimes fell before the wrecking crews, but new ones took their place. Five years after the 1906 law had taken effect, the Labor Office stated: "It is realistic to admit that in spite of the ample and generous terms established by the Law of February 20, 1906, the dispositions of the Law have in reality gone almost unapplied."[26] In 1919, more than one-third of the 3,200 conventillos examined in Chile by the Labor Office had no running water or plumbing facilities on the premises, flagrantly in violation of the law.[27] Like most of the "social legislation" passed by the Chilean Congress before 1927, the housing law of 1906 was largely ignored.

More legislation appeared as a result of the rent strike of January–February, 1925. As we shall see later, the decree cutting rents by 50 percent in "unsanitary" housing was a stopgap attempt by the revolutionary junta to defuse what appeared to be the most widespread and radical grass roots movement since the turn of the century. A housing law in March, 1925, and its regulatory acts created a new bureaucracy to deal with the construction of worker homes and the improvement of conventillos. Liberal funding available to individuals, contractors, and "legally recognized" labor unions differentiated this bill from its 1906 predecessor.

Various "model housing" projects for workers were drafted during the 1902–27 period, but few advanced past the planning stage. Furthermore, when "low-cost" and "worker" houses in model projects finally reached completion, the vast majority of working people could not afford to buy them. In 1904, for example, the State Railway planned a model project for its employees which called for rent payments of $300–500 per year when most workers made two or three pesos a day.[28] That project, the "Población San Eugenio," and another, the "Población Huemul," were inaugurated with great pomp by the President of the Republic in 1911. By 1920, the cheapest homes in the Huemul sold for $7,000, with $700 as a down payment and $42 per month, an impossible sum for workers to raise.[29] Model homes built by the Santiago Savings Fund (Caja de Ahorros) in 1919 cost between $14,000 and $32,000, with a down payment of 10 percent.[30] After taking into consideration that a well-paid worker in 1919 made approximately $2,000 per year and that these were considered inexpensive dwellings, it is apparent that the great majority of Santiago workers could not hope to be homeowners.

DIET AND COST OF LIVING

Food constituted by far the greatest single expense of the working classes in Santiago and Valparaíso. Studies by the Labor Office of a total of ninety-four families between 1912 and 1925 indicated an average expenditure of 64 percent of total income on food. Family size appears to have partially influenced the percentage of the budget spent on food. Families spending more than the average 64 percent had an average of 4.65 members, while families spending less contained only 3.88. Income also partly determined the size of food expenditures. Studies of these families indicated that those with higher than median incomes spent proportionately less for food, and vice-versa.[31]

Urban workers normally ate three meals a day. Breakfast typically consisted of coffee with milk and bread. Workers whose jobs took them far from home either carried their lunch with them or ate in one of Santiago's many popular restaurants in order to save the money and time involved in riding the tram.[32] Otherwise, they ate at home. Lunch was usually a two-course affair, the heaviest meal of the day. The first course invariably consisted of a stew of some kind (*cazuela, ajiaco*) with meat, potatoes, rice, and vegetables. Beans, rice, noodles, or potatoes formed the basis for the second course. Bread nearly always accompanied the working class lunch. Leftovers from the noon meal or freshly prepared beans or potatoes were served for dinner, which was normally eaten after eight o'clock.

Some foods in Chile were consumed only by certain classes, while other dishes were enjoyed by all strata of society. On a per capita basis, Chileans ate nearly twice as much bread as any other food, followed in order by potatoes, meat, sugar, beans, corn, and rice.[33] In their 1903 study of one working class family in Santiago, Errázuriz and Eyzaguirre found that potato and bread consumption were nearly the same.[34] When food costs rose rapidly between 1919 and 1920, many relatively better-off Chileans substituted potatoes for bread, indicating that the working class may have been doing so all along, since a kilogram of potatoes generally cost less than a third of a kilo of bread.[35] Workers consumed coffee and sugar in spite of their high cost, although certainly in lesser quantities than did the middle and upper classes. In spite of Chile's lengthy seacoast, the working classes of Santiago and Valparaíso ate almost no fish, mainly due to its high price.[36]

Meat (beef) and beans, aside from being the working class's main sources of protein, came to cause much discussion and controversy during the 1902–27 period. According to Labor Office figures, the Province of Santiago in 1924 led all others in meat consumption, with an average of 100 kilos consumed per person. Valparaíso placed second with sixty-three kilos per person, while in the urban area of Santiago, the figure was seventy kilos. Many sources claimed, however, that workers ate meat only when their wages rose and prices remained stationary.[37] The nine people in the Errázuriz-Eyzaguirre study together consumed an average of only one pound of meat per day.[38] Beef and more expensive types of meat occupied a major role in the middle/upper class diet, and it is therefore certain that per capita figures for beef consumption in Santiago and Valparaíso were highly skewed in their favor.

If most workers did not eat much beef, at least they wanted to. On two different occasions, the issue of beef consumption became the rallying cry around which working class organizations and several political parties united for joint agitation. Labor groups during both the October, 1905 "meat riot" and the agitation in 1918–19 by the Workers' Assembly on National Nutrition (AOAN) called for lowered food and especially meat prices. Complaints against high food costs proved an excellent vehicle for the mobilization of great masses of people, since even small price increases greatly affected the budget of the urban workforce.

Food prices in Santiago and Valparaíso skyrocketed during the first quarter of the twentieth century. The wholesale cost of second class white flour, from which working class bread was made, rose from $5.30 in October, 1902, to $33.00 in October, 1925. A hundred kilos of beans, which sold for $9.25 in 1902, commanded $70.00 in 1925. Second class beef at the municipal slaughterhouse cost $.34 per kilo in 1902 and rose to $1.80 in 1925.[39] Food costs for working people nearly doubled between 1902 and 1909, as demonstrated by the price index in table 3.2.[40]

Wholesale prices fell slowly during most of the 1909–12 period and then rose again, so that by 1913 they were nearly the same as in 1909. Between 1913 and 1925 great fluctuations occurred in the price structure of food, with costs peaking immediately following World War One and in 1924–25, as

Table 3.2
Weighted Price Index of the Wholesale Cost of Food Staples in Santiago, 1902–9[a]
(April, 1902 = 100)

Date	Index	Date	Index
April, 1902	100	October, 1905	152
July, 1902	106	April, 1906	144
October, 1902	93	July, 1906	169
April, 1903	111	October, 1906	176
July, 1903	93	January, 1907	159
October, 1903	101	April, 1907	145
January, 1904	88	July, 1907	171
April, 1904	84	October, 1907	190
July, 1904	92	January, 1908	181
October, 1904	104	April, 1908	177
January, 1905	103	July, 1908	201
April, 1905	112	October, 1908	196
July, 1905	126	January, 1909	167

Source: Commercial section of *La Lei*, first Sunday of the month.
[a]Foods included are second class flour, corn, second class beef, beans (bayos), and potatoes.

shown in graph 3.1. The upward trend of food costs and the price peaks of 1920 and 1925 are notable. Food in general appears to have been slightly more expensive in Valparaíso than in Santiago, although in 1920 the difference grew to more than 12 percent.

Food prices rose and fell for several reasons. The most important appears to have been the sharp rise in the international prices of basic food commodities which stimulated Chilean landowners to export many of their crops between 1916 and 1921. Prices then rose in Chile as the wholesalers competed for the remainder of the harvests. When the international and internal prices fell, producers in the south of Chile held their crops in reserve until prices rose again.[41] The cost of imported food items in the working class diet, especially coffee, tea, sugar, and rice, depended on international prices and the foreign exchange value of the Chilean peso. As the peso rose in value during the First World War, prices for imported goods remained stable, in spite of their higher international price. Working class and elite groups alike placed the blame for high food prices at the end of the war on the shoulders of the exporters-landowners, and on several occasions the maritime unions refused to handle Chilean food products destined for foreign markets.[42]

High prices were further exacerbated by Santiago's system of distribution and marketing. Agricultural products shipped to Santiago from the surrounding countryside and nearby provinces were brought to the Vega Central, the city's principal market, to be auctioned off in huge lots to a small group of wholesalers. The wholesalers then divided their original purchases into smaller lots and sold them to retailers at great profit. A reporter from one Santiago newspaper traced a shipment of 3,500 heads of lettuce into the Vega. The entire load was purchased for twenty-five pesos by a wholesaler, who then sold it at a price of six pesos per 100 heads.[43] Retailers further raised prices by an average of 47 percent, according to a 1910 study.[44]

Many workers did not even pay the retail cost of an article. Habitually short of cash, the proletarian shopper sought and received credit for his daily purchases from the local butcher, baker, and greengrocer, but at a price above the normal retail level. Food was bought in small quantities and its cost calculated according to volume rather than weight, enabling the retailer to collect even higher prices.[45] To make matters worse, working class consumers could never be sure of what they were buying, whatever its price. A municipal hygiene inspector reported in 1918: "It has been repeated many times and with complete validity that the food consumed by the population of this vast metropolis, aside from being of such a high price that few can afford it, is in most cases adulterated and falsified with components foreign to its legitimate state."[46] A study in 1925 by a municipal chemist found that of 1,536 food samples tested, 34 percent were either adulterated or rotten.[47] Sawdust added weight to coffee, water found its way into milk and wine, and horse meat magically became pork sausage. Clandestine slaughterhouses in Santiago sold uninspected, tubercular, or rotten meat to workers at reduced prices. Chilean consumers enjoyed no effective legal protection against adulterated and unsanitary food during the first quarter of the twentieth century, and workers suffered more than any other class from such falsification.

CLOTHING

Urban workers spent a relatively small portion of their budget on clothing, approximately 11 percent according to research by the Labor Office.[48] Some proletarian clothing was made at home from native wool, while nearly all workers and their children had a suit of store-bought "Sunday clothes" (*ropa dominguera*).[49] Men normally wore a dark suit, white shirt, and tie as their Sunday outfit. Holidays and social events of nearly every kind, even demonstrations or rallies called by the labor unions, were also considered worthy of special clothing. Santiago newspapers issued on days of great protest meetings are filled with photographs of these well-dressed workers. Portraits of labor union leaders normally captured them in their finest garb. Aside from the custom of wearing good clothing for "social" occasions, which indicates that strikes and rallies served a social function, workers may also have dressed up to demonstrate their respectability to bourgeois onlookers, to the press, and to themselves.

Women wore skirts, blouses, and shawls as their main articles of dress. Children were given outfits much like those of their parents for holiday and everyday use. In very few pictures do urban workers appear in typically rural dress, with short pants, poncho, or the like.

Like all other items in the working class budget, clothing costs grew rapidly during the 1902–27 period. Between 1902 and 1912, the wholesale price of wool rose more than five and a half times.[50] A rising international price of cotton, coupled with fluctuations in the value of the peso and a purely revenue-seeking tariff of 30 percent on cotton fabric, caused the price of cotton goods to climb quickly.[51] According to Labor Office statistics, the price index for working class clothing grew by more than 125 percent between 1913 and 1924.[52]

HEALTH

Despite its benign climate, Chile ranked among the unhealthiest countries in Latin America during the first quarter of the twentieth century. Its national mortality coefficient (deaths per 1,000 people) remained above thirty-one during the entire 1900–1924 period, twice as high as Argentina's and two and a half times higher than Uruguay's.[53] Santiago, often dubbed a "deadly" city by its residents, scored a death rate (thirty-four to thirty-six per 1,000) even higher than the national average during the first decade of the century; it then dropped to twenty-two in 1929, a figure slightly lower than the national average.[54]

To dramatize the city's unsanitary condition, the newspaper *La Lei* compared the number of deaths in Santiago with mortality in Buenos Aires during the months of October and November, 1902. Despite the fact that Buenos Aires contained three times the population of Santiago, the number of burials during those months were nearly the same in the two cities—2,455 and 2,245, respectively.[55] Valparaíso's mortality coefficient in 1929 was 24.7, lower than the national average and considerably better than most other Chilean cities, which averaged 37.5 deaths per 1,000 inhabitants.[56]

Infants less than one year old accounted for one-third or more of total deaths during the years 1902–27. Vital statistics normally recorded cause of death for adults and children in such general categories that it is difficult to determine the number of deaths attributable to specific illnesses. Between 1924 and 1927, tuberculosis and respiratory ailments (such as pneumonia) accounted for an average of 26.8 percent of total deaths.[57] Influenza and gastrointestinal infections were common killers of all ages. A 1921 study of 1,064 working class children in Santiago conducted by doctors from the University of Chile determined that only fifty-two could by considered "healthy."[58] The rest suffered from intestinal infections (357), infectious hereditary diseases (216), tuberculosis (80), rickets (50), and other diseases.

Epidemic diseases tormented the residents of Santiago and Valparaíso on a regular basis. Smallpox brought from Bolivia to the north of Chile in 1902 reached Santiago the following year and remained until 1907, leaving thousands dead in its wake.[59] Valparaíso narrowly escaped an epidemic outbreak of bubonic plague in 1903, but in 1905 suffered much more from smallpox than did Santiago. Typhoid fever made a yearly appearance in Valparaíso with the first autumn rains in April–May. In 1911 and 1921, Santiago was hit by further smallpox epidemics. Unemployed nitrate workers from the North were the carriers for the latter outbreak when they were resettled in the Capital. By August of 1921, more than 1,000 santiaguinos were dying of smallpox per month. Typhus killed more than 6,000 in Santiago between 1919 and 1921.[60]

Epidemic disease and premature death victimized the working class home in Santiago and Valparaíso far more frequently than those of the middle and upper classes. The first reason was the unsanitary condition of working class neighborhoods in both cities. *El Mercurio* of Valparaíso commented in 1905: "This city . . . today presents the picture of those towns of the Middle Ages, in times in which public hygiene was unknown; . . . [it is] fetid, infected, pestilent, with its streets covered with a thick layer of fermenting filth."[61] Santiago was described by its chief of police in 1906 as "one of the unhealthiest cities in the country."[62] Open sewers in the Capital carried human excrement and garbage from the central portions of the city to the Mapocho River and the Zanjón de la Aguada, a turgid stream on the southern edge of town. During the heavy rainstorms, these sewer canals overflowed their banks and filthy water seeped onto streets and into homes. Garbage found its way to makeshift dumps usually located in working class neighborhoods. Municipal and private garbage collectors used the so-called "slaughterhouse" neighborhood in the southeast corner of Santiago as a dump as late as 1917. In Valparaíso, the gullies or *quebradas* behind working class hills became the resting place for mountains of garbage and the subsequent breeding ground for swarms of rats.[63]

Although unsanitary conditions characterized all of Santiago and Valparaíso, sewage disposal, public works, and hygiene were first improved in the "better" neighborhoods. As noted earlier, closed sewage lines and paved streets first appeared in the Centro of Santiago and the upper class Third Precinct just west of it. When major sewage lines did reach working class neighborhoods, little or no attempt was made to connect them with conventillo latrines.[64] Dust from unpaved streets spread disease in proletarian barrios long after concrete and asphalt streets were laid in the Centro.

Control over public health was given to the municipalities by the decentralizing legislation of 1891. The following year, Congress created the Superior Council of Public Hygiene with departmental branches to regulate public health in the cities. Lack of funds, the political unpopularity of higher property taxes for increased revenue, and corruption in the municipal administration greatly hampered efforts to better hygienic conditions in Santiago and Valparaíso.[65] Municipal regulations concerning public health, such as the housing laws, went unenforced due to lack of personnel and motivation. The national government and private charity were increasingly forced to intervene in matters of urban public hygiene.

Superstition and ignorance regarding sickness further contributed to the unhealthy state of the working class. Women especially turned to witch doctors or folk healers (*curanderos, médicas*) when they were ill, at times with fatal consequences. Santiago police periodically rounded up the curanderos, but many more appeared to take their places, especially during the threat of an epidemic.[66] The ignorance of most working class mothers combined with filthy living conditions and poor medical care to create Chile's staggering infant mortality rate during the first quarter of the century.

A third cause of proletarian ill health was the difficulty involved in obtaining proper medical care. During the entire 1902–27 period, some form of free medical care was available to working people in Santiago, but few took advantage of it, either because they did not know that these services existed or because they were unwilling or unable to present themselves for treatment. In 1904, the municipality created a series of clinics in each precinct of the city where workers could at least be examined by a doctor. According to 1908 figures, some 44,000 consultations took place in these municipal dispensaries, mainly with mothers and their children.[67] A free gynecology clinic also operated at this time, but a mere 1,627 women used it in 1908 because few people in the city knew of its existence.[68] Charity clinics run in conjunction with the Municipality of Santiago served another 100,000 people in 1908, although many of the "consultations" merely involved the dispensation of small quantities of milk or other basic foods.

In 1911 a central public assistance clinic was opened in Santiago, providing, perhaps for the first time, hospital care for emergency cases and seriously ill working people.[69] The formation of other charitable organizations, many of which received the endorsement of Santiago labor organizations, intensified the effort to combat alcoholism, venereal disease, and tuberculosis. Between 1908 and 1926, the number of people entering hospitals in Santiago grew from 23,000 to 53,000, including a reasonable number from the working class.[70]

In spite of the growing availability of health care facilities and the drop in the death rates of Santiago and Valparaíso by the late 1920s, many people remained without proper medical service. Few workers could afford to see a private doctor or spend time in a hospital. Drugs were very expensive and required experience and knowledge to procure and take. The fact that Chile's infant mortality rate continued to be notoriously high between 1902 and 1927 indicates that the health conditions of the working class remained exceptionally poor.

WOMEN AND THE FAMILY

The position of women in Chilean society during the first quarter of the twentieth century was likened to "legal slavery" by a leading Santiago newspaper.[71] Aside from being disenfranchised by the constitution of 1833, Chilean women were made legally subservient to their husbands. According to the Civil Code of 1855, unmodified in this respect during the 1902–27 period, "the husband gives protection to his wife and the wife must obey her husband." Employment possibilities, even for well-educated women, were limited to low-paying, low prestige jobs. By all but the most chauvinistic Latin American standards, the Chilean woman was treated as a second class citizen and person.

While upper and middle class women may have been dominated by their fathers and husbands and trained to merely reflect the image of a "proper" upbringing, working class women fared much worse. The most proletarian women could hope for was marriage to a vice-free, highly paid worker and a minimum of children.[72] For most, life in the city meant poverty, ignorance, and early death. Unlike their alcoholic menfolk who avoided harsh reality by turning to the bottle, working class women faced misery squarely and were more directly affected by it.

Proletarian girls appear to have received the same inadequate primary education as boys and also began work at an early age. Jobs for girls paralleled the occupations of women, either helping mind the home, or working as a washerwoman, seamstress, or in industries such as textiles. Many girls became domestic servants in wealthy and middle class families.

Thousands of young women turned to prostitution as a means of employment. *Casas de tolerancia,* as houses of prostitution were called, enjoyed legal status so long as they complied with regulations outlined by the municipalities. Free-lance whores who registered with city officials were also allowed to ply their trade without harassment. More than 400 women were registered with Valparaíso authorities at the beginning of the century. Between 1906 and 1920, some 200–500 prostitutes per year entered their names in the Santiago register, totaling 8,582 in all.[73] Registered prostitutes received an identification book to which municipal doctors would affix a hygiene stamp after completing a periodic inspection. The legality of prostitution reflected its social function in Chile. Men of all classes frequented the *casas de tolerancia* which, of course, varied in lavishness according to the customers they served.

Most of the thousands of prostitutes in both Santiago and Valparaíso were not registered, however. An underworld of white slavers, pimps, and thieves ran most of the urban houses of prostitution. Working class girls, generally recruited in the provinces for service in Santiago and in Santiago for the provinces, provided the raw material for the operation.[74] Of registered prostitutes in Santiago in 1920 and Valparaíso in 1898, some 39 percent had no previous occupation before turning to prostitution, 32 percent were formerly employed as seamstresses, and 15 percent were domestic servants.[75] Most claimed to be between eighteen and twenty-five years of age and almost all were unmarried. Friendly women or dandies called *caftenes* enticed the working girl with small gifts, free train tickets, and promises of a high-paying job in another city. When the victim arrived at her destination with the *caftén,* she was sold to a *rufián,* or pimp, who convinced her by either threats, beatings, or further gifts to become a prostitute. Once engaged in her new occupation, the working girl, either because of the shame brought upon herself and her family or because of the easy money she made as a whore, usually remained one for several years.

At all levels of Chilean society, women tended to marry at a younger age than men. According to the 1920 Census, 11.6 percent of Santiago girls between the ages of fifteen and nineteen, compared to only 2.1 percent of boys that age, were married. By age 20–24, 34 percent of women as opposed to 21 percent of men were married. Between age twenty-five and thirty-four, more than half of both sexes took a legal spouse.[76] The trend was similar in Valparaíso in 1920 and 1930, although porteños appear to have married at a slightly older age than santiaguinos. Many working class couples lived together and had children out of wedlock. In Santiago in 1903, for example, 49 percent of all births were illegitimate.[77]

Few working class Chileans practiced any method of contraception during the first quarter of the twentieth century.[78] Working class women frequently resorted to self-induced or midwife-aided abortions to terminate an unwanted pregnancy, despite the great health risks involved. It is difficult to determine what the average size of the working class family was during the 1902–27 period. The families studied in Labor Office monographs contained 4.31 members on the average, a seemingly low figure.

The death of infants and children was an integral facet of Chilean daily life during the early twentieth century. In the country-side, dead infants, termed *angelitos* (little angels), received the prayers of parents and friends in hope that the new arrival in heaven would intercede on behalf of their own salvation. Custom transformed the tragedy of an early death into a social occasion, the ascendence of an innocent to paradise amidst songs and celebration. Infant mortality—an urban as well as rural phenomenon—may also have served the function of lessening the long-term misery of the family by eliminating another mouth to feed. A single worker could always survive on his earnings. Married men might also remain solvent if their wives worked or if their own jobs were highly paid. As the family grew, however, the ability of husband and wife to live within their means declined.

Chile led most other Spanish American countries in infant mortality during the first quarter of the twentieth century. In 1920, for example, 250 infants per 1,000 born alive died during their first year of life as compared with 100 in Argentina.[79] The rate of infant mortality within the urban limits of Santiago dropped significantly between 1900 and 1930, however. In 1903–5, nearly one-third of all infants died in their first year of life, while by 1928, the figure shrank to less than one-quarter.[80] A careful study of infant mortality in two urban and two rural districts in the Department of Santiago by Luis Calvo Mackenna, Chile's leading pediatrician, showed the average rate in 1929 to be 232 per 1,000.[81]

Many children were doomed before birth by inherited disease. Calvo Mackenna estimated that in 1929 syphilis caused nearly 9 percent of all infant deaths. Children nursed by undernourished mothers lacked the strength to resist the onslaught of infections and diseases which flourished in the conventillo environment. Gastrointestinal infections, especially diarrhea, were common causes of infant death. Working mothers often left their children with neighbors or friends who, out of ignorance, gave cow's milk or unboiled water to the newborn. More infants died in the summer months, when the incidence of gastrointestinal infections and resulting dehydration peaked, than at any other time of the year. Blame for the high infant mortality rate in Santiago and Valparaíso was placed by nearly everyone on the lack of care infants received from their mothers. The working class press vigorously defended these women by claiming that their ignorance in matters of hygiene, rather than mistreatment, caused the deaths of their infants.[82] Filthy living conditions, poor food, and lack of proper medical attention compounded the problem.

Little has been written about working class children aside from their lack of education and their early entry into the workforce. Children of very poor parents often became beggars at an early age, and many left home permanently or were abandoned. Packs of vagrant children roamed the streets of Santiago and Valparaíso, either begging or stealing to keep themselves alive. Santiago police claimed that in 1904 these vagabond juveniles committed some 40 percent of all reported crimes in the city.[83] Charitable organizations, reform schools, and periodic campaigns to improve the lot of these children accomplished little.

EDUCATION

Public instruction in Chile in the early twentieth century was fairly advanced compared to its development in other Latin American nations, with a comparatively high (and, according to the censuses, steadily growing)

73

Table 3.3
Literacy Rates in the Provinces of Santiago
and Valparaíso and in Chile, 1885–1930

	1885	1895	1907	1920	1930
Santiago	36.2	45.2	50.5	61.8	86.4
Valparaíso	40.7	43.9	53.5	63.9	—
Chile	28.9	31.9	40.0	50.3	56.1

Sources: Chile, *Censo de 1920*, p. 303; *Censo de 1930*, vol. 2, p. 434.

literacy rate. Even so, the working classes of Santiago and Valparaíso received very little formal instruction during the years 1902–27. Few workers even completed primary school.

Men achieved slightly higher percentages of literacy than did women, and many more city dwellers learned to read and write than did people in rural areas. Within the Municipality of Santiago, literacy rates fluctuated significantly. According to the 1930 Census, only 1.5 to 3 percent of males living in the aristocratic districts of the Avenida Brasil, Calle Ejército, and Avenida España, could not read and write, while male illiteracy ranged from 12 to 19 percent in working class neighborhoods such as the Población Chuchunco and the Gasómetro District.[84] Nearly fifteen times more eight to fourteen-year-old children living just west of the Central Station in 1930 were illiterate than their counterparts along the elegant Avenida España, despite the fact that the latter district contained 2,000 more people than the former.[85]

Enrollment in public schools grew slowly until 1920 and then accelerated rapidly after the passage of the Obilgatory Primary Education Law in August of that year. Primary education was not mandatory in Chile until the 1920 law, which required all children to receive four years of schooling before their thirteenth birthday. Children not meeting this stipulation were nominally prevented from working on a full-time basis until they reached sixteen years of age. Before 1920, only an estimated 57 percent of school-age children received any primary education at all.[86] By 1936, primary school enrollment in Chile had grown to 557,000 from 170,000 in 1895, but only one child in ten actually completed six years of primary education.[87] Three of every ten school-age children received no education at all in 1921, a figure which had dropped to one in six by 1936.[88] The great majority of those children not attending school after the 1920 law took effect lived in rural areas.

Secondary education was a luxury reserved for upper and middle class youth. Proletarian children rarely attended primary school for more than a few years before taking a job to help support their families. Although very few working class children were qualified for, or even considered, a secondary education, those who did wish to pursue higher learning were effectively barred from doing so by a public school system designed to serve elites. Public secondary schools, called *liceos,* were bound by law to accept all students with six years of primary education, but they successfully excluded the few working class youths with a complete primary education by requiring clean uniforms to be worn to class every day, an impossibility for most proletarian families. Santiago's prestigious Liceo Number One for Girls served an expensive lunch each day which all students were required to purchase.[89] In 1926, only 12,400 students were enrolled in all the liceos of Santiago and Valparaíso combined.[90] Several thousand other students attended religious and private secondary schools, which normally charged a high tuition fee. Only one Chilean in 10,000 held a university degree in 1936.[91]

Public primary schools in most districts of Valparaíso and Santiago were mainly attended by working class children. In 1926, some ninety-eight primary schools operated in the Department of Valparaíso and 255 in Santiago.[92] The state built very few schools, but instead rented buildings in areas where more instruction was needed. As a result, most primary schools did not conform to any standards of construction or hygiene which would make them suitable as places of education. An inspection of eighty-eight of the 121 primary schools functioning in urban Santiago in 1903 showed one to by hygienically "optimal," twenty-one "good," thirty-eight "mediocre" (in need of major repairs), twenty-four "bad" (should be closed immediately), and four "horrible."[93] Classrooms lacked proper ventilation and light. In the winter, they went unheated and unprotected from the chilling dampness which seeped through their adobe-plaster walls and brick floors. The meagre portion of the national budget devoted to primary education left few funds for the construction of bathrooms in these buildings, not to speak of providing soap and towels. Little education could have taken place in these schools. In most cases, they simply provided a dreary, often filthy meeting ground where miserably paid teachers and undernourished students passed time.[94]

Some urban workers obtained basic and advanced training in industrial arts in schools run by the state, by the Sociedad de Fomento Fabril, and by the labor unions. A School of Arts and Crafts in Santiago provided instruction in technical fields. Between the early years of the century and the 1920s, a dozen or more SOFOFA schools trained workers in linear drawing, mathematics, stucco sculpture, and other skills. In the SOFOFA classes, students were required to be able to read and write, know the four basic operations of mathematics and fractions, and pay a fee of three pesos or more, conditions which few workers could meet. An average of only 440 students per year attended SOFOFA classes in Chile during the 1903–21 period.[95] Since a basic primary education was necessary for admittance to classes in advanced technical training, few workers qualified. Night classes sponsored by labor unions provided instruction in reading, writing, arithmetic, and other subjects during the entire period, although it is difficult to determine how many workers took advantage of them. Sympathetic public school teachers, university students, and even professors taught night courses for workers, especially in the case of the "popular universities" founded in 1912 and afterward. Technical training provided by professional teachers or masters in a given craft was available to members of several labor unions. Here again, few workers qualified. Nevertheless, union men enjoyed considerably greater access to education than did unorganized workers.

RELIGIOUS BELIEFS

While nearly all Chileans, according to the 1895–1930 Censuses, professed membership in the Catholic Church, few actively practiced their religion. Many factors eroded the power of the Church and weakened the hold of religion. Freemasonry, the rise of the Liberal and later the Radical and Democratic Parties, bitter Church/state conflicts, and an active spirit of anticlericalism fostered by freethinkers and positivists helped turn large numbers of Chilean males of all classes against the Church. Migration from the countryside to the city freed the former *campesino* from any control which landowner and priest may have exercised over him, although the many agricultural laborers of the peón-gañan class who came to the cities probably held few religious convictions to begin with.[96] Church power and prestige were systematically curtailed during the nineteenth and early twentieth centuries until the final separation of Church and state took place in 1925.

Working class people in Santiago and Valparaíso appear to have been no more or less religious than anybody else in urban society. Men typically avoided mass and the sacraments except on very special occasions, while women took a more active role in the Church.[97] Working class organizations maintained a hostile attitude toward the Church, which many regarded as an ally of the Conservative Party and an agent of the anti-union movement. Anarcho-Syndicalist and Socialist-influenced labor unions were especially vociferous in condemning the "opiate" effect of religion on the masses, although there is little indication that the Church held practical sway over urban workers. Catholic unions did not make much headway in Chile until the 1920s, when a group of "Christian Democrats" broke away from the Conservative Party to form the ephemeral "Federation of Chilean Workers" and "Federation of White Syndicates."

Occasionally, however, workers did express opinions about the Church. Elite groups, especially the Conservative Party, were convinced that the Church could both pacify the working class and eventually improve its lot through the practice of Christian charity.[98] When, for example, an outbreak

76

of strikes and violence in the nitrate fields caused a special investigatory commission to be sent in 1904 and the final report of the commission indicated great unrest among workers, the government responded by despatching priests into the nitrate camps to stabilize the situation.[99]

On other occasions, workers were stirred to violence at least partly because of religious or antireligious sentiment. During Holy Week of 1905 in Santiago, a priest who had only recently been defrocked for attempting to interpret the teachings of the Church in a "popular" manner convinced a crowd of workers to attack a religious procession. This extraordinary figure, named Juan José Julio Elizalde but popularly known as "Pope Julio," had a unique capacity for arousing the passions of what newspapers of the time called the "lowest class." On April 21, 1905, Pope Julio harangued a crowd of several thousand workers who had gathered to hear him and convinced them to march through the center of Santiago to demonstrate against the Good Friday procession then in progress. On the way, they were joined by members of the Anarchist group *La Luz* and by the Socialist Alejandro Bustamante. As the crowd came into contact with the procession, people began to hurl rocks at the marchers and the police guarding them, provoking a bloody clash during which over 100 workers and thirty police were injured.[100] Pope Julio, with his strange appeal as orator, quasi socialist, and ex-priest, played a notable role in the October, 1905 riots which rocked Santiago, and continued to preach his sermon of anticlericalism into the 1920s.

On other occasions, labor unions showed some deference towards religion. The mutualist Gran Federación Obrera de Chile inaugurated its new member unions by having their costly, hand-stitched banners blessed by a priest during a solemn ceremony.[101] Both the Communist and Anarchist press used the figure of Christ for their own propaganda purposes as if it held some meaning for workers. Their most common description of Christ was that of the "first Anarchist" or "first Communist," a convinced revolutionary who, were he to reappear on earth, would vigorously condemn the present-day Church for its support of the repressive capitalist system.[102] From all we can learn, the cause of Anarchism and Communism was not noticeably furthered by the use of the Christ figure, nor did an appeal to religious sentiment greatly benefit any group attempting to influence workers.

ENTERTAINMENT

As the size of the average workday gradually shrank and the organizational strength of the urban working class grew between 1902 and 1927, more forms of entertainment became available to the Chilean proletariat. Certain basic leisure-time activities, those most deeply rooted in custom and tradition, remained constant, however. Many of the urban proletariat's favorite pastimes could be classified as both vice and entertainment, with the distinction often blurred.

Perhaps the most common form of family entertainment available to the working class was outings to a park or to the countryside. Both Santiago and Valparaíso contained many parks and plazas, often in the heart of working class neighborhoods, where families could have a picnic or take a leisurely stroll. By the 1920s, public parks in Santiago, especially the huge Parque Cousiño, the Quinta Normal, and Cerro San Cristóbal, were considered entirely "popular" in the sense that the middle and upper classes seldom frequented them except in their carriages and motor cars.[103] On weekends and during the summer, urban Santiago practically belonged to the working class, as upper class families abandoned the Centro for their second homes in Providencia, their farms in the provinces, or their beach houses at Viña, Cartagena, Zapallar, and other mushrooming resorts. Workers also had access to the countryside. A tram ride, a brief train trip, or even a half-hour's walk could take them out of the city. Picnics, labor union outings, and visits to friends out of town proved no problem for most workers.

Movies, plays, and other forms of visual or staged entertainment commanded prices which most workers could not afford. In 1908, for example, only four cinemas and three theatres operated in Santiago, charging average admission prices of $2.10 and $3.60 respectively at a time when the mean daily wage was less than $2.00.[104] By the 1920s, however, the price of movie tickets had fallen and wages had risen to the point that the cinema became a popular working class pastime.[105] More cinemas sprang up to meet the rising demand, and advertisements for the films of Gloria Swanson, William S. Hart, and Charlie Chaplin crept into the working class press.

Sports did not enjoy wide popularity among the urban working class until the 1920s, and even then remained mainly a diversion for the wealthy. Soccer emerged early in the twentieth century as a game played by resident Britishers and their upper class Chilean friends, but the sport gradually filtered down to the pueblo. Sporting clubs and labor organizations were major promoters of soccer and boxing, probably the only sports in which working class Chileans became highly involved.

Perhaps the most important form of entertainment for men was drinking. Whether he drank to relax, ease the pain of a hard day's work, forget family and financial problems, or satisfy a habitual craving, the average Chilean worker consumed tremendous quantities of alcoholic beverages. Two 1909 studies placed per capita consumption of 100 percent grade alcohol at seven to ten and fifteen liters per year.[106] The figure for France at that time was 13.8 liters, the highest in Europe. A 1919 study pegged per capita consumption of wine in Valparaíso at 56.18 liters per year.[107] Drinking was an integral

78

part of the lives of most working men, forming the basis for social contact when other means of entertainment did not exist. Wine and *chicha,* a fermented fruit drink, were the beverages most consumed by the working class because they were very cheap.

Most drinking took place in bars, where the worker could socialize with friends and other customers. By law, bars and liquor stores in Chile required a license in order to operate, but more than a third of the establishments selling liquor went unregistered.[108] Drinking establishments, both legal and bootleg, tended to center in working class neighborhoods, above all in the San Pablo, Central Station, Mapocho Station, and San Diego barrios.[109] The solidly working class Fourth Precinct contained nearly four times as many illegal liquor establishments as any other precinct in Santiago in 1922.

Drinking in bars was a ritual. Men most frequently drank immediately after work late in the afternoon and on Sunday, although consumption of wine at lunch and even in the morning before work was not uncommon.[110] Workers generally drank with the purpose of getting drunk, considering inebriation essential to any successful night out. Although a 1902 law made intoxication illegal in itself, little social stigma appears to have been attached to drunkenness. During major holidays, especially Chile's independence day (celebrated at that time from September 17 to 21 or later), the streets of cities became littered with staggering drunks. Women and even children rounded out the group in many bars, despite laws prohibiting the presence of minors in places serving alcohol.

Another form of entertainment for men and a hallowed tradition among all classes in Chile was prostitution. For single men, whores provided their main source of sexual satisfaction as well as social contact, but married men by no means gave up old habits after taking a wife.[111] Gambling was another cherished pastime among workingmen, who often lost a day's wages at cards, dominoes, or the Club Hípico racetrack.[112] Liberal amounts of wine encouraged the workingman both at the *casa de tolerancia* and the track.

As in the case of education, union men enjoyed a great advantage over the unorganized in their access to entertainment, since labor unions during the entire 1902–27 period placed great emphasis on leisure and cultural activities. The working class press is filled with accounts of outings, plays, concerts, poetry readings, recitals, sporting events, lectures, and dances held by unions for the benefit of their members and often for the general public. Labor leaders perceived the glaring need of workers for constructive entertainment and sought to provide it in such a way as to further the integral development of each member and at the same time attract new *socios.* For the great mass of unorganized labor, however, the park, the tavern, and the *casa de tolerancia* remained the main centers of leisure.

ALCOHOLISM

Nearly everyone who wrote about the "social question" in Chile considered alcoholism, along with poor housing, to be the gravest problem facing the working class. Employers blamed drunkenness for high rates of absenteeism and job-related accidents.[113] Labor unions considered alcoholism a major force inhibiting the organization, economic betterment, and revolutionary potential of the working class.[114] Police officials and civic reformers claimed that alcohol was a major cause of violent crimes in Chile. Aside from the powerful Vintners' Association (Asociación Vinícola), all elements of Chilean society agreed that something had to be done to counter the destructive effects of drinking.

Alcoholism in Chile reflected the institutionalized nature of excessive social drinking. While upper and middle class men drank heavily, their habits did not appear to have had the same economic and social effects as alcohol consumption among the urban proletariat. Lower class drinking more frequently crossed the boundary between entertainment and vice, and was linked in the public mind with economic deprivation and moral degeneration. As mentioned earlier, workers drank as a response to many factors. Escape from the reality of poverty, the need for social exchange, conformity to customary male behavior, and the easing of tension and physical pain were all cited as causes of alcoholism. Alcoholic beverages remained extremely cheap in relation to any other product of consumption during the entire 1902–27 period, and were always available, in either licensed or illegal establishments. A powerful lobby of wine producers prevented anti-alcohol legislation from acquiring teeth, and municipal authorities generally did not enforce those regulations which were passed.

The famous *Ley de Alcoholes* of 1902 for the first time made drunkenness itself a crime. Before that date, drunks were not liable to arrest unless they became bothersome to other people; under the terms of the new law, anyone found "in a manifest state of inebriation" in a public place could be arrested and sentenced to either three to five days in jail or a fine of not less than five pesos.[115] In effect, however, the 1902 law did not lower the rate of alcoholism, because Congress intended it to be a producer of revenue rather than a social reform. During the latter nineteenth century, the wine producers and alcohol distillers in Chile fought a running battle for control of the alcoholic beverages market. The 1902 law recognized the final triumph of the vintners by placing a high tax on factory-produced alcohol, limiting its sale in bars and restaurants, and allowing the sale of wine to go virtually unregulated.[116] The designers of the bill undoubtedly felt that the municipal treasury could be further padded by fines collected from arrested drunks.

During the first year in which the Ley de Alcoholes took effect (1902), arrests and convictions nearly doubled in Chile.[117] Between 1903 and 1909,

Santiago police arrested an average of 17,300 persons per year for drunkenness, of which only 10 percent were women.[118] In 1908, only one-fifth of all those arrested for drunkenness actually went to jail. Drunk arrests during the 1903-9 period accounted for slightly more than half of total arrests among both men and women. The number of arrested drunks appears to have remained within the range of fifteen to twenty thousand per year in Santiago during the 1902-27 period.[119]

Rather than curbing alcoholism, the Ley de Alcoholes had an unfavorable effect on the well-being of the working class. As one observer noted in 1909: "The police arrest no one but the worker and the poor unfortunate: the drunken aristocrat, the rich man, the elegant youth, and even the office worker escape the clutches of the patrolman."[120] Even if he were to be arrested, a fine of five pesos meant nothing to a wealthy person, but for the worker it was more than a day's wages.

In 1915 and 1916, a series of laws passed which limited consumption of wine, beer, and chicha to establishments classified as hotels, restaurants, and clubs, and at the same time prohibited these places of business from serving alcoholic beverages from Saturday afternoon to Monday morning except at stipulated mealtimes.[121] Although this law struck at one of the real causes of alcoholism, the ready availability of liquor, its provisions were easily sidestepped by bar owners, who began serving meals and took out second class licenses as "restaurants" and "clubs."[122] In 1924, a new municipal law in Santiago reopened bars from 8 A.M. to 8 P.M. and allowed restaurants to serve liquor from 8 A.M. to 4 A.M. Even with apparently preventive legislation on the books between 1916 and 1924, it is highly unlikely that lower class access to cheap liquor was inhibited in any way, since arrests for drunkenness remained at pre-1916 levels. Pressure from the vintners, bribery, and widespread municipal corruption doomed even the most will-intentioned reform legislation to failure.

Private organizations and labor unions undertook their own campaigns to lower working class consumption of alcohol, apparently with little success. A *Liga Contra el Alcoholismo* patterned after the French Anti-Alcohol League operated during the second decade of the century with support from the Santiago mutual aid societies, but could do little more than distribute pamphlets and hold lectures.[123] Efforts by other charitable organizations, such as the *Liga Defensa de la Raza,* received the endorsement of many labor unions in Santiago and Valparaíso, but appear to have accomplished very little to counter alcoholism. The labor unions themselves found it difficult to stop their members from drinking during union meetings, let alone convince them to give up the bottle altogether. In general, the weak and halfhearted anti-alcohol campaign in Chile appears to have failed completely between 1902 and 1927.

81

CRIME

As in the case of drunkenness, the vast majority of people who went to jail or prison for non–alcohol related crimes were of working class background. Classifications of the professions of prisoners in jails and penitentiaries invariably listed unskilled laborers, day laborers, small-scale peddlars, service workers, unemployed men, and agricultural workers most frequently.[124] Among women, domestic servants, cooks, laundresses, prostitutes, and seamstresses were those most commonly jailed. In 1920, no convict serving more than a sixty-day sentence in Chilean jails had any high school education, a further indication of the working class nature of crime and unequal enforcement of the law.[125]

Violent crime appears to have been far less common in Santiago and Valparaíso than in mining and rural areas. Homicide rates for both cities were considerably lower than the national average during the 1905–8 period.[126] In 1909, 92 percent of all crimes committed in Santiago did not involve the use of a weapon. Those violent crimes which did take place in the Capital occurred overwhelmingly in working class neighborhoods. In 1902, for example, five times more people were wounded in criminal attacks in the totally working class Fourth Precinct than in the aristocratic Third.[127] Although anti-alcohol reformers often claimed that violent crime and drunkenness went hand-in-hand, statistics indicate otherwise. According to Santiago police, only one of the city's nineteen reported homicides in 1906 was committed by a drunk, and in 1912, only 11 percent of all prisoners sentenced to terms of six months or more had been intoxicated when committing their crime.[128] Few captured criminals used firearms in the commission of their misdeeds, although between 1901 and 1909 the number of violent crimes committed in Santiago with the use of revolvers grew steadily from thirty-one to 196, and continued to rise into the 1920s. More than ten times as many violent crimes were carried out by people armed with knives and clubs, the typical weapons of the working class criminal.[129]

Just as workers in the cities appear to have committed the great majority of crimes, given the fact that drunkenness, begging, vagrancy, and disorderly conduct constituted the most frequent infractions of the law, so did workers most directly suffer from the effects of crime. In 1906, more than six times as many homes were robbed or broken into in the Fourth Precinct of Santiago than the Third or First, where houses and shops certainly contained more goods worth stealing.[130]

After the riot of May, 1903, in Valparaíso and the October, 1905 sack of Santiago, a great fear of lower class crime welled up among property holders and members of the "aristocracy." Events between 1902 and 1927 demonstrate, however, that very little urban violence or crime crossed class lines.

Only a handful of elite homes were broken into by mobs during the riots of 1903 and 1905, and few upper or middle class persons were killed. Incidents of violence against members of the upper class by workers received much publicity whenever they occurred, but by all indications they were infrequent. Police units normally protected upper class property quite effectively during major urban disturbances, even when the mob appeared to have complete control of the town, as in 1903 and 1905. Crime in the cities, therefore, appears to have affected the upper classes very little, remaining a working class problem.

A group that had a singular ability to provoke the hatred of the working class was the police.[131] Despite the fact that most policemen were recruited from the lower classes, urban workers from childhood learned to look upon the patrolman (*guardián*) as their natural enemy, an oppressor who enforced the law only to harass them. Mounted dragoons charged into crowds without mercy during riots and demonstrations, policemen broke up countless labor union rallies and picket lines, and agents of the Security Police infiltrated every important working class organization. This deep-seated hatred for law enforcement officers had the long-range effect of intensifying industrial conflict and deepening the alienation of the working class.

CREDIT

Many working class families could not meet their basic expenses for food, housing, heat, and clothing with the wages they brought home.[132] Barring a loan from a well-off friend or relative, the urban worker had nowhere to turn for the extra money he needed for survival but to the pawnshop (casa de préstamo). Bakers and butchers extended credit only so long; the landlord could be put off for one month but not two. Sickness and death in the family created unexpected costs which surpassed income. In cases like these, a member of the urban proletariat had no choice but to pawn yet another personal belonging. According to the newspaper of one labor federation in 1922, "The pawnshop business has arrived at the point of being a necessary evil for our proletariat."[133] Urban workers hated the predominantly Spanish pawnbrokers who paid so little for their possessions and resold them at a handsome profit, but they desperately needed the extra pesos derived from the unhappy transaction.[134]

Exchanges in the *casas de préstamo* occurred frequently, as workers reacted to the need for additional cash by pawning only enough to meet their current needs. In 1918, 70 percent of goods pawned were articles of clothing and 20 percent tools and furniture.[135] Typically, about 70 percent of all transactions involved an article valued at between one and five pesos, further evidence of the stopgap nature of pawnshops as a means of obtaining credit.[136]

As the 1902–27 period wore on, workers relied increasingly on pawnshops. The value of transactions in Chile nearly doubled between 1913 and the depression year 1914, as unemployed workers and those suffering from pay cuts sold more of their goods in order to survive.[137] Between 1916 and 1927, the total value of goods pawned in Santiago and Valparaíso rose 266 percent, and between 1916 and 1925 per capita loans climbed from $102.12 to $169.65.[138]

According to the 1877 law which first regulated pawnshops, written contracts for each transaction had to be given to the person hocking his possession, but no limit was placed on the amount of interest he could be charged.[139] By the early twentieth century, further legislation provided for regular inspection of pawnshops and fixed the monthly rate of interest at a maximum of 4 percent. Pawnbrokers normally made their profit by appraising the article at half of its real value, subtracting a portion of the interest to be paid from the sum of money advanced, and reselling the article after its former owner failed to redeem it. Public outcry against the abuses of the pawnshops caused the interest rate to be lowered to 3 percent per month in 1920 and stimulated the creation of a Popular Credit Fund which raised money for interest-free loans to workers by collecting a fixed percentage of auction sales. Pawnbrokers overcame the potentially harmful effects of regulatory legislation by bribing the pawnshop inspection functionaries and by cleverly juggling their books to hide profits. As in the case of housing and other social legislation, pawnshop regulations went unenforced.

CONCLUSION

By all appearances, the standard of living of workers in Santiago and Valparaíso was lower than that of nitrate workers during the first quarter of the twentieth century. Lawrence Stickell, in his excellent study of the nitrate industry, concluded that "nitrate workers (were) relatively well-off compared to their counterparts elsewhere. . . ."[140] A comparison of the socioeconomic state of unskilled workers in the North and central cities indeed shows the nitrate workers to have been in better shape on nearly every count. Salaries in the North were far higher, so much so that the typical unskilled nitrate miner received better pay than many semiskilled workers in Santiago and Valparaíso.[141] While the cost of food was normally higher in the North, the disparity never equaled pay differences, and in at least one year the cost of living in the nitrate fields actually fell below that of the urban center. Workers in the nitrate camps generally inhabited quarters that, besides being more spacious than conventillo rooms, were provided free. The company store, long described by historians as a means of robbing workers of their wages through high prices, actually appears to have held prices down in most oficinas. Retailers in Santiago marked their prices up an average of 47 percent at a time when nitrate camp stores took a 15 percent profit. Furthermore, nitrate workers could obtain free credit at the company store while their urban counterparts had no choice but to pawn their belongings on unfavorable terms. Savings appears to have been a real possibility for even unskilled nitrate miners, while the concept was rarely discussed among any but the most highly paid urban workers.

In 1913, the mortality coefficient for the Provinces of Tarapacá and Antofagasta was slightly lower than those of Santiago and Valparaíso, despite the more easy access to hospitals enjoyed by urban workers. Illiteracy on the pampa was much higher, but schools may have been neither less available nor worse in quality than in urban Chile. Alcoholism appears to have been a lesser problem in the nitrate camps, where the consumption of liquor was often prohibited and the isolation imposed on the pampino stimulated overtime work and greater savings.

While the urban worker had to fend for himself when unemployed, the out-of-work nitrate miner could be resettled at government expense and find a new job. Nitrate miners suffered many privations during these forced relocations, but they could expect to be rehired for work in the North after a relatively brief period of unemployment, so quickly did the nitrate industry rebound following periodic downturns in production.

Although some urban workers undoubtedly lived better than others, no clear pattern of a "labor aristocracy" emerges. There is little indication that artisans or highly paid workmen lived in separate neighborhoods, wore clothing of different design from most other workers, ate different foods, or lived dissimilar lives. The higher-paid worker and his family consumed more food, perhaps lived in a two-room conventillo apartment or a cité, owned a few more articles of clothing, etc., but no significant patterns of elitist behavior appear to have emerged as a result of better living standards. Perhaps the mutual aid societies of the period most closely resembled an "aristocracy," although their conservative outlook hardly reflected elitist ideals or rejection of proletarian values. Nor did comparatively high pay guarantee a worker what could be considered "decent" living conditions by middle class standards, which normally reflected the ideal of conspicuous consumption. The gap between working and middle/upper class life-styles remained too great to be bridged by higher salary or increased literacy.

When working people did rise above the urban mass to become political or labor union leaders, they appear to have either remained closely identified with the pueblo or left it altogether for middle class status. Most labor leaders, as will be demonstrated in the following chapters, were better educated than other workers and possessed work skills guaranteeing them an above-average wage. They do not, however, appear to have identified with the middle class, although they were better equipped than their compatriots to deal with people of middle and upper class background. Instead, labor leaders quite closely related to the working masses and to the rank and file of their unions.

Rather than "rising out" of the working class, many labor leaders may have instead been "sinking into" working class status from what in the nineteenth century may have more closely resembled a labor aristocracy composed of skilled and prosperous artisans. The speed and direction of Chile's industrialization eroded traditional skills less rapidly than in the case of European nations during the Industrial Revolution, but between 1902 and 1927, gradual mechanization as well as a growing disdain for manual labor among the upper and middle classes may have set the artisan on a downward track. Inflation ate steadily into real wages, especially after 1891, resulting in downward socioeconomic mobility for wage earners while property owners and speculators prospered. In such a situation, identification with the proletariat and even a revolutionary outlook would have been likely reactions.

Several aspects of the condition of the urban working class hindered the growth of labor organizations. Alcoholism was probably the most important factor, since it caused absenteeism, lowered the worker's weekly income considerably, and generally added to the impoverishment of the working class. Labor unions found it difficult to recruit workers who had no funds available for dues and could not sustain themselves during strikes or periods of blacklisting. Even without the curse of alcohol, most urban workers had no savings or monthly surplus to invest in union dues, strike funds, or organizational activities.

The dependent, subservient position of women in Chilean working class society, as well as their disadvantageous industrial role, made them extremely difficult to organize. A woman's income often meant the difference between food or starvation for her family, between paying the rent or being evicted. Husbands and fathers greatly feared having that supply of income cut off and therefore were reluctant to run the risk of layoffs or firings due to union activity. Without the support of women, strikes in industries such as shoes, leather, textiles, and food preparation had far less chance of success. When labor organizations were able to overcome this problem, as in the case of the Shoeworkers' Federation, they prospered.

Other working class conditions favored the formation of labor unions. The miserable housing situation appears to have united much of the urban working class on at least a temporary basis. Since the conventillo was something of a communal house, families sharing its facilities appear to have developed a high degree of solidarity among themselves. The rent strike movement of 1925 revealed unprecedented levels of grass roots participation in a social movement which notably occurred in both Santiago and Valparaíso. (See chapter 8.) People fed up with high rents and filthy living conditions rallied by the tens of thousands to demand rent reductions from the government, and later resorted to direct action when all else failed. Most Chilean workers enjoyed a bare minimum of privacy at home and consequently developed a certain sociability derived from sharing common experiences, which facilitated collective action.

High food costs, while driving down real wages, also provided workers with a common grievance which, like poor housing, helped to mobilize them. Unions offering the opportunity to better wages through collective action appealed to workers with rising but frustrated expectations. Needs neglected by society, such as education, entertainment, and aid for financial emergencies, were met at least in part by labor unions. In this respect, the union held out a richer life for Chilean workers who could perceive the benefits of organization membership and were able to pay the costs involved.

In a very real sense, the Chilean worker functioned as an independent actor during the first quarter of the twentieth century. The Church exercised no practical control over him, political parties paid him attention only at election time, few employers showed concern for his well-being, and the government ignored him almost completely. Only the unions actively tried to recruit working class support on a long-term basis. They alone offered the worker a dignified place in society and a sense of belonging to something other than an amorphous mass. With no serious competition, the unions built an independent labor movement before 1924 which social legislation, cheaper food, better housing, and more attention, even of a repressive nature, on the part of government might have prevented.

4

The Rise of Labor Unions, 1902-8

THIS AND THE REMAINING CHAPTERS discuss labor organizations in Santiago and Valparaíso between 1902 and 1927. My division of the quarter century into periods is somewhat artificial, since none of the years selected, except perhaps 1927, involved cataclysmic changes in the nature of labor unions. However, since the purpose of my research has not been to trace the historical development of a single political or working class organization, the years chosen reflect widespread trends rather than specific occurrences. The growth of working class organizations in Chile was a steady process. Alternating periods of rapid unionization and retrogression did take place, but the long-range trend was of increased membership in unions. Nearly every labor union or federation could point to a precursor which laid its foundation. The temple of organized labor in Chile rose by placing stone upon stone. No single law, political event, or charismatic leader built or destroyed this edifice.

It is therefore mistaken to view the nineteenth century as a "prehistory" of the proletariat or to consider the first strikes as constituting a "heroic" period in Chilean labor history. I have chosen to study the years between 1902 and 1908 in this chapter to underline a trend in the historical continuum. The "resistance societies" of this period were an important force in increasing the organizational capacity of Chilean workers. The first strike of a resistance society occurred in 1902, to be followed by many more. Great gains in the size and strength of organized labor in Santiago and Valparaíso were realized between 1905 and 1907, and important changes in the industrial relations system began to take place. Increased strike activity and working class organizational strength forced employers and the government to seek new methods of dealing with the "social question." Labor became a more active, although not always welcome, participant in the economic and political life of the country. The year 1908 marked the end of this expansive period of urban labor unions.

Organized Labor Before 1902

Until the last years of the nineteenth century, almost all labor organizations in Chile were mutual aid societies (*socorros mutuos*) formed by artisans and skilled workers. They provided members with sickness or accident pay, a "dignified" burial, death benefits paid to dependents, and, in some cases, retirement payments. Other activities of the mutual aid societies included the establishment of savings plans, night classes for workers and their families, cultural and social events, and consumer cooperatives. The first mutualist groups were established in Santiago during the 1840s, but it was not until the formation of the printers' societies in Santiago and Valparaíso in 1853 and 1855 that a working class organization achieved any institutional stability.[1] Other skilled or semiskilled workers, such as tailors, carpenters, bricklayers, bakers, and railway workers, also organized mutual aid societies. While many were established along purely craft lines, other *socorros mutuos* admitted workers of several industries, served all the employees of a single establishment, or included only female or Catholic workers.

Mutual aid societies generally solicited and nearly always received recognition as legally constituted bodies according to the Civil Code of 1855. Aside from those statutes in the Code regarding the freedom of citizens to associate and form legal organizations, no Chilean laws before 1924 in any way regulated the formation of labor unions. All associations, including mutual aid societies, solicited legal status by directly petitioning the President of the Republic. After examining the bylaws and statutes of an applicant organization to see if they conformed with Chilean law, the President was empowered to issue a decree establishing the legality of the association. Once legal, a mutual aid society could enter into binding obligations with its members and with other institutions, acquire goods of any kind, be legally represented in court, and enjoy legal protection against the theft of its funds.[2] Legal regulation of the dues, savings, investments, and benefit payments of the *socorros mutuos* bolstered their economic stability and furthered their attraction for artisans and skilled workers.

A study by Labor Office functionary Oscar Parrao claimed that some seventy-five societies existed in 1890, 240 in 1900, 433 in 1910, and 735 in 1922.[3] Parrao further estimated that another sixty-five nonlegal mutual aid societies operated in Chile in 1922, and that the 800 together contained some 135,000 members and capital of between nine and ten million pesos. A Labor Office survey of working class societies in 1909 found that the Provinces of Santiago and Valparaíso contained one-half of total mutual aid society membership.[4]

In spite of the rapid growth of mutual aid societies during the second and third decades of the twentieth century, mutualism ceased to be a dynamic force in the history of the movement after the 1905–7 strike wave. During the last quarter of the nineteeth century, however, the *socorros mutuos* played a key role in furthering the cause of organized labor in Santiago and Valparaíso. Many of the artisans and skilled workers who composed the bulk of mutual aid society membership actively participated in politics, either as revolutionaries during the conspiratorial disturbances of the 1840s and 1850s, or as founders and supporters of the Democratic Party (Partido Demócrata— PD) in 1887.[5] Mutualist societies furthered the knowledge of revolutionary and reformist ideologies by bringing together those who espoused such ideas. Their meetings became the sounding board for social democrats, freethinkers, utopian socialists, Marxists, and Anarchists, while their libraries contained the works of Proudhon, Saint Simon, Blanc, Marx, Bakunin, Kropotkin, and many others. Although the mutualist societies made no provisions for strikes in their bylaws, it is certain that they unofficially participated in those strikes which occurred in urban areas during the nineteenth century. The role of the early mutual aid societies was therefore a broad one. They provided members with greater financial security, brought them into contact with people of different political and ideological persuasions, afforded further opportunity for political participation (especially through the PD), and, on several occasions, mobilized them for job action.

"Revolutionary" ideology of every strain arrived in Chile from abroad (mainly France) and won converts among artisans and intellectuals. The famous *Sociedad de la Igualdad* formed by Francisco Bilbao and Santiago Arcos in Santiago in 1850 could claim as its ideological predecessor the liberal-democratic, mutualist, and utopian Socialist movements of the 1840s.[6] France continued to supply both ideas and revolutionaries to several Latin American countries, especially after the destruction of the Paris Commune and the subsequent emigration of many Communards. French exiles founded an Argentine section of the First International in Buenos Aires in 1872 and an Uruguayan branch in 1878.[7] While some Communards did arrive in Chile during the 1870s and a few aided organizers from Montevideo in establishing sections of the International in Valparaíso and Santiago in 1881, their long-term effect on working class movements in Chile proved minimal.[8]

Very few foreigners took part in the growth of labor organizations in Chile during the half-century from 1870 to 1920. We have already seen that Chile received insignificant numbers of working class immigrants at a time when millions of European workers flocked to Brazil, Argentina, and Uruguay. Immigrants founded and staffed labor unions, Socialist clubs, and Anarchist federations in the Atlantic seaboard countries of Latin America long before Chilean workers established similar organizations. Only a handful of foreigners rose to positions of importance within the Chilean labor movement, the most notable being the intellectual Mario Centore (Peruvian) and the Anarch-

90

ist organizers Julio Rebosio (Italian) and Inocencio P. Lombardozzi (Argentine).

Libertarian and Socialist ideas were instead transmitted to Chile by printed sources and through contact with workers and intellectuals in Argentina. The original French editions of works by Louis Blanc, Proudhon, Fourier, and Saint Simon could be purchased in Santiago and Valparaíso as early as 1850, but Spanish versions of Anarchist and Socialist literature did not become available before the arrival of Pi y Margall's translations of Proudhon in the 1870s.[9] Anarchists in Argentina, Mexico, Cuba, and Uruguay printed several short-lived newspapers before 1890, but it was not until the appearance of *El Perseguido* of Buenos Aires (1890–97) that the libertarian press became firmly established. Revolutionary groups in Chile did not publish any periodicals of widespread importance until the first decade of the twentieth century. The arrival of Anarchist books and newspapers from Argentina, the rest of Latin America, and Europe during the 1890s, however, provided steady ideological nourishment for Chile's first generation of libertarian workers until they were able to produce their own propaganda.

The political awareness and organizational capacity of Chilean urban workers grew rapidly between 1888 and 1902. As a response to the extension of the franchise to all literate male adults by an 1884 law which eliminated property-holding as a requirement for suffrage and the reluctance of the Radical Party (PR) to accomodate demands for reform, a group of middle class professionals and artisans broke away from the PR to form the Partido Demócrata in November, 1887. The PD considered itself to be the workingman's political party, and from its inception counted on the support and active participation of many members of the mutual aid societies. Most of the founders and early leaders of the PD were less than thirty years old when they became Democrats. Young men of different backgrounds became attracted by the party's early reputation for combativeness, reformist zeal, and willingness to support strikes and public protests. Party leadership during the PD's first twenty years remained in the hands of two groups: professional/white collar employees and worker/mutual aid society representatives.[10] The former group included the party's *jefe máximo* Malaquías Concha (lawyer), Francisco Landa (doctor), Alejandro Bustamante (doctor), and Lindorfo Alarcón (white collar employee). Representatives of the second group were: Zenón Torrealba (pipe fitter), Artemio Gutiérrez (tailor), Abraham Leckie (barber), Bonifacio Veas (tinsmith), Luis Emilio Recabarren (printer), and Vicente Adrián (jeweler). In 1894 the PD elected its first deputy to Congress, followed by others in 1897, and 1901, and six in 1906. The party eventually abandoned its stance as the reformist opposition by joining coalitions formed by traditional political parties. Marxists, quasi anarchists, and social democrats periodically attempted to steer the PD on a more leftist course, and usually abandoned the party after failing to do so. These defections occurred mainly among members of the PD's labor wing, although ideological conviction, personal differences, and regional factors rather than class background caused rifts in the party to occur. Democrats continued to exercise much influence within the mutual aid societies, but the party's unpopularity with Anarcho-Syndicalist and Marxist-led labor unions eroded much of its labor support by the 1920s.

Early attempts by splinter groups from the PD to form effective Marxist political parties enjoyed little success. A Socialist Party of Chile was formed in 1897 in Santiago, followed by the Francisco Bilbao Socialist Workers' Party in 1898, the Socialist Party in 1900, and, in Valparaíso, the Social Democratic Party in 1901.[11] These ephemeral socialist groups convinced few of their viability as a political alternative to the PD. The Democrats, meanwhile, continued to expand their influence within the mutualist movement by assisting in the formation of a series of organizations which united mutual aid societies on a regional basis. From 1900 until approximately 1906, the Democrats further increased their labor support by fostering the development of the labor "brotherhoods," or *mancomunales*, of the North, central cities, and coal mining zone near Concepción.

Significant numbers of urban workers rejected politics altogether and became Anarchists. The Anarchist movement in Chile grew slowly, staffed continuously by Chilean nationals but greatly influenced by foreign ideology and propaganda. Early issues of the libertarian newspaper *El Perseguido* were sent from Buenos Aires to Anarchist sympathizers in Valparaíso, and in 1891 a Chilean correspondent began reporting news of the Civil War.[12] The following year, a small group of Anarchists in Valparaíso formed what was probably Chile's first "social studies center" (*centro de estudios sociales*), the typically libertarian institution whose basic purpose was to promulgate Anarchist ideology.[13] Other such centers appeared in both Valparaíso and Santiago, and one managed to issue four numbers of Chile's first Anarchist publication, *El Oprimido* of Santiago, in 1893.[14] Thirty-eight contributors, most of whom sent their donations under false names to avoid persecution by the police, sustained *El Oprimido* during its short life.

By 1897, the number of Anarchist workers in Santiago and Valparaíso had grown to perhaps a hundred or more. A group of Anarchist sympathizers and Socialist-oriented renegades from the PD attempted in October of that year to organize a "Socialist Union" among Santiago workers as a revolutionary vehicle. Although they managed to recruit some 250 workers from the ranks of the mutual aid societies, the secretary in charge of registering these men was an undercover agent of the Santiago police who turned the list over to the authorities.[15] Police promptly raided the hall of the Socialist Union, arrested several of its leaders, and effectively dissolved the organization. The founders of the Union then began their effort to influence workers by "boring from within" the mutual aid societies and forming more social studies groups.

In early 1898, the Anarchist firebrand Magno Espinoza organized the *Grupo Rebelión* in Santiago, and the Chilean disciples of the Argentine Socialist José Ingenieros, led by Alejandro Escobar y Carvallo, began to publish the weekly magazine *La Tromba*.[16] These early proponents of libertarianism in Chile had not yet reached a level of ideological sophistication worthy of being called Anarchist-Communist or anything else, but rather borrowed heavily from many sources. They did, however, concur in their stance against politics, the Church, the military, capitalism, and the mutual aid societies. Kropotkin's *The Conquest of Bread*, which outlines the basic conceptions of Anarchist-Communism (as opposed to the collectivist ideas of Bakunin), was widely read by Chilean libertarians as early as 1895, but few declared themselves to be followers of the new doctrine.[17] Marxian economics were accepted wholeheartedly by Chilean Anarchists, while many also were drawn to the Bakuninist conception of "revolution by deed." Violence and destruction became fixations for the early Anarchists, a fact which the police and worried elites quickly perceived. Statements such as the following outburst by Escobar y Carvallo frequently appeared in the Anarchist press:[18]

> Capital, Private Property, and Government will tomorrow all be eliminated and taken along with other filth to death's door. . . . Nothing will be left of the political, economic, and religious garbage of this sodomitic society. . . . Everything will be destroyed by the new communists of the new Commune.

Such statements may have accomplished little more than inciting the wrath of the police. Magno Espinoza was jailed for publishing the Anarchist paper *El Rebelde* in 1898, but again tested Chile's freedom of the press law in a second number which appeared six months later. His defiant claim, "We wipe our asses with the paper on which you print your laws," cost him another term in jail and the permanent closing of *El Rebelde*.[19]

Anarchist doctrine became somewhat more sophisticated as contact with Latin American and European libertarians increased. Chilean workers enthusiastically sent copies of their newly established newspapers to foreign Anarchists in order to receive other literature in return and to participate in what they rightly considered an international revolutionary movement. Greatest contact was maintained with Argentina, less with Brazil and Uruguay, and very little with the Caribbean, United States, and Europe.[20] Argentine workers, on the other hand, remained in constant touch with Europe, due mainly to the large number of immigrants in the workforce and the shorter distance between Western Europe and the Río de la Plata. From the 1890s into the 1930s, Chilean Anarchists continued to be somewhat isolated from the mainstream of Anarchism in Europe, although European influence did reach Chile via Argentina. The noted Italian revolutionary Errico Malatesta spent many years in Argentina during the 1880s but did not travel to Chile. His chief lieutenant, Pietro Gori, did, however, give several lectures in Santiago and Valparaíso in April, 1901.[21] Other Anarchist notables, such as the Peruvian Eulogio Otazú, the Spaniard Rodolfo González Pacheco, and the Spanish terrorists Buenaventura Durruti, Francisco Ascaso, and Gregorio Jover, visited Chile for brief speaking tours or "fund raising" (bank robberies) between 1913 and 1925.[22] As mentioned earlier, the overall effect of their presence on Chilean workers was slight. Syndicalist and Anarchist-Communist ideas normally reached Chile in the form of printed matter, although the industrial syndicalist doctrines of the U.S.-based Industrial Workers of the World were transmitted to Chile after 1917 by the personal contact of foreign sailors with Chilean dockers. Given the lack of immigration to Chile and her geographic isolation, the Chilean Anarchist movement remained something of an ideological maverick during much of its existence.

Anarchists in Chile sought to put their revolutionary ideas into practice by forming resistance societies within existing mutualist labor organizations and by staging frequent protest meetings. Most of the early Anarchist leaders were young, well educated, skilled workers, members of the same socioeconomic group which played an active role in the Partido Demócrata, the mutual aid societies, and the early Socialist endeavors. Among them were: Esteban Cavieres (machinist), Mango Espinoza (bronze worker), Manuel J. Montenegro (printer), Ignacio Mora (sailor), Luis Morales (shoemaker), Luis Olea (painter), Nicolás Orellana (printer), Amador Parry (tannery worker), Luis A. Sosa (printer), and Julio E. Valiente (printer). A few, such as Escobar y Carvallo, Marcos Yáñez, and Inocencio Lombardozzi, came from middle class families. These worker-Anarchists were already active in mutual aid societies before their conversion to libertarianism, and thus used "boring from within" tactics to recruit menbers for resistance organizations.

The basic differences between a mutualist society and a resistance society involved goals and tactics. While the *socorros mutuos* had as their basic goal the financial security of the membership through dues payments, the resistance societies attempted to better the lot of the worker by strikes. The Anarchists criticized the mutual aid societies for their overwhelming concern with decent burials and social security, claiming that workers would never win better conditions or pay from employers unless they took to the offensive.[23] Resistance societies, on the other hand, were organized for action. Their dues were low, and nonpayment did not result in expulsion. Dues payments were used not for purposes of mutual aid but to sustain propaganda campaigns and strikes. The extraction of material benefits from employers through job action was the first stage in the Anarchist long-term plan, to be followed by the consolidation of working class strength and the elimination

94

of the capitalist system through a revolutionary act. The manner in which the final defeat of capitalism was to occur remained undefined until the widespread acceptance after 1905 of the concept of the revolutionary general strike. The young Anarchists rejected political participation as a waste of time, and encouraged other workers not to vote and to abandon the PD.

"Boring from within" tactics began to bear fruit for the Anarchists. In 1898, Esteban Cavieres formed the first resistance society among metal workers in the State Railway shops of Santiago, while bakers and sailors in Valparaíso and coal miners near Concepción established similar organizations by the end of 1901.[24] Most of the men who formed the *sociedades de resistencia* appear to have remained nominal members of the mutualist societies, probably because they were unwilling to sacrifice precious benefits payments and because they hoped to further exploit their position as mutualist members to spread the cause of Anarchism. More libertarian study groups were formed in Santiago and Valparaíso, often with the active participation of freethinkers, intellectuals, and literary figures. Two utopian colonies were established by Anarchists and their hangers-on, one a Tolstoyan settlement of artists and writers just outside Santiago in San Bernardo, and the other an Anarchist-Communist colony in the city itself.[25] At the same time that organizational efforts within the working class societies took place, leading Anarchists held a series of public rallies to protest unemployment, the high price of food, the threat of war with Argentina, and other issues affecting the working class. By 1902, Anarchist influence among urban workers had grown appreciably.

Few strikes occurred in Chile before 1902. The government first began to record the incidence of strikes in 1907, but studies by several scholars indicate that the occurrence of strikes between 1849 and 1900 was very low.[26] Strike activity centered in the northern ports, central cities, and the coal mining zone. Some strikes, like those of dockers in Iquique and Valparaíso in 1890, assumed large-scale proportions and had to be broken by troops, resulting in much bloodshed. Strikes in the North were mainly unorganized, spontaneous responses to rising prices or unpopular working conditions.[27] The prevalent view of nineteenth-century employers and government officials that equated strikes with rebellion persisted into the twentieth century, exacerbating class hatred.

THE UNIONIZATION DRIVE, 1902–7

Organized labor in Santiago and Valparíso reached hitherto unattained levels of numerical and practical strength during the years 1902–7. Mutual aid societies proliferated under the watchful eye of the PD, while the Anarchist-led resistance societies continued to incorporate increasing numbers of urban workers into job-oriented labor unions. The activities of these two major types of working class organization conflicted sharply on the ideological-political level, although a certain amount of coordinated action took place when economic issues were at stake.

It was not until the inflation and strike wave of late 1905–7 that the resistance societies reached a high level of prestige or power in the cities. Pre-1905 societies were extremely short-lived, since many workers regarded them as useful only in carrying out strikes. A reduced group of tradesmen, notably printers, metal workers, and bakers, showed much zeal in breaking out of the mutualist orbit to form unions capable of protecting and advancing labor's position *vis-à-vis* employers. As mentioned earlier, Anarchist organizers managed to set up a small but influential resistance society in the metal shops of the State Railway in Santiago as early as 1898. Santiago tram drivers and conductors formed a resistance society in March, 1902, and were followed three months later by printers, who established a Printers' Federation (FOI) on the eve of an important strike.[28] The agitator and organizer Magno Espinoza had by early 1902 formed a Workers' Resistance Federation in Valparaíso based on a cadre of Anarchist bakers and a few sailors.[29] Unionization in Santiago furthered the rise of resistance societies in the Port when State Railway metallurgists and printers sent organizers to establish parallel unions as a brake on scabbing. Small numbers of shoemakers, carpenters, and cigarette makers also formed resistance societies in Santiago in 1902.

Resistance societies, although claiming to be organized by craft, were in reality industrially oriented at the time of their formation. The railway metal workers, bakers, printers, and tram workers made no distinction between the various jobs within each industry, since the main purpose of their oganizations was to foment strikes capable of stopping operations. As soon as more than one or two different trades contained a handful of Anarchist union men, a "federation" of resistance societies was formed to coordinate the activities of member groups. Most strike action involved workers of several different skills or crafts within each industry or establishment, and the resistance societies excluded no one from their ranks because of his trade. On the contrary, as few as twenty representatives of a trade might be encouraged to form their own *sociedad de resistencia* and join the federation.

True to form, most resistance societies wasted little time in putting their ideology to practice by going on strike. Railroad metallurgists, tram workers, and printers in both Santiago and Valparaíso struck for better wages and working conditions in 1902. Bakers, sailors, and shoemakers followed suit in 1903. While such strikes marked the beginning of the active life of many resistance societies, they also proved their undoing. The society formed by Santiago tram workers failed to outlast their unsuccessful strike of March,

1902, mainly due to persecution of the union by the government and the tram company.[30] In other industries, the reverse proved true; workers joined the ranks of the resistance societies only for the purpose of winning a single strike. Within a year after its highly successful 1902 strike, the Printers' Federation in Santiago was forced to disband due to lack of interest from the rank and file. The Sailors' Resistance Union, which helped foment the rioting in Valparaíso in May, 1903, and brought about a favorable solution to what had been a doomed strike, broke up immediately after victory was achieved.[31] Other resistance societies among carpenters and cigarette workers disintegrated before they could bring about a strike.

By early 1904, the resistance societies had all but disappeared from the urban scene. Few workers had participated in the societies on a steady basis, but several thousand were for the first time introduced to strikes and job-oriented labor unions, if only for a brief period. The sacrifices necessary for membership in a resistance society often outweighed the benefits. Arrests, firings, blacklisting, and economic privation faced many workers who chose to join or support a resistance society. Until a pressing need for strike action to counter inflation arose during the latter part of 1905, resistance societies languished in a state of inactivity.

Chilean Anarchism in general suffered a decline during 1904 and most of 1905. A number of libertarian organizations which had been established in Santiago between 1898 and 1902 also fell into disrepair at the same time that the resistance societies disintegrated. These included the Worker Athenaeum (*Ateneo Obrero*) founded by libertarian workers, intellectuals, and freethinkers near the end of the nineteenth century; the *Casa del Pueblo*, established as a consumer cooperative in December, 1901; and the small Anarchist study groups which published the newspapers *La Revuelta, La Ajitación, La Luz, La Campaña, Lo Nuevo, El Martillo, El Faro,* and *La Defensa* between 1900 and 1903. By 1904, the entire Anarchist press of Santiago had been replaced by only one paper (*Jerminal!*) due to lack of funds.[32] Until their expulsion in March, 1902, the Casa del Pueblo, FOI, Ateneo Obrero, and Anarchist study centers were members of the *Congreso Social Obrero,* an organization of mutual aid societies and social democrats led by Alejandro Bustamante.[33] Anarchist delegates to a National Worker Convention in September, 1902, were excluded from positions of power by the mutualist majority.

While the Anarchists in Santiago and Valparaíso attempted unsuccessfully to form an active labor movement from the ranks of the mutual aid societies, new labor organizations were being created in the northern ports and the coal mining zone near Concepción. Iquique maritime workers, led by their long-standing boss Abdón Díaz, formed the first labor brotherhood or mancomunal in 1900.[34] The mancomunal combined all of the different maritime craft unions and mutual aid societies into a loose federation for coordinated job action, including strikes. Non-maritime societies later joined, making the brotherhoods of the North the first regionally based labor groups of any consequence in Chile's history. Other mancomunales were formed in Tocopilla (1902); Antofagasta, Chañaral, Taltal, and Copiapó (1903); Coquimbo, Ovalle, and Valdivia (1904); and La Serena (1905). In May, 1904, these organizations held a convention in Santiago for the purpose of coordinating their activities and petitioning the President of the Republic for a series of reforms. Some Anarchists held positions of importance in the mancomunales, in spite of the fact that Chilean libertarians generally branded the brotherhoods as boss-ridden, conservative, and politically motivated. These complaints were partially true. Many mancomunal leaders did attempt to build successful political careers on the basis of the labor vote, and the Democratic Party exercised considerable influence over the activities of the brotherhoods.[35]

By 1906 the mancomunales had lost most of their influence, and within a few years all were dissolved.[36] Persecution by national authorities and employers was certainly the most important cause of their decline. Unlike the generally passive mutual aid societies, most mancomunales chose to strike for better wages and conditions. These strikes more often than not were met with armed force by the government. Soldiers and sailors arrested labor leaders, confiscated the presses used to print labor newspapers, sacked union halls, and, on several occasions, slaughtered workers indiscriminately. Although the ideology expressed by most mancomunales was consistently reformist, their strikes and wage demands set them up for repression.[37] The Anarchist-led Federation of Lota and Coronel in the coal zone fared little better when it unleashed a series of yearly strikes between 1902 and 1904.

Workers in Santiago and Valparaíso began to reorganize their resistance societies during the latter months of 1905. By March, 1906, the urban labor movement had grown to proportions never before witnessed, and began a wave of strikes which culminated in the general strike of June, 1907, in Santiago and Valparaíso. Many factors appear to have caused this sudden spurt of organizational activity. The nitrate industry and national manufacturing experienced a period of great prosperity during the years 1905–6. Heavy capital investment in manufacturing provided new jobs for both production and construction workers. Increased government revenues from the nitrate tax bolstered the state's potential to pay higher wages to its employees. The Valparaíso earthquake of August, 1906, created a boom in the construction industry. All sources point to an acute shortage of both skilled and unskilled labor in Santiago and Valparaíso in 1906. Labor quite naturally responded to this situation with demands for higher wages, and required labor unions to carry out the strikes that were often necessary to achieve them. A rapid rise in food prices beginning in May, 1905 also encouraged workers to join unions and go on strike.[38]

Political parties actively courted the working class vote for the presidential and parliamentary elections of 1906. In the process, many rallies and demonstrations, culminating in the so-called "Meat Riot" in Santiago in October, 1905, began to awaken feelings of class identity and dissatisfaction among workers. A split in the Democratic Party in early 1906 favored the continued growth of labor unions in Santiago and Valparaíso when the radical wing of the PD, led by Luis Emilio Recabarren, aligned itself and its influential daily newspaper, *La Reforma,* on the side of the resistance societies. Major clashes between workers and police during 1905 in Santiago, added to the fresh memory of the bloodshed of the Valparaíso riot of 1903 and labor disturbances in the North, caused many workers to listen more attentively to the Anarchists and Recabarren Democrats, who assured them that bosses and the government would grant nothing without a show of force on labor's part. Early organizational and strike successes stimulated further gains. By mid-1906, the daily example of successful strikes and effective wage bargaining by resistance societies constituted the strongest impetus to further unionization.

Anarchist carpenters in Santiago attempted to form a resistance society in the early months of 1905, and finally succeeded in September when they created the Carpenters' Federation.[39] According to the federation's statutes, any carpenter or carpenter's helper over fifteen years of age could join. All members were required to pay the low monthly dues of fifty cents (one-half peso; twenty-five cents for apprentices), attend union meetings, and refrain from political and religious activities. No honorary or nonworker members (foremen, for example) were allowed. The federation was governed by a board (*concejo*) of seven members elected by general secret ballot every six months. The goals of the federation as outlined in its statutes included the eight-hour day, thirty-six consecutive hours of rest per week, recognition of the union's right to organize and bargain, and the establishment of a job placement service for members. The federation declared May 1 to be an official holiday for all carpenters.

Other crafts followed suit in establishing resistance societies. Shoemakers and female assemblers formed a resistance federation in December, 1905, and within a few months, cigarette makers, printers, teamsters, upholsterers, tannery workers, locksmiths, blacksmiths, and bakers had established similar organizations.[40] A 1906 May 1 demonstration and picnic held jointly by the PD and the Anarchists attracted over 3,000 workers and closed down many of Santiago's industries for the day.[41]

In June, 1906, several resistance societies banded together to form the

Federation of Workers in Chile (FTCh), perhaps the most influential working class organization in Santiago to that date. At the height of its power in May, 1907, the FTCh counted as members twenty-four of Santiago's thirty-three resistance organizations.[42] The purpose of the federation was to coordinate the activities of current working class organizations in Santiago and stimulate the formation of new unions. The FTCh, as indicated by its title, considered itself the nucleus of what was eventually to be a national labor federation. Although this dream was never realized, the FTCh did help stimulate unionization in other parts of Chile through solidarity and propaganda. To belong to the federation, a union had to agree not to engage in political or religious activities. Unions of twenty or more members whose statutes did not conflict with FTCh rules were eligible for membership. Each member union contributed monthly dues of ten cents per male and five per female to the federation. In an effort to cut down on dual unionism and lure workers away from the mutual aid societies, the FTCh recognized only one union for each craft in any given area.

Realizing that many of the resistance societies, such as the federations of printers, shoeworkers, and carpenters, already provided their members with some mutual aid benefits (paid through voluntary contributions at the time of need rather than by dues), the FTCh did not deal with matters of social security or mutual help. Instead, it attempted to coordinate the strike activities of member societies by regulating the flow of funds to a striking union and providing for solidarity action.[43] Unions were required to obtain the prior consent of the federation before going out on strike, and were encouraged to submit formal petitions to employers in order to facilitate a settlement. Because employers frequently broke agreements signed during collective bargaining, the FTCh *required* member unions to automatically go on strike against any employer who refused to honor his contract obligations.

The power of organized labor in Santiago and Valparaíso peaked between May and June of 1907. By that time, the mancomunal established in Valparaíso in 1904 had grown to include the resistance societies and federations of shoemakers, bakers, tram drivers and conductors, some textile workers, metal workers, and cigarette makers.[44] Although they remained organized in mutual aid societies, Valparaíso printers, dockers, and sailors nevertheless struck on several occasions. A mancomunal was also organized in Santiago in 1907, the most influential of its nine resistance society members being the Printers' Federation.[45] Organization had by 1907 spread to workers having no previous union background, including many women. A Resistance Society of Garment Workers, containing some 150 young women, was created in July, 1906, and many other female workers joined resistance societies in the leather and tobacco industries.[46] Thus, by June of 1907, both highly skilled and unskilled workers had organized resistance societies in Santiago and

100

Valparaíso. Although the most successful unions proved to be those of skilled workers, especially printers, metal workers, and shoemakers, resistance societies of female and unskilled workers did win better wages and conditions through strike activity in 1906-7.

The decentralized labor movements of Santiago and Valparaíso produced many leaders during the 1905-7 unionization drive, but no single figure dominated any one union or federation.[47] Some, like Recabarren and Magno Espinoza, acquired wide popularity among all workers because of their propagandistic zeal and willingness to go to jail in defense of working class interests. Several PD figures, such as Vicente Leiva, leader of the 1907 general strike in Valparaíso, Manuel Hidalgo, and Recabarren, remained members of their respective mutual aid societies while participating in politics. Bonifacio Veas and other Democrats were able to influence the activities of some labor unions by means of their position as deputies. As we shall see later, the intervention of PD parliamentarians in major strikes was common.

Most labor leaders during the period of organizational expansion, however, aspired to no political position. Indeed, many were Anarchists who roundly condemned politics as detrimental to working class needs. The leaders of major resistance societies were all workers, and none received any pay for his efforts. The Printers' Federation without doubt produced more able union leaders than any other organization. Most were convinced Anarchists, but of a strongly syndicalist orientation. Dedicated to strengthening the power of the FOI in order to improve the economic lot of its members, they also aided in the formation of other labor unions and frequently assumed the direction of Anarchist newspapers. Considering that Recabarren was himself a *tipógrafo,* it could fairly be said that Chilean printers formed the vanguard of the urban labor movement during the first decade of the twentieth century and continued to be very influential into the 1930s. The careers of many of these men spanned the entire twenty-five years between 1902 and 1927. Among them were Julio E. Valiente, Luis A. Soza, Nicolás Orellana, Manuel J. Montenegro, Pedro N. Arratia, Luis Víctor Cruz, and Elías Lafertte.

Other Anarchist labor leaders of regional stature, including Marcial Lisperguer, Daniel Labbé, Luis A Pardo, and Adolfo Hernández, sprang from the important construction and leather workers' unions of Santiago. Early death claimed the lives of several founders of the Anarchist/resistance society movements. In 1906, Magno Espinoza succumbed to tuberculosis, perhaps the most common killer of young workers. Recabarren's newspaper, *La Reforma,* received so many requests for Espinoza's portrait from Santiago workers that thousands of extra copies had to be printed.[48] During a nine-year period, he led several successful strikes, organized resistance societies in at least four different industries, published Anarchist newspapers, directed countless rallies, and suffered imprisonment on a number of occasions. Had

101

he been a member of a political party or a Marxist rather than an Anarchist, his name would today be well known and honored by the Chilean left. Tuberculosis also claimed the life of printer-Anarchist Agustín G. Saavedra in 1906, while Esteban Cavieres, the agitator who founded Chile's first resistance society, died a year earlier. Luis Olea, a *compañero* of Espinoza and Cavieres, went to the North after the decline of the urban resistance societies in 1904. He miraculously escaped death during the massacre at the Escuela Santa María de Iquique in December, 1907 (he was apparently the only leader of the movement to have done so), and spent the next four years of his life in exile, writing for the Anarchist press of Peru and Ecuador. He died of yellow fever in Guayaquil in 1911.[49] The Argentine Anarchist Inocencio Lombardozzi was imprisoned in 1903 after leading a baking strike in Santiago and was later expelled to Peru, where he died in 1908.

STRIKES, 1902–8

An editorial in the Santiago daily *La Lei* (January 26, 1902) claimed that as of January, 1902, strikes in Chile were extremely "rare."[50] This statement appears to have been true, given the government's early perception of strikes as acts of rebellion and the general public consternation which followed the strike/riot of May, 1903, in Valparaíso. By 1907, however, the people of Santiago and Valparaíso had become well acquainted with strikes, as their number increased dramatically. Although the occurrence of industrial disputes was not recorded in Chile until 1907, several attempts have been made to tabulate their number between 1902 and 1908 by scanning newspapers of the period. Table 4.1 is a compilation of data gathered by Floreal Recabarren Rojas for strikes in the Provinces of Tarapacá and Antofagasta, by Jorge Barría S. and Manuel Barrera for all of Chile, by myself for the cities of Santiago and Valparaíso, and by the Labor Office for all of Chile in 1907 and 1908.[51] It demonstrates a rapid increase in strike activity beginning in 1905 and culminating in the "strike wave" of 1906–7 which swept across the country. Economic recession and the bloody suppression of strikes in the North led to a drastic decline in the number of strikes occurring in 1908.

Anarchists led ten of the thirteen strikes recorded in Santiago and Valparaíso during the short-lived burst of organizational fervor in 1902–3. In each case, members of a resistance society in the affected industry or establishment convinced other workers of the need to strike and then directed the operation. The first of such strikes took place in March, 1902, as the result of the government's demand that State Railway metallurgists in the Santiago and Valparaíso *maestranzas* work four extra hours on Saturday with no increase in pay.[52] Cavieres and the resistance societies in both cities generated a strike involving thousands of workers which quickly persuaded Rail-

Table 4.1
Incidence of Strikes in Chile, 1901–8

Year	Tarapacá-Antofagasta[a]	Santiago, Valparaíso[b]	Sum of Preceding Two Columns	All Chile (Barría-Barrera)[c]	All Chile (Labor Office)[d]
1901	3	—	—	5	—
1902	4	8	12	21	—
1903	6	5	11	17	—
1904	7	3	10	11	—
1905	17	12	29	23	—
1906	20	31	51	48	—
1907	31	22	53	80	52
1908	3	3	6	15	29
TOTAL	91	85	176	220	81

[a]Source: Floreal Recabarren R., *Historia del proletariado de Tarapacá y Antofagasta, 1884–1913*, chart, p. 227.

[b]Source: See note 51.

[c]Source: Figures cited in Manuel Barrera, "Perspectiva histórica de la huelga obrera en Chile," in *Cuadernos de la realidad nacional*, no. 9, September, 1971, p. 125. Information from Jorge Barría, *Los movimientos sociales de principios del siglo, 1900–1910*, pp. 120–70.

[d]Source: 1907 figure from ADGT, *Primeros documentos desde la organización de la oficina, 1907-8* Document 364/6, letter of Simón Rodríguez, December 19, 1907. 1908 figure cited in Luis Galdames, "Los movimientos obreros en Chile," Pan American Union, Fourth Scientific Conference, 1908, tomo 3, vol. 10, section 7, p. 361.

way authorities to reinstate the previous English Saturday arrangement. Striking workers paraded down Santiago's main boulevard, the Alameda de las Delicias, massed in their traditional meeting place in front of the statue of O'Higgins on the Alameda near the Calle San Martín, and briefly clashed with police when they tried to stone the offices of *El Mercurio*, the daily newspaper which over the years had won the undying hatred of workers in both Santiago and Valparaíso.[53]

Later that month, the Anarchists decided to try their luck with a tram strike in Santiago. The moment they chose for their job action was optimal; the tram company had recently doubled its fares, provoking a hostile reaction in the press and among the general public.[54] A resistance society of drivers and conductors (both male and female) was established with the encouragement of Anarchist printers and railway shop workers. While further recruitment continued, the resistance society outlined its demands for shorter hours, higher pay, and lower fines which they intended to present to the company before striking. Police agents, however, infiltrated the union, stole its membership registry, and turned it over to the company. Widespread firing of resistance society members resulted, and the union had to call its strike prematurely to avoid elimination. Only a few electric trams ran during the first day of the strike, but service gradually increased when scabs and policemen were recruited to drive the cars. Workers responded with violence typical of a tram strike. Scab-driven cars were attacked and stoned, provoking police to raid the union's hall and arrest scores of strikers. Anarchist participation in the strike, combined with violence and the disruption of service, turned the daily press against the tram workers. Within eight days, service was restored to normal, the strike broken, and many of the resistance society leaders blacklisted by the company. Future strikes of electric tram workers followed the same pattern of violence, heated emotions, and rapid arousal of public opinion.

In June of 1902, nearly a thousand Santiago printers recently organized in the Anarchist-led Printers' Federation won a spectacular victory against most of the city's large newspapers and publishing houses.[55] The strike began when the FOI's proposed contract calling for increased wages and better conditions was turned down by most employers. Within a week, all employers had capitulated in the face of a model effort. The federation choked off the supply of scabs from Valparaíso and the provinces by sending delegates to insure the solidarity of other printers. Several employers gave in quickly, and the federation allowed their workers to return under the terms of the new contract in order to sustain those still on strike. Attempts by several of the large publishers to recruit scabs from the ranks of civilian printers under contract with the army failed, and they too surrendered. The FOI emerged from this strike as the most prestigious and powerful of Chile's resistance societies.

The Anarchist contention that "direct action" and violence could be employed by workers to bring strikes to a successful end proved true during the famous Valparaíso maritime strike of April–May, 1903. No previous strike in either Santiago or Valparaíso had acquired the same magnitude, captured similar public attention, or ended in such spectacular fashion. Chilean workers and elites would remember the events of May 12, 1903, for many years, although the blood spilled in the strets of Valparaíso did not prevent, but rather stimulated, further violence and death.

The strike began quietly on April 17, when demands for higher pay by stevedores employed by the British-owned Pacific Steam Navigation Company (PSNC) were turned down by the company's manager.[56] With no settlement in sight, other mutual aid societies of lightermen, sailors, and customshouse workers joined the strike, first in solidarity with the stevedores and soon after as participants with their own petitions. By April 20, activity in the Port ground to a halt as the number of strikers reached 4,000, nearly the entire workforce engaged in cargo handling.

Magno Espinoza used the strike as an occasion to revitalize the resistance society of sailors, but the other idled workers ignored the Anarchist call for a common front. Employers, meanwhile, steadfastly refused to enter into collective bargaining and sabotaged efforts by state maritime authorities, other labor societies, and interested politicians to set up an arbitration committee. They had been able to gradually recruit strikebreakers from the ranks of the unemployed in Valparaíso and from dock workers in other ports. Activity at the customshouse dock resumed on April 27, with police on hand to protect the 100 strikebreakers the contractor (Espejo & Co.) had managed to recruit. Maritime authorities greatly assisted the shipping companies by allowing them to sail with smaller crews than legally permitted. Police and workers clashed for the first time on the twenty-seventh when strikers attempted to prevent scabs from entering the customshouse. By May 1, all daily newspapers noted the increased activity in the Port and predicted that the strike would soon be broken. The workers, meanwhile, sought the intercession of political figures such as PD Deputy Angel Guarello in setting up arbitration.

The morale of the strikers had begun to waver noticeably, but the Anarchists pumped new life into the strike during a rally on May 4, at which Espinoza was the featured speaker. He urged the workers to adopt direct action tactics to force employers to the bargaining table. Despite the increasingly aggressive behavior of the Anarchist-led sailors, the companies were able to recruit more strikebreakers, and attempts by the unions to set up an arbitration committee proved fruitless. By May 9, the strike appeared doomed to total failure.

Completely frustrated by the intransigence of the shipping companies, which refused to meet or even correspond with the strikers, workers embraced the Anarchist tactic of direct action as a last resort. Early in the morning of May 12, strikers began to gather in large numbers on the docks to prevent blacklegs from going to work. Within a few hours, all activity in the bay had ceased, and crowds of several thousand people began to mass in the Port section of the city. When the predictable tram stoning and burning began, a police official shot a worker dead, and a riot ensued. Infuriated mobs began to sack the headquarters of the shipping companies and the many warehouses along the docks. Some 600 naval marines stationed in the Port area stood idly by and then joined the crowd in looting the warehouses. Another mob attacked the offices of *El Mercurio,* the newspaper which had most enthusiastically supported the shipping companies during the course of the strike. The newspaper's management took the precaution of arming its employees with repeating rifles, and they were able to defend the fortress-like building with ease, killing seven attackers in the process.

With the bulk of the Chilean battle fleet still on high seas maneuvers that had begun May 4 and the marines dispersed and useless, the city lay at the mercy of the mob, and looting became general. Military units began to arrive from Santiago around midnight, but it was not until the afternoon of the thirteenth that order was finally restored. Nearly 100 people died during the rioting, and several hundred more were wounded. Few police or people of high socioeconomic extraction were injured and none was killed, but the lifeless, sometimes headless corpses of workers littered the streets and hills of Valparaíso.

Although many lives were lost in the process, the maritime strike ended successfully for workers. In the afternoon of the thirteenth, representatives of the shipping and contracting companies and the four striking unions met in the office of PD Deputy Angel Guarello and signed an agreement establishing procedures for binding arbitration. Workers agreed to return to their jobs under prestrike conditions, but would receive retroactive wage increases when the arbitrators set the new pay scale. On the nineteenth, all parties agreed on two arbiters whom they empowered to name a third. The arbiters reached their settlement on July 31, 1903. Wages were increased for all workers by 10–20 percent, overtime pay was granted to some, and stevedores received shorter hours. The arbiters rejected all other demands outright. Had labor established the arbitrational procedures while bargaining from a position of strength, this settlement would have been less than satisfactory. Considering, however, that the strike was all but lost on May 11, the tactic of direct action was successful because it drove employers to the bargaining table.

The only other major strikes in 1903 took place in the baking industry of Santiago and Valparaíso. In both cases, employers held out against resistance society demands for nearly a month before reaching a compromise with their workers.[57] The strikes proved exceptionally violent, with scabs beaten, property destroyed, and many arrests made. During these strikes, as in many others to follow, bakers practiced direct action tactics as a result of their ideological attraction to Anarchism and their particular job situation.

Very few strikes took place in Santiago and Valparaíso in 1904. Wholesale food costs declined during most of the year and did not reach 1902–3 levels again until April of 1905. Workers in the most successfully organized industries (baking, printing, maritime, metal) were probably satisfied with their increased real wages and showed little interest in further agitation. The resistance societies consequently entered a period of decline or disappeared altogether.

As food prices rose sharply beginning in early 1905 and real wages fell, urban workers began to reorganize their resistance groups and initiate strikes. The "strike wave" itself did not begin until October, 1905. Ten strikes were initiated during the months of October, November, and December, 1905, as opposed to only five during the preceeding twenty-one months. The connection between rising food prices, popular discontent, and an increase in strikes is clear. Wholesale prices of bread, potatoes, flour, beans, meat, and corn (grouped together and weighted) rose by 48 percent between January and October, 1905.[58] The inflationary period continued well into 1908, while the strike wave came to a halt by July, 1907.

Santiago tram workers won higher pay, shorter hours, and lower fines after a two-day strike early in October, 1905, but their union was afterwards broken when the company fired and blacklisted the strike leaders.[59] An industry-wide strike of several hundred tannery workers won shorter hours later that month. Small-scale strikes of shoemakers, metal workers, teamsters, cigarette makers, bakers, and factory workers constituted most job action taking place until the general printing strike in Santiago in June, 1906. Printers had not received a raise in pay since their successful strike in 1902, and therefore sought piece rate increases of 20 percent and more. The reestablished Printers' Federation combined with the mutualist Federación Gráfica to bring about total victory after ten days.[60] Less than two weeks later, the Universo Printing House, with branches in both Santiago and Valparaíso, refused to comply with the contract and locked out its workforce. Other employers followed Universo's example in what was to become the first industry-wide lockout in Chilean history.[61] After sixteen days, however, the employers failed to recruit enough new workers or coax many locked-out printers into signing a nonunion contract. The lockout was therefore lifted and the union contract honored. In typical fashion, Valparaíso printers used coercive comparison to win 20 percent pay increases from their employers after a ten-day strike in July, 1906.[62]

No strikes occurred in Valparaíso between the August 16 earthquake and a boatmen's strike in November. By the end of 1906, however, employers began forming their own organizations to present a united front to labor and stem the tide of union successes. The first industries to have employers' associations were those in which a high degree of competition prevailed and unions were strongest, including baking, printing, shoemaking, tanning, tobacco, and metal work.[63] Especially powerful unions overcame the resistance of employers' organizations. An eighty-four-day strike begun in December, 1906, won a 40 percent wage increase for Valparaíso shoeworkers in spite of dogged efforts by employers to break the movement.[64] An industry-wide strike involving more than 3,000 male and female shoemakers in Santiago began while the Valparaíso strike was still in progress, and eventually resulted in large pay increases.[65]

Attempts by employers in the metal, construction, and food processing industries of Valparaíso to cut wages in March, 1907, led to a massive general strike. The power of employers in Valparaíso was still weakened by a scarcity of labor, and their attempt to roll back recent wage gains quickly failed when the unions closed ranks to meet the challenge. Former pay scales were reinstated within two days, and the strike was called off.[66]

The labor movement and the strike wave reached their high-water marks in May–June, 1907. Forty strikes had taken place during the twelve-month period between May, 1906, and May, 1907. Santiago's mammoth May 1 demonstration, planned nearly a month ahead of time by the FTCh and the city's mancomunal, clearly indicated that the power of organized labor had grown to unprecedented heights. Thirty thousand working people marched along the principal avenues of the city, and for the first time, virtually no production or commercial activity took place.[67] Between them, the FTCh and mancomunal could not claim more than about 10,000 members, but the appeal of the resistance societies among mutualists and unorganized workers had obviously grown during the strike wave. Feelings of solidarity ran high, as borne out by the willingness of workers in the resistance societies to aid the strikes of other workers.

The combative spirit and organizational capacity of the urban labor movement was put to its greatest test during the general strike of June, 1907. Within a month, organized labor in Santiago and Valparaíso would be in full decline.

The general strike began as a wage dispute among a group of unskilled workers in the State Railway shops of Santiago.[68] Their petition had gone unanswered for thirty days, leaving them no choice but to walk off the job on May 27. Railroad blacksmiths quickly seconded their strike on the May 28, and by the twenty-ninth, the entire maestranza workforce had quit work for the first time since 1902. The director of the State Railway system offered small wage increases to the original strikers, which were refused. Maestranza workers throughout the central and southern zones of the State Railway adhered to the strike on May 30, affecting shops in Valparaíso, Talca, Concepción, and Valdivia. In an unprecedented display of solidarity, switchmen and couplers joined the strike on June 2, and by the fourth, railroad traffic from Valparaíso to Valdivia ground to a halt as the engineers and firemen also walked off. On June 5, the FTCh and the Santiago mancomunal joined the strike, shutting down operations in foundries, textile factories, construction projects, booteries,tanneries, and cigarette factories. Tram service halted when the drivers and conductors refused to work. *La Reforma* correctly described the movement as "the most important and colossal which this country has ever witnessed."[69] At least 15,000 workers in Santiago alone were on strike.

Fearing violence and the extension of the strike to other industries, the government deployed large numbers of troops and police in the strike zone. Military engineers and firemen protected by infantry units ran the trains which carried coal and food into the cities, while all important railroad installations were heavily guarded in order to prevent sabotage. Naval electricians placed at the service of the Santiago Power and Light Company kept

108

electric current flowing during the strike, and military telegraph operators filled in for striking communications workers. The government also took steps to break the strike by force. Valparaíso police began to arrest strikers in that city, while much pressure was put upon striking government workers to return to their jobs. Most contract employees who had struck illegally (telegraph operators, railroad engineers) resumed work when threatened with arrest.

The government could not, however, break the strike by repressive measures alone, and appears to have reached this conclusion within a few days after the strike's inception. More workers were joining the strike every day, and the walkout was crippling the economic life of the entire country. When the petition of the strike committee reached President Montt on June 2, he therefore quickly acceded to workers' demands by appointing a three-man committee composed of political figures and State Railway functionaries to mediate a settlement. On the fourth, the government offered an across-the-board wage increase of 30 percent for maestranza personnel and future payment at a fixed exchange in gold set at 16d (British pennies) to the peso. Workers refused to back down from their demand that wages be paid at an exchange of 18d, since they feared that the precipitous decline in the value of the peso which occurred during the first half of 1907 would continue. Offers of shorter hours and no retribution were also extended to the line personnel of the railway to lure them back to work.

The position of the shop workers was extremely favorable. Massive solidarity on the part of the line workers and urban labor unions provided them with a kind of bargaining leverage that they had never before enjoyed. The Strike Committee which led the action chose PD Deputy Bonifacio Veas as its chief, and was itself composed of men known for their lack of revolutionary fervor. Anarchists had not been able to re-establish their resistance societies within the State Railway shops, but prolibertarian sentiment among the rank and file appears to have remained significant. The reformist, nonideological nature of the strike leaders probably increased the government's willingness to arrive at an early settlement.

The government repeated its offer of a wage fixed at 16d on the seventh, only to have it immediately rejected by the Strike Committee. Veas boasted that the workers possessed funds to maintain the strike indefinitely.[70] The following day, however, the committee held a secret meeting and decided to accept the government's offer of 16d. Veas announced the decision to the state mediators and proceeded to call off the strike. Much of the rank and file, however, refused to abide by the decision, which the committee had neither considered as an issue for bargaining nor ratified. An assembly of maestranza strikers met on the evening of the eighth to receive word from the committee, but no committee members arrived. The following day another meeting was held, but members of the Strike Committee refused to attend. Greatly angered by what they and *La Reforma* (normally a spokesman for the Recabarren-Veas wing of the PD) considered a "sellout," the workers marched to strike headquarters near the Central Train Station, only to find its doors tightly bolted.[71]

The general strike was still expanding at the time of the settlement on May 8. Maritime workers in Valparaíso stopped work on the seventh, and other unions appeared willing to join the movement. Few of the striking resistance societies proposed any demands other than the settlement of the *maestranza* strike at the 18d rate. *El Diario Ilustrado* of Santiago remarked, only hours before the secret settlement was reached:[72]

> We have no reason to silence the revelation of brotherhood within the working class which this strike has demonstrated. We see workers of various jobs who stand to gain nothing from winning a fixed rate of pay for railway workers making common cause with them. This movement has assumed very special characteristics which men of political influence should bear in mind.

Given the widespread solidarity of other unions and the strong bargaining position enjoyed by the railroad workers, why did the Strike Committee end the strike so quickly? The editors of *La Lei* and *El Heraldo* postulated that the government's resolve to recruit strikebreakers for work in the maestranzas and the subsequent fear of strike leaders that the rank and file would abandon the strike once their jobs were threatened influenced Veas to accept the conciliatory 16d.[73] *La Reforma* claimed that Veas had sold out to the government, and *El Diario Ilustrado* implied that the Strike Committee agreed to the government's offer because it substantially raised wages.[74] None of the newspapers voiced the most obvious conclusion, that Veas called off the strike in order to win political favors from the government. Veas and the "Doctrinaire" wing of the Democratic Party (including Recabarren) had split with the Concha wing over the presidential election of 1906 by supporting the candidacy of Pedro Montt, while Concha backed the losing faction. By ending the strike early, Veas may have hoped to further demonstrate his loyalty to Montt in return for political rewards, perhaps the help of the government in wresting control of the PD from the Concha faction of the party. Notably, *La Reforma* did not pursue the "sold out" interpretation of the matter, and refrained from any further criticism of the role played by Veas.

More than 10,000 workers remained on strike in both Santiago and Valparaíso after the "settlement" was announced. Over a thousand maestranza workers in Santiago and all railroad personnel in Valparaíso decided to press ahead for pay fixed at 18d. The Santiago FTCh declared the strike to be general on the thirteenth, although it had been a de facto general strike long before. Dockers, maritime metal workers, sailors, shoemakers, blacksmiths, teamsters, lightermen, and factory workers totaling some 15,000 in all either remained on strike in Valparaíso or joined it by June 17.[75] Many of the unions which had hitherto struck as a gesture of solidarity now began to press their own wage demands.

The position of employers and the state was greatly enhanced by the decision of the Strike Committee to come to terms. The line personnel of the State Railways (engineers, firemen, conductors, couplers, switchmen, etc.), who struck for reasons of solidarity and in the process had their workday shortened, returned to their jobs on Monday, June 10, along with about half of the Santiago maestranza workers. At a stroke, the greatest single source of pressure against the government was eliminated when train service regained full capacity. With a "settlement" reached and the strike "over," the state threatened to fire those public service employees still on strike and began more actively to employ the armed forces as strikebreakers. On June 11, naval officials in Valparaíso met with the Minister of Finance, the chief of police, and the intendant to announce that in the future, sailors were available for strikebreaking duty.[76] The Valparaíso and Santiago maestranzas began firing strikers on the twelfth, starting with those most closely connected with the walkout. On the fifteenth, the customshouse in Valparaíso announced that its entire workforce was permanently laid off, and the shipping companies declared an industry-wide lockout to be in effect on the seventeenth. Police in both cities began rounding up strike leaders, raiding union halls, and closing down the publishing establishments which printed strike handbills. Patrolling cavalry units gave the impression that a state of war had been declared in the Port.

The striking unions could not hold out against such pressure. On June 15, one week after the Veas settlement, maestranza workers in Santiago decided that a wage increase was preferable to unemployment and returned to work. Under the threat of firing, the customshouse workers in Valparaíso gave up the strike on the eighteenth. By this time, most of the resistance societies in Santiago had returned to work. The last group of original strikers, the Valparaíso railroad shop workers, surrendered on June 22. Lightermen returned on the twenty-fifth, and the Port strike collapsed the following day. Valparaíso metal workers held out for several weeks longer and won small wage increases from their employers.

The general strike of 1907 demonstrated that the strength of organized labor in Chile had grown tremendously in just a few years but that the decentralized nature of its institutional structure precluded any effective action on either a regional or interindustrial basis. Despite the fact that the original strikers of the railway shops won much higher wages as well as important safeguards for future wage security, the strike must be considered a failure.

111

The fixed demand of 18d was not met, nor were subsequent petitions put forward by the solidarity strikers. After employers and the government forced the unions back to work on a one-by-one basis, a wave of union-breaking occurred, with principal strike leaders fired and blacklisted. In many cases, the strike not only resulted in the loss of potential wage increases, it also meant the weakening or demise of the union.

Observers from the mancomunal of Coquimbo claimed that the strike failed because the activities and demands of the various unions involved were not coordinated and for that reason, the government easily drove a wedge between them.[77] The solidarity issue held them together until Veas undercut the strike by prematurely settling the issue. Once abandoned by the railroad workers, the other strikers failed to harmonize their efforts and in almost all cases went down to defeat. Much of the blame lay in the original planning of the railroad walkout. According to one labor leader, "the impetus [of the maestranza strike] shook up almost all workers in the country and led them into the depths of struggle without any preparation, idea of what they were doing, organization, strike funds, or unity of purpose."[78]

THE NATIONAL LABOR SCENE

Labor organizations developed principally in three areas of Chile during the 1902–7 period: the northern ports and nitrate zone, the urban center (Santiago and Valparaíso), and the coal mining area and ports near Concepción. By most appearances, organized labor was strongest and most effective in the urban center, and the differences grew even more pronounced after 1910. Strikes in the urban center often succeeded, while the historian is hard put to find anything but failed strikes elsewhere. Government repression, however vigorous in the central cities, was not as freely applied as in the mining North and South, where it accounted for many failed strikes. The general picture which emerges for the 1902–7 period is more activity, better organization, sounder tactics, and greater success for labor in the urban center.

Anarchists competed with the PD for control of labor in the coal zone at the turn of the century, and by 1902 had formed a resistance society amoung miners in Lota and Coronel. A series of disastrous and violent strikes between 1902 and 1904 resulted in military intervention, loss of life, and the crushing of the resistance societies. No labor organizations of importance rose to take their place until almost thirteen years later.

In the North, the record of the labor brotherhoods in winning strikes proved equally dismal.[79] Iquique dockers lost a major strike in 1902, nitrate and maritime workers had their strikes broken by force in Tocopilla in 1904, port workers in Iquique failed again in 1905, a general strike of transport workers in Antofagasta dissolved in the face of a massacre in 1906, and machine guns put an end to a port and nitrate strike at the Escuela Santa María de Iquique in December, 1907.[80] While these strikes were apparently better organized than pre-1900 movements, they nonetheless attracted massive repression from the Chilean government, which depended heavily on the nitrate export tax and took energetic steps to see that its major source of revenue was not cut.

Anarchists vied with the PD for influence in the North as in the South. By 1906 they appeared to be getting the upper hand in the port of Iquique and had already established some newspapers and social studies centers in several pampa towns as the influence of the mancomunales waned.[81] Compared with the resistance societies in the urban center, however, the Anarchist movement in the North was very weak.

It is important to note that nitrate miners during the 1902-7 period by no means constituted a vanguard of the national labor movement. During this time they did carry out some strikes, but not as many as did their brothers in the ports, and with more uniform lack of success. They had few organizations of their own, and in many cases responded to developments in port cities rather than initiating their own actions. Workers from the central cities and northern ports attempted without much success to organize them. Viewed nationally, their contribution to the formation of the labor movement in the first decade of the twentieth century was much smaller than has been thought.

STRIKE STATISTICS, 1902-8

The following statistical analysis of the eighty-four strikes identified as having occurred in Santiago and Valparaíso between 1902 and 1908 underlines several important trends in industrial relations during those years. Although more than eighty-four strikes must have taken place, the most important and widespread are included in the sample. In the case of some variables, unknowns account for as much as 30 percent of total examples, but interesting conclusions can still be drawn from the remaining complete information. The general picture of strike activity which emerges is that of labor and private capital settling their own disputes without the intervention of government.

Of the eighty-four strikes, fifty-four took place in Santiago and thirty in Valparaíso. The imbalance was partly due to the earthquake of 1906, which drove wages up and at least partly eliminated the need for strikes in the Port. In 1907, for example, eighteen of the twenty-two strikes recorded took place in Santiago.

Strike activity peaked in the spring and autumn months. (See Appendix, table A.1.) More strikes (eighteen) began during April than during any other

113

month. Relatively abundant supplies of food during the autumn harvest months probably encouraged workers to strike, as well as the realization that fuel costs in the winter would put an extra strain on the family budget. May, June, and November placed second, with eleven strikes apiece. The month in which fewest (two) strikes were undertaken was September, probably due to the reluctance of workers to disrupt their five-day "Dieciocho" holiday (celebrating Chile's independence from Spain) or lose pay at a time when everyone tried to save money to meet the extra expenses involved in the festivities.

Strikes took place in twenty different industries, although they tended to be concentrated in printing (seventeen strikes, 20 percent of the total) and shoes and leather (fifteen strikes, 18 percent of the total). (See table A.2.) A total of seventeen strikes (20.2 percent) occurred among transport workers, sixty-four (76.1 percent) among those engaged in manufacturing, and only one in the construction industry. Three general strikes on a regional (city-wide) basis involved workers in many different industries. The small to medium-scale nature of shoe and printing strikes accounts for their over-whelming predominance in the total number. General industrial strikes did take place on occasion in those industries, but the normal tactic of the shoeworkers' and printers' federations was to isolate a single employer or a small number of establishments to be struck while allowing the rest of the membership to continue working in order to support their comrades. Once a settlement was reached, another group of employers was presented with demands.

A total of sixty-eight of the establishments struck (82 percent) were private companies. State-employed workers struck in only seven cases, and the Municipalities of Santiago and Valparaíso were the employers involved in five strikes.

By all indications, strikes in Santiago and Valparaíso were carried out by organized workers who planned their course of action before walking off the job. A typical strike involved the articulation of grievances by workers, often at the same time that the resistance society itself was established, the drafting of a petition reflecting these grievances, the presentation of the petition to the employer, and further action depending on the employer's response. Between 1902 and 1908, 86 percent of all strikes were carried out by workers who had been organized in a union prior to the initial walkout (tables A.7, A.8). In 85 per-cent of cases, workers presented their employers with a grievance petition before the strike was called, further indication that the great majority of strikes were planned rather than spontaneous events (table A.9). On several occasions, workers became unionized and a petition was drawn up after the initial walkout had taken place. Organizers from other unions generally intervened to help establish a resistance society in such cases.

114

The type of organization leading the strike was named or indicated in fifty-nine of the eighty-four strikes taking place. Several strikes involved more than one type of labor organization. Resistance societies (those using the words *de resistencia* in their title or described by the press as being a resistance union) directed far more strike activity than any other group. While resistance unions took part in fifty-two different strikes, mutual aid societies participated in only seventeen.

Female workers in Santiago and Valparaíso played an active role in strikes, mainly in 1906 and 1907. Only a few strikes were carried out by women without the help or participation of men, but *obreras* did show themselves to be willing strikers once their male counterparts decided to take action. Women participated in 23 percent of all strikes between 1902 and 1908, although only 3.6 percent of total strikes were carried out entirely by women (table A.6).

The direct cause of strikes during this period appears quite clear. In fifty-eight cases, or 69 percent of the total, the refusal of employers to meet the demands of worker petitions led to a walkout. Pay cuts (seven cases), the firing of workers (four cases), and attempts by employers to break the labor union involved (four cases) were the only other major causes of strikes.

Striking workers normally voiced few demands in their petitions, unlike the practice of unions of the 1917-21 period. In only fourteen cases did petitions contain more than three demands. Higher pay was the issue most frequently at stake in labor disputes, appearing in sixty-six strike petitions, followed by shorter hours (eighteen), insistence on no reprisals for striking (fourteen), the dismissal of a foreman (ten), rehiring a fired worker (nine), fines (eight), and so on.

Both national and local government appear to have taken a neutral or mildly procapital stance in most strikes, although there were cases in which important strikes were broken by government intervention (discussed above). A purely subjective categorization of responses of the government and government officials shows that state interference was not an important ingredient in most strikes. In fifty cases, the government took no action at all. When it did take steps to end a strike, its efforts normally benefitted capital, although state support for employers waned when they allowed strikes in their establishments to drag on, especially if the general public was affected.

Employers showed little conciliatory spirit at the start of most strikes. The most frequent response (50 cases, 63 percent) of employers during the first twenty-four hours of a strike was to refuse to bargain with their workers (table A.12). In only 10 percent of cases did employers offer any kind of compromise. The very low percentage of compromise solutions reached when the strikes were finally settled (table A.22) is further evidence of the unwillingness of both employers and workers to compromise on major issues.

Few strikes lasted more than two weeks. The mean duration of the sixty-five strikes for which both the beginning and ending dates are known was 11.3 days. The range was a low of one day to a high of eighty-four days.

Strikebreakers were introduced in twenty-four strikes and were not used in forty-two; in eighteen cases the information regarding the strike was insufficient to know whether they were used or not.

Strikes in Valparaíso and Santiago appear to have been less violent than those of the mining areas of the North and South. Small groups of police patrolmen were dispatched to guard the premises of each establishment struck; major intervention on the part of police, army, or navy units was reported in thirty-two cases. Violence, or at least reported violence, occurred in about one in five strikes. Strikebreakers were probably assaulted away from the job site, arrests made without the press reporting them, and property destroyed without being immediately detected. Nevertheless, of eighty-four strikes, only one led to fatalities—that of May 12, 1903, in Valparaíso.

Just as government refrained from interference during the course of most strikes, so did it play only a minor role in bringing them to a close. Between 1902 and 1908, only nine strikes, or 13 percent of the total, were settled through government action, in these cases mediation or binding arbitration by a representative of the government (table A.20). The great majority of strikes (68.1 percent) found their solution in direct concilation between workers and employers.

Strikes between 1902 and 1908 ended with remarkable success for labor, perhaps due to the fact that workers struck when the occasion was most favorable, such as during the years 1902-3 and 1905-7. Of the seventy strikes for which complete information is available, thirty-three ended in complete success for workers, twenty-two in a compromise solution, and only fifteen in total failure (see table A.22).

LABOR IN DECLINE

A combination of factors resulted in the rapid decline of the labor movement after June, 1907. Only three more strikes took place in Santiago and Valparaíso during the remainder of 1907 and, according to figures compiled by the Labor Office, eleven occurred in 1908.[82] The strength of many resistance societies had been seriously weakened by the firing and blacklisting of union leaders after the unsuccessful general strike of June, 1907, and continued to decline during the next year. Santiago bakers survived a general lockout in the industry during August, 1907, but failed to win the recognition of their union by employers as a condition for returning to work.[83] Strikes in the tram and glass industries failed miserably. The financial panic of 1907 resulted in a disastrous decline in the value of the Chilean peso and hardened the determination of employers not to give in to further union demands. Labor did win a victory against the government in December, 1907, when it threatened to call a giant rally similar to that of October, 1905, to demand the repeal of the beef tax. Congress quickly abolished the tax to avoid trouble, but the government met further labor unrest in the North with machine gun fire.

Savage repression in Iquique struck fear into the hearts of urban workers. In order to avoid further bloodshed, *La Reforma* urged the resistance societies not to hold rallies or gather in "shootable groups."[84] By May, few resistance societies were functioning in Santiago and Valparaíso, and the FTCh had disappeared altogher. *La Reforma* noted that the victories of 1906-7 had been forgotten and that workers drifted away from the labor unions, probably under pressure from employers.[85] Further purges of labor organizers took place in the shops of the State Railway in Santiago. In March, 1908, a walkout in sympathy with Concepción workers resulted in widespread firings, and an even more diastrous month-long strike in May crushed the union altogether.[86] Later that year, the state forced a 10 percent pay cut on railway workers. Santiago printers won an industry-wide strike for higher wages in June, 1908, both by the end of the year, their once-strong federation had fallen apart for lack of interest.[87]

The reasons for the notable decline of labor after 1907 are not entirely clear. No single event, save perhaps the 1907 general strike, hastened the process appreciably. The increased resolution of employers and government to rid themselves of the resistance societies certainly played an important role, as did the business slump of 1907. Thousands of workers, either content with their 1906-7 gains or fearful of losing their jobs during a time of financial crisis, deserted the resistance societies, some to rejoin the secure, persecution-free mutual aid groups. The resistance society movement by no means died after 1908, but neither did labor totally regain its strength until the great organizational effort of 1917-20.

POLITICS AND URBAN LABOR

Certain sectors of the urban workforce had played an active role in Chilean politics since the early days of the Republic. While only those artisans holding property of a stipulated value voted before the electoral reforms of the 1880s workers constituted an "infantry" which supported or opposed the electoral campaigns, insurrections, and demonstrations of political elites.[88] Politicians of every faction courted the support of urban labor, both for electoral events and to produce visual expressions of "popular" support. After the removal of property requirements for voting, which granted all literate males over twenty-one years of age the right to vote, political parties

117

increased their demogogic courtship of the working class. Traditional parties, such as the Liberals and Conservatives, as well as the Radicals and Democrats, established working class clubs and founded newspapers with "popular" titles such as *La Comuna, El Obrero,* and *El Trabajo* to encourage workers to join the party. The Liberals, for example, urged Santiago workers to support them in the elections of 1896 to defeat the "oligarch millionaires" (Conservatives), while the Conservatives in the same election challenged workers to stand up for their rights "like big boys" and vote Conservative in their own self-interest.[89]

The nature of the Chilean political system in effect after 1891 greatly encouraged the spread of demagoguery by Chile's six major political parties. No single party could by itself elect a President or control enough votes in the nation's all-powerful Congress to exercise power. Instead, politics revolved around the making and unmaking of coalitions and alliances.[90] Coalitions were formed by normally antagonistic parties, while alliances bound together parties of similar political outlook. The instability of these groupings, and consequently of the national cabinets which reflected the political compromises inherent in such an arrangement, caused politics to be in a constant state of flux between 1891 and 1924.

All parties except perhaps the Democrats used any means at their disposal to win more votes. Officeholding, which led to the increased power (and wealth) of the coalition, party, and individual in question, was a universal goal. Since a few hundred votes often spelled the difference between victory or defeat in congressional elections, the parties used every possible means to gain support. Because the ballot deposited in the election box was provided the voter by each political party, vote-buying and selling constituted perhaps the most widespread means of obtaining working class votes. A U.S. diplomat in Chile summed up this process in a 1912 report:[91]

> Vote buying has always been a feature of Chilean politics. It is practised openly by all parties and is regarded as an almost legitimate means of success. The striking difference between the educated and governing class and the ignorant *roto, inquilino,* and laboring element explains and in Chilean eyes justifies the practice. The educated class claims that the adoption of universal suffrage in the country was an unreasoned, overenthusiastic mistake and that as the lower classes, here at least, do not know for whom or for what they are voting, no injustice is done to them, and it is further agreed that a man's vote is his property which he can dispose of as he sees fit.

Major parties employed many other corrupt practices to insure victory. Youths of less than twenty-one years were registered as eligible voters, urban and rural patrones signed up their illiterate workers in the election registries and later provided them with party ballots, and many qualified voters were prevented from registering for political reasons.[92] Dead and absent people frequently exercised the franchise, and in some cases the ballot boxes themselves were "lost" or "stuffed" by party zealots. Under such a system, the traditional elites which had dominated Chilean politics since the first days of the Republic maintained their influence within all parties but the PD. Despite the lack of discipline within the political parties and the fierce interparty rivalries, the political "game" during the so-called "Parliamentary Republic" in Chile remained in the hands of the upper class. Groups such as the PD which rose to challenge the hold of elites over politics in any given area and demonstrated an ability to attract significant numbers of votes were eventually absorbed into the system by admittance to an alliance or coalition.

While all parties claimed to represent the needs of the urban pueblo, only the Democratic Party had working people among its leaders. Because it did not enjoy a secure enough financial position to buy votes and was ideologically repelled by the idea of doing so, the major task of the PD was to convince workers not to sell their votes but instead to vote Democratic. Connections with the mutual aid societies and the northern mancomunales provided the Democrats with a major source of support and a base from which to expand their influence. Between 1902 and 1908, the party either organized or participated in many of the congresses and conferences aimed at unifying the mutualist and brotherhood movements, and sponsored or supported several strikes, rallies, and large-scale demonstrations. In every case, the PD's goal was to build a political base of power around the urban working class. Recabarren effectively stated the party's gradualist faith in politics in a 1905 newspaper article:"Politics is the principal weapon for taking power, and after that, from the top, we will capture the rest of the holdings of the bourgeoisie."[93]

The prestige of the PD expanded as it elected more members to Congress. In 1906, six Democrats won seats in the Chamber of Deputies, although two were later disqualified for past "subversive" activities. Angel Guarello, for example, played an important part in mediating the Valparaíso port strike of 1903. The PD actively encouraged workers to join the demonstration to protest the tax on Argentine beef which took place in Santiago on October 22, 1905. Party members helped lead the neighborhood committees which organized the march itself, and many Democrats also held leadership positions in the mutualist organizations participating in the demonstration.[94] It is probably no coincidence that the October demonstration took place during the registration period for the presidential and congressional elections of March, 1906.

The Santiago branch of the Democratic Party proved something of a maverick during the years 1905–8, much as the Santiago section of the Communist Party of Chile resisted central authority during the 1920s. In both cases, the strength of Anarchist ideology and the subsequent failure of political caudillos to emerge from labor unions in the Capital prevented the Democrats and Communists from winning political power. In Tocopilla, Antofagasta, Concepción, and Valparaíso, the Democrats used their influence over the mancomunales and mutual aid societies to elect deputies and many municipal councilmen in 1906, while in Santiago the party's candidates for deputy and senator were roundly defeated, and only one Democratic councilman (of a total of thirty) was elected.[95] Recabarren, Veas, Guarello, and Concha each built a local power base in a provincial city, but none could establish himself as a political boss among Santiago workers. The Santiago branch of the PD was dissolved less than a week after the Meat Riot in Santiago in order to purge "outside and unruly elements" who had enthusiastically supported the lawlessness.[96] The official party line condemned the government's lack of foresight in leaving the city undefended, praised Malaquías Concha's role in quieting the "mob," and blamed most of the violence on Anarchists and Socialists.[97] In Congress, Concha argued that the respectful and law-abiding mutualists had nothing to do with the rioting and that the PD was innocent of charges that it planned the violence before the rally began.[98] By purging the Santiago branch, the PD proved Concha wrong.

In 1906, the PD split, with Santiago again becoming the focus of opposition to Concha's authority. Branches in the North and in Santiago supported the candidacy of Pedro Montt for President, while the main sector of the party favored Fernando Lazcano. The rump group, led by Veas and Recabarren, formed the short-lived Doctrinaire Democratic Party, which took an ideological stand far to the left of the Concha Democrats while at the same time remaining politically loyal to the oligarch Montt. Its principal mouthpiece, the Santiago daily *La Reforma,* attacked both the Anarchists on the left and the Concha position. The Doctrinaires branded the Anarchist FTCh as a "wolf in sheep's clothing," claiming that the "boring from within" tactics of the resistance societies sought the destruction of mutualism.[99] Ironically, the pages of *La Reforma* were thrown open for use by the resistance societies, and their strikes, proclamations, and even ideological statements were reproduced with regularity. Despite the accusations hurled back and forth between Recabarren and the Anarchists, the Doctrinaires moved closer to the ideological position of the resistance societies as increasing numbers of Santiago workers deserted the mutualists. An editorial in *La Reforma* declared in October, 1907: "We repeat what we said eight months ago, the general strike is the *only means* which the workers have to *oblige* public authorities and even private exploiters [employers] to slacken their homicidal noose."[100] The Doctrinaires walked a thin line between the leftist, or at least activist, position of the resistance societies and continued support for the Montt government. Conflict of interest between the two positions was clearly apparent during the general strike of June, 1907, and would become even more so later in the year. The massacre of more than a thousand workers by army units in Iquique on December 21, 1907, seriously strained relations between the Doctrinaires and the government.

The two sections of the Democratic Party were reunified in April, 1908. The Iquique massacre and subsequent repression of the labor movement, coupled with Veas's suspension from the Chamber of Deputies for refusing to vote for a measure expressing official grief over the assassination of Carlos I of Portugal when no action had been taken to punish those responsible for the Iquique killings, all but extinguished Doctrinaire support for Montt. During its brief flirtation with the resistance society movement, the PD in Santiago and Valparaíso encouraged the growth of organized labor by contributing to strikes, coordinating solidarity campaigns in *La Reforma,* providing militant workers with daily news presented from a prolabor viewpoint, and helping solve organizational problems of the resistance societies. Yet it was the workers who prodded the Doctrinaires into taking a more aggressive stance, not vice-versa. By the time of the Concha/Doctrinaire split, the strike wave of 1906 was already in full swing.

While tens of thousands of workers voiced their discontent with government or support for a political party by "informal" political activity, such as protest marches, rallies, rioting, and looting, far fewer engaged in "formal" political participation. Although the number of voters who participated in the elections of the 1902-8 period is unclear, government statistics for the following decade indicate that the great majority of workers did not vote. Given the total population of 100,000 adult males in the Department of Santiago in 1912 and a literacy rate of approximately 73 percent among them, some 73,000 people were eligible to vote in that year. Of these, only 26,163, or 35.8 percent cast ballots in the 1912 congressional-municipal elections.[101] Assuming that all illiterate adult males in Santiago were of working class extraction, and that (in line with contemporary accounts) workers normally refrained from voting, the percentage of workers who cast ballots in the 1912 election must have been significantly lower than the overall figure of 35.8 percent. The presidential election of 1920 captured tremendous popular interest, and yet only 22.6 percent of eligible adult males voted in that election.[102] Fraud at the polling places may have cut down on the size of the working class vote, although, by all indications, only one in five or six workers appears to have cast a ballot. It is unlikely that the working class vote was larger between 1902 and 1908, unless the traditional parties were somehow more successful in buying votes during those years than in 1912 or 1920. Even when the PD elected a deputy to Congress in cities such as Antofagasta, Tocopilla, and Valparaíso, voter turnout was very light, and the Democrats were able to win only because the percentage of

121

working class men over age twenty-one in the total population was much higher than in Santiago.

The fact that all parties courted the working class vote indicates that some workers certainly did receive and cast ballots during the years 1902 and 1908. A handful of working class candidates were elected to office in some areas, but these men could do virtually nothing to better the lot of the workingman through politics. That "reform" legislation which did pass Congress was the work of the traditional elite parties, not the PD. Within a few years after 1908, however, the Democratic Party would itself receive ministerial positions and become a fully legitimate participant in Chilean politics.

An aggressive campaign mounted by the Anarchists against electoral politics may have had some effect in holding down the size of the working class vote, especially in Santiago.[103] The Anarchists argued that all politicians, including the Democrats, were demagogues who had no intention of fulfilling any of their campaign promises. Criticism of electoral politics stemmed from the libertarian belief that by voting, a man surrendered his personal rights to the politician representing him. Furthermore, no dedicated Anarchist would admit the legitimacy of the state by voting in elections. Anarchism strengthened its appeal to Chilean workers by persistently underscoring the futility of exercising the franchise as compared with direct action tactics to improve living conditions and bring about change in the social order. The FTCh and the individual resistance societies which composed it obviously agreed with the anti-electoral spirit of libertarianism, inasmuch as they refused to allow any political activity within the unions.

ELITES AND THE SOCIAL QUESTION

Elites in Chile became increasingly concerned with the so-called "social question" between 1902 and 1908, mainly as a result of the growing occurrence of strikes and mass demonstrations. Fear of the "mob" tormented upper class Chileans and foreigners long before 1902, but the series of urban riots and strikes after that date brought the issue of working class violence into national prominence. The social question resulted more from dread of social upheaval than from increased concern for the well-being of the pueblo on the part of elites. The frequent use of violence in dealing with the working class and the paucity of social legislation before 1924 reflect the government's perception of the problem.

The appearance of Anarchist newspapers of an inflammatory nature in the late 1890s concerned police officials, who feared that agitators would establish themselves within the Santiago labor movement.[104] Once relations with Argentina were normalized after the war fever of 1900-1902, elites began to worry that an influx of foreign Anarchists from the neighboring republic might cause labor unrest similar to that of Buenos Aires.[105] The passage of the Residency Law of 1902 in Argentina, which allowed for the deportation of undesirable aliens, constituted further proof for Chilean elites that international Anarchism might be a threat to their country.

It was not until the Valparaíso riot of 1903, however, that the upper class in Chile began seriously to consider the social question. Reports describing the sack of the city by thousands of infuriated, drunken rotos and the incompetence of local authorities greatly upset elites throughout the country.[106] Even though public opinion generally distinguished between the legitimate grievances of the strikers and the excesses of lower class rioters, most elitist newspapers or pressure groups called for increased police protection from the government. *El Diario Ilustrado* of Santiago expressed the concern of many when it asked:[107]

> If simultaneously the workers of the Mancomunal of Iquique, those of the Railroad Shops in Santiago, workers in Viña del Mar, Concepción, Lota, Coronel, and Talcahuano were to rise up against constituted order, what means would the authorities have to maintain control? On which troops of the line do they depend to re-establish order?

British businessmen in Valparaíso and Santiago, as well as in the nitrate camps and ports of the North, lived in constant fear of an uprising directed against foreign lives and property. After each strike or outbreak of violence, they petitioned the Foreign Office to send one or more of His Majesty's men-of-war to patrol Chilean waters and to pressure local authorities into providing better police protection. One British diplomat in 1905 expressed fears similar to those of *El Diario Ilustrado:*[108]

> The police is entirely inadequate to deal with the situation and whenever an outburst of lawlessness occurs, recourse is made to vessels of war or troops of the line. As long as these outbursts are isolated, they can be suppressed, but if general discontent in the country broke out into simultaneous riots, I think the government would be pressed to find means of quelling them.

Although strikes and public assemblies were legal in Chile, the government reacted to large-scale rallies or strikes, especially in mining zones, as if they were rebellions. As indicated by the British diplomat, local police could not by themselves control large crowds, and government authorities (usually the intendant) frequently called on units of the armed forces to maintain order. On other occasions, troops or sailors were sent to break strikes, either by force or by serving as scabs. In February, 1903, the Chacabuco Regiment of the army crushed a strike among coal miners in Lota, leaving three workers dead in the process. Several other strikes in the region provoked authorities into calling for the intervention of the armed forces. Men-of-war carrying cavalry detachments were sent to break a strike of nitrate workers and dockers near Tocopilla in 1904. Major or particularly violent job actions in Santiago, such as the printers' strike of 1902, most tram strikes, and the bakers' strike of 1903, all resulted in the use of troops as scabs.

The events of May 12, 1903 were repeated two years later in Santiago. Rising meat prices and the impending registration period for the 1906 elections prompted the PD and its labor ally, the *Congreso Social Obrero,* to plan a "great demonstration" in the Capital to demand the removal of the tax on beef imported from Argentina. The idea of holding a rally was decided upon as early as September 2, 1905, and on September 29, the Chillán convention of the Congreso Social Obrero committed itself to the election of Democrats in 1906.[109] Food prices had in fact risen sharply in Santiago from April to October, 1905, but the Democrats and mutualists decided to focus their attention only on the beef tax, undoubtedly hoping to win greater prestige and more votes by having it abolished. It seemed an obtainable objective capable of producing a handsome political return.

By early October, a planning committee had been formed to coordinate the activities of the many groups scheduled to participate in the demonstration. On October 12, the committee decided to hold its rally on Sunday, October 22, 1905.[110] The sizable military garrison of Santiago began leaving the city on October 15 for the annual army maneuvers held near Talca, more than a hundred miles to the south. The last detachments of the garrison departed by train on the twentieth. The government obviously did not feel that the demonstration would pose a threat to public security, in spite of the lesson of Valparaíso and the serious rioting which occurred in the Capital on Good Friday of 1905. The Chief of Police of Santiago received prior warning that the demonstration might result in violence, but he felt that such fears were unwarranted. The highly respected mutual aid societies had already drafted a petition which politely called on President Riesco to remove the beef tax, and the daily press considered the approaching demonstration "living proof of a cultured populace." The Democrats and mutualists at least in public declared their action to be that of respectful protest.

Some 30,000 people massed in the Centro of Santiago at 1 P.M. on the twenty-second, and by two o'clock, a procession had been formed to march on the Presidential Mansion (*La Moneda*) and present the Committee's petition to Riesco. The President, however, had decided to spend the day at his nearby private residence. While the bulk of the crowd waited at La Moneda, a smaller group took the petition to the President's home. Riesco received the Committee leaders and promised to intervene on behalf of the workers by urging Congress to repeal the tax. Satisfied, the Committee thanked Riesco and returned to the Presidential Mansion. Before its arrival, however, word had gotten out that Riesco refused to grant an audience to the Committee, and a group of demonstrators began hurling rocks at La Moneda. A police guard fired on the crowd, which dispersed and then began a rampage of destruction throughout the Centro. All available police units were mobilized to guard public buildings and the homes of influential citizens in the zone. The crowd smashed light fixtures, overturned and destroyed tram cars, and began looting undefended stores. By nightfall, most of the demonstrators had returned to their homes, leaving the Centro in the hands of the police.

Early in the morning of the twenty-third the attack on the semidefenseless city was resumed. Workers in factories, foundries, construction crews, and in the State Railway shops declared themselves on strike, although they neither drafted nor presented any lists of grievances. The bajo pueblo poured into the central part of the city from slums in the outlying districts to loot the goods they could not afford to buy. Desperate to maintain order, the police formed a "white guard" by arming some 300 young men from the "upper social classes," who had earlier volunteered for service. One thousand firemen also received rifles and were sent out with the aristocratic youths to guard stores and homes. October 23 was drowned in blood. Workers, agricultural laborers from nearby farms, and members of the so-called "lowest classes" attempted to loot whatever they could, and the white guards and the police shot them down by the score. Looting occurred all over the city, in working and upper class neighborhoods alike, although the police showed particular zeal in protecting the well-to-do Centro.

The first troops recalled from the South arrived in Santiago early in the morning of October 24. Order was immediately restored, but the cost of two days of rioting had been heavy. The bodies of fifteen people shot by police and the vigilantes were brought to the morgue, but authorities admitted that countless more had been killed and dragged home by friends.[111] Hundreds of workers were wounded, but few reported to hospitals for fear of being arrested. No policemen or members of the white guard were killed, although 185 policemen received wounds.[112] Over 690 arrests took place, many of them after the arrival of army units on the twenty-fourth. Police reported 149 stores looted, mainly of the same type sacked in Valparaíso in 1903, including pawnshops, food stores, cobbler shops, and liquor stores.

Elites blamed the riot not on the honorable "men of labor" who planned the demonstration, but on the Anarchists, lower classes, and "criminal element" of the city.[113] Evidence to support or refute this interpretation is mixed. Arrest records for all but fifty-five of the nearly 700 persons taken into custody by police have been lost or destroyed by fire. The fifty-five cases which exist include some of the people arrested in unspecified locations on October 22 and 23.[114] Their median age was twenty-one years, all but one were male, thirty could neither read nor write, thirty-seven had been arrested on at least one other occasion, and only two were members of a working class organization. This lends credence to the elite claim that the mutual aid society members had not engaged in looting or acts of destruction. Yet, the great majority of these men were urban workers. Only three were unemployed at the time of their arrest. The PD claimed that "respectable" members of the Democratic Party participated in the violence, and for that reason purged the Santiago branch. The Chief of Police of Santiago noted in his report to the Minister of the Interior that the rioters on the twenty-third included both workingmen and the bajo pueblo, but that patrolmen considered the industrial workers to be superior to the "mass" and normally did not arrest them.[115] The then-Anarchist Escobar y Carvallo, who was in the Centro on October 22, claimed that the workers assembled under the mutualist banners also took part in the destruction and that the Anarchists, as "recognized captains of the proletarian multitude," played an active role in fomenting violence.[116] Such evidence indicates that organized workers as well as Anarchists and the "lowest class" took part in the rioting. The Santiago dailies obviously did not wish to alienate the mutual aid societies and strengthen the political position of the PD by outwardly attacking them. The ill-defined "rabble" and "foreign Anarchists" thus bore the blame for what the labor organizations and PD had begun.

Elite fear of social upheaval and Anarchist inroads among Chilean workers heightened after the Santiago riot and the strike wave which followed. More far-sighted members of the upper class realized that miserable living conditions and high food prices were major factors in fostering a rebellious spirit in urban workers. The handful of "social laws" passed by Congress during the first decades of the century reflected this minority perception of the social question, although elites arrived at their ideas only after much violence and agitation on the part of labor. Most employers and key government officials, however, attributed the cause of working class discontent not to the failure of elites to ease the dire situation of the pueblo, but to the work of domestic subversives and foreign Anarchists who sought to use the naive Chilean workers for their own ends. The death of foreign notables at the hands of Anarchist assassins sent shivers down the collective spine of Chilean elites, who wondered when their turn would come. Most upper class Chileans associated Anarchism with bombings, murder, and destruction, and therefore called upon the government to do something to prevent it form flourishing in Chile.[117] The day after Santiago's mammoth May 1 rally in 1907, *El Mercurio* suggested that Chile adopt a residence law similar to that put into effect by Argentina as a means of preventing the influx of foreign undesirables.[118] Such legislation was not introduced in Congress until 1912 nor acted upon until December, 1918. I have already noted that the label of "foreign subversive" attached to Anarcho-Syndicalist leaders in Chile was a myth, either devised by the government to shift widespread criticism of its handling of labor affairs onto a scapegoat, or actually believed by confused aristocrats who were certain that "it couldn't happen here."

Sincere in their beliefs or not, government authorities and employers moved energetically to halt the rise of labor unions. Small-scale strikes generally did not require government interference, but were left in the hands of labor and capital. Those strikes which threatened to seriously disrupt the economic life of the country, have an adverse political impact on the government, or cause great inconvenience to a powerful employer were often dealt with by force. Labor disputes in the coal, nitrate, and maritime industries were those most frequently repressed, although the government also used force during strikes in important urban industries such as baking or transportation. Tension built steadily during the years 1905–7 as labor increasingly flexed its muscle. In 1906, the small-scale strikes in Santiago and Valparaíso did not receive much adverse public attention, but the cumulative effect of the strike wave, the success of many job actions in forcing employers to raise wages, rising labor discontent with the high cost of living, and the general strike of June, 1907, stimulated a repressive response. Capitalists, as we have already seen, began to counterattack the unions late in 1906 when they formed employers' associations. They were aided in their union-breaking campaign by the government's willingness to assign police and troops to strike duty. The most fearful use of repression employed by government during the entire 1902–8 period occurred in Iquique on December 21, 1907, when army units machine-gunned an utterly defenseless crowd of striking nitrate workers, killing perhaps a thousand.

The government had several forces at its disposal which were used to control and repress labor. Municipal police, normally under the command of a high-ranking army officer and the local intendant, saw the most action on the labor front. Working class organizations in both Santiago and Valparaíso were kept under constant surveillance by the security section of the police force, a group of plainclothes career detectives and part-time spies recruited from the ranks of labor itself. As the unions expanded, so did the skill of the Security Police agents in penetrating them. Strikes, which the Santiago police characterized as "hostile" activity of workers against employers, received close attention from law enforcement authorities.[119] Once a strike was under way, agents began gathering information concerning its cause and nature, while patrolmen were sent to guard the jobsite and watch the union hall. Mounted police accompanied all meetings or demonstrations, while plainclothes policemen mingled among the strikers. Police were under orders to break up all "Anarchist" demonstrations displaying banners "offensive to

127

public authorities and institutions'' and to arrest speakers who too enthusiastically criticized the President or other high officials. Patrolmen were normally armed with clubs and revolvers, but during strike or riot duty they received Mauser rifles.

When widespread strikes or demonstrations could not be contained by police alone, military units were brought in. The effectiveness of troops varied greatly according to the units involved. Almost all private soldiers and sailors came from working class or rural backgrounds and were unwillingly drafted into service. The low pay and severe discipline of military life caused working class youths to fear military conscription and to do whatever possible to avoid it. Middle and upper class youths evaded the Universal Military Service Act of 1902 by bribing the proper authority or simply by filing a form soliciting exemption from service for one of a dozen reasons.[120] Eighteen-year-old workers resisted the draft by not reporting to their units when called up. In 1907, for example, only 20 percent of army conscripts reported to induction centers, while in 1908, 857 of 1,200 navy conscripts called up did not present themselves.[121] Military authorities were therefore forced literally to hunt down these recruits and drag them off to their designated units.

The zeal of Chilean soldiers and sailors in controlling social unrest was frequently called into question. The best example of reported insubordination among the armed forced was that of the marine units during the riot of May 12, 1903, in Valparíso. The government afterwards took care to see that units sent to break strikes had not been recruited from or based in the affected area. Some units proved especially effective against large crowds, most notably the mounted lancers, *Cazadores,* and Escort Regiment, which terrified workers with their long lances and rapid-firing carbines. The gradual creation of *carabinero* units from volunteers who had successfully completed their military service placed a disciplined, more reliable force at the service of the government by the early 1920s. Machine guns played a major role in intimidating labor during demonstrations, but the only reported case of their use was during the 1907 Iquique massacre. While large crowds of workers could isolate police units and force them to retreat by hurling paving stones, they did not even attempt a stand against military forces.

5

Decline, Recovery, and Depression, 1909-16

THE YEARS 1909 TO 1916 constitute something of a "lost period" in Chilean history, or at least one which has attracted very little attention from historians. Aside from the centennial celebration in 1910 and the depression of 1914–15, few events emerge to capture the scholarly eye. Marxist historians have traditionally isolated the formation of the Chilean Workers' Federation (FOCh) and the Socialist Workers' Party (POS) in 1909 and 1912 respectively as key events, since both organizations later merged in the 1920s to form the labor and political wings of the Communist Party. Although these institutions, after first undergoing many fundamental changes, rose to prominence during the 1920s, their formation did not, as Jorge Barría claims, open a "new era" in the history of the labor movement.[1] As we shall see, the role of the FOCh and the POS in stimulating the spread of unionization and revolutionary ideology has been greatly overstated by Chilean and non-Chilean scholars alike. The history of Chilean labor to 1927 is not one of institutions and organizations, but of masses of people and what they did. Single unions or federations did from time to time make an important difference in accelerating the spread of organized labor, but most important working class activities, especially those which altered the social order in Chile, resulted from the combined action of many groups.

THE LABOR UNIONS

Between 1909 and early 1914, workers in Santiago and Valparaíso enjoyed considerable success in rebuilding many of the resistance societies which had fallen victim to repression and lack of rank and file interest after June, 1907. Mutual aid societies, largely unaffected by the events of 1907–8, continued to expand their total membership until 1914, according to Labor Office figures.[2] As the overall strength of labor grew between 1909 and early 1914, the number of resistance societies rose to twenty or more in both Santiago

Table 5.1
Estimates of the Number and Total Membership of Working Class Organizations
in the Provinces of Valparaíso and Santiago
and in Chile, 1909 and 1912–13

Year(s)	Number of Organizations	Total Membership
Valparaíso		
1909[a]	85	10,551
1912–13[b]	116	20,886
Santiago		
1909[a]	72	9,796
1912–13[b]	97	17,931
Chile		
1909[a]	372	65,136
1912–13[b]	463	91,609

[a]Source: ADGT, *Estadística de la Asociación Obrera,* Santiago, 1910, pp. 24, 26, 57.
[b]Source: *BOT* 7, 1913, p. 183.

and Valparaíso.[3] In similar fashion to the events of 1905–7, these few resistance groups were far more visible than the numerically superior mutual aid societies.

The resurgence of labor organizations after 1909 was associated with economic prosperity. A booming nitrate industry, increased state revenues, the rapid expansion of the State Railway system, and greater manufacturing production combined to create new jobs and lessen the ability of employers to thwart the spread of labor unions. Food costs fell after the tremendous inflation of 1907–8, remained more or less stationary until 1912, when they began to rise and then skyrocketed during the 1914–15 depression. Thus, a period of economic prosperity and stable prices strengthened the financial position of workers, and growing inflation from 1912 to 1914 gave them further reason to organize. A slump in nitrate production during the recession of 1913 does not appear to have slowed the growth of urban labor unions, but the widespread unemployment caused by the depression of 1914–15 eventually led to the collapse of many.

By 1909, many of the important labor unions of 1906–7 had disappeared altogether. Gone were the federations of shoemakers, printers, and construction workers, as well as the FTCh, the Valparaíso mancomunal, and nearly all of the once-influential brotherhoods of the northern ports.[4] Many ex-members of these resistance societies may have drifted back to the mutualist groups from which they had originated. Workers fearful of losing their jobs due to labor union membership retreated to the safety of mutualism. The

Gran Federación Obrera de Chile (FOCh) exemplified the conservative mood of many Chilean workers. Formed among the workers in the Santiago and Valparaíso shops of the State Railway in September, 1909, the main purpose of the organization was to press for the payment of money withheld from workers' salaries as a result of a 10 percent wage cut imposed by the government in 1908.[5] After a year of petitioning Congress and the courts to order the State Railway to pay the back wages as it had promised to do, the FOCh finally realized its objective in September, 1910.

The FOCh continued to operate as a mutual aid society whose goal was "to aid the membership, increase the cultural level of the working classes, and further the economic, moral, and intellectual well-being of members."[6] Like most mutualist organizations, the FOCh collected monthly death, burial, and membership dues from each member. Reflecting the economic security of workers in the State Railway shops, who remained the only proletarians in Chile paid in pesos at a fixed rate of exchange (16d) with the pound, the FOCh exuded patriotism and conservatism. As opposed to the combative unions organized by railroad shop workers in Santiago and Valparaíso before 1907, the FOCh of 1911 regarded strikes as "already antiquated" as a working class weapon, and no member council of the federation participated in a strike before 1916.[7]

The significance of the FOCh lay not in its size or effectiveness, but in its institutional structure. Although it was at first organized by shop workers of the State Railway, the federal council (concejo) established in each city as its main organizational unit later admitted mutual aid groups of many different crafts as members. The FOCh therefore became the first labor organization in Chile to unite workers of a similar craft (railroad metal workers) in more than two cities and to combine regional federations at the national level. As the federation grew, newly matriculated trade unions were allowed to retain their craft autonomy by forming a local concejo and electing representatives to the Concejo Federal, or Regional (city) Council. The Regional Council in turn elected a president and an Executive Council to preside over the national organization. In May, 1911, the FOCh contained federal (regional) councils in fifteen different cities from Coquimbo to Valdivia, including Santiago and Valparaíso. Most regional councils contained a single concejo formed by railroad workers, although electricians in Valparaíso and tannery workers in Valdivia also joined the organization.[8] At its peak of predepression influence in 1911-12, the FOCh probably contained some 2,500 members, the great majority of whom resided in Santiago (800) and Valparaíso (830).[9] The economic recession and brake on railroad construction in 1913 severely undermined the financial position of the FOCh and sent it into decline. Wage cuts among railroad workers in 1914 and 1915 and the disastrous showing of the federation in the 1916 general rail strike further eroded membership. In

May, 1917, the FOCh councils in Santiago and Valparaíso contained only 600 members between them.[10]

The successful campaign by the FOCh to win the release of wages withheld from maestranza workers since 1908 reaffirmed the faith of many urban mutual aid societies in legalistic behavior. Strikes, the FOCh argued, were not only destructive but unnecessary, since the President of the Republic and his ministers looked favorably on the "just" petitions of the organized working class.[11] This attitude predominated in the protest rallies and demonstrations controlled by the mutualists and later by the semileftist FOCh of the 1917–19 period. The threat of rioting, constantly on the minds of government officials after the bloody events of 1903–7 and other disturbances to follow, remained a silent, muscular ally of the mutualists, who benefitted from it by obtaining some of their own objectives. Before 1917, however, the public activities of the FOCh and the majority of urban mutual aid groups remained at a very low level.

Most strike activity, protest rallies, and public demonstrations between 1909 and 1916 were planned and carried out by the comparatively few resistance societies of the Capital and Port. Among the most combative unions, however, was the Union of Stevedores and Sailors, a resistance/mutual aid group formed in Valparaíso during the general strike of June, 1907.[12] Marine workers of Valparaíso had traditionally been more aggressive and strike-prone than other mutualist workers, and between 1911 and 1914, the Union behaved like a typical resistance organization. Other mutual aid societies, including glass workers in Santiago and printers in Valparaíso, also went on strike during this period.

It was the Anarchist-inspired resistance societies, however, which continued the tradition of job-oriented labor unionism. Between 1909 and early 1914, a core of Anarcho-Syndicalist union men rebuilt many of the labor organizations which had flourished during the strike wave of 1905–7. The spirit of ideologically or at least economically motivated labor unionism leading to strikes and wage demands had not been totally suppressed during the years of decline, but only six resistance societies (among cigarette workers, seamstresses, bakers, woodworkers [two], and electricians) existed in Santiago in 1909.[13] Slow growth occurred during 1910 and 1911, but in the next two and a half years, great strides were made in rebuilding the strength of many resistance unions. The important Shoeworkers' Federation was reorganized in both Santiago and Valparaíso in 1910, as were unions of tailors, blacksmiths, foundrymen, and upholsterers.[14] Two important fortnightly newspapers, El Productor and La Batalla of Santiago, went into print in 1912 to spread the Anarchist creed and further the growth of resistance societies. In October, 1913, the Workers' Federation of the Chilean Region (FORCh) was formed by five resistance societies in Valparaíso.[15] The

FORCh, which grew to twenty member unions by February, 1914, served the same coordinating purpose as had the FTCh of Santiago in 1907, and, like its predecessor, failed to become a national organization. Among the new resistance societies were those of the building trades, tinsmiths, metal workers at the shops of the Pacific Steam Navigation Company and Compañía Sud Americana de Vapores, some railroad line personnel, stevedores, and workers at the vegetable oil factory and sugar refinery of Viña del Mar.[16] Thus, except for the Viña factory workers, the same trades formed resistance societies during both the 1905-7 and 1911-14 organizational drives. Many worked at skilled or semiskilled jobs, although by no means did all of the skilled trades become involved in the resistance movement.

Few changes took place in the nature of the urban resistance societies between 1909 and 1916. They continued to be job-oriented rather than merely concerned with mutual aid, conducted their usual antivote campaigns, and cultivated the previous tactics of "boring from within" the mutualist groups to win new converts. Anarchist ideology became more strongly entrenched among workers in Santiago and Valparaíso between 1912 and 1914 than it had previously been, as reflected by the regular publication of *La Batalla* and *El Productor* and the proliferation of the *centros de estudios sociales*. Further evidence of the spread of ideological conviction among Chilean workers was provided by the large crowds participating in rallies protesting the arrest of Anarchists in Argentina and expressing solidarity with the Mexican Revolution.[17] Union leaders took an active part in the social studies centers, and Anarchist ideology was diffused to the rank and file during union meetings and social events. The resurrection of May 1 as a day of work stoppage and protest was a further indication of the growth of Anarchist influence and the strength of organized labor between 1909 and 1914. Fearful of repression and lacking organizational capacity, only a hundred or so die-hard Anarchists turned out for Santiago's May 1 demonstration in 1909.[18] The crowd swelled to 10,000 in 1910, and between 1912 and 1914, the May 1 demonstrations of Santiago and Valparaíso were judged "colossal triumphs" by the press.[19] After the full effects of the depression of 1914 were felt, May 1 rallies shrank in size, and did not reach 1913 proportions again until 1918.

Several resistance societies were formed among port workers, skilled tradesmen, and nitrate workers in the Provinces of Tarapacá and Antofagasta after the disappearance of the mancomunales, but the main base of Anarchist/ resistance society activity, as well as labor organization in general, continued to be Santiago and Valparaíso.[20] With the nitrate companies competing with each other for laborers and production booming between 1909 and 1913, wages for miners rose substantially, and the labor movement in the North nearly disappeared altogether.[21] Nitrate workers appear to have been in a most conservative mood, in great part due to their rising real wages. In the words of the Anarchist newspaper *Luz y Vida* of Antofagasta, they became "drugged by a deceitful well-being" and shunned labor unions.[22] It would not be an exaggeration to say that the Anarchists, through their resistance societies in the urban center, were responsible for keeping labor unionism alive in Chile from 1908 to 1916. Total membership in resistance organizations perhaps reached 3,000–4,000 in Valparaíso and several thousand in Santiago, but as in the case of the 1905–7 resistance societies, the small size of the membership did not preclude successful job action. The effectiveness of the 1913 general strike in Valparaíso amply demonstrated the prestige of the Anarcho-Syndicalist FORCh to other workers.

Organized labor declined once again during the depression of 1914–15, perhaps reaching its nadir in late 1915. The Anarchists responded to the widespread unemployment and misery among workers after August, 1914, by carrying out a series of protest rallies demanding work for the unemployed and by setting up soup kitchens in Santiago to feed the jobless.[23] When tenement rents more than doubled during 1914, the Anarchists formed tenant leagues (*ligas de arrendatarios*) in both Santiago and Valparaíso.[24] The tenant leagues held several public demonstrations to demand overall rent reductions of 50 percent for conventillo rooms. Although rents were not lowered, the tenant leagues brought many unorganized workers and their families into contact with Anarchist union men and paved the way for the growth of more effective rent reduction movements during the 1920s.

A new generation of labor leaders assumed positions of importance in the resistance society movement and the Socialist Workers' Party between 1909 and 1916. A handful of pre-1908 figures, notably Recabarren, Manuel Hidalgo, Julio E. Valiente, and Luis A. Pardo, continued to play an important role in the labor movement of the second decade, but the great majority of the old leaders disappeared from view. Nearly all new union chiefs continued to be active in labor affairs throughout the 1920s, many of them as members of the Industrial Workers of the World or the various Anarcho-Syndicalist unions of Valparaíso and Santiago. Like their predecessors of the 1902–8 period, these men were highly educated by working class standards, extremely literate, and generally employed in semiskillled or skilled trades. Many wrote for *El Productor* and *La Batalla* and actively participated in a social studies center while also serving as union leaders. Almost all were Anarchists, and none received pay for union work.[25]

Perhaps the most notable figure in the new generation of Anarchists was Juan Onofre Chamorro, a part-time sailor and operator of a butcher shop in Valparaíso's market. In 1913 he was elected secretary of the Union of Stevedores and Sailors of Valparaíso, and later became secretary general of the FORCh. Chamorro directed the general strike of 1913, founded several social studies centers, and was arrested on numerous occasions. Even after the depression he continued to organize maritime workers, rebuilt the FORCh in 1917, directed the massive port strike of that year, and became one of the leading figures in the Anarcho-Syndicalist IWW during the 1920s. Other prominent IWW members, including Luis Armando Triviño, and Augusto Pinto, first became involved with Anarchism and labor unions through participation in *La Batalla*. The Shoeworkers' Federations of Santiago and Valparaíso produced three important leaders during their period of expansion in 1913-14: Pedro Ortúzar, Ramón Contreras, and Eugenio Retamales. All three held important positions in the IWW and the shoeworkers' unions during the 1920s. Another leader of 1913 FORCh, Moisés Oyarzún, went on to direct the Anarchist newspaper *Verba Roja* in 1918.

Anarchism began to attract many young intellectuals to its ranks, several of whom were of working class origin. These proletarian members of the "generation of 1920" embraced libertarian ideas several years before the Federation of Chilean Students (FECh), the associaton of university students in Santiago, was won over to Anarchism. The most famous of these were Manuel Rojas, José Santos González Vera, and José Domingo Gómez Rojas. All three were young workers who began their careers as revolutionary propagandists by writing for *La Batalla*.[26] Rojas later joined the IWW and wrote of life as a maritime worker in his first novel, *Lanchas en la bahía*. That and further works won him a reputation as one of Chile's foremost novelists. González Vera also joined the IWW after many years as a propagandist, became secretary general of the IWW local in Concepción, and gained recognition as an important literary figure during the 1930s and 1940s. Gómez Rojas wrote his celebrated poems *Rebeldías Líricas* at age seventeen while serving on the staff of *La Batalla*. A member of the IWW's first Administrative Council, he was arrested during the dragnet raids ordered by President Juan Luis Sanfuentes in August, 1920, and died in prison a month later. Other important libertarian propagandists included the university student Carlos Caro and the Italian/Peruvian worker Julio Rebosio.

Several founders of the Socialist Workers' Party (POS) in 1912 became important figures in the labor movement. Recabarren, of course, enjoyed prestige among workers throughout the country. Manuel Hidalgo came from a lower middle class family, attended high school for three years, and was apprenticed to a watchmaker. His political career spanned nearly four decades, but his link with the labor unions was never as close as Recabarren's. Another cofounder of the POS, Enrique Díaz Vera, joined the FOCh and later became its secretary general. Carlos A. Sepúlveda, another POS notable, became one of the most effective and highly respected labor leaders of the 1920s by successfully walking the thin ideological line between membership in the FOCh, the Anarcho-Syndicalist Shoeworkers' Federation, and the

Table 5.2
Incidence of Strikes in Chile, 1907–16

| | Number of Strikes According to: | |
Year	Barrera-Barría[a]	Oficina del Trabajo[b]
1907	80	52
1908	15	29
1909	5	—
1910	3	—
1911	8	—
1912	26	10
1913	27	18
1914	8	17
1915	7	5
1916	21	16

[a]Source: Figures cited in Manuel Barrera, "Perspectiva histórica de la huelga obrera en Chile," in *Cuadernos de la realidad nacional*, no. 9, September, 1971, p. 125.

[b]Source: Labor Office figures cited in U.S. Bureau of Labor Statistics, *Monthly Labor Review*, vol. 21, no. 1, July, 1925, p. 195.

POS at the same time. Ramón Sepúlveda Leal, a future Communist Party chief and propagandist in Viña del Mar, also joined the POS in 1912.

STRIKES

The occurrence of strikes in Santiago and Valparaíso paralleled the growth and decline of the labor movement. As labor reorganized its forces between 1912 and 1914, the number of strikes increased substantially, but still remained far below 1906–7 levels.[27] The rise in the number of strikes between 1908 and 1913 reflects the gradual strengthening of the organized labor movement. Rising food and rent costs between 1912 and 1914 helped stimulate the desire of workers to engage in job action. Few strikes took place during 1914–15 as the effects of the 1913 recession and the depression to follow completely undercut the bargaining position of workers throughout the country. By 1916, urban industry began to recover, employment rose, and strike activity increased again.

Labor Office information indicates that approximately half of all strikes in 1912 and 1913 took place in Santiago and Valparaíso, a pattern similar to that of 1905–6.[28] Unlike the earlier period, however, the greater share of strikes occurred in Valparaíso. Strike activity centered in the transportation industry, especially among maritime and State Railway workers. The frequent strikes in the leather and printing industries between 1905 and 1907 were not repeated between 1911 and 1916. Manufacturing workers in general appear to have refrained from strike activity, either because they were able to negotiate wage increases without going on strike or because they lacked the proper organizational strength. Given the general prosperity of 1911 to early 1913 and the presence of several important resistance societies among manufacturing workers in both Santiago and Valparaíso, it appears likely that wage increments may have been obtained without resorting to strikes.

Several transportation strikes reached large-scale proportions. On June 11, 1912, stevedores, lightermen, and sailors engaged in unloading coal in Valparaíso struck the Pacific Steam Navigation Company, the Compañía Sud Americana de Vapores, and the German-owned Kosmos Line, the three principal shipping companies operating in Chile. Their demands included shorter hours, higher pay, and better working conditions.[29] The strike involved the coordinated effort of several resistance societies and came at a time when the unions were certain that the coal reserves of the State Railway and the Santiago and Valparaíso electric companies were very low. Within two days, 2,000 maritime workers had walked off their jobs. In what was to become a typical pattern in all important port strikes since that of 1903, the intendant of Valparaíso mobilized the troops of the Maipú Batallion in Viña del Mar and called in 100 cavalrymen of a crack Santiago regiment.

The lightermen settled with their contractors on the thirteenth, receiving sizable wage increases. They refused to return to work, however, until the companies and contractors came to terms with the stevedores and sailors on the fifteenth. Work was finally resumed for Kosmos and the British PSNC, while coercive comparison tactics were applied to the Chilean-owned CSAV. Several days later, the Compañía Sud Americana de Vapores also capitulated, but the wages agreed to in the new accord remained below those paid by the foreign companies.

The most significant strike of the 1909-16 period proved to be the general strike of October, 1913, in Valparaíso. At its height, some 10,000 workers of twenty or more different unions were out, indicating a definite resurgence of labor strength since the low point of 1909-10. The 1913 general strike differed fundamentally from that of 1907 in that some central organization existed and most of the participating unions put forward their own list of demands at the time of the walkout rather than striking purely for solidarity. Many workers did win higher wages or better conditions, but several important unions suffered adverse effects from the strike in similar fashion to 1907.

In April, 1913, State Railway authorities ordered all workers to be photographed for identification purposes. Among the several workers who refused to comply with the new rule was vice-president of the union of loaders, couplers, and switchmen.[30] When the company expelled him from work and had him arrested, the union struck on October 16, demanding his reinstatement and the suppression of the photo-identification rule. Within days, some 900 railroad line workers, only 100 of whom were actually members of the union, left their jobs. The government steadfastly refused even to discuss the issue at stake, claiming that the proper identification of railroad workers was necessary to cut down on thefts. Workers objected to being photographed because they feared the increased capability of the Railroad to blacklist.

On October 19, stevedores and other port workers organized in an Anarchist-dominated resistance society struck for higher pay, and their leader, Juan O. Chamorro, immediately became the coordinator of both the railroad and maritime strikes. The other resistance organizations of the Anarchist FORCh, including some construction and metal workers, joined the strike. By the twenty-seventh, the number of strikers had swelled appreciably with the adherence of tram workers, foundrymen, and employees of the Sugar Refinery of Viña del Mar and the Compañía Chilena de Tabacos. The FORCh committee organizing the strike put forward a list of common demands for all unions, including the eight-hour day, effective Sunday rest, pay fixed at an exchange of 18d, and indemnity payments for work-related accidents. Workers began referring to the walkout as a "general strike" on the twenty-seventh and attempted to increase its effectiveness by staging daily rallies in the Plaza O'Higgins.

The strike remained nonviolent during its first two weeks. Troops had been brought in to guard railroad installations and tram cars, but the government did not begin arresting strike leaders until the thirtieth, when the Peruvian Anarchist and labor organizer Eulogio Otazú was detained by police. Attempts by the intendant to prohibit further public rallies led to clashes between police and workers during which several people were wounded. Further arrests took place when FORCh sailors in small boats came into contact with warships anchored in the harbor. Recalling the disobedience of marines in 1903, *El Mercurio* claimed that the workers hoped to foment mutiny by urging the sailors of the fleet to come ashore and fraternize with the strikers.[31] The arrested workers insisted that they were merely searching for the whereabouts of Otazú.

More unions joined the strike in early November, including enough railroad engineers to grind transportation service to a near halt. Notably, the railroad shop workers of the FOCh did not support the strike. More rallies and protest marches were held, all under the careful supervision of carabineros and mounted troops brought to Valparaíso from other areas. By November 6, many of the strikers offered to return to work if no retaliation would be taken against them and if the photo-identification order were rescinded. Railroad functionaries insisted on firing many of the striking workers, and efforts by PD Senator Angel Guarello to intervene on behalf of the workers also failed.

On November 8, the first victory of the general strike was achieved by workers in the Sugar Refinery of Viña del Mar, who returned to work with better pay, shorter hours, and several other benefits. The strike committee also authorized CSAV workers to return to their jobs after winning improvements in their job situation. Shoeworkers joined the strike en masse on the ninth, closing down Valparaíso's major shoe factories. A series of meetings between employers and the strike committee presided over by Guarello failed to reach a general agreement. Some unions were beginning to give in while others successfully bargained with their employers. Between November 15 and 19, the strike came to a halt. Many port workers, shoemakers, and factory workers gained conciliatory agreements and returned to their jobs. The railroad strike ended in total failure when the strike leaders were fired and the identification card rule strictly applied.

The general strike of 1913 did not end as unfavorably for most workers as did that of 1907. The first strikers in the 1907 walkout were the only ones to obtain benefits, while the reverse proved true in 1913. The government adamantly refused to even consider the basic grievances of the railroad workers, and the other labor organizations, perhaps fearing results similar to those of 1907, did not hold out for solidarity after some of their own demands had been met. Strikebreakers were recruited from the army to run the trains, which remained in good functioning order thanks to the nonadherence of the FOCh to the strike. The fact that the strike lasted a month, even in the face of arrests, suggests that labor had indeed recovered a good portion of its former strength. Nevertheless, the government did not move with exceptional force to break the strike, but rather sought to bring the railroad union to its knees while allowing private employers and their workers a free hand in settling their differences.

No other major strikes occurred in either Santiago or Valparaíso until the railroad strike of 1916. The weakness of labor unions and widespread unemployment nearly precluded strike activity. Successive pay cuts in 1914 and 1915, added to the government's decision to discontinue the payment of wages to maestranza workers at the 16d exchange, led to the presentation of grievances by railway workers in February, 1916.[32] Unfortunately for the Democrats, their first cabinet appointment, Angel Guarello, happened to be serving as Minister of Railroads. The party judged the petitions of workers for the reinstatement of the 16d wage and higher pay scales to be "just," but Guarello for several weeks refused to respond to the demands.[33] Finally, the personnel of the entire State Railway system, both line and shop, struck on March 2, 1916.

The government wasted no time in attempting to break the strike, which threatened to paralyze the country from Coquimbo to Valdivia.[34] Military engineers began running the trains, guarded by armed troops. Carabineros patrolled the tracks and railyards to prevent sabotage, while Santiago's Pudeto and Buín Regiments were mobilized for active guard duty at the Central

Station and other key installations. Railroad authorities claimed they could not possibly meet the wage demands put forward by workers, and on the first day of the walkout threatened all strikers with permanent expulsion from their jobs. Within a few days, the *Regimiento de Ferrocarrileros* (Railroad Regiment), a special army unit dedicated to railroad building and maintenance, had enough trains running to provide needed supplies for the cities. On March 7, the workers of the Santiago and Valparaíso railroad zone petitioned President Sanfuentes to intervene in their favor and were granted an audience. Sanfuentes promised that if the strikers returned to their jobs immediately, a favorable solution to their demands would be forthcoming. The workers refused, insisting that their original petition be met in full. Guarello, meanwhile, appears to have been at odds with State Railway officials over the strike settlement, he being anxious to reach a face-saving compromise, they hoping to break the strike.

The strike remained totally nonviolent. All unions participating in the affair, the FOCh, the Federación Santiago Watt (engineers and firemen), and the Unión Gremial de los Ferrocarriles del Estado, were mutual aid societies forced into striking because of a more than 40 percent loss in real wages over a two-year period. Rallies were held in Santiago and other cities, but the mood of the strike was generally unemotional.

Several more meetings were held between Sanfuentes, Guarello, and the strike committee. The fact that a reasonable number of strikebreakers were at work in the shops and a few trains were operating became the government's trump card in dealing with the unions. On March 13, Sanfuentes appointed the Commander of Carabineros to arbitrate the strike, and invited all former railroad workers to reoccupy their old positions. Those who chose to remain on strike would be immediately replaced.

Grasping at the straw of arbitration, the engineers returned on March 14, much to the displeasure of the lesser-skilled line workers and the maestranza personnel. The following day, a crowd of strikers atttempting to prevent the engineers from reaching their trains was repelled by police. The railroad shops then opened their doors, and many strikers entered. Fights broke out among scabs and ex-strikers, resulting in arrests and firings. Many strikers were never allowed back to their old positions and were blacklisted from further employment. No arbitration ever took place.

The strike failed totally, mainly because the Railroad Regiment succeeded in keeping a few trains running and because the government could count on a glutted labor market to recruit strikebreakers. No other urban workers responded to the strike call, undoubtedly because the few unions which survived the depression of 1914 were weak and workers feared the loss of their jobs. The presence of Guarello in the Railroad Ministry had no favorable effect on the strike from the worker's point of view. Guarello could not raise funds with which to pay the wage increases and therefore was forced to put on the appearance of a concerned friend of labor while allowing his underlings to crush the strike.

LABOR AND POLITICS

The nature of working class participation in politics changed very little from pre-1908 patterns during the years 1909–16. The Democratic Party began to lose at least a portion of its labor support at the same time that it gained greater national stature by electing its first senators and filling several ministerial posts.

In February, 1912, the FOCh's lawyer, honorary president, and editor of its newspaper, Paulo Marín Pinuer, attempted to use the federation to build a political career by declaring himself the FOCh candidate for deputy from Concepción.[35] In the past, only members of the Democrat Party had been elected to Congress by virtue of the working class vote. Those attempting to form "labor" parties or work outside the PD often failed to win the votes of even their fellow union men. The miserable showing of Abdón Díaz, founder and president of the powerful mancomunal of Iquique, in the elections of 1906 was perhaps the best example of labor's lack of interest in political alternatives to the PD.[36] Marín's bid for office was not permitted according to the bylaws of the FOCh, but those statutes outlawing formal political action easily fell victim to a "reinterpretation", and the Marín campaign rolled on.[37] Unfortunately, Malaquías Concha also stood for re-election as the PD's candidate in Concepción. Four of five hopefuls were elected, with Marín the loser. The FOCh claimed that fraud on the part of the *Conchistas* robbed the federation of its votes in order to spare the PD boss an embarrassing defeat. The FOCh did not become a suitable vehicle for political aspirations until new blood was pumped into the organization in 1917–21.

Recabarren and the "Doctrinaires" of 1906 finally broke with the PD in 1912 by forming the Socialist Workers' Party in Iquique. Although several branches of the party were set up in Santiago, Valparaíso, and other cities, the center of POS strength remained in the North. Manuel Hidalgo became the first "socialist" to be elected to public office in Chile when he won an aldermanship on the Santiago Municipal Council in 1913. The Anarchists vigorously condemned his candidacy as a step backward for labor, claiming that he would only instill "false hopes" in the working class.[38] Hidalgo was probably elected because of his long-term membership in the mutualist movement and former association with the PD rather than his appeal as a Socialist. His election as alderman did nothing to better the lot of the Santiago proletariat, but the victory was nonetheless significant because no other non-Democrat had ever been elected to office on the basis of an appeal to working class votes.

The POS itself remained powerless in Santiago and could not elect candidates in other cities. Anarchists both criticized and tolerated the appearance of the POS in Valparaíso and Santiago. Hidalgo participated in the Anarchist-organized May 1 rally in Santiago in 1915, but an attempt by the Socialists to break away from the main group and hold their own meeting failed when nobody joined them.[39] The leaders of the Santiago section of the POS also found their collaboration in 1906 with the hated Pedro Montt difficult to live down.

ELITES AND LABOR

The laissez-faire attitude of government towards the industrial relations system of Chile continued during the 1909–16 period. No attempt was made to establish formal procedures for settling strikes, nor did any significant labor legislation except the 1916 Work Accident Law pass Congress. The "social question" remained much the same issue as before, although elite fears of foreign Anarchists were more clearly expressed.

The one important change in the government's relationship with labor was the formation of the Labor Office (Oficina del Trabajo) as part of the Ministry of Industry and Public Works in 1907.[40] Lack of funds and personnel hampered the efforts of the OT from the start. Its main function was to gather statistical information, but by the early 1920s, the Oficina del Trabajo regularly intervened in the affairs of labor and capital, often serving as a go-between or referee. During times of high unemployment, such as in 1914–15, 1919, and 1921, the OT attempted to find jobs for workers soliciting its aid. Congress officially sanctioned the independence of the OT in 1910, and a full-time inspector began directing the collection of statistics in 1912.[41] More functionaries were hired to handle cases involving work accidents in 1916, but the OT remained greatly understaffed until Arturo Alessandri became President in late 1920.

Governing elites before Alessandri paid little attention to either labor affairs or the Oficina del Trabajo. Except for its practical role during the 1914–15 depression, the OT constituted little more than window dressing to disguise the government's lack of interest in industrial relations. The effectiveness of the OT was undercut by lack of congressional zeal in passing or enforcing social legislation and the resistance of employers in complying with their legal obligations to workers. The employees of the Oficina del Trabajo described the miserable living and working conditions of the Chilean proletariat in countless reports, but their suggestions for reform fell upon deaf ears.

Elite interest in the urban working class deepened noticeably during times of economic crisis and social unrest. As in the pre-1908 years, the "social question" between 1909 and 1916 was equated with a fear of labor unions and the pueblo on the part of upper class Chileans. With the riots of 1903-7 still fresh in their memories, Chilean and foreign elites were treated to a series of events between 1909 and 1916 which further convinced them that subversive elements within the working class planned to overturn the social order.

The assassination of Buenos Aires Police Chief Ramón Falcón by a Russian Anarchist in 1909 greatly upset police authorities in Santiago and deepened their hatred of "repugnant anarchism."[42] Fear of popular disturbances during the 1910 Centennial of Chilean independence prompted Deputy Alfredo Irrarázaval to introduce a bill in Congress strengthening the Santiago police force during the festivities.[43] Unlike their Argentine counterparts, Chilean workers had not planned a general strike to disrupt the celebration of the Centennial, but elites feared that their well-laid plans for an ostentatious display of patriotism during the festivities might be sabotaged by popular unrest.

Elite concern with Anarchism was heightened on December 21, 1911, when three bombs thrown from the street exploded in the Carmelite Monastery in Santiago's Independencia neighborhood. Police claimed that members of a resistance society had bombed the monastery to mark the fourth anniversary of the Santa María de Iquique massacre, and proponents of a residence law cited the incident as evidence of foreign terrorism.[44] The resistance societies protested their innocence, insisting that *agents provocateurs* of the police hurled the bombs, an interpretation shared by British diplomats in Santiago.[45] A 1920s labor leader commented that it was common knowledge among Santiago workers that the police had correctly placed the blame for the bombing on the Anarchists, none of whom was brought to trial for the incident due to lack of evidence.[46]

Pressure for a residence law increased during 1912. On June 13 of that year, the supreme nightmare of urban elites became reality. A young worker named Efraín Plaza Olmedo walked to the corner of Huérfanos and Bandera in Santiago's Centro and began shooting at well-to-do passersby, killing two and wounding others.[47] Plaza admitted to having been driven by hatred for the bourgeoisie and revulsion at upper class nationalism. Although not himself an Anarchist, Plaza immediately became a *cause célèbre* of Chilean libertarians. In 1918, while serving time for his crime, he led a strike at the prison shoe factory in Santiago and had to be transferred to the Talca Penitentiary.[48] The Anarchists on various occasions demanded that authorities commute his long sentence, but it was not until the threat of a mass rally led by the IWW in February of 1925 that the fearful military junta released Plaza. Two months later, Plaza Olmedo's battered and lifeless body was found outside Santiago, a bullet through his head and a pistol in his hand. His death was ruled a suicide, although it is likely that police authorities, incensed at his early release, had beaten and then murdered him.[49]

The Plaza Olmedo affair, coupled with a successful May 1 demonstration and the port strike of June, 1912, in Valparaíso, probably influenced Deputy Guillermo Subercaseaux to introduce his residence law (ley de residencia) in Congress on July 6.[50] The terms of the law prohibited the immigration of Anarchists to Chile and facilitated the deportation of subversive foreigners. A residence law was not passed until 1918, however. The xenophobic nature of such legislation demonstrated the misconception of Anarchism and the Chilean labor movement held by some elites and the desire of others to find a scapegoat upon which to cast the blame for social unrest. A mere handful of foreigners had taken part in strikes and union activity in Chile, and none remained in a position of influence for more than a brief period. Yet, the myth of the "subversive foreigner" persisted.

Mass action in 1913 and 1914 kept elite fears alive. The Valparaíso general strike of 1913 led to clashes between police and workers and increased the awareness of the upper classes that Anarchists were active within the labor movement. The spectre of rebellion and mob violence similar to that of 1903 and 1905 reappeared in Valparaíso in December, 1914. When the value of the Chilean peso dropped below 9d, the Valparaíso tram company was by the terms of its contract allowed to double fares from ten and five cents (first and second class) to twenty and ten respectively.[51] A few months after the outbreak of the depression of 1914, the peso's value fell below the established rate and the company announced a fare increase effective December 1. Public outcry was instantaneous, and a series of working class and political organizations, including the FORCh, tenant leagues, PD, and scores of mutual iad societies, staged a huge protest rally on November 28, during which they called on the intendant not only to prohibit the fare hike but also to lower the price of train tickets, provide public works employment for the jobless, and place a moratorium on rent increases. The daily press and municipal authorities all agreed with the populace that the fare increase at a time of widespread misery was "most inopportune."

Undaunted, the company put its new fares into effect. People boycotted the trams as previously planned, and the municipality harassed the company by fining it for the most trivial transgressions in its service obligations. Great legal leeway was offered bus, carriage, and taxi operators in order to provide an alternate means of transportation.

On the evening of December 1, the labor unions and political leaders called another protest rally which erupted in violence. In what the Anarchists termed an act of "unconscious rebellion," crowds of working class porteños smashed and burned trams in the Centro of Valparaíso, attacked the headquarters of the tram company, hurled rocks through the windows of banks and commercial establishments, and took to looting.[52] Police units made many arrests and wounded several of the rock-throwing rioters. Further clashes between police and the populace occurred on the third and fourth. The Maipú Batallion from Viña took up positions in Valparaíso, but the intendant of the province allowed protest meetings to continue. More trams were attacked until the company decided to suspend service on December 10. When the cars ran again on December 27, people grudgingly accepted the increased fare, and the conflict came to an end. Between the first and tenth of December, however, municipal and provincial authorities harnessed mob fury for their own ends. The tram fare hike adversely affected nearly all porteños, and the humiliation of Chilean authorities at not being able to control a foreign (British) company was more than they could bear. Consequently, tram smashing was condoned as a means of striking back at the company, although the violence on several occasions threatened to get out of hand.

A further attack on the elite occurred on December 14, 1914, when a Spanish worker stabbed and nearly killed General Roberto Silva Renard, commander of army units at the Iquique massacre of 1907. The would-be assassin, Antonio Ramón, hoped to avenge the death of his brother in the massacre by eliminating the man who carried it out. The General lived and his assailant went to prison, but the deed received widespread attention in both the daily and labor press. Pressure for the passage of Subercaseaux's residence law increased, since Ramón was a foreigner and thought to be an Anarchist.[53] Elite fears therefore remained aroused during the 1909–16 period, but labor's perceived threat to the established order appeared far less ominous than it would during the unionization drive and strike wave of 1917–20. Uneasiness had not yet evolved into hysteria.

6

Organizational Successes, 1917-20

THE ROLE OF ORGANIZED LABOR in Chilean society changed greatly during the ten years between 1917 and 1927. As a result of the unionization drive from 1917 to 1920, labor unions in Santiago and Valparaíso achieved sufficient institutional stability to survive the kinds of economic fluctuations and employer counterattacks which on occasion drove pre-1917 unions completely out of existence. Afterwards, only massive repression directed by an authoritarian government such as that of Carlos Ibáñez in 1927 was capable of suppressing the important urban labor federations.

Much of labor's newly acquired power stemmed from the ability of workers in a dozen key industries to re-establish the resistance societies of 1905–7 and 1912–14, strengthen these organizations through structural modifications, and then form unions among previously unorganized workers. Large numbers of unskilled and female workers joined the union fold during labor's 1917–20 period of expansion, often under the guidance of organizers from the skilled trades. The number of organized workers in Santiago and Valparaíso consequently skyrocketed after 1917.

The political influence of urban workers increased dramatically as their unions became more effective. Politicians began to recognize the power of labor in a number of ways, ranging from the drafting of social legislation to increased repression. The wave of strikes initiated in 1917 prompted the government to establish procedures for settling labor disputes. Communist Party members claiming to represent sectors of the labor movement were elected to Congress on several occasions during the 1920s. Other parties vigorously courted the working class vote, and the military juntas of 1924 and 1925 proved equally anxious to enlist working class support for their movements.

Political recognition resulted from success on the economic front. For the first time in the history of Chile, employers were forced to surrender many of their cherished managerial prerogatives to aggressive labor unions. Collective bargaining grew more sophisticated than in pre-1917 times, industry-wide contracts became more commonplace, and many unions extracted agreements from employers to recognize them as bargaining agents for the workforce. Organizational power within the factory and jobsite formed the basis of labor's resurgence and stimulated the government to curtail the influence of important unions and federations.

The next three chapters reflect fluctuations in the growth of organized labor as described above. This chapter discusses the great spurt of unionization from 1917 to July of 1920. Chapter 7 treats the subsequent decline of most urban labor organizations from that date until 1924. Chapter 8 deals with labor's resurgence between 1924 and 1925, and then analyzes the decline of the labor movement during the following two years. As in the case of preceding chapters, those boundary dates often reflect trends rather than specific events.

The Unionization Drive

The tremendous growth in the number of labor unions in urban Chile between 1917 and 1920 was due mainly to the revival of nitrate production after the depression of 1914. As the production and exportation of salitre increased, tens of thousands of workers became re-employed, the size of the domestic market expanded, and industrial production rose.[1] The ranks of the urban unemployed dwindled when factories reopened their doors, construction projects were initiated, and the spending power of the state was broadened. Reasonably full employment provided one of the most important preconditions for the reorganization of many labor unions.

Further stimulus to unionization came from the wage cuts of 1914–15 and a rise in the cost of living between 1916 and 1917. Workers since 1914 had suffered from a painful drop in real wages and were willing to take to the offensive to restore and better their predepression pay scales. By early 1917, employers could no longer count on a large pool of the unemployed in thwarting union activity, and workers took advantage of their improved bargaining position by unleashing a wave of strikes between 1917 and 1920 that far outdistanced the strikes of 1905–7 in both scope and effectiveness.

The rise of a few powerful labor federations in 1917 further stimulated the union movement by providing unorganized workers with funds, experienced leaders, and the example of successful activity. Unions which achieved early prominence in 1917 were generally those which had flourished during 1905–7 and 1912–14. Their re-establishment marked the opening phase of a process which culminated in the unionization of previously unorganized workers.

Of the newly reorganized labor unions of 1917, none played a more important role than the Shoeworkers' Federation (FZA). The leather industry had traditionally been a stronghold of trade unionism in both Santiago and Valparaíso, but the establishment of mechanized shoe factories after 1910 and the effects of the depression in 1914 hamstrung the union movement. Until the formation of the FZA, only a handful of shoemakers in Santiago's small booteries were organized.[2] Workers in several shoe factories in Valparaíso formed a short-lived federation during labor's recovery in 1912–14, but the depression killed it.

Santiago shoe factories, which produced a large percentage of Chilean shoes, became the principal focus of labor's reorganization in 1917. The industry had regained its predepression prosperity, and employment and production were high. Workers in the shoe factories were in some cases displaced shoemakers and assemblers from the small booteries, while many others had no training in leather work. Several participants in the 1905–7 Shoeworkers' Federation remained active in 1917, providing the new organization with experienced union men.

The Federación de Zapateros y Aparadoras was formed in February, 1917, during an open-air meeting in Santiago.[3] The original membership, some 500 men and women, worked in five of the more than forty shoe factories in Santiago. The Santiago branch of the Socialist Workers' Party allowed the fledgling Shoeworkers' Federation to use its headquarters as a union hall until enough money was raised to rent a separate building. Within a month after its foundation, the FZA staged a series of strikes which obtained higher pay for those involved. By June, 1917, eight factories in Santiago, including two of the largest in Chile (Sureda, Antonio Ferrer), recognized the FZA as the bargaining agent for its workers, raised wages, and instituted the closed shop.[4] Successful strikes caused other shoeworkers to join the federation and finally prompted employers to strike back in December, 1917, when the owners of forty-five shoe factories in Santiago formed an employers' association (the Unión de Fabricantes del Calzado) to combat the spread of unionism in their plants. The Unión de Fabricantes established a tribunal composed of five of its members to arbitrate all future disputes between labor and capital. Employers warned that any further strikes by the FZA would be met with an obligatory, industry-wide lockout.[5]

The lockout agreement among employers was a baited trap which the factory owners hoped would be the undoing of the FZA. Its terms could not possibly have been met by any labor union intent on preserving its independence. The issue was forced shortly before the date on which the lockout condition was to take effect, (December 22, 1917). Several federation members were fired from their jobs in the large Ferrer shoe factory, and the FZA struck when management refused to rehire them. As Ferrer's 300 employees filed out of the plant, the longest and one of the most important strikes in Santiago's history commenced. The employers' lockout did not begin until January 27, 1918, but was immediately effective in forty-one of the forty-five companies which had eventually joined the Unión de Fabricantes.[6] The FZA in turn called a general strike, although it had plant delegates in only thirteen of the forty-one factories shut down by the lockout. During the following two weeks, however, the employers' plan to crush the federation backfired as several thousand locked-out shoe workers joined the FZA en masse, raising total membership from less than 1,000 to over 3,000. The lockout had in fact driven hitherto-unorganized workers into the arms of the union.

Employers reopened their factories on April 6 and offered conciliation to the FZA. No work was performed until April 11, when several of the largest companies signed a contract with the FZA establishing a nine-hour workday, higher wages, a standardized minimum wage, cleaner shops, and the recognition of a union delegate. Other companies signed the union contract and resumed work, but Ferrer refused to capitulate for several more weeks. He at last signed on April 29, ending a 128-day strike which resulted in humiliating defeat for him and the Unión de Fabricantes. A further series of strikes proved necessary to force employers to comply with the terms of the contract, but the general industrial strike/lockout of 1918 was nonetheless a landmark victory for labor in Santiago.

The FZA emerged from its victory as the largest and most prestigious labor organization in central Chile. By October, 1918, the daily newspaper La Opinión claimed that it had enrolled 4,500 of the 6,000 leather workers of Santiago. Further strike activity in 1919 won the federation official recognition in forty-two shoe factories and a checkoff system for collecting dues in eight plants.[7]

The Shoeworkers' Federation owed its success to several factors. The prosperity and high employment of the shoe industry was one. Other factors had to do with the organization of the federation itself. By adopting a federal system which allowed for local autonomy and flexibility in dealing with employers, the FZA harnessed and further stimulated rank and file interest in the affairs of their own plants.[8] Workers in each factory with more than twenty-five employees elected their own directorate, which included a plant delegate who also served as secretary of the directorate, four officers, and shop stewards for the various sectors of the factory.[9] The plant directorate met every week and members received no pay for their work.

The federation itself was governed by a secretary general elected by the direct vote of the membership and a council composed of plant delegates. Mutual aid funds were collected by the plant directorates, and each worker paid small monthly dues to the federation. The secretary general of the FZA received pay for his work only when forced to leave his own job (as a shoeworker) to attend to union business. Each federal council served for one year and could not be re-elected. The major role of the federation was to coordinate strike activity, take part in the collective bargaining process, and handle the interunion relations of the FZA.

In spite of the presence of Anarchist notables Ramón Contreras and Marcial Lisperguer and the Socialist Carlos A. Sepúlveda in the federation, the bylaws of the FZA prohibited the organization from declaring its adherence to an ideology. The Shoeworkers' Federation and its heir, the Federation of Male and Female Shoeworkers (FOOC) termed themselves "syndicalist" in nature in order to prevent ideological infighting from undermining the union's strength.[10] This combative yet undogmatic ideological position prevailed until 1921, when Anarchists within the federation got the upper hand.

The prestige and importance of the FZA between the middle of 1917 and 1920 was enormous. No single industry in Santiago and Valparaíso was as successfully organized as that of footwear. For the first time, men and women became equally integrated in an industry-wide union. The presence of the female assemblers in the Shoeworkers' Federation (FZA) proved crucial to the success of the union. Women actively participated in union affairs, served on every plant directorate as shop stewards, and enthusiastically carried out their duties during strikes.[11] Although no woman ever rose to the rank of secretary general, the presence of thousands of female workers in a labor union must certainly have served as an example to their unorganized sisters in the textile and food processing industries.

Soon after its founding, the FZA began organizing workers in other industries and collecting funds to spread the union movement. Unions of painters, tram workers, and garbagemen in Santiago all received help and encouragment from the FZA in launching their own organizations.[12] In February, 1918, the FZA reorganized the Resistance Union of Shoeworkers in Valparaíso, apparently to prevent the recruitment of strikebreakers during the general strike.[13] Shoeworkers actively supported popular front organizations such as the Workers' Assembly on National Nutrition (AOAN), and generally provided "a wonderful and practical lesson" in successful union activity to workers in both Santiago and Valparaíso.[14]

Organized labor penetrated several other industries in 1917. A Federal Union of Furniture Makers and Carpenters was formed in August, 1917, among workers of several furniture factories in Santiago. Successful strike activity in August and September cemented the organization's stability by winning increased wages and attracting more than five hundred workers to the union.[15] More than twenty different factories employing between ten and 100 or more workers produced furniture in Santiago. Furniture workers benefitted from the highly competitive nature of the industry and their own position as skilled craftsmen, both of which greatly enhanced their organizational prospects. The Union of Furniture Makers later moved to include carpenters in its ranks by joining with two other small resistance societies in May, 1919, to form the Union of Woodworkers.[16] The merger effectively united furniture workers and their less skilled brethren in the carpentry shops. Woodworkers took a further step towards unification when they organized themselves along industrial lines by joining the IWW in early 1920.

Resistance societies also sprang up among workers in the building trades during 1917. By August, the Union of Plasterers and Bricklayers in both Santiago and Valparaíso had carried out successful job actions.[17] Similar organizations of carpenters were established in both cities, but only a small percentage of carpenters appears to have joined. Probably less than 1,000 carpenters, bricklayers, and plasterers in both Santiago and Valparaíso were unionized as late as 1918. A Resistance Society of Painters established at the end of 1917 in Santiago brought yet another group of building trade workers into the union fold, but widespread and effective organization in the construction industry did not come about until the formation of the IWW in 1919.

Workers in the maritime trades of Valparaíso made a desperate attempt to revitalize their unions by means of a campaign aimed at canceling the government's order to photograph and register all port workers in Chile. As in the case of the railwaymen in 1913, the maritime unions feared greater government control over the hiring and discharging of workers, and resorted to strike action to prevent the use of identification cards. A six-day strike of nearly 4,000 workers occurred in April, 1917, when the government first attempted to implement its order. Surprised by labor's tenacity in resisting his will, the Maritime Governor postponed the photographing of workers until July 31, 1917, and guaranteed that all expenses involved would be assumed by the government.[18]

The moving force behind the anti-identification campaign was Juan O. Chamorro, leader of the newly reorganized FORCh and the Union of Stevedores and Sailors. Workers struck again in July when the government moved to photograph port workers, but this time employers were ready with strikebreakers, and troops from Santiago arrived to break the strike by force.[19] The FORCh immediately disintegrated, as did the Union of Stevedores and Sailors. In 1918, the sailors formed a new semimutualist group, the Federación de Gente de Mar, and the lightermen and stevedores drifted into the Industrial Workers of the World local union established in Valparaíso by Chamorro in 1918.[20] The strength of organized labor on the docks of Valparaíso peaked in 1920–21 when both the Gente de Mar and IWW established a high degree of job control over work in the bay.

Bakers in Santiago formed a resistance society in 1917 and later established a federation, but their organization remained decentralized and weak until 1921.[21] Valparaíso bakers were more combative and efficient in limiting the quota of bread processed and baked by each worker per shift.[22] The union movement among bakers in Valparaíso did not grow substantially, however, until the early 1920s.

Santiago's Tailors' Federation, which had flourished on various past occasions, was reorganized in October, 1917, by both male tailors and female dressmakers. As in the case of printing workers and shoeworkers, the Tailors' Federation first consolidated its strength in the largest establishments in the industry, the Gath y Chávez store and the Casa Francesa.[23] Both catered to upper and middle class tastes, and the tailoring work done for these stores was by necessity of the highest quality. The Tailors' Federation won further converts in other establishments, so that by May, 1919, it numbered 1,700 men and women. As its strength grew, the federation undertook several important job actions.

Still other resistance societies were organized among workers in skilled jobs, including glass makers, coopers, and foundrymen, but none achieved any real strength or importance. Except for workers in the railroad and maritime shops, labor unions failed to effectively penetrate the metal industry until 1924. Tannery workers reformed their federation in 1917 and carried out a series of strikes soon afterward.

Printers failed to reorganize their labor union in Santiago until September, 1918. At that time some 600 tradesmen left the venerable Typographers' Union, Chile's oldest mutual aid society, to re-establish the Federation of Printing Workers (FOI).[24] Falling real wages at a time of prosperity in the industry propelled these printers to realize the dream that many had held since the disappearance of the original FOI in 1908. The Printers' Federation quickly swept the entire industry in Santiago with a series of strikes in November and December, 1918. When employers granted higher wages and shorter hours, the ranks of the FOI swelled to 1,400.[25] As in the case of the shoeworkers, a successful strike against the largest firms resulted in spectacular gains in membership and the launching of the union. By early 1919, membership in the FOI had risen to perhaps 2,000.[26]

Organizational success in Santiago prompted Valparaíso printers to take to the offensive. Immediately after the 1918 strike in Santiago, the mutualist Federation of Graphic Arts presented similar wage demands to employers, several of whom also operated in Santiago and were still smarting from defeat. Most of the large firms, including the Imprenta Universo, gave in before a strike could be called.[27] Easy success probably thwarted the transformation of the Federation of Graphic Arts into a more combative organization, but it nevertheless developed a higher degree of militancy than normal in a mutual aid society. In November, 1921, its members finally voted to establish a chapter of the FOI in Valparaíso.

All printing workers regardless of craft were eligible for membership in the FOI. The federation took care to include apprentices as members in order to bolster its strike potential and groom young men for leadership positions in the union. A plant committee composed of shop stewards from the four traditional crafts (pressmen, typesetters, binders, and linotype operators) and a delegate to the federation were responsible for intra-establishment affairs. The FOI contained an executive committee presided over by a secretary general who served a one-year term. Printers, like the shoeworkers, used the federal system to their advantage by allowing much local autonomy and at the same time benefitting from the effective leadership of the federation during strikes and collective bargaining.

The organization which most successfully united workers of several industries during the 1917–20 organizational drive was the Federación Obrera de Chile (FOCh). In 1917, the FOCh contained only 400 members in Valparaíso and 200 in Santiago, all metal workers in the State Railway shops.[28] The strength of the organization had been drained by the railroad strike of 1916, and morale fell to new depths when the FOCh's honorary president was accused by some union members of embezzling funds. However, the incorporation into the FOCh of Socialists from the northern ports and Santiago produced a marked swing to the left during the federation's 1917 convention in Valparaíso. In essence, the FOCh dropped its mutualist outlook by changing its bylaws to allow for direct action tactics in pursuit of economic gains. It thus became a job-oriented union after eight years as a mutual aid society. Many of the pre-1917 councils (concejos) remained legally recognized bodies, while the new federation did not seek legal status.

The FOCh grew rapidly in 1918 by mustering a strange assortment of highly skilled and totally unskilled workers to its ranks. Tram conductors and drivers, tinsmiths and gas fitters, glass workers, flour millers, and textile workers all formed FOCh councils in Santiago in 1918.[29] In 1919, brewers, teamsters, hatters, tobacco workers, and metal workers joined, bringing the total number of Santiago concejos to twenty-seven in July, 1919, from what had been one in late 1917. Not all of these councils functioned at the same time, however, since the FOCh did not revoke the charters of the many concejos which folded after a few months of life. The FOCh newspaper *La Comuna* of Viña del Mar claimed that only sixteen concejos actually functioned in Santiago in January, 1920, and only eight in Valparaíso.[30]

The most remarkable aspect of the FOCh organizational drive was its success among hitherto-unorganized, unskilled, and female workers in textile, beverage, and food processing plants. Several strikes by unorganized textile workers occurred in Santiago in 1917 and 1918, indicating that factory labor may have been riper for unionization than most labor leaders had previously thought. Workers at the Corradi textile factory and several hundred hatters joined the FOCh in 1918.[31] In early 1919, organization spread to the Vender, Brussadelli, and Tumagalli textile factories and the Girardi hattery, adding approximately 500 new members to the federation. The Federation of Tailors also made gains among dress and shirt makers at this time. Food, candy, and tobacco workers joined the FOCh in large numbers in 1919, most notably those of the McKay cookie factory in Santiago, the Compañía Chilena de Tabacos in both Santiago and Valparaíso, the Compañía de Cervecerías Unidas of Santiago, a host of Santiago pastry shops, the sugar refinery of Viña del Mar, a vegetable oil factory in Valparaíso, and the match monopoly's Santiago plant.[32]

The FOCh claimed 12,000 members in Santiago in January, 1919, an inflated figure for that particular moment, when the major gains in textiles and manufacturing had not yet been realized.[33] Judging by the experience of the 1920s, few of the urban *fochistas* of 1917–19 paid dues or actively participated in union affairs. Nevertheless, the FOCh could mobilize the support of thousands for strike action in Valparaíso, Viña del Mar, and Santiago as it built its strength within the factories.

A final participant in the urban labor movement of 1917–20 was the Industrial Workers of the World (IWW). The establishment of an IWW branch among Valparaíso port workers in 1918 resulted from contact between members of the New York and California–based Marine Transport Workers' Industrial Union of the IWW and Chilean dockers.[34] Chamorro and other leaders of the FORCh became disillusioned with the federal system of organizing port workers, and listened carefully to IWW claims that industrial unionism could greatly strengthen the bargaining position of labor in Chile. After its founding, the Valparaíso local of the Marine Transport Workers was quickly recognized by IWW headquarters in Chicago, although the North Americans neither financed nor staffed the new branch. Other Marine Transport Workers locals sprouted up in Antofagasta and Iquique, and in December, 1919, a national convention was held in Santiago which formally established the Chilean IWW.[35] Between 1919 and 1927, the IWW founded local unions in nineteen different Chilean cities, but few functioned for more than a year or two.

The new organization pledged itself to the destruction of capitalism and its replacement by a society based on industrial unions grouped into six departments: agriculture, mining, marine transport, land transport, manufacturing, and construction and public services. IWW leaders planned first to organize maritime, construction, and manufacturing workers on an industrial basis, and then spread out into other sectors of the economy. Their practice of industrial syndicalism clashed with the brand of federalism employed by several important unions in that it centralized control over decision-making

154

to a greater degree and eliminated plant or shop organizations. It is no wonder that maritime and construction workers turned most enthusiastically to the IWW while printers and shoeworkers retained their federations in order to preserve local autonomy. The basic organizational unit of the FOI and FZA was the plant directorate, and their strike action frequently involved only one or two establishments. Job action in the maritime and construction industries, on the other hand, required the solidarity of many different crafts. When the IWW demonstrated the effectiveness of industrial organization, it quickly gained adherents among such workers. The IWW thus partially or totally replaced the resistance societies of stevedores, lightermen, sailors, dockers, teamsters, bricklayers, carpenters, plasterers, and painters, while reorganizing these workers into maritime and construction industrial departments.

Early successes in the port of Valparaíso earned the IWW a widespread reputation for combativeness and provided labor with a concrete example of the effectiveness of industrial unionism. In spite of the IWW's more centralized structure, other labor groups, including the FOI, FZA, Bakers' Union (USP), and several FOCh councils took an active interest in IWW affairs and regarded the IWW as a natural ally in the struggle against mutualism and capitalism. During the hardening of ideological lines after 1921, however, the IWW drifted away from both the Anarchists and Socialists.

Ideology played a lesser role in the urban labor movement of 1917–20 than it later would. Both the leadership and rank and file of most unions appeared to be in a syndicalist mood, that is, one which placed the stability and success of the union above ideological considerations. Nearly all labor unions and federations willingly admitted workers of various ideological persuasions to their ranks in an effort to bolster organizational effectiveness. The presence of varied elements within several unions, most notably the FOCh and the IWW, produced rounds of vicious infighting after 1920, but during the initial unionization drive, harmony and cooperation generally prevailed.

The federations of shoeworkers and printers in both Santiago and Valparaíso espoused a Syndicalist ideology until formally embracing Anarchist-Communism after 1921. Among the pre-1922 FZA leaders were the Socialist, Carlos A. Sepúlveda, the Anarchists Ramón Contreras, Marcial Lisperguer, Eugenio Retamales, and members of the IWW Manuel A. Silva, Amaro Castro, Alberto Baloffet, and Augusto Pinto. All agreed that the FZA had one basic goal, to extract as many material concessions as possible from employers and subsequently to institutionalize the power of the federation. While leaders may have held particular ideas regarding the establishment of a future society, specifically Anarchist or Marxist doctrine was not forced

155

upon the rank and file. Consequently, the ideological level of most shoe-workers was low, but the great majority of *federados* did take an active part in union affairs.[36]

The Federation of Printing Workers also elected members of diverse ideological backgrounds to positions of leadership. Evaristo Ríos was an active member of the POS (as well as an agent of the Security Police) while serving as secretary general of the FOI in 1919. Luis A. Troncoso, secretary general in 1920, was neither a Socialist nor an Anarchist. Experienced Anarchists in the FOI, especially Julio Valiente and Manuel J. Montenegro, maintained good relations with both Marxists and libertarians. Pedro N. Arratia, secretary general in 1924, was also a member of the IWW. In every case, these men were elected to office because of their commitment to the federation. After 1923, when the FOI declared itself an Anarchist federation, ideological deviation at the upper leadership level became rare.

No labor organization in Chile contained a greater assortment of ideological tendencies than the FOCh. Among its most important leaders during the 1917–21 period were the dedicated mutualist Carlos A. Martínez, Democratic Party Deputy Juan Pradenas Muñoz, the commercial employee and nonideologue Enrique Bunster, the social democrat Enrique Díaz Vera, and the increasingly radical Marxists Recabarren, Hidalgo, and Sepúlveda Leal. The FOCh officially moved to the left between 1917 and 1921, at first by dropping its mutualist trappings, then in 1919 by declaring that "once the capitalist system is abolished, it will be replaced by the Federación Obrera de Chile," and finally in 1921 by joining the Red International of Labor Unions as the labor wing of the Communist Party of Chile.[37] Many of the non-Marxists left the federation before its 1921 convention in Rancagua which resulted in the linkage with the Communist Party, and those not willing to subordinate themselves to the Communists (Bunster, Díaz Vera, Martínez) were later purged.

Before 1921, however, the FOCh maintained no clear-cut ideology. Firebrand Marxists such as Sepúlveda Leal, leader of the FOCh in Viña del Mar, declared the federation to be a "revolutionary" organization in 1919.[38] The evolutionary Socialists and Democrats who controlled the national organization rejected radical changes in the federation's ideology, however. During the great repression of labor by the Sanfuentes government in July, 1920, the FOCh sought desperately to avoid persecution by procuring a document from the Ministry of Justice certifying the legality of the FOCh through its direct descendence from the legally constituted Gran Federación Obrera of 1912.[39] A hastily assembled convention of the FOCh in Santiago contradicted previous declarations of revolutionary intent when it pronounced:[40]

> We are the first to ask for social order, the maintenance of internal peace, but naturally we wish that this social order be guaranteed on the basis of mutual

respect and strict compliance with the law. We wish nothing more than the enforcement of the laws which now exist.

Thus, the FOCh deviated widely in its ideological moods, one moment posing as the revolutionary wave of the future, the other bowing humbly to the will of "His Excellency," the President.

Anarchists and independent Syndicalists occasionally attacked the pre-Communist FOCh for its lack of revolutionary zeal, but it was not until the worldwide Anarchist/Communist split after 1921 that the federation became the sworn enemy of the IWW and the libertarians.[41] Before this ideological rift, the FOCh, the IWW, and the resistance societies merely accused each other of "divisionism," since unions frequently raided each other's membership and established dual unions in several trades.[42] Politics was another point of friction between the electorally prone FOCh and the antivote IWW and Anarchist federations.

Despite such rivalry, an antimutualist consensus permeated the urban labor movement during its period of expansion. Tens of thousands of workers rejected the passivity of the mutual aid societies and joined labor unions. Direct action became the watchword of the day, the means to achieve higher wages and better working conditions. Labor was in a combative mood and readily accepted the Syndicalist strike call, not because urban workers suddenly became converted to an ideology, but because they perceived the value of unionization as a means of bettering their lives. The strike wave of 1917–20, however, combined with several other important factors, such as massive inflation and the Bolshevik Revolution, did gradually foster a sense of class consciousness among many Chilean workers.

Many Marxist and Anarchist zealots held important union positions, but they were unable to transmit their ideological convictions to the rank and file during the basically Syndicalist mood of 1917–20. The mainstay of Marxism in Chile was the POS, an organization which enjoyed far less prestige among Santiago workers than it did in the North and the coal mines. Ramón Sepúlveda successfully carved out a POS fief in Viña del Mar, where he published the Marxist newspaper *La Comuna,* but it was the Syndicalists, Democrats, and ex-mutualists in the FOCh who held sway in Santiago and Valparaíso.[43]

Anarchists enjoyed more prestige among workers in Santiago and Valparaíso than did Marxists or the reformists within the FOCh. Libertarian ideology was propagated through countless rallies and lectures, and by the fortnightly newspapers *Verba Roja, Numen, Acción Directa, Mar y Tierra,* and several others of lesser importance. The many social studies centers founded in both cities during the unionization drive sharpened the ideological awareness of workers who participated in them and furthered the spread of

Anarchism within the labor unions. As in the case of Chilean Marxists, the heated ideological discussions of the *Verba Roja* Anarchists and the social studies centers filtered down to the rank and file of labor unions in a simpler and less dogmatic form.

Labor's only ally outside the working class was the Federation of Chilean Students (FECh). Since its founding by socially conscious medical students in 1906, the FECh had fallen under the influence of libertarian intellectuals and became closely aligned with Anarchists in the labor movement. Early worker-student contact took place at the high school extension set up by the FECh in 1911 to teach academic subjects to workers in Santiago, and at the Lastarria Popular University established the following year.[44] The FECh began to actively support the labor movement in Santiago during the 1917–20 period by financially backing and helping to issue publications of the working class press, setting up clinics where workers and their families received low-cost medical attention, and defending arrested labor leaders free of charge. Many of the FECh's presidents were declared Anarchists, including Alfredo Demaría, Oscar Schnake, and Eugenio Gonzáles. Libertarian propagandists José D. Gómez Rojas and Carlos Caro enjoyed great popularity among university students. The young physician Juan Gandulfo became one of the outstanding popular figures of his day as a writer for *Verba Roja*, leader of the IWW, humanitarian doctor, and revolutionary agitator.[45] Many a union man would have languished in prison had it not been for the dedicated legal efforts of Daniel Schweitzer and Carlos Vicuña Fuentes, both FECh notables. The overt sympathy shown the labor movement by the Student Federation proved the most genuine expressed by any non–working class sector of Chilean society during the early twentieth century. Accordingly, the FECh also became a target of government repression.

JOINT ACTION

Organized labor demonstrated a united front to the rest of urban society between 1917 and 1920. Because no single federation or union was by itself strong enough to influence government or public opinion, unions in Santiago and Valparaíso banded together on many occasions to form short-lived organizations aimed at pressuring the government into improving the lot of the working class through legislation or special decrees. Such popular front tactics demonstrated the basic solidarity of urban labor and its unity of purpose, although after 1920 rivalry and ideological conflict greatly hampered attempts to coordinate the activities of urban workers.

The willingness of different labor unions to cooperate with each other became apparent during the May 1 celebrations in Valparaíso and Santiago in 1917 and 1918, when giant rallies staged by Anarchists and the FOCh attracted large crowds for the first time since 1913.[46] The May 1 demonstrations in 1919 and 1920 reached gigantic proportions and curtailed virtually all economic activity in both cities.[47] In every case, the events of May 1 were planned months ahead of time by a committee formed by representatives of all important labor organizations and the FECh. Workers poured into the main squares and boulevards of Valparaíso and Santiago by the thousands on May 1 to be harangued by orators speaking from the several platforms erected beforehand. The scheduled speakers at each soapbox normally espoused different ideological points of view, although the Anarcho-Syndicalists were usually better represented than the Socialists. Because of its highly emotional, ideological, and rebellious nature, May 1 more than any other single event instilled a sense of class identity in urban workers.

Coordinated action by labor unions gave birth to several organizations, most of which were geared to the attainment of a single reform. Anarcho-Syndicalists and Socialists alike staffed pressure groups such as the Central Committee in Favor of Obligatory Primary Education, the "pro-prisoners" organizations which sprang up during times of government repression, and the tenant leagues of Santiago and Valparaíso. Without doubt, however, the most important pressure group created by the Chilean working class before 1925 was the Workers' Assembly on National Nutrition. The effects of the AOAN, both positive and negative from the workers' point of view, influenced events taking place long after the Assembly was itself dissolved. Politicians, economic elites, and workers stood in awe as they witnessed or participated in the AOAN rallies, which by their massiveness seemed to foreshadow a future revolution. Not since the great riots and massacres of 1903–7 had labor captured so much national attention.

The AOAN had its roots in past efforts by labor unions and the PD to limit the export of foodstuffs from Chile and lower the price of meat and cereals to the proletarian consumer. A new wave of protests against the high cost of food began in early 1917 when the FOCh, Democrats, mutualists, and a few Catholic labor societies demanded that the government halt the growing export of food products.[48] The cost of living in Santiago had fallen during 1916 after having risen dramatically during the depression years 1914 and 1915. During 1917, however, prices for basic foodstuffs in Santiago rose by 33 percent and the cost of living index climbed from 115 to 130, a gain of 13 percent.[49] Food prices rose at least in part because of increased exports of cereals, especially wheat. In 1917 the combined tonnage of wheat, beans, lentils, and potatoes exported from Chile rose 83 percent over 1916 levels and in 1918 climbed another 68 percent.[50] The cost of living index dropped to 129 in 1918 and then rose quickly to 152 in 1919. Given the fact that many workers in 1917–18 were striking to restore 1913 wage levels (at which time the price index was 100), further inflation could not be tolerated.

By the end of 1918, the labor movement in both Santiago and Valparaíso had acquired enough institutional stability to make coordinated action against high prices feasible. The FOCh in October, 1918, organized a Committee for the Lowering of Food Costs in Santiago which representatives of Catholic, mutualist, and Anarcho-Syndicalist organizations quickly joined.[51] Within a month, the new organization named itself the AOAN and decided to hold a massive rally in Santiago on November 22, 1918, at which time a petition drafted by the AOAN committee would be presented to President Sanfuentes. In it, the AOAN demanded a halt to cereal exports, the abolition of the reinstated tax on Argentine beef, the creation of a National Subsistance Council presided over by workers to enforce the new regulations, the establishment of "free markets" in the cities to allow farmers to sell their products directly to consumers, and a number of other reforms.

From the outset, the government apparently comprehended the scope and importance of the AOAN movement. Several days before the scheduled rally Sanfuentes declared the "free market" to be in effect in Santiago and named a special committee to formulate a law aimed at lowering food costs.[52] Before this committee could meet, Deputy Pablo Ramírez of Valdivia introduced sweeping legislation in the Chamber which, if passed, would have met all AOAN demands.[53]

Despite these eleventh-hour concessions, the rally proceeded as scheduled. "A considerable crowd," measured at between sixty and 100 thousand people, converged on the Centro of Santiago at 5 P.M. on November 22.[54] The Organization Committee of the AOAN was led by fochista Carlos Alberto Martínez. Its vice-president was the Anarchist woodworker Moisés Montoya, and other officials represented Catholic, mutualist, and Valparaíso workers. Speakers at the rally also reflected the popular front nature of the AOAN. After making public its petition and peacefully marching down the Alameda, the workers disbanded and the AOAN committee awaited the results of their very convincing show of strength.

The government responded to the AOAN petition in two ways. Between November 23 and 27, two more bills were introduced into the Chamber of Deputies and one into the Senate which regulated food prices. They ranged from a token gesture of appeasement to strict rules fixing the cost of foodstuffs.[55] On the twenty-eighth, the AOAN declared these steps "deficient" and voted to set a fifteen-day deadline for the creation of a National Subsistence Council with wide regulatory powers. It further demanded the introduction of property and income taxes, free meals for school children, minimum wage legislation, and a nationally funded campaign against alcoholism, as well as other reforms in the exportation of food. On December 12, only hours before the AOAN's deadline was to expire, Sanfuentes formally promised that a National Subsistence Administration would be created.[56] Working class pressure had been applied directly to Sanfuentes from the outset of the AOAN campaign, just as the 1905 rally in Santiago had dealt personally with President Riesco. Petitioning the President was a time-honored tactic of working class lobbyists, reflecting the tremendous power of the Chilean Presidents before 1890 and the futility of trying to apply pressure to a hopelessly splintered Congress after that date. The weight of decision therefore rested on Sanfuentes, who sought to appease labor with the barest minimum of reform.

When the AOAN expressed dissatisfaction with his conciliatory measures, Sanfuentes and his allies in Congress set the repressive state machinery into motion. Each contrary move by the AOAN produced a further stiffening of government resistance. Ominous "patriotic" rallies began to take place in Santiago the week following the AOAN parade of November 22, allegedly to show popular support for the government at a time when it was widely believed that Peru planned hostile action against Chile. By strange coincidence, Peruvian plots to recapture Tacna and Arica from Chile often surfaced during times of great labor unrest in Santiago. On November 26, only four days after the AOAN rally and in the midst of the nationalistic outburst, the residence law first introduced in Congress by Deputy Armando Jaramillo during the general port strike in Valparaíso in July, 1917, was taken up. Similar pieces of legislation had been under discussion for six years, but both chambers of Congress passed the "Jaramillo Law" in one day, so great was their fear of "subversives."[57] After the AOAN voiced its displeasure with pending reform legislation, Sanfuentes ordered that soldiers conscripted in 1917 have their service extended for several more months. The government thus girded itself for battle, be the enemy Peruvian or Chilean.

The year 1919 opened in disconcerting fashion for elites. A tram strike in Santiago in January was followed by general strikes and bloodshed in faraway Puerto Natales and Punta Arenas and a massive coal strike in the Concepción region. Added to this, the AOAN decided to press its demands more vigorously than ever. The Assembly vehemently condemned the "parliamentary indifference" shown when night after night, special sessions of Congress devoted to the National Subsistence Administration bills were canceled due to lack of a quorum. On January 14, the AOAN decided to stage another rally, this time to be held in Valparaíso on the twenty-seventh. Sanfuentes responded with the following declaration:[58]

> The workers are well-inspired and very worthy of the attention of Public Authorities. They are educated, respectful of the law, and lovers of their country. Therefore, there is no reason why their needs cannot be attended to. . . .
>
> It is also certain that subversive elements are attempting to penetrate their ranks, and workers know that such [elements] should not be tolerated, because if they are, the Government will have no choice but to proceed with great force.

Above all, the Government must preserve the public order and assure the country of the tranquility it now more than ever needs.

The Valparaíso rally drew 50,000 people, encouraging the AOAN to expand its activities to other provinces and prepare another massive demonstration for February 7 in Santiago.[59] Congress responded by passing a law granting Sanfuentes extraordinary powers to dispense with constitutional guarantees and declare a two-month state of siege in Santiago, Valparaíso, and Aconcagua Provinces effective February 3.[60] Only Malaquías Concha voted against the bill in the Senate, and three other Democrats in the Chamber abstained from voting. For the first time since 1894, the Capital and principal port of Chile would be under state of siege. The daily press heartily praised Congress for its patriotism, noting that "subversives" in the labor movement undoubtedly planned to use the February 7 rally as a springboard to violence.[61]

With arrests of FOCh and Anarchist leaders already taking place, the AOAN decided that the government would use its state of siege powers to crush the movement, and therefore, on February 4, canceled the rally. A petition was, however, presented Sanfuentes by a group of workers on the seventh as scheduled. Catholic mutualists withdrew from the AOAN on the eighth, claiming that the Assembly had become too ideological for their taste.[62] In fact, the AOAN did move to the left after being thwarted by the state of siege. A conference held in March declared that "the AOAN will become the permanent representative of all the working class societies in the country" and insinuated that Assembly was henceforth to be a revolutionary organization.[63]

During the following months, the Assembly regrouped its forces for another rally, to be held simultaneously in Santiago and other cities on August 29, 1919. The event occurred as scheduled, with General Luis Altamirano placed by Sanfuentes in charge of Santiago's defense for the day. Perhaps a hundred thousand workers took part, including members of all the major labor unions in the Capital. *El Mercurio* claimed that the demonstration was the largest ever witnessed, and marked "the start of a new era in Chile, in which the people [pueblo] begin participating more directly in the affairs of the national Government, indicating by themselves what their own aspirations and ideals are."[64] Hour after hour, the seemingly endless column of workers filed past the presidential balcony of La Moneda while the AOAN petition calling for sweeping reforms in nearly all aspects of social and economic activity was presented to Sanfuentes.

Despite the impressive performance of the labor unions in recruiting a massive crowd, the 1919 rally did not produce any beneficial results for workers. Less than a week after the demonstration, the FOCh declared a general strike in Santiago to support its three councils of brewery workers (in Limache, Santiago, and Valparaíso), which were at the point of collapse due to a lockout by the Compañía de Cervecerías Unidas. Adverse public opinion, a hostile press, intransigence on the company's part, and finally government pressure forced the FOCh to call off its strike after four days. The general strike diverted national attention away from the AOAN and hardened the antilabor attitude of many governing elites. Furthermore, many Anarchists became disillusioned with the "Prussian regimentation" of the AOAN at its August 29 rally and rightly assumed that further petitioning of the President would bring no results.[65] After the FOCh backed down from its general strike, allowed the brewery unions to be smashed, and did not raise a protest when employer-worker conciliation guaranteed by Sanfuentes himself failed to come about, the government may have reached the conclusion that FOCh and the AOAN posed no immediate threat to national security and thus did not have to be placated with reforms.

By December, 1919, only a handful of people attended the biweekly meetings of the Santiago AOAN, and the daily press refused to print any more of its declarations.[66] Ironically, the Assembly's council voted to discontinue all attempts to petition the President or Congress for reforms. The AOAN was finally dissolved in early February 1920.

La Opinión, the prolabor daily newspaper in Santiago which sympathetically covered the rise and fall of the AOAN, considered the entire movement to have been a failure because the basic legislation it espoused became hopelessly "entombed" in Congress.[67] Given the radical (for that time) demands put forward by the AOAN, its lack of support in Congress, and the realization by the state that the AOAN would not resort to violence to achieve its goals, it is little wonder that no meaningful legislation resulted from AOAN efforts to apply pressure. The Conservative Party, however, introduced a series of labor laws in Congress on June 2, 1919, perhaps as a result of the demonstration effect of the previous AOAN rallies and the threat of future activity. While such legislation was intended to defuse an independent labor movement through regulation of the industrial relations system, the Ley de Residencia and the state of siege law more clearly reflected elite fear of social upheaval.

It is unlikely that the AOAN had any positive economic effect on workers. Food exports (wheat, beans, lentils, and potatoes) dropped 24 percent in 1919 and another 40 percent in 1920, but there is no indication that AOAN activities had anything to do with it.[68] The cost of living index shot up by 30 percent between 1919 and 1920 despite reductions in food exports. Perhaps the "free markets" of 1918–19 and the removal of the beef tax temporarily benefitted consumers, but the overall inflationary trend was not reversed.

163

The main effect of the AOAN was the sudden appearance of labor in the national spotlight, exposing its real and potential strengths and its weaknesses for all to see. Politicians, especially the future presidential candidate Arturo Alessandri, must have been impressed by the eagerness of workers to participate in the AOAN rallies. These demonstrators, once recruited for political action, could mean the difference between victory or defeat in the upcoming election. Government authorities were forced by the AOAN to reconsider the "social question" and how to deal with it. Organized labor suddenly found itself commanding vast armies of disciplined, although temporarily recruited, troops. No reliable figures exist for the size of the organized labor movement in Chile at this time, but the number of active, dues-paying members of labor unions in Santiago could not have been greater than about 10,000, with perhaps another 15,000 nominally enrolled but financially inactive.[69] Yet, a hundred thousand or more people answered the call of the AOAN to march in its demonstrations. Many workers received their first exposure to labor unions and organized activity of any kind through participation in the AOAN. The failure of the AOAN to achieve its basic goals may have enhanced the appeal of revolutionary labor unionism by demonstrating to these workers the futility of petitioning for reform legislation.

STRIKES

The expansion of the organized labor movement in Santiago and Valparaíso between 1917 and 1921 produced a strike wave of great intensity which in turn stimulated the further development of labor unions. The number of strikes taking place during the strike wave far surpassed that of 1905–7, and 1919 proved to be the most strike-prone year in Chilean history until the 1950s. Using many different periodical sources, it is possible to identify and analyze large numbers of strikes in both cities which have escaped the attention of government officials and historians. A comparison of the number of strikes identified as having taken place in Santiago and Valparaíso between 1917 and 1921 (table 6.1), with figures given by the Labor Office and the Jorge Barría–Manuel Barrera studies for the entire country, demonstrates that the strike wave began earlier than previously thought and was more intense.[70] The strike wave developed slowly throughout 1917 and most of 1918, suddenly accelerated in the spring (October–December) of 1918, peaked during the first half of 1919, declined to 1917–18 levels by early 1920, and then fell to almost no strike activity at all during the remainder of 1920 as a result of the tremendous repression applied to organized labor by the Sanfuentes regime in July of that year. Strike activity quickened during the first half of 1921 and then declined again when the effects of the depression of 1921 were

Table 6.1
Incidence of Strikes in Santiago, Valparaíso and Chile, 1916–22
According to Various Sources

Year	Santiago-Valparaíso[a]	All Chile (Barrera-Barría)[b]	All Chile (Labor Office)[c]
1916	—	21	16
1917	39	18	26
1918	48	18	30
1919	92	71	66
1920	22	58	105
1921	28	59	24
1922	—	29	19
TOTAL	229	224	251

[a]Source: See note 70.

[b]Source: Manuel Barrera, "Perspectiva histórica de la huelga obrera en Chile," in *Cuadernos de la realidad nacional*, no. 9, September, 1971, p. 133. Information derived from: Jorge Barría, *Los movimientos sociales de Chile desde 1910 hasta 1926*.

[c]Source: *Bot* 22, 1924, pp. 222–23.

felt in central Chile and employers initiated their anti-union campaign. (Graph 6.1 more clearly demonstrates the ebb and flow of strike activity during this period.)

Increased strikes reflected the growing strength of organized labor. As workers in a given industry of craft became organized, they often undertook immediate job action. On several occasions, workers formed their labor union during the process of carrying out a strike. Leather workers called a majority of all strikes in 1917 and 1918, during which time the unions of shoe and tannery workers were consolidated. Printers did not engage in job action until November of 1918, when the FOI was re-established. Similarly, strikes among textile workers increased dramatically in 1919 when the FOCh set up concejos in several establishments. (See table 6.2.)

The organizational success and combativeness of the FZA skewed figures for the occurrence of strikes in 1917–19 heavily in favor of Santiago (see table 6.3). Strikes in Valparaíso generally affected more workers and took place in larger establishments than those in Santiago. A single maritime strike usually involved as many people as a series of printing, construction, leather, or textile walkouts.

Shoeworkers in Santiago initiated the strike wave by undertaking job actions aimed at increasing pay and gaining the recognition of the union as a bargaining agent. Employers frequently reneged on their contract agreements, forcing the FZA to strike the same establishment more than once. Almost invariably, the federation struck only one employer at a time in order

Table 6.2

Incidence of Strikes by Industry, Santiago and Valparaíso, 1917–21

| Industry | Number of Strikes Per Year | | | | | | Percentage of Strikes in All Industries |
	1917	1918	1919	1920	1921	total	
leather	24	25	24	6	5	84	36.7
printing	1	4	12	1	1	19	8.4
textile and garment	1	1	9	4	3	18	7.9
construction	5	1	6	2	3	17	7.4
wood and furniture	2	3	5	1	1	12	5.2
marine transport	2	0	2	2	4	10	4.4
food processing	0	1	6	1	1	9	3.9
metal	1	4	2	0	1	8	3.6
tramways	0	2	2	1	2	7	3.1
baking	0	1	0	0	4	5	1.8
other	3	6	24	4	3	40	17.6
TOTAL	39	48	92	22	28	229	100.0

Source: See note 70.

Table 6.3

Incidence of Strikes in Santiago and Valparaíso, 1917–21

Year	Santiago	(Percentage)	Valparaíso	(Percentage)	Total
1917	34	(88)	5	(12)	39
1918	42	(88)	6	(12)	48
1919	75	(82)	16	(17)	92[a]
1920	11	(50)	11	(50)	22
1921	17	(61)	11	(39)	28
TOTAL	179	(78)	49	(22)	229

Source: See note 70.

[a]Includes one strike affecting both Santiago and Valparaíso.

to insure the flow of union funds to sustain the strikers and their families. Not until the lockout instigated by the employers' association in February, 1918, did more than a handful of establishments strike together. Once employers were forced to concede, the FZA resumed its tactic of isolating one or two employers for job action.

The only major strike of 1917 was the general maritime strike which closed Valparaíso and several other ports in July and August. As mentioned earlier, the strike involved several thousand lightermen, sailors, and steve-dores who refused to accept a system of mandatory identification cards to obtain work. The Sanfuentes government responded to the strike by sending carabineros and regular army units to Valparaíso, facilitating the recruitment of scabs, and finally declaring martial law in order to break the strike by force.[71] Organized labor in Valparaíso appears to have suffered greatly from this failed strike, and undertook few further job actions until the latter months of 1919.

The pace of the strike wave quickened notably during the second half of 1918 and early 1919 (graph 6.1). The major strikes of 1918 were those called by the newly reorganized Federation of Printing Workers in November. In two lightning movements, the FOI forced thirty-four of Santiago's largest printing houses to sign a union contract which provided for the recognition of union delegates by employers.[72] In August, 1919, the FOI struck again on an industry-wide basis to win further wage increases and a one-year work contract.[73] Further strikes proved necessary to bring delinquent employers into line or impose the union contract in other establishments, but major gains for printing workers after 1919 often came about as the result of industry-wide negotiations between the FOI and the Instituto de Impresores, the employers' association formed by the printing houses.[74]

The rapid increase of strikes in 1917 caused the government to take its first steps toward more actively regulating industrial relations. With the prospect of an industry-wide strike threatening Santiago shoe factories in December, 1917, an executive decree called the Yáñez Decree after its sponsor, Eliodoro Yáñez, took effect which established procedures for mediating strikes.[75] As an appointed representative of the Minister of the Interior, the intendant of each province enjoyed the executive privileges of a governor and was considered the ideal person for settling labor disputes. Under the terms of the Yáñez Decree, the intendant of each province was given the responsibility for joining three labor and three employer represen-tatives in a "conciliation committee" (junta de conciliación) within twenty-four hours after the beginning of a strike. If the parties involved accepted conciliation, the intendant was to serve as mediator and cosigner of all resulting agreements. Should no settlement be reached, the Decree empow-ered the intendant to name an "arbitrational committee" composed of a worker, employer, and neutral member to decide the issue. If one or both sides in the dispute refused either the mediation or arbitration of the inden-dant, the case was to be turned over to the Ministry of the Interior. Although the decree did not establish any means of forcing either party to come to the bargaining table, it contained a clause implying that the "right to work" of employees would be protected: "The administrative or local authority in each case will provide the services of public forces [i.e., police] to guard

Table 6.4

Means of Settlement of Strikes in Santiago and Valparaíso, 1917–21

Means of Settlement	1917	1918	1919	1920	1921	Total
workers return— strike broken	1	2	1	2	1	7
workers replaced— strike broken	2	1	2	0	1	6
worker-employer conciliation	15	11	25	8	5	64
private mediation	0	1	0	0	0	1
government mediation	1	12	27	1	6	47
private arbitration	0	0	1	0	0	1
government arbitration	0	0	2	1	2	5
other	0	1	1	0	1	3
TOTAL KNOWN	19	28	59	12	16	134
UNKNOWN	20	20	33	10	12	95
TOTAL	39	48	92	22	28	229

Source: See note 70.

workers and employees who wish to continue working or return to their jobs."[76] The government thus bolstered its legal right to provide protection for strikebreakers, although the invocation of the Yáñez Decree did not necessarily mean that extra police would be sent to aid employers.

Government mediation became a more important factor in labor disputes after the announcement of the Yáñez Decree. The number of mediated strikes rose from one in 1917 to twelve in 1918, peaking at twenty-seven in 1919 (table 6.4).[77] The decline in mediated settlements in 1920 and 1921 reflected the lower level of strike activity in Santiago, the only province where the Yáñez Decree took effect. In most of the strike settlements classified as "mediated," the role of intendant was limited to invoking the Yáñez Decree and arranging for a conciliatory meeting between workers and their employers. Agreements signed as a result of government-encouraged conciliation were generally countersigned by the intendant, although his signature did not have any legal effect. These settlements were, of course, not imposed, but have been categorized as "mediated" to distinguish them from strikes settled without government interference. All "arbitrated" decisions were considered binding. Since the great majority of labor unions were extra-legal entities, however, the contracts they signed with employers had no legal significance and thus could be broken by either party at any time.

An executive decree of September 20, 1919, established a Permanent Conciliation and Arbitration Committee in the Province of Santiago with the head of the Labor Office as its secretary.[78] Government authorities appear to have taken this step as a reaction to the general strike staged by the FOCh in

Santiago earlier that month. The new organization had little effect in settling future strikes.

Labor unions in Santiago and Valparaíso maintained two basic policies regarding the mediation and arbitration of strikes. The FOCh generally favored mediation and actively sought government participation in settling the strikes of its councils. Of the forty-seven mediated strikes between 1917 and 1919, twenty-four involved FOCh concejos. No ideological reasons prohibited the FOCh from soliciting the mediation of public officials, and in many cases the unions involved were recently formed and so weak that they could not withstand an unregulated square-off with employers. The willingness of government authorities to mediate FOCh-led strikes stemmed from the fact that many took place in public services (tramlines and communications) and because of a precedent established by Senator Ismael Tocornal in settling the Santiago tram strike of January, 1919. The newly formed FOCh Tram Council Number 2 had struck for higher wages, lower hours, and the recognition of the FOCh as the bargaining agent of the company's workforce. The manager of the tram company refused to bargain with the workers, claiming that the FOCh was not a legally recognized organization and therefore could not enter into a binding agreement. Under pressure from the government, the tram company agreed to the arbitration of Senator Tocornal, who eventually ruled that the FOCh Concejo 2 was a legal entity because the original Gran Federación Obrera de Chile, of which it was a member, had been granted legal recognition in 1912.[79] Thus, by claiming legality through association with the old mutualist Gran FOCh, the more radical FOCh of 1919 gained recognition as the bargaining agent for tram workers.

Within months, the intendant of Santiago mediated settlements through which the FOCh gained recognition in textile factories, the sugar refinery of Viña del Mar, Santiago's McKay cookie factory, the State Telegraph system, and the Compañía Chilena de Tabacos. Other employers refused to accept the FOCh as a bargaining agent, but the total effect of government mediation in cementing the power of the FOCh proved considerable. Perhaps because it had gained so much from government mediation, the FOCh called off its general strike of September, 1919, after five days, and placed the fate of its brewery councils in the hands of arbitrators.

Most Anarchist and Syndicalist labor unions rejected government participation in labor disputes. The FZA refused mediation during its general strike in February, 1918, and the Federation of Male and Female Shoe Workers which succeeded the FZA forbade its members from bargaining with anyone other than employers.[80] The terms of the Yáñez Decree were carried out in only five shoe and four tannery strikes between 1917 and 1921. Several other unions with Anarcho-Syndicalist leaders allowed the government to intercede in a few strikes, but the general trend was to reject mediation altogether.

Printers steadfastly refused to submit to government intervention, as did IWW construction and maritime workers unless gravely threatened by powerful employer associations. Many workers who had a libertarian distaste for the state and government regulation of industrial relations branded the Yáñez Decree as a ploy to aid employers, and rejected its application in their labor disputes.[81]

Only six strikes, five of which involved public service industries (tram, electricity, garbage collection), were solved by arbitration. As in the case of mediation, the FOCh was willing to honor the decisions of arbitrators while the Anarcho-Syndicalists were not. The FOCh could not guarantee a favorable solution from the government, however, and on at least one occasion paid dearly for its trust.

In early August, 1919, FOCh brewery workers struck the giant Compañía de Cervecerías Unidas (CCU) at its three plants in Santiago, Valparaíso, and Limache when the company failed to respond to demands for higher wages and overtime pay. After two weeks, the CCU declared its entire workforce locked out, and began recruiting strikebreakers. Company officials refused to bargain with workers, confident that the three-month supply of beer they had stockpiled before the strike would permit them to outlast the union.[82] By the time of the AOAN rally on August 29, the brewery workers' concejos faced certain destruction.

Hoping to capitalize on the combative mood of most Santiago labor unions, the FOCh Executive Council met on the evening of August 31 and decided to call a general strike in Santiago effective September 3 to demand a favorable settlement of the brewery strike.[83] No strike vote was taken among the individual FOCh councils which were to spearhead the operation, but the Executive Council counted on their complete cooperation. The FOCh advised all solidarity strikers to remain at home to avoid "street incidents" and begged for financial support.

Organized labor in Santiago once again demonstrated its high spirit of solidarity by shutting down the city on September 3. FOCh tram drivers and conductors stayed home, the FZA forced most shoe factories to close, bakers refused to work, and the Anarcho-Syndicalist federations of furniture and construction workers stayed out. Several councils, including those of railroad metal workers and teamsters, remained on the job during the strike's first day, but later adhered to the movement, as did other railroad personnel and the AOAN. The Santiago section of the Democratic Party also voted to support the strike, but was unable to convince national party leaders to withdraw from their ministerial positions or express sympathy with the FOCh. None of the striking unions put forward any other demand than the favorable solution of the CCU strike, and all bargaining was left in the hands of the Executive Council of the FOCh.

Sanfuentes met with FOCh Secretary General Enrique Cornejo on the first day of the strike, received the FOCh petition, and promised to study it. Meanwhile, the government mobilized police, carabineros, and army units to break the strike. General Altamirano, fresh from his duties during the August 29 AOAN rally, was renamed commander-in-chief of all armed forces in Santiago. Troops began moving trains and trams on September 6, after first unleashing a series of repressive measures against organized labor. Altamirano declared all meetings of twenty or more people to be illegal, and proceeded to raid the hall of the Anarcho-Syndicalist Union of Woodworkers, arresting its secretary general and several members.[84] Police forcibly closed the FOCh local in Limache on September 3, and in Santiago raided the offices of the radical newspaper *Numen*. When the Federation of Chilean Students expressed its official solidarity with the strike, police closed the Lastarria Popular University. Several street battles between bakers, teamsters, and police took place as a result of the strike, but in general, labor appears to have followed the wishes of the FOCh by refraining from provocative or retaliatory action.

Except for the predictably prolabor *La Opinión,* the daily press in Santiago vehemently condemned the general strike as the work of subversives or an irresponsible minority who willingly crippled the economic life of a great city to settle a mere wage dispute in one company. *El Mercurio*'s editorials goaded the government for "tolerating" subversive activity in Chile and warned its readers that the FOCh posed a grave threat to national security:[85]

> As we said a few days ago, the federation of all working class trades and even those of certain administrative categories, such as railwaymen, telegraph operators, etc., signifies the beginning of a new state of affairs in which the Government is merely *tolerated* for an indefinite period of time.

El Mercurio repeated the long-standing contention of Chilean elites that strikes involving wage issues were acceptable, while those seeking any other ends were subversive. *La Nación* also claimed that agitators had caused the "deplorable" general strike to further their own subversive designs.[86]

Since the CCU had all but broken up the FOCh brewery councils by the time of the general strike and refused to bargain with workers or agree to mediation under the terms of the Yáñez Decree, the government could do nothing to solve the strike. Workers approached both the Minister of the Interior and the indendant of Santiago with their petitions, but neither one would even consider the demands. Sensing that their petitions for a successful settlement of the brewery strike could not be answered through a formal agreement, members of the Executive Council of the FOCh met with Sanfuentes on September 6 and extracted from him a promise to establish a Permanent Conciliation and Arbitration Committee which would in turn

171

arbitrate the CCU strike.[87] In return for Sanfuentes' word, the FOCh called off the general strike on the afternoon of the sixth. The brewers' strike continued in partial form until September 19, when it finally collapsed. At a stroke, the CCU once again became a nonunion firm, and the FOCh lost three councils as a result of what *La Opinión* termed "a most total defeat."[88] The conciliation committee promised by Sanfuentes began meeting on September 23 and a few weeks later announced that it could make no decision in the CCU case because the strike was no longer in progress.[89]

The general strike of September, 1919, reached larger proportions than any other in Santiago during the 1917–21 strike wave. Despite the widespread solidarity shown by many labor organizations and the resonable effectiveness of the FOCh in controlling its own councils, the strike ended in failure. In the process it exposed a major miscalculation on the part of the FOCh's Executive Council. Had the original strikers been state employees, such as railroad or telegraph workers, the general strike might have been successful because the government had the power to grant higher wages whenever it wished. In the case of a tram or baking strike, state officials might have intervened to force a settlement in order to shield the public from hardship or inconvenience. The government, however, saw no reason to intervene in favor of the brewery workers, and the FOCh proved too weak to combat the CCU without the aid of the state. As later events proved, the needs of most workers could be best defended by the trade unions themselves, rather than through attempts to invoke the friendly interference of government. State intervention at times produced favorable settlements for workers, but only when labor held a trump card. Otherwise, the state was under no obligation, nor did it harbor any inclination, to aid workers in their strikes. Perhaps because of its mutualist infancy, the FOCh looked to the state as its guardian and ultimate hope in settling labor disputes. The Anarcho-Syndicalists, on the other hand, distrusted state interference and welcomed it only as a final, desperate resort.

A statistical analysis of the 229 strikes which I recorded as having taken place in Santiago and Valparaíso between 1917 and 1921 demonstrates several important patterns in industrial relations and organized labor's evolution since the 1905–7 strike wave. Strike activity became increasingly centered in the manufacturing trades, the government's role in settling labor disputes increased, female workers went out more frequently than before, and the establishment and consolidation of labor unions became a major issue in collective bargaining. A clear picture of an expanding, combative labor movement emerges.

The overwhelming number of strikes between 1917 and 1921 occured in the private sector, some 217 (95 percent) of the 229 strikes recorded. Strikes in state-owned enterprises shrank from 8.4 percent of the 1902–8 total to 3 percent in 1917-21. Except for their participation in the general strike of September, 1919, railroad workers did not go on strike in Santiago or Valparaíso during the entire five-year period. State Railway workers were granted a standard eight-hour workday in 1917 and an extension of retirement benefits, explaining at least in part their lack of interest in strikes.

Slightly more strikers were organized at the beginning of their walkouts than during the 1902-8 period (88 percent compared to 86 percent; see table A.7). Anarcho-Syndicalist labor organizations participated in 148 strikes, or 73 percent of all those which occurred in Santiago and Valparaíso between 1917 and 1921 (Table A.10). The bulk of the strikes in the "Anarcho-Syndicalist federation" category were carried out by the FZA and the FOI. Strike activity by the FOCh was limited to 23 percent of the total and concentrated in 1919, when most of the federation's textile, food processing, and communications councils were organized.

As the FZA, the FOCh, and the Tailors' Federation expanded their membership, greater numbers of female workers participated in strikes. Women took part in 24 percent of all recorded strikes between 1902 and 1908, a figure which doubled to 47 percent in 1917-21. Almost all shoe strikes involved female assemblers, and nearly all the workers who participated in the 1919 textile and food processing strikes were women. Men in most cases planned the walkouts and represented the union during collective bargaining, but women played an important role in maintaining the strikes through hard work and sacrifice. Few if any women reached positions of prominence in the pre-1927 urban labor movement, despite their numerical importance in many unions.

Strikes between 1917 and 1921 were concentrated in middle-sized and large-scale establishments. Some 68 percent of all strikes involved 100 workers or more, while in nineteen cases, more than 1,000 workers were out.[90]

The principal cause of strikes from 1917 to 1921 was the rejection of worker grievances by employers, but a new trend of great importance also stimulated strike activity. Unlike their counterparts of 1902-8, urban workers in the latter period often struck to establish or protect their labor unions and to limit the ability of employers to exercise complete control over the work environment. For that reason, a very large number of strikes were caused by the firing of workers, often union organizers or officials. Consequently, while higher pay nearly always appeared on the workers' lists of demands put to employers, demands for the recognition of a labor union and the reinstatement of fired workers were voiced very frequently as well.[91] As in the strikes between 1902 and 1908, fines and hygienic conditions on the job were minor points of contention.

The government normally responded to strikes by taking a neutral position, which included sending police to guard company property as established by law. Employers maintained the same intransigent attitude toward worker demands that they demonstrated between 1902 and 1908, generally refusing to compromise or enter into conciliatory talks during the first days of the strike (table A.12). They did, however, more readily accept government mediation in 1918 and 1919, when their bargaining position was at its ebb.

Most strikes lasted two weeks or less, with a mean duration of 13.7 days. The longest strike recorded during the entire 1902–27 period was that in the Antonio Ferrer shoe factory in Santiago, which began in December, 1917, and went on for 128 days.

Extraordinary numbers of police or armed forces units were present during fifty-two of the 146 strikes for which there is complete information concerning the conduct of the strike. Of these fifty-two strikes, at least thirty-five resulted in clashes between police and workers, thirty in arrests, eighteen in bloodshed, and two in fatalities. The ratio of violent strikes (the number of strikes in which violence occurred divided by the number in which no known violence occurred and for which information was complete) rose and fell from .166 in 1917 to .454 in 1918, .196 in 1919, .444 in 1920, and .727 in 1921. The high figure for 1921 resulted, as we shall see, from attempts by employers to crush several key labor unions.

Strikebreakers were used by employers in fifty-two (36 percent) of the 146 cases for which I was able to find complete enough information regarding the strike to be able to make a judgement. In nine instances, these strikebreakers were provided by the government, either in the form of police or units of the armed forces. Only one case of a union scabbing on another was reported.

A much larger percentage of strikes ended in a compromise solution between 1917 and 1921 (50.0) then between 1902 and 1908 (31.5). (Table A.22.) This appears to have been due to the willingness of both workers and employers to make greater concessions during the bargaining process and the more complex nature of collective bargaining itself. Grievance petitions became longer after 1917 as workers learned the tactic of asking for more than they hoped to receive in order to show a compromising spirit and obtain what they most desired. The large number of mediated settlements in 1918 and 1919 also raised the percentage of strikes ending in a compromise solution.

LABOR AND THE ELECTION OF 1920

The election of Arturo Alessandri to the Presidency on June 25, 1920, is considered by most scholars of modern Chilean history to have been a crucial event, one which precipitated a new era of political and social change.

Alessandri's fervent appeal for working class support, his promises of wide-spread socioeconomic reform, and his role in drafting the constitution of 1925 are the principal facts which have conditioned this standard interpretation of the first Alessandri Presidency (1920–25). When "Lion of Tarapacá" took office in December, 1920, the "oligarchy" experienced its first political setback in thirty years, the "middle classes" assumed an important governmental role, and the working class enjoyed more presidential sympathy than ever before.

This interpretation obscures several important facts regarding the relationship between Arturo Alessandri and organized labor in urban Chile. Election figures indicate that labor did *not* cast any more votes in 1920 than in other years and did not throw its support entirely to Alessandri. Not long after his inauguration, Alessandri began repressing the organized labor movement as zealously as his predecessors had done and saw his working class support evaporate. Rather than providing a reformist alternative for Chilean workers, the Alessandri presidency witnessed and in part stimulated a sharp deviation to the left by many important labor unions. The penetration of revolutionary ideology in the labor movement had begun before December, 1920, to be sure, but the process greatly accelerated when Alessandri failed to live up to the ideal promoted by his demagogic campaign.

Historians as diverse as James O. Morris and Hernán Ramírez have concurred with Julio César Jobet in his perception of the electoral victory of Alessandri as being brought about by working class votes.[92] A brief look at the campaign and election of 1920 indicates, however, that the working class did not vote Alessandri into office. Paul Drake's observation that "fear of the masses, not the masses themselves, elected Alessandri to the presidency" is a more realistic interpretation.[93] Labor in fact played an important role in elevating Alessandri to the Presidency, but not by the ballot.

Alessandri hoped to lure as many elegible workers as possible into voting for him in 1920 while at the same time preventing the widespread sale of working class votes to the candidate of the National Union, Luis Barros Borgoño. As Frederick Pike points out, the platform of the Liberal Alliance (the pro-Alessandri coalition of Liberals, Radicals, and Democrats) appealed to many conservative interests and was by no means radical.[94] It was, rather, Alessandri's campaign oratory, blasting away at the "oligarchy" and promising social reform, which deviated from normal patterns of political behavior. Demagoguery had always been a factor in Chilean politics, but Alessandri stretched this tactic to the limit during the hard-fought and extremely bitter campaign of 1920.

The campaign revolved not around issues, but rather around the ability of each candidate to win votes by emotional appeals to the public, fraud, strong-arm tactics, and vote-buying. Barros Borgoño and the National Union (of

Liberals and Conservatives) claimed to be friends of the worker, and attempted to win over the working class support by paying off important figures within the labor movement and by simply buying the votes of individual workers. The most successful police agent within the labor movement, Evaristo Ríos, worked for the Barros campaign until he was unmasked by a pro-Alessandri bureaucrat who provided several working class organizations with documents linking him to the police.[95] *La Opinión,* the Santiago daily most favorable to organized labor and most highly trusted by labor unions, declared Alessandri to be "a sworn enemy of the working class and an oligarch of the highest category," and formally endorsed the Barros candidacy on June 2.[96] A principal tactic of the National Union was to refute Alessandrist claims of friendship with the working class by reminding the readers of *La Opinión, La Unión, El Diario Ilustrado,* and *El Mercurio* that Alessandri had voted to expel Recabarren from the Chamber of Deputies in 1906 and, as Minister of the Interior in 1918, ordered troops to forcibly eject large numbers of poor settlers from government land in the South, resulting in the so-called "massacre" of Lake Buenos Aires.[97] To reinforce its anti-Alessandri propaganda, the National Union sent scores of electoral agents to buy working class votes on the day of the election.[98]

Alessandri sought both the working class vote and the support of the urban poor in staging demonstrations and forcibly preventing the *cohecho* (vote buying and selling). From the time of his senatorial campaign in 1915, which earned him his famous title, Alessandri cultivated a "popular" image despite his antilabor activities in government and his own personal fortune. In an extraordinary gesture of solidarity with labor, he contributed $10,000 to maintain the strike of coal miners at Curanilahue in April, 1920.[99] On May 1, Alessandri spoke for several hours at FOCh headquarters in Santiago and received an enthusiastic ovation from those present.[100] The "Lion of Tarapacá" harangued workers and the poor as no candidate had ever done, addressing them in their own language and paying them a degree of attention unheard of before. In speech after speech, he pounded away at the anti-oligarchy theme, claiming that "after thirty years of a Democratic dream, the people shall awaken and join the struggle for their economic and social redemption."[101] Alessandri's reputation and popular appeal grew to unprecedented heights, stimulating the interest of the disenfranchised masses throughout the country. Manuel Rivas Vicuña described the Alessandri campaign in the provinces:[102]

> His [Alessandri's] able campaign organizers had staged great demonstrations all along the route. For the people, he was a thaumaturge, almost a Messiah. Workers, women, and children flocked to the railroad station to greet him. They claimed he had the power to heal the sick and work miracles.

The National Union smeared Alessandri as a "maximalist" and revolutionary as a result of his rhetoric, but the urban and rural poor loved every word.

Aside from the support of the PD, which could still deliver votes from mutualist workers, Alessandri could not depend on any other working class organization to formally aid him. FOCh leaders in Santiago toyed with the idea of forming a Workers' Labor Party in February, 1920, but nothing became of their efforts.[103] The FOCh in Santiago refused to officially endorse Alessandri but left its members free to individually participate in his campaign. In the North, the POS attempted to convince fochistas in Iquique and Antofagasta to reject both Barros and Alessandri and vote for its candidate for President, Luis Emilio Recabarren.[104]

Rather than working through the FOCh, the Liberal Alliance set up a Pro-Alessandri Labor Committee and "anti-vote-selling leagues" to work for an Alessandri victory. A major function of these groups was to organize goon squads to disrupt the Barros campaign, beat up pro–National Union workers, and prevent Barros supporters from voting on June 25.[105] Several workers died during clashes between crowds supporting the rival candidates. As a last resort, the Liberal Alliance bought votes on a massive scale.[106]

The results of the election were very close and the winner was not officially proclaimed until a specially constituted "Tribunal of Honor" named Alessandri the victor in September. Official figures from the Departmental councils in charge of tabulating votes gave Alessandri 179 electoral votes to 175 for Barros. Only 166,115 people voted in the election. Alessandri's major support came from the Provinces of Tarapacá, Antofagasta, and Atacama, where he won twenty-nine electoral votes to four for Barros, but the National Union easily defeated Alessandri in the rural areas of the Center-South. Some 21,388 people voted in the Department of Santiago, 4,785 less than in the congressional election of 1912, and only 22.5 percent of eligible voters.[107] The Alliance won 9,448 votes to 7,066 for the National Union in urban Santiago, hardly a landslide or a sweeping endorsement of Alessandri. In Valparaíso, 3.226 porteños voted for the Union's candidates as opposed to 2,728 for the Alliance.[108]

It appears unlikely that workers played an important electoral role in winning the Presidency for Alessandri. Recabarren claimed that 80 percent of the fochistas in Antofagasta voted for Alessandri, but a mere 5,500 people in the entire province voted in the election.[109] Only 527 people voted Socialist in Antofagasta and 154 in Tarapacá, both supposed strongholds of the FOCh and areas where Recabarren was ostensibly popular.[110] In Santiago and Valparaíso, there is little reason to believe that many more workers voted for Alessandri than for Barros. Many certainly sold their votes, although the presence of Alessandrist toughs at the polling places probably held down the number of votes that the National Union could buy and prevented workers who had already sold their votes from casting the ballots given them by the National Union. Furthermore, it must be remembered that Santiago and Valparaíso were power centers of the nonvoting Anarchists, who urged workers to boycott the elections. The importance of the urban crowd lay in its visual support for Alessandri and its vocal, often threatening enthusiasm for the "popular" candidate. Fear of an Alessandrist coup supported by the masses may have prompted the National Union to halt its attempt to deny Alessandri the Presidency after the June 25 election.[111] It is, therefore, fair to say that labor played a significant "unofficial" role in Alessandri's election and inauguration.

The 1920 presidential campaign undoubtedly raised the expectations of many urban workers that the government would do something to ease their plight. Soon after election day, the Sanfuentes regime lashed out at organized labor through mass arrests and police violence, driving many important unions underground and forcing others to curtail their activities. Alessandri slackened government repression when he took office, but he too, within a short time, not only tolerated but directed an anti–labor union reaction.

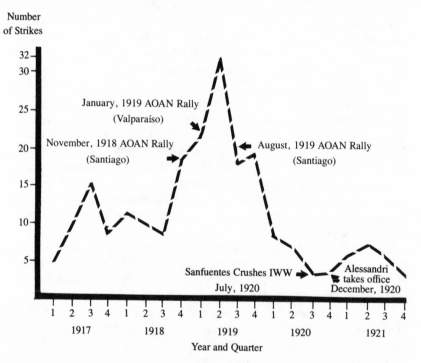

Number
of Strikes

January, 1919 AOAN Rally
(Valparaíso)

November, 1918 AOAN Rally
(Santiago)

August, 1919 AOAN Rally
(Santiago)

Sanfuentes Crushes IWW
July, 1920

Alessandri
takes office
December, 1920

| 1 | 2 | 3 | 4 | 1 | 2 | 3 | 4 | 1 | 2 | 3 | 4 | 1 | 2 | 3 | 4 | 1 | 2 | 3 | 4 |

1917   1918   1919   1920   1921

Year and Quarter

Fig. 6.1. Strikes initiated in Santiago and Valparaíso, by quarter, 1917–21. 1 = January–March; 2 = April–June; 3 = July–September; 4 = October–December.

7

Depression and Decline, 1920-23

THE STRENGTH of the organized labor movement in Santiago and Valparaíso peaked between 1920 and 1921. While labor unions in some industries, notably printing and construction, continued to consolidate their power after 1921, most working class organizations experienced a sharp decline in membership and effectiveness as bargaining agents. Government repression of key labor federations, a concentrated effort by employers to roll back the gains won by unions from 1917 to 1920, and the depression of 1921 all combined to bring this decline about. None of these factors alone could have inflicted such great damage on organized labor.

This chapter begins with the purge of labor by the Sanfuentes regime in July of 1920, goes on to discuss labor's brief revival during its "honeymoon" with President Alessandri in early 1921, and then treats the general weakening of labor unions from 1921 to 1923. During these years, the nature of the urban labor movement was significantly altered by a wide diffusion of revolutionary ideology, a round of infighting which changed the composition of several important labor federations, and a growing lack of consensus among unions. Despite their overall decline between 1921 and 1923, most unions emerged ready to resume a more aggressive stance by 1924.

THE SANFUENTES PURGE

Elite groups in Chile experienced a growing fear of subversion and social upheaval as the strike wave of 1917–20 progressed. Employers proved unable in most cases to withstand the onslaught of militant labor unions, and began surrendering many of their managerial prerogatives to workers. The failure of combined action by employers, the most notable example being the disastrous lockout called by the owners of shoe factories in Santiago in 1918, indicated that the "new" labor movement could not be easily intimidated. As the pace of the strike wave quickened, the AOAN arose to

179

further frighten the upper class. The spectacle of a hundred thousand protesting workers parading through Santiago greatly upset elites, who reasoned that subversive, probably foreign elements were behind it all. Violence, more strikes, demonstrations, chaos in Europe and Anarchist propaganda at home caused upper class Chileans to fear that their socioeconomic hegemony was under attack.

Just as the Bolshevik Revolution encouraged many Chilean workers, so it terrified elites. Important newspapers, such as *La Unión* of Valparaíso and *La Nación* of the Capital, as early as April, 1918, carried a series of front page cartoons depicting the brutality and sadism of the "maximalist" regime in Russia.[1] The passage of the Ley de Residencia after the AOAN's November, 1918 rally reflected the fears of political leaders that Chile was becoming a haven for foreign subversives. Earlier that year, the arrival in Valparaíso of eight Wobblies deported from Australia caused great concern in the daily press.[2] Despite the fact that only a handful of people were deported under the terms of the Ley de Residencia and that nearly all of the leaders of the labor movement were Chileans, mythical "foreign subversives" continued to be blamed for the intensified social unrest of 1919 and 1920.[3]

Fear and repression waxed and waned in urban Chile as the number of strikes fluctuated. Violence in another part of the country or a large-scale demonstration generally triggered a reaction by the government. For example, the Ley de Residencia and the arrest of several important labor leaders (Triviño, Silva, Gandulfo) followed on the heels of the AOAN's November, 1918 rally in Santiago.[4] In January, 1919, a tram strike in Santiago, a general strike in Punta Arenas, a walkout in the coal mines of Concepción, and the death of five carabineros at the hands of strikers in Puerto Natales caused great fear among elites of the Capital.[5] When the AOAN decided to schedule a mass rally for February, the government declared a state of siege. Santiago briefly became an armed camp for the May 1 demonstration, then pressure slackened again until the AOAN rally in August. As before, the threat of mass action by urban workers provoked reaction. Police agents raided and closed down the labor newspapers *Numen* and *Verba Roja*, arrested their publishers, and harassed other labor leaders by searching their homes or arresting them without charge.[6] The night of the September 29 AOAN rally, police *provocateurs* in Santiago placed a time bomb in a magazine kiosk in the Centro which killed the two newsboys who habitually slept there.[7] Blame for the bombing was, of course, placed on the Anarchists.

After a brief relaxation of tension in late 1919, the Sanfuentes Regime became more aggressive in its antilabor campaign as the skyrocketing cost of living produced widespread discontent among urban workers. Several mining strikes, including the traditional January 1 walkout in the Lota and Schwager coal mines, resulted in an increased use of the armed forces as strikebreakers.

180

In March, 1920, *Verba Roja* was again raided by police and its editorial board arrested. *La Opinión* vigorously protested "the new tendencies of authorities to violate individual rights which guarantee citizens freedom of association and freedom to express their ideas."[8] On March 21, the IWW, the FOCh, the Shoeworkers' Federation (now the FOOC), the Federation of Chilean Students, and most of the Anarcho-Syndicalist labor unions staged a twelve-hour work stoppage in Santiago, Valparaíso, and Viña del Mar to protest these arrests.[9] Six hundred extra carabineros and troops under the command of General Altamirano looked on in the Capital as the unions shut the city down and held a mass rally on the Alameda. The government responded with more arrests in the days following the walkout. A court of appeals, however, ruled that the detention of the *Verba Roja* editors constituted an abridgement of freedom of speech, and ordered their release.

On April 20, a group of IWW stevedores wielding knives and grappling hooks disarmed a group of carabineros whom they found beating a small boy. More police entered the docks and arrested sixteen workers. The IWW responded with a twenty-four hour protest work stoppage which halted all port operations.[10] The growing prestige of the IWW among port workers in Valparaíso became a source of concern for employers and police authorities. After leading a highly successful May 1 demonstration, the Wobblies undertook a series of lightning strikes intended to win material benefits for its members and at the same time consolidate its power. In early June, 100 IWW dockers struck for higher pay. When employers refused to bargain, the Wobblies paralyzed the port with a general strike of lightermen, teamsters, and stevedores, and realized all their demands within three days.[11]

In July, the IWW boycotted a major shipping contractor who would not recognize an IWW job delegate, and began their much-publicized refusal to handle any food products destined for export. A wildcat strike of cargo handlers on July 13 was followed the next day by yet another general port strike by the IWW. Many contractors immediately gave in to union demands for higher wages, but the Wobblies decided to enforce their strike until victory was complete. An editorial in *La Unión* expressed the consternation of employers at the new and effective IWW tactic:[12]

> Given the state of permanent agitation regarding propaganda and collective action in which the maritime workers now find themselves because of the activity of IWW leaders, it is now almost certain that once a grievance is voiced and not settled in the same day, a strike or a general work stoppage of all unions will be called immediately.

Until July, 1920, government-directed repression occurred as a reaction to strikes, demonstrations, or protests organized by the labor unions. While many workers were arrested, few remained in prison for long periods of time, and no unions suffered permanent damage as a result of such harassment. It appears likely that the Sanfuentes regime did not wish to further alienate the working class before the presidential election of 1920. As a sympathizer of the National Union, Sanfuentes favored the candidacy of Barros Borgoño and probably assumed that massive repression would drive more workers into the Alessandri camp. After the June 25 election, however, it became clear that a vocal segment of the working class in Santiago and Valparaíso stood solidly behind Alessandri and would take to the streets to impede a move by the National Union to deprive him of victory. With the urban crowd firmly on the side of Alessandri and apparently willing to back a coup by the Liberal Alliance, Sanfuentes risked nothing by unleashing massive repression.

Elite fear peaked during the last months of the presidential campaign and immediately afterward. Strikes, rallies, and political demonstrations took place on a daily basis. The conservative press linked Alessandri with subversives and foreign agents in Chile, branding him a "maximalist" and "the Peruvian candidate."[13] Santiago Assistant Chief of Police Ismael Torrealba warned his fellow officers in May: "It is necessary to detain by all possible means the advance of maximalism, which threatens us with an age of terror, countless murders, extermination, and brutal tyranny, in sum, of all imaginable horrors."[14] U.S. Ambassador Shea voiced the fear of foreign elites in a telegram sent to the Department of State on July 1:[15]

> Atmosphere charged with revolution. Recent demonstrations have convinced Chile people that danger is ahead due social unrest, high cost of living, and proletariat believing that their cause will be favored by Alessandri against old Aristocratic regime. If Alessandri is not seated, much agitation and disorders expected. Though army acted well in recent disorders, future action not certain. In view of all the facts, I think it would be advisable and perhaps favorable for salutory effect if one or two American battleships could be sent unostentatiously to west coast so as to arrive here about August.

A further factor was added to the already turbulent atmosphere of July, 1920. While the forces of the Alliance and the Union quarrelled over the manner in which the presidential election was to be resolved, the Sanfuentes government attempted to tip the balance in favor of Barros by creating an "international crisis." A coup in Bolivia on July 12 overthrew the government of Gutiérrez Guerra and installed a regime more friendly to Peru. Official sources in Chile implied that the Peruvians had assisted the rebels in Bolivia and afterward planned to recoup the territorial losses of both countries incurred during the War of the Pacific. To "defend" Chile from her hated enemy, the Sanfuentes regime ordered a general mobilization of the armed forces on July 15. During the tremendous outburst of patriotism which followed the mobilization call, Sanfuentes hoped to divert public attention from the election, crush elements in the working class which had shown great organizational strength or support for Alessandri, remove pro-Alessandri army units from Santiago, and then have Barros elected President by Congress.[16] War was avoided when Peru and Bolivia did not respond to Chilean aggression by mobilizing their own forces. While nationalistic hysteria briefly gripped the country, however, several of the government's enemies were effectively silenced and Alessandri forced to back down from his aggressive position.

The Sanfuentes regime chose the local union of the IWW in Valparaíso as its first target for repression. Police agents posing as marine workers had long since infiltrated the IWW and plainclothesmen attended all public meeetings held by that and other working class organizations.[17] Both Chief of Police Enrique Caballero and the Maritime Governor regarded the IWW as a dangerous adversary, undoubtedly because the combative Wobblies had established themselves a major force among port workers and a threat to traditional authority. After the IWW called its general port strike on July 14, Caballero and the Maritime Governor began "informing" the provincial intendant of the IWW's subversive intentions. Caballero warned of foreign demolitions experts who were then training Wobblies in the use of dynamite bombs. Convinced that the IWW planned a revolution or at least to disrupt the transfer of troops to the "threatened" northern provinces, the intendant wrote the Minister of the Interior to warn him that the IWW was "openly subversive."[18] Acting under orders from the Ministry, the intendant instructed Caballero to raid the IWW hall. Since his alarming reports of an arms cache in the IWW headquarters had been fabrications, Caballero ordered his chief of investigation to have a package of dynamite planted in the IWW hall shortly before the commencement of a union meeting.[19] At 2 P.M. on July 21, heavily armed police broke into the Wobbly headquarters and arrested the 200 people in attendance. The general port strike collapsed immediately.

The bourgeois press reacted predictably to the announcement that dynamite had been "discovered" in the IWW hall. *La Unión* commented the day after the raid: "These cursed people (IWW) who are members of an institution of foreign origin and led by foreigners, among whom are many Peruvians, hatched the dastardly plan of inhibiting the embarcation of troops."[20] The tactic of linking domestic enemies of the government with foreign subversives worked well. "Patriotic leagues" had been organized among army reservists and well-to-do youths soon after the mobilization was ordered. Xenophobic and reactionary fervor ran high in these circles, transforming them into violent mobs at the service of the Sanfuentes regime. On July 21, the same day as the IWW raid, a patriotic crowd in Santiago assembled at the Mapocho Train Station to send off a detachment of troops to Valparaíso.

It then marched through the centro to be congratulated by President San-fuentes, after which the army officers directing it ordered an attack on the headquarters of the Federation of Chilean Students. The FECh had long since taken a pacifist, antimilitary stance, and was known to have among its leaders many Anarchists and IWW members. Radical Party militants in the FECh had also been vocal supporters of Alessandri. While police stood by, the angry crowd broke into and completely sacked the FECh headquarters. On the twenty-fourth, Sanfuentes officially dissolved the FECh, while the press of both Santiago and Valparaíso branded the students as traitors. *El Diario Ilustrado* summed up the public impression of the FECh by claiming: "The lance of defense has pricked the pedagogic, internationalist, and bol-shevik pus which these students constitute; it has made us turn our heads in horror to avoid its pestilence."[21]

In rapid succession, *Verba Roja, Numen, Acción Directa, Mar y Tierra, El Surco*, and other working class publications were forced to suspend publication after police raids. Leaders of the IWW, POS, FECh, and several labor federations were hunted down and arrested, and on August 2, a dragnet raid hauled in an additional sixty-seven Wobblies in Santiago.[22] When the FOCh attempted to resist Sanfuentes' antilabor campaign, it too became a target for repression. As a gesture of solidarity with the FECh and a protest against the arrest of workers, the FOCh called an indefinite general strike to take effect at noon on July 26.[23] The Anarcho-Syndicalist federations (print-ers, shoeworkers, woodworkers) immediately joined the strike, and Alessan-dri attempted to bring about a settlement. A rally held the following day was broken up by police, and many of its participants were arrested. With the government threatening further repression, the FOCh called off its strike that afternoon. The daily press of Santiago reacted very unfavorably to the gen-eral strike, and government officials began to publicly consider revoking the legal status of the FOCh. Fearful of guilt by association, the FOCh railroad concejos quickly disclaimed any support for the general strike or the leftist reforms made in the FOCh bylaws in 1917 and 1919. C. A. Martínez and Enrique Díaz Vera, leaders of the FOCh and bosses of the Santiago and Valparaíso regional councils, also declared the federation to be nonrevolu-tionary, but at the same time protested government repression.[24]

Sanfuentes continued to harass labor throughout the last months of his regime. The IWW case was turned over to the Ministry of Justice, which ordered the arrest of many more Wobblies before the end of the year. Fochistas were also placed under arrest by order of the intendant of Santiago and the Minister of the Interior. Further protest demonstrations occurred, the most notable being the funeral of IWW leader José Domingo Gómez Rojas on September 30 in Santiago, which attracted a gigantic crowd. Periodic arrests and the constant threat of legal action against the FOCh, however, held union activity to a minimum until Alessandri took office in December. Only five strikes occurred in Santiago and Valparaíso after July 20, while eighteen had taken place during the first six months of the year. The IWW in Santiago was driven underground during the investigation by the Ministry of Justice, and the local union in Valparaíso could mount nothing more than a one-day work stoppage in the port to protest the continued imprisonment of its leaders.[25]

The Sanfuentes repression failed, of course, to prevent Alessandri from being named President. Nor did it permanently damage the labor movement. The raids and arrests of July–December, 1920, did, however, put a brake on the strike wave and deepen feelings of class hatred between elites and workers. The conviction of many upper class Chileans that subversives planned the overthrow of society was undoubtedly reinforced by the raid on IWW headquarters and all that followed. Workers who saw and felt the fury of the "patriotic leagues" and police became more receptive to the preachings of Anarchists and Marxists. Alessandri also backed down from his golpista stance for fear of associating himself with "anti-Chilean" or revolutionary elements (the FECh, the IWW) at a time of great nationalistic fervor.[26] His conduct during the mobilization crisis may, in fact, have convinced many of his former detractors that he posed less of a threat to the established order than previously thought.[27]

THE HONEYMOON

Alessandri promised the earth and the sky to workers during his presidential campaign. It is no wonder, therefore, that labor counted on him to respond favorably to the many demands that urban workers would make of him in early 1921. The cost of living index had risen 30 percent during 1920, the collapse of nitrate production made depression and unemployment in the cities inevitable, and hundreds of workers still languished in jail as a result of the Sanfuentes purge. Jobless nitrate miners by the thousands were resettled in the hostels provided for them in Santiago and Valparaíso. Falling real wages and general misery dictated a new round of strikes. The expectations that Alessandri's rhetoric awoke would have been difficult to meet in times of prosperity. With Chile's worst economic crisis since 1914 unfolding at the moment of his inauguration, however, the *León de Tarapacá* faced an insurmountable task in attempting to please labor. Yet, his campaign promises and the need for working class support in the congressional elections of March, 1921, forced him to do everything possible to be the people's President. For a brief while he was.

Even before receiving the presidential sash from Sanfuentes, Alessandri expressed his concern for labor by touring the factories of Santiago in

185

November, 1920, and talking informally with workers.[28] As President, he intervened in most of the key labor disputes which flared up during the first half of 1921. The Federación de Gente de Mar in Valparaíso struck for higher pay and recognition of job delegates on January 7. A week later, Alessandri dispatched his Minister of Justice to urge workers and employers to submit their differences to binding arbitration, pledging a fair decision which he guaranteed would be enforced.[29] The union leaders refused to call off the strike, fearing that rank and file distrust of employers was too great to risk going back to work. On the seventeenth, the IWW joined the strike, its only request being the immediate release of Juan Chamorrro from prison. A few days later, Alessandri sent Minister of the Interior Pedro Aguirre Cerda to arrange a settlement. The IWW called off its strike, apparently after receiving Aguirre's promise to have Chamorro released. It was not until Alessandri himself came to Valparaíso, however, that the sailors ended their strike. The final settlement mediated by Alessandri granted them the right to name job delegates and established inspection procedures to insure employer compliance with the ruling.[30]

In late January, railroad workers in Santiago began agitating for a general wage increase of 30 percent. State Railway authorities offered only 10 percent, and the workers took their petition directly to Alessandri at La Moneda. Despite protests from Railway executives, who claimed that the government could not afford large wage increases, Alessandri ordered 15 to 40 percent pay hikes to take effect on a gradual basis beginning April 1, 1921.[31]

Other workers benefitted from the intervention of the Alessandri government in their labor disputes. A tram strike in Valparaíso was avoided in February when a representative named by Alessandri arbitrated a settlement granting labor most of its demands.[32] In April, Alessandri helped solve a similar dispute between workers and employers of the Santiago tram company. More than any other president in Chilean history up to then, Alessandri made himself available to workers. Most rallies and protest marches staged by labor unions in Santiago ended with Alessandri addressing the assembled crowd or personally receiving a petition from labor leaders.[33] Police brutality, unemployment, high food prices, and low wages were only a few of the complaints which workers voiced directly to the President. Alessandri's ministers and disciples in the Labor Office dedicated themselves to solving conflicts between labor and capital, especially in the maritime industry of Valparaíso. The government's role in the industrial relations system thus became a far more active one than during previous regimes.

Alessandri's popularity among urban workers remained very high or even grew during the first half of 1921 as a result of his favorable intervention in labor conflicts. Even the death of seventy nitrate workers at the hands of troops at the Oficina San Gregorio (Province of Antofagasta) in February,

1921, did not dampen the enthusiasm of the urban masses for their leader.[34] Less than a week after the San Gregorio killings, the FOCh in Santiago organized and later held a large rally in support of Alessandri. When the Senate refused to approve Alessandri's choice for ambassador to France, the FOCh called another demonstration to demand that the appointment be confirmed.[35]

Labor appears to have supported the Liberal Alliance in the congressional elections of March, 1921, in the same way that it had in 1920. True to its bylaws, the FOCh did not endorse any party, but several FOCh leaders ran for office on the POS ticket. Once again, pro-Alessandri workers organized pickets to prevent the buying and selling of votes on election day.[36] The number of people voting in Chile rose by 18 percent over the 1920 figure, indicating that new elements, perhaps of working class extraction, were added to the electorate. The number of voters in Santiago actually declined, however, from 16,551 in 1920 to 15,558 in 1921, while in Valparaíso it climbed to 11,467 from 6,070 in 1920.[37] The Liberal Alliance increased its majority in the Chamber but failed to achieve its goal of winning control of the Senate.

POS candidates Luis Emilio Recabarren and Luis Víctor Cruz were elected to the Chamber of Deputies from Antofagasta and Tarapacá, despite the fact that a total of only 2,700 people voted for them.[38] Elsewhere, Sepúlveda Leal won a seat on Viña del Mar's municipal council, but FOCh leaders Enrique Bunster and Roberto Salinas failed to win election as aldermen in Santiago.

Relations between Alessandri and labor became increasingly strained as 1921 wore on. In May, Alessandri rebuked the FOCh coal miners in Lota and Coronel for threatening to strike if their demand for a government investigation of police brutality in the coal zone were not met.[39] Disruptive strikes at a time of economic crisis added to the growing alienation between Alessandri and his labor supporters. In June, the IWW and the FOCh shut down both Santiago and Valparaíso with general strikes in support of bakery workers. After arranging a settlement in Santiago, Alessandri paternalistically reproached the workers:[40]

> You know that a father who loves his children has the right to scold them when they make mistakes.
> In the same way, I, because of the affection I have for you, consider myself the father of the people and therefore have the right to chastise you when I feel that your activities are blameworthy. Therefore, don't be surprised when I tell you that you commit an error by going on strike without any real cause.

The hard-fought, often violent strikes of June–August, 1921, stretched Alessandri's patience to the breaking point. Foreign elites considered him a quasi-Socialist whose government sided with workers against employers.[41] Rising labor agitation, the effectiveness of the IWW in Valparaíso, and Alessandri's unwillingness to use force against the working class turned native capitalists even more vehemently against him. Criticism of Alessandri from the left, mainly by the POS and the Anarchists, began soon after he took office and may have shaken his confidence in his own popularity among workers.[42] Worsening unemployment and economic privation in all sectors of the working class further tarnished Alessandri's image as a friend of labor.

Finally, in July, Alessandri aided the Santiago tram company in breaking a strike of drivers and conductors.[43] When the Valparaíso Merchants' Association declared a lockout against the IWW the following month, Alessandri attempted to bring about a settlement, but soon discontinued his efforts when he realized that the shipping companies had no intention of submitting to arbitration. Later in the year, he allowed his relationship with labor to degenerate much further by abolishing the redondilla system of labor recruitment for port workers, thereby dealing the maritime unions a crippling blow. Criticism by the FOCh of his campaign to prevent agricultural workers from forming labor unions and a series of highly publicized scandals in the administration of the hostels for unemployed workers in Santiago further angered and embarrassed Alessandri. By the end of 1921, his government began using the typical tools of repression, including police raids, searches, arrests, and violence, to subjugate a labor movement which refused to respect the will of its "father."

EMPLOYERS COUNTERATTACK

Bosses in Chile took advantage of widespread unemployment and labor's growing dissatisfaction with the Alessandri regime to launch a counteroffensive in July, 1921, aimed at rolling back the gains won by labor during the 1917–20 strike wave. The number of employers' associations grew rapidly between 1921 and 1923, and a series of lockouts cut deeply into union membership and effectively reduced the power of most labor unions until economic recovery in 1923 began to improve the bargaining position of urban workers. The number of strikes in 1922 and 1923 fell substantially.

On June 2, 1921, the Bakers' Union (USP), a recently constituted organization with strong Anarcho-Syndicalist tendencies, struck all bakeries in Valparaíso.[44] Union demands included higher wages, better working conditions, and the closed shop. Employers scrambled desperately to form a united front, but the rapid capitulation of many bakeries made coordinated action impossible. The aggressive bakers drove reluctant employers into signing the union contract by force. One bakery attempting to operate with scabs was destroyed by a bomb, and in another, a nonunion worker was shot and killed by a striker. After eighteen days, the thirty-two largest bakeries in Valparaíso signed the contract, and the strike ended.

Anxious to avoid defeat in a strike which would inevitably follow the one in Valparaíso, Santiago bakery owners declared an industry-wide lockout on June 19, and on the following day invited their employees to return on a nonunion basis. This first attempt at union-breaking failed when the IWW and the FOCh declared a general strike in Santiago, which prompted Alessandri to intervene in the affair.[45] Employers finally rehired all of the blacklisted union workers.

Valparaíso seethed with labor unrest during the winter (June–August) of 1921. A strike for higher pay in June by the unorganized workers of the Hucke Brothers cookie and candy factory was taken over by the IWW and eventually brought to a successful conclusion after a two-week boycott of Hucke's products and raw materials.[46] A FOCh-led strike of some 2,000 tobacco workers at the Compañía Chilena de Tabacos went unsettled for eighteen days and eventually triggered a general sympathy strike by the IWW, the FOCh, and most of the Anarcho-Syndicalist federations.[47] Economic activity in the port and city came to an immediate halt, and extra troops were brought in from Viña del Mar. A clash between strikers and police left a railraod worker dead and prompted other unions, including some reluctant FOCh councils, to join the strike. While its employees struck in sympathy with the tobacco workers, the recently formed employers' association of bakery owners voted to cancel the union contract and lock out all members of the USP.[48]

After five days of general strike, the intendant of Valparaíso finally mediated a settlement between workers and the Compañía Chilena de Tabacos which raised wages but did not recognize the FOCh. The bakery strike continued in spite of the termination of the general strike on July 4, and a group of IWW maritime workers presented their own list of grievances on July 5. Both the bakery lockout and the maritime strike were settled by the intervention of Aguirre Cerda on the seventh.[49] The dockers received higher pay, and the bakery owners agreed to fire their strikebreakers until 50 percent of the workforce in each bakery consisted of USP members.

When tram drivers and conductors in Santiago called a strike on July 18, the company declared all FOCh members locked out. Policemen drove the cars and guarded those workers who stayed on duty. Despite threats of a general work stoppage by the FOCh, the strike quickly collapsed, and some 400 fochistas were left without work.[50]

By far the most damaging blow to the urban working class in 1921 was dealt by the Merchants' Association of Valparaíso to the IWW. Wobbly strength in the maritime industry had been revitalized during the first months of 1921, and by July, the IWW threatened to establish itself as the single, dominant force among port workers.[51] By means of brief walkouts, boycotts, and threats of strike action, the IWW isolated employers one by one, forced them to raise wages, and established a closed shop situation for all work performed. Chamorro further attempted to solidify IWW power by enlisting allies among FOCh transport workers (streetcar drivers and teamsters), and Anarchist bakers and shoe and construction workers. Lightermen, stevedores teamsters, steam crane operators, and railroad cargo handlers formed the bulk of IWW membership, although several hundred female workers at the Hucke factory and some 360 merchant sailors also belonged to the organization.[52]

The Wobblies created many enemies en route to establishing their control over labor in the port of Valparaíso. Mutual aid societies complained of "boring from within" tactics and strong-arm methods used by the IWW to raid their memberships.[53] The Labor Office vacillated between outright condemnation of the IWW and a position of mild support for its continued existence. While Moisés Poblete Troncoso, head of the Labor Office, and Labor Inspector Alfredo Weber feared what they considered the "evil work" of the Wobblies, they did not want the companies to smash the independent labor movement and replace it with employer-controlled mutual aid societies.[54] Neither could the Labor Office tolerate frequent disruptions in maritime service at a time of economic distress. Weber, aided by the intervention of Aguirre Cerda, therefore attempted to forestall what appeared to be a showdown between the IWW and the Merchants' Association. Aguirre finally obtained a no-strike, no-lockout promise from the IWW and the Merchants' Association as part of the general strike settlement on July 7.[55]

The IWW did not require strike action to further consolidate its power, because it could easily boycott goods handled by nonunion workers and cripple the operations of the company involved. Wobblies could and did press for higher wages by the mere threat of a boycott. In the face of this very grave challenge to its hegemony, the Merchants' Association decided to strike an all-out blow against the Wobblies by declaring a general lockout in the marine transport industry on August 18.[56] All of the major shipping lines and their contractors shut down operations while the Association posted notices in the Valparaíso newspapers urging workers to sign its "registry," in reality a yellow dog contract promising not to join the IWW. Work resumed on August 26, the Association claiming that 1,500 workers, or about 30 percent of the total, had signed the registry and returned to work, while the IWW counted only 300 men on the job. On the twenty-eighth, the IWW declared a general strike, which was later seconded by the Wobbly locals of Antofagasta and Talcahuano. It would be war to the death.

The Association had two important factors in its favor. By postponing the lockout until August, when the volume of shipping was low due to prevailing winds which made anchorage in Valparaíso's harbor difficult, they faced lower financial losses. The large number of unemployed workers in Valparaíso also made the recruitment of strikebreakers a far easier task. The Wobblies untypically counted on government help to solve the strike in their favor. They allowed coal for the State Railways to be unloaded in order to curry government favor, and demanded that public authorities defend each man's "right to work" by ordering the Association to close its registry. Aguirre Cerda and the intendant of Valparaíso did in fact attempt to bring the shippers to the bargaining table, but employers steadfastly refused to conciliate.[57] Labor Office inspectors agreed with the IWW that the lockout had been planned well in advance and was intended to rid employers of all previous contract obligations and break the IWW.[58] Despite its initial partiality towards labor, the Alessandri regime did nothing, or perhaps found itself unable to force a settlement on the Merchants' Association.

In rapid succession, other ports joined the strike: Antofagasta, Mejillones, San Antonio, Talcahuano, Coronel, and Punta Arenas. With the coal zone in a state of great unrest, Alessandri found himself in an extremely difficult position. Lockouts by recently formed merchants' associations in Antofagasta and Talcahuano, combined with the general strike, had closed Chile's nitrate and coal-handling ports, and employers were determined to keep them down until the redondilla system of labor recruitment, which established a "turn" system and allowed for greater employment (see chapter 2), was abolished.[59] Workers, on the other hand, wished to submit to arbitration in order to break the lockout. On September 13, Alessandri wired the intendant of Concepción to recruit his cooperation in settling the Talcahuano strike, reminding him of the vital importance of coal to Chile's economy and the desperate financial state in which the government found itself.[60] Four days later, Alessandri's worst fears materialized when the coal miners of Lota and Coronel struck in solidarity with the Talcahuano dockers. Presidential intervention during the next two days settled the matter by guaranteeing the continuation of the redondilla system in that port.[61] Satisfied, the maritime unions and miners returned to work.

Under extreme pressure from the employers' associations of Talcahuano and Antofagasta, Alessandri finally promulgated a decree abolishing the redondilla on October 24, only a few days after his government promised to preserve it.[62] By doing so, he recognized that the lockout by the Valparaíso Merchants' Association had already crippled the IWW and that the maritime unions in the other ports faced similar defeat. The local unions of the IWW and the Syndicalist *Federación Obrera Marítima* had withered in the face of capital's all-out counteroffensive, and could not maintain their bargaining position at a time of high unemployment without the redondilla. Certainly unable and probably unwilling to back labor in a showdown with its stronger enemy, Alessandri capitulated to employer demands. As a result, organized labor was set back in every Chilean port and especially Valparaíso, where the IWW admitted that it had been "pulverized" by the lockout.[63]

The successful lockouts of August–October, 1921, charged the anti-union movement throughout Chile with tremendous force. A national employers' association, the Asociación del Trabajo, was formed in the heat of the maritime conflict (October, 1921) by many of the largest companies and employer organizations in the country, including the Merchants' Association of Valparaíso.[64] Labor immediately accused the Asociación of seeking to destroy the independent labor movement through lockouts and anti-union activities disguised as a "right to work" campaign.

During 1922 and 1923, employers did in fact establish many company unions at the expense of independent labor organizations, while seriously weakening other unions through lockouts. The FOCh was handed a severe setback by the Lota and Schwager coal companies in early 1922. On December 31, 1921, the annual contract between the FOCh councils of coal miners and the companies was allowed to expire as workers prepared for their customary strike on January 1. The companies in turn announced that a two-shift workday resulting in more work for each miner and massive layoffs would go into effect immediately.[65] They further warned that a lockout would be called if the workers struck on January 1. These changes in the work schedule were designed to cut costs as well as to smash the FOCh by laying off hundreds of its members and establishing company unions for those who remained on the job.

Both the strike and the lockout occurred as scheduled on January 1, 1922. Employers had stockpiled a four-month supply of coal in preparation for the strike, and the workers were also resigned to a drawn-out battle. It soon became apparent, however, that the employers held the upper hand and had no intention of allowing government interference to limit their potential victory. The FOCh provincial council in Concepción wished to call a general strike in solidarity with the miners, but its plans were vetoed by the Executive Council. Instead, a nationwide general strike was planned for February 10, 1922.[66] By this time, the FOCh had already dropped all demands for wage increases and concentrated its efforts on preventing layoffs and changes in the work schedule. It was hoped that a massive display of solidarity in Santiago, Valparaíso, and other cities would induce Alessandri to press for a settlement or at least bring employers to the bargaining table.

One day before the general strike, representatives of the coal companies met with Alessandri in Santiago and agreed to limit their layoffs to seventy-five workers per establishment.[67] The FOCh refused this offer and went ahead with its strike, confident that a better settlement could be reached. Despite the exemplary solidarity of the Anarcho-Syndicalist federations in

Santiago and Valparaíso, including the IWW, FOI, and FOOC, the strike proved a dismal failure. The State Railways operated at near-full capacity throughout Chile, thanks to the nonadherence to the strike of the mutual aid society of engineers and firemen and the unofficial decision of FOCh railway workers to remain on the job.[68] Tram service in Santiago improved markedly on the second day of the strike, and the morale of the strikers rapidly weakened. After less than forty-eight hours of what was intended to be an indefinite movement, the FOCh called the strike off, absurdly claiming that it had been a great success.[69]

On March 20, the FOCh finally accepted the terms of the companies, which called for the firing of at least 150 of its most valuable militants in the Lota and Schwager councils.[70] A parallel company union was set up by employers in an effort to do away with the FOCh altogether. The wording of the agreement reflected the basic desire of the coal companies to defend their managerial prerogatives: "Recognizing in the presence of the President of the Republic the *inalienable right* of the companies to fix the number of employees who work in their establishments and to choose them, . . ."[71] Employers had thus seriously weakened the IWW and the FOCh in two of their strongholds by laying off, firing, and blacklisting union members while creating company unions to insure the docility of the workforce.

Further lockouts assaulted labor unions in other industries. The FOOC endured a series of lockouts in 1922 and 1923 which greatly undermined its strength and cost it representation in many shoe factories.[72] IWW tile and furniture workers found themselves locked out in 1922 in Santiago, and in October, 1923, a failed strike in the Hucke candy factory of Valparaíso resulted in the replacement of the IWW by a company union.[73] The IWW received another punishing blow that month when its local union of port workers in Iquique was smashed during an eighty-three-day strike.[74] FOCh tobacco workers were laid off in large numbers when the Compañía Chilena de Tabacos began introducing cigarette-making machines in early 1923.[75] The tram workers' concejo of Santiago saw its power rivaled by a company union during 1923.

The story was the same nearly everywhere. When layoffs occurred, union men and women were the first to go. Wage cuts and company unions often followed. Only in the printing industry and among IWW tile makers did workers succeed in breaking lockouts to win further benefits.

The success of the employers' counteroffensive from 1921 to 1923 was due in part to worsening relations between Alessandri and the major labor federations. After July, 1921, labor could no longer count on the aid or even the neutrality of the Alessandri regime. Police and carabineros were given a freer hand in repressing demonstrations and carrying out their traditional anti-union activities. Labor in return assumed a more militant attitude.

A major source of friction between Alessandri and the FOCh was the presence of up to 20,000 unemployed nitrate workers and their families in the hostels set up by the government in Santiago during most of 1921 and 1922. Some of these men had probably been members of the FOCh while in the North, and in order to retain their loyalty, the federation organized them into a "various trades" council in Santiago.[76] Since they had nothing to do and were fed and housed by the government, a portion of these workers provided the FOCh with a mobile, dependable force which could be put to use in a number of ways. The main function of the "various trades" council was to provide an audience for the many protest meetings called by the FOCh in Santiago. On one such occasion on November 23, 1921, a crowd of several thousand unemployed workers under FOCh direction marched down Santa Rosa Street towards the city limits and the farm of Eliodoro Yáñez to join the agricultural workers on strike there.[77] Seventy mounted carabineros blocked their route near the municipal slaughterhouse and eventually opened fire, killing one worker and wounding several others. FOCh tram workers staged a walkout on the twenty-fifth, in protest, and police retaliated by raiding the FOCh headquarters. Afterwards, violent clashes occurred between residents of the hostels and police, who had orders to search for arms and limit the mobility of the workers.

During the coal strike of January–March, 1922, Alessandri sent troops into the Lota-Coronel area and allowed employers to form armed vigilance committees. His response to the general strike of February 10 was basically the same as that of his predecessors: Santiago became an armed camp. On February 11, a youth was shot dead by police while attempting to halt a tram in Santiago. Another rally of *albergue* residents in May resulted in the death of one worker and the wounding of several others by police. Carabineros were increasingly placed at the service of employers for strikebreaking duty in Santiago during 1923. When Alessandri personally directed the police in breaking up a crowd protesting a raise in tram fares, the workers involved furiously insulted him.[78] Labor soon learned that Alessandri no longer wished to entertain grievance petitions or settle industrial disputes. His working class support consequently dwindled, and whatever plans he and the Labor Office had of forming a reformist, controllable labor movement evaporated.

The Size of the Unions

While the labor movement clearly declined in strength between 1921 and 1923, membership figures which could quantitatively describe that decline have proven very difficult to obtain. I have until now presented very little information regarding the size (membership) of the various labor unions in Santiago and Valparaíso, but have instead concentrated on their activities and relative strength *vis-à-vis* employers and each other. Figures for the number of organized workers in urban Chile do exist, but they are for the most part unreliable and often fantastic. These figures have, unfortunately, often been repeated by modern historians. Government officials of the 1920s also tended to believe the false figures given them by the unions, and thus further perpetuated the myth of labor's numerical strength. In fact, the labor unions of 1917-27, especially the FOCh, had far fewer members than they claimed. This does not mean, however, that the role of organized labor in Chilean society was of less importance. We have already seen that many small groups of men and women combined their efforts to bring about large-scale, significant events. Labor unions held great sway over the unorganized mass. A few union men in a factory could lead hundreds or even thousands of workers out on strike. Massive demonstrations and riots involving tens of thousands were provoked by relatively small groups of organized workers. This visible influence which organized labor exercised led many observers and perhaps even the labor leaders themselves to believe that legions of workers militated in the union fold when, in reality, their membership files contained few names.

The Labor Office and other government bureaus released no official statistics regarding the size of labor unions because they did not attempt to obtain such information. Legal mutual aid societies were surveyed from time to time by the Labor Office to determine the size of their membership, but the government wasted little effort on the labor unions, because they either refused to reply or could not be properly identified in the first place.[79] Attempts to estimate the membership of the labor unions, such as that of Moisés Poblete Troncoso in 1926, were, therefore, pure guesswork.[80]

The best, and, ironically, the worst possible means of comparing the strength of labor unions is by using figures compiled by the unions themselves. All of the important labor federations of Santiago and Valparaíso overstated their numerical strength on one occasion or another. The FOCh was notorious in this respect, dreaming up round figures in the hundreds of thousands which it hoped would impress elites and workers alike. *La Nación*, for example, printed without comment an article stating that the FOCh had 300,000 members in March, 1921, despite the fact that the federation claimed in some industries to have more members than the total number of workers employed.[81] The unwary reader of *La Nación* might have considered the FOCh a very powerful organization indeed, a belief further solidified by the frequency of Santiago's FOCh-led tram strikes.

By using other sources of information provided by the FOCh itself, we see a very different picture. The FOCh claimed between ten and fifteen thousand members in Santiago in September, 1919, at the height of its organizational drive.[82] These figures are probably inflated, but nevertheless are more realis-

Table 7.1

National FOCh Membership as Claimed by Various Sources
and Measured by Dues Payments, 1921–25

Year	Month	Claimed Membership		Dues-Paying Members	
		Source	Membership	Number	Number × 2
1921	unspecified	Ramírez[a]	60,000	—	—
1921	December	Alvarez[b]	80,000	—	—
1922	unspecified	Ramírez[a]	30,000	5,738[c]	11,476
1923	December	FOCh[d]	30,000	4,290[d]	8,580
1924	unspecified	Ramírez[a]	140,000	6,161[e]	12,322
1924	October	FOCh[f]	150,000	8,280[g]	16,560
1925	December	FOCh[h]	120,000	10,601[i]	21,202
1925	unspecified	Jobet[j]	100,000	10,601[i]	21,202
	MEAN		88,750	7,611	

[a]Source: Ramírez, *Origen y formación del partido comunista de Chile*, p. 93.
[b]Source: Oscar Alvarez, *Historia del desarrollo de la industria en Chile*, p. 222.
[c]Source: *La Federación Obrera* (S), December 27, 1923, p. 1 (average per month in 1922).
[d]Source: ibid., January 3, 1924, p. 1 (average per month, 1923).
[e]Source: *Justicia* (S), December 6, 1924, p. 8 (average for first six months of 1924).
[f]Source: ibid., October 29, 1924, p. 1.
[g]Source: ibid., March 19, 1925, p. 5.
[h]Source: ibid., December 20, 1925, p. 5.
[i]Source: ibid., April 19, 1926 (figure for February, 1925, the month of highest dues contributions for the entire year).
[j]Source: Jobet, *Luis Emilio Recabarren*, p. 147.

tic than those for the size of the national organization. Recabarren, Salinas, and other FOCh notables continuously overstated the number of members in the organization, mainly to bolster their contention that the federation spoke for all organized workers in Chile. The number of dues-paying fochistas, however, came to a fraction of the total number claimed by the national organization. FOCh organs *La Federación Obrera* and *Justicia* periodically released figures for the number of workers who paid their twenty-cent-a-month dues to the Executive Committee. At the 1923 Chillán convention, the FOCh contended that the number of members represented by the delegates present should be considered twice that of the number of dues-payers.[83] Table 7.1 therefore compares the membership figures given by FOCh leaders and several historians with the average number of dues-paying members per month and those same figures doubled.

The discrepancies between membership claims and the actual number of dues-paying members clearly demonstrate that membership figures given by FOCh leaders and echoed by later historians are gross exaggerations. We also know, for example, that in 1922 and 1923, the FOCh sold only 9,763 and 7,945 dues books to new members.[84]

The strength of the FOCh in Santiago and Valparaíso was slight compared to that of the Anarcho-Syndicalists. The federation had by July, 1919, organized some twenty-seven concejos in the department of Santiago, but many were unstable and short-lived.[85] At the time of the Rancagua convention in December, 1921, the number of concejos in urban Santiago had fallen to eleven, while only five operated in the entire Province of Valparaíso.[86] In October, 1922, only 3,000 fochistas in the Province of Santiago voted in the union elections to fill four important positions on the provincial executive board.[87] A mere 1,061 in urban Santiago voted in the August, 1923 election which determined half of the Executive Council.[88] Of the 11,098 dues-paying members represented at the 1923 Chillán convention, official FOCh sources listed only 2,220 from Santiago and 540 from Valparaíso Provinces.[89] In January, 1926, only 1,075 fochistas in urban Santiago and 700 in Valparaíso paid dues to the federal Executive Council.[90] Such evidence indicates that the FOCh probably had fewer than 5,000 active members in Santiago and perhaps 1,500 in Valparaíso between 1922 and 1926. Considering the large numbers of concejos which disappeared during the repression and employer counterattack of 1920–23, it is very likely that the FOCh contained more members beforehand, perhaps reaching its peak of strength in late 1919 and early 1920. Most of its support in Santiago came from tram workers, teamsters, glass workers, textile factory laborers, and communications workers. Tram, textile, and food processing workers made up the bulk of membership in Valparaíso and Viña del Mar.

With the information at hand, it is difficult to accurately judge the numerical strength of the FOCh in other areas of the country. Dues payments to the federation show greater FOCh strength in the nitrate and coal mining areas than in the urban center, but by no means reflect the level of influence that previous histories of labor unions in Chile have attributed to the federation. Michael Monteón and Alan Angell, for example, claim that the FOCh contained 40,000 nitrate workers as members in 1919 and 1925, respectively, or 90 and 67 percent of the total workforce in the industry those years.[91] Federation financial records from 1923 to 1926, however, show that membership was concentrated in a few nitrate towns and surrounding oficinas, and indicate an absolute maximum of about 9,500 dues-paying fochistas in the Provinces of Tarapacá and Antofagasta combined at the height of the FOCh's influence in 1924–25.[92] At the January, 1924, national convention, delegates represented 918 fochistas in Tarapacá and 3,160 in Antofagasta, a total of 4,078.[93] Doubled, this figure would also indicate less than 10,000 members of the FOCh in the entire North, both ports and pampa.

While membership in the FOCh was concentrated in the nitrate towns and oficinas, the federation's regional leaders in the North operated out of Iquique, Antofagasta, and Tocopilla, publishing newspapers which were the joint organs of the FOCh and the POS and PC. In Iquique, the IWW controlled maritime labor from 1920 to the end of 1923, when its power was broken by employers and the government during an eighty-two-day port strike.[94] The FOCh enjoyed more prestige in Antofagasta than Iquique, but the port was an IWW stronghold until the nationwide lockout of 1921, although the Wobblies regained some of their former strength in Antofagasta after 1923. Smaller ports, such as Pisagua and Tocopilla, had active but numerically small FOCh concejos during the 1920s.

Strike activity in the North during the 1916–23 period appears to have been less intense than in the cities of Santiago and Vaparaíso. The great majority of northern strikes took place among non-nitrate workers, and the most strike-prone groups seem to have been maritime laborers in the principal ports and transport workers in the cities and small towns.[95] The FOCh never attempted to use whatever influence it may have exercised over nitrate workers to call for solidarity in support of its general strike efforts in the urban center and coal zone. The only nationwide strikes which took place from 1917 to 1925 resulted from efforts by Anarcho-Syndicalist maritime workers.

The FOCh also had regional strength in the coal mining cities of Lota, Coronel, and Lebú (Curanilahue), where it carrried out a series of hard-fought strikes between 1916 and 1922.[96] Records of dues payments to the federal Executive Council of the FOCh show less than 5,000 federados in the coal mining zone and city of Concepción during the 1920s, although the FOCh minority managed to carry out strikes involving many more workers on several occasions. FOCh strength in the city of Concepción was never great, and in the port of Talcahuano, maritime workers formed an FOCh council which promptly affiliated with the IWW as well.[97] The FOCh in the South suffered from intense competition. The IWW established an active local in Concepción, and at one time attempted to form dual unions among coal miners. After 1921, the coal companies fought a partly successful battle to set up company unions in the Lota-Coronel and Schwager mines. Furthermore, Concepción had traditionally been a PD stronghold, and the political aspirations of many fochista and Communist candidates for elected office in that city were blocked by Democratic and Anarchist influence. Given these circumstances, the institutional survival of the FOCh among coal miners indicates dedicated regional leadership and conviction and fortitude on the part of the rank and file.

By comparison, the Anarcho-Syndicalists were far stronger in both Santiago and Valparaíso during the entire 1917–27 period, although almost all of their federations and unions suffered losses in membership between 1921 and 1923. The Shoeworkers' Federation in October, 1918, claimed to have 4,500 members (of a total workforce in the leather industry of some 7,000) at a time when they maintained a union shop contract in almost all shoe factories in Santiago.[98] It is certain that not all of these union members paid dues, but rank and file participation in internal union affairs was high, judging from the fact that FZA general meetings had to be held in theatres or small stadiums to accommodate the large number of people in attendance. It is likely, therefore, that the Shoeworkers' Federation alone contained nearly as many members as the FOCh in Santiago in early 1921.

A series of lockouts and unemployment in the leather industry sent the FOOC into rapid decline, however. In the latter part of 1921, it maintained a union shop in only seventeen shoe factories in Santiago, whereas at the beginning of the year, forty factories were organized.[99] At its low point in early 1923, the FOOC held on in only thirteen establishments, although many were the largest in the industry. By 1925, the number rose to twenty-five shoe factories and three tanneries, but only about 300 union members paid their monthly dues.[100] The various shoeworkers' federations thus contained at least 1,500 workers at all times during the 1920s, judging by the number of factories signing the union contract, although they had a difficult time extracting dues payments.

The Federación de Obreros de Imprenta claimed a high of 2,500 members in February, 1919, an exaggerated figure given the fact that the federation had not organized newspaper workers.[101] A more realistic figure would place membership at about 1,800–2,000. The FOI managed to win wage increases in 1921 despite an anti-union campaign by employers, and weathered the 1921–23 years better than any other union in Santiago. In July, 1924, it maintained union shops in twenty-five printing houses in Santiago, indicating a membership of about 1,800. The FOI in Valparaíso controlled nearly the entire printing workforce of some 700 men by 1925, with a union delegate in each of twenty-six establishments and a monthly average of 413 dues-payers.[102]

At the time of its 1921 contract granting it a 70 percent closed shop on board all Chilean merchant steamers, the Federación de Gente de Mar probably contained several thousand members. The Gente gradually lost its power as a result of depression in the shipping industry, the loss of its 70 percent agreement, corruption within the union, and IWW raids on its membership. It collapsed in 1924.[103]

Several sources have estimated the size of both the national IWW and its local union in Valparaíso. Wobbly leaders Chamorro and Gandulfo claimed that the IWW contained from nine to ten thousand members before the Sanfuentes purge of July, 1920.[104] This figure is not improbable, given the large number of maritime workers in several ports who were enrolled in the union. An investigation by the court of appeals of Valparaíso in November, 1920, claimed that the IWW had 2,000 active members and 10,000 "allies" in other unions, despite widespread arrests and persecution.[105] The Wobblies contended that their membership peaked at ten to fifteen thousand around July of 1921 and afterward fell to only 3,000 in late 1922, a figure neverthe- less superior to the size of the FOCh in Santiago at that time.[106] Membership in Valparaíso may have reached 4,000 or more on various occasions, although thousands of Wobblies were effectively blacklisted after the disastrous mari- time lockout in 1921. During its resurgence in Valparaíso in 1924 and 1925, the IWW contained some 1,140 sailors as members, most of whom had recently joined and paid the IWW's comparatively high initiation fee of $5.20.[107] A Labor Office inspector reported in June, 1925, that the IWW controlled "at least" 70 percent of labor in the harbor, or approximately 3,100 workers.[108] While the Oficina inspector probably overrated the strength of the IWW, ita appears certain that the Wobblies contained at least as many members in Valparaíso as the FOCh in Valparaíso and Viña del Mar com- bined. IWW membership in Santiago may have been as high as 3,000, centered mainly in the construction industry.

Information concerning most other labor unions is even less plentiful and trustworthy than the figures I have just presented. Several conclusions can be drawn from these findings, however. The strength of the FOCh in Santiago and Valparaíso was far weaker than that of the Anarcho-Syndicalists. Judging by financial statements and frequent complaints by union treasurers, the majority of nominal union members did not pay dues on a regular basis. Many union members could barely meet the basic economic needs of their families, and in no reported cases were people expelled from membership for nonpayment of dues. Chilean urban workers did contribute generously to mutual aid and strike funds whenever the need arose, but probably consid- ered union dues to be of secondary importance.[109]

Perhaps another reason why workers showed reluctance to pay regular dues and why the Anarchists spent their money as quickly as possible was the frequent embezzlement and theft of union funds. The vast majority of labor unions in Chile neither sought nor obtained legal status, and therefore the safety of their funds was not regulated by the Civil Code. Santiago and Valparaíso police, who usually were at odds with organized labor, showed little zeal in tracking down union officials who absconded with funds. In one case, the FOCh had to pay private detectives to locate and arrest the secretary general of the tram concejo in Santiago who cleaned out the treasury and fled to a small town outside the Capital.[110] Loss of funds through theft plagued many unions and, in some cases, seriously weakened or destroyed them. [111] Anarchist, Syndicalist, and mutualist organizations as well as the FOCh were affected. Informality in the collection, spending, and accounting of union dues encouraged thefts and probably caused rank and file members to think twice before parting with their hard-earned centavos.

THE ADVANCE OF IDEOLOGY

Great changes took place within the labor movements of Santiago and Valparaíso during the employers' counterattack of 1921–23. As late as September, 1920, the major labor federations and unions in both cities maintained a basically Syndicalist outlook, one which subordinated Anarchist or Marxist ideology to the growth and well-being of the organization. This attitude gradually changed, however, so that by the end of 1923, almost all important labor groups in urban Chile had become defined according to their ideological point of view. We have already seen that these ideologies influenced early labor unions, but no working class organizations before 1921 were as exclusivistic or hard-bound in their acceptance of revolutionary philosophy as they were to become after that date. Ideological penetration affected both internal affairs of individual organizations and their relationships with other working class and elite groups. The ultimate result of this ideological onslaught was a disunited and weakened labor movement.

Anarchist ideology was nothing new to Chilean workers, having been the most influential revolutionary doctrine in shaping the nature and tactics of the urban labor unions since the turn of the century. Marxism enjoyed less prestige among workers and intellectuals alike, but rose in stature in the years following the Bolshevik Revolution. The increasing acceptance of both Anarchist and Marxist dogma by Chilean labor leaders and, to a far lesser extent, the rank and file, came about as the result of several factors. The strike wave of 1917–20 acquainted thousands of workers with labor unions and industrial conflict for the first time. These often desperate battles to restore wages which had been drastically lowered by cuts and inflation since 1914 were carried out in an atmosphere charged with the rhetoric of the class struggle. The unwillingness of bosses to concede higher wages, their frequent counterattacks, and the presence of troops and police at the service of capital during many strikes undoubtedly fostered a sense of class identification among workers. Chilean society was based on a rigid distinction between the "popular" and the "better" classes. The activities of the AOAN, massive in their display of working class might and yet powerless to bring about reform, certainly awakened in many workers a feeling of class pride and a determination to take more drastic action.

The lockouts of 1921–23, coupled with the failure of the Alessandri regime to comply with its campaign promises of 1920, undoubtedly quickened the pace of radicalization. Rampant inflation and unemployment low-

201

ered the real wages of most workers in 1920 and 1921. Police raids, arrests, violence, and blacklisting followed attempts by workers to publicly express their dissatisfaction with the socioeconomic order.

Finally, international events furthered the spread of revolutionary ideology in Chile. IWW concepts of industrial Syndicalism arrived from the United States at a time of great working class agitation in Chile. The success of the Bolsheviks in Russia and later revolutionary events in Germany and Hungary inspired Chilean Anarchists and Socialists alike. The formation in Europe of the Red International of Labor Unions (RILU) and the International Working Mens' Association (IWMA), the Communist and Anarcho-Syndicalist internationals, greatly influenced interunion affairs in faraway Chile.

Many important industrial and trade federations moved noticeably leftward in 1921. The Printers' Federation, at its second convention held in September of that year, called for the destruction of capitalism and declared itself to be based on "Communist" (i.e., collectivist) principles, although it still considered its tactics to be "Syndicalist."[112] The name of the FOI was changed to Federación de Obreros de Imprenta de Chile to reflect the formation of a provincial federation in Valparaíso and a desire to extend the union to other cities. In 1923, the FOI(Ch) moved totally within the ideological camp of the Anarchists by declaring the basic goal of the federation to be the realization of a society based upon "libertarian Communism." Santiago and Valparaíso printers formed the vanguard of the Autonomous Organizations and the Federación Obrera Regional Chilena (FORCh), both Anarcho-Syndicalist federations created between 1924 and 1926.

Shoe workers also assumed a clearly defined ideological position in 1921. The FZA was renamed the Federación de Obreros y Obreras en Calzado (FOOC) in January, 1921, but the old FZA bylaws, including its self-identification as a "Syndicalist" organization, remained in effect. At its November, 1921, convention, however, the FOOC committed itself to "libertarian Communism," reaffirming its belief in the federal system of organization and the tactics of direct action.[113] Despite its apparent marriage to Anarchism, the FOOC continued for several years to allow noted Socialists, such as Carlos A. Sepúlveda, to remain in positions of leadership, and openly favored the "common front" between the IWW and the FOCh.

Bakers in both Santiago and Valparaíso remained divided and weak until the formation of the USP in 1921. A revolutionary minority committed to extreme direct action tactics (including bombings) called itself the Communist Center of Bakers and formed a Red Guard, or flying squad, for use in strikes. The bakers received generous support from the IWW and the FOCh in Valparaíso and soon consolidated their position, both institutionally and ideologically. The USP considered itself a "revolutionary" and "libertarian" organization until its destruction by Ibáñez in 1927.[114]

A host of resistance societies, mainly Anarchist in inspiration, gravitated in the orbit of the Anarcho-Syndicalist federations (FOI, FOOC, USP) or the IWW. These included resistance craft unions of foundrymen, locksmiths, plasterers, tile makers, carpenters, furniture makers, painters, bricklayers, and teamsters. Resistance societies often contained less than one hundred members, especially if two or three other labor organizations actively recruited workers of the same trade.

From the time of its establishment on the national level in late 1919, the IWW attempted to unify important sectors of the Chilean working class under the industrialist banner. Its strength lay in the struggle, the ability to stimulate coordinated and effective strike action between workers of several different crafts and industries. While the industrial federations such as the USP, FOI, and FOOC willingly cooperated with the IWW, they refused to surrender their automony and join the Wobblies as members of a local union or industrial department. When the lockouts of 1921-23 rolled back IWW gains in the maritime industry, a debate arose among Wobblies as to whether autonomous unions should be admitted into the IWW and the rules regarding industrial organization relaxed to accommodate them. Anarchists within the IWW also pressed for changes in the organization's goals regarding the industrial Syndicalist future of society, which they and other libertarians outside the IWW found "authoritarian" and "centralized."[115] After a heated debate at its third convention in March, 1924, the IWW voted to declare itself in favor of "Anarchist-Communism" and to decentralize the organization in hope of attracting new support from the Anarchists.[116] Unable to maintain itself as a separate force between the Anarchists and the FOCh, the IWW fell into disrepair after 1924, its only remaining strength centered among maritime workers in Valparaíso and San Antonio and construction workers in Santiago. Many of its former adherents, such as woodworkers, factory laborers, and even craftsmen and laborers in the building trades, drifted off to join the various Anarchist federations formed after 1924.

The FOCh followed the Anarchists to the left in a series of moves destined to link it to the Chilean Communist Party and the worldwide Communist movement. We have already noted the FOCh's lack of ideological definition and its vacillation in public statements made before 1920. The bylaws of the federation had, nevertheless, been changed to reflect an openly Syndicalist position from what had previously been mutualist. Several of the concejos formed among railroad workers found the 1917 and 1919 statutes incompatible with their conservative outlook, and dropped out or were purged from the FOCh even before its link with Communism in 1921.[117] In September, 1921, the Painters' Council quit the FOCh to form an independent union, apparently over a dispute with the provincial board.

Socialists within the FOCh, especially Recabarren, Cruz, Hidalgo, Sepúlveda Leal, and Carlos A. Sepúlveda, steered the federation into affiliation with the RILU during the FOCh convention held in Rancagua in December, 1921. After initially refusing an alliance with the Democratic Party and voting down (by 71–42) a measure introduced by ex–Secretary General Enrique Díaz Vera to postpone the debate on affiliation, the FOCh voted by 106–12 to join the RILU.[118] Immediately after the adjournment of the FOCh convention, the POS voted to become the Communist Party of Chile (PC) and seek admission to the Third International.

Despite its affiliation with the RILU, and the presence of many Communists in important leadership positions, the FOCh of January, 1922, was by no means under Communist control. The decidedly non-Communist Carlos Alberto Martínez became secretary general of the Federal Executive Board, and many of the councils, especially those in Santiago and Valparaíso, remained under the influence of FOCh conservatives such as Enrique Bunster and Díaz Vera. Some 35 percent of FOCh delegates at the Rancagua convention expressed a desire to postpone the decision to affiliate with the RILU, and many probably accepted adherence because of the RILU's supposed independence from political parties.[119] The Socialists who published the FOCh organ *La Federación Obrera* fraternally claimed that the federation in early 1922 contained "Catholics, Protestants, Radicals, Socialists, Anarchists, and Communists," as well it may have.[120]

The days of the non-Communist leaders were numbered, however. Using *La Federación Obrera* as its principal weapon, the Communist Party began to consolidate its position within the FOCh. Articles describing the ideology of the PC and urging workers to join drew criticism from the Syndicalist wing of the FOCh, which argued that politics had no place in the columns of the federations's newspaper.[121] In August, 1922, a convention of FOCh railroad concejos voted by twelve to eleven to leave the FOCh and join with the Federación Santiago Watt (engineers and firemen) and several mutual aid societies in forming an independent railwaymen's federation called the Federación Ferroviaria.[122] Railway workers in Santiago and Valparaíso had been particularly unhappy with the post-1917 FOCh. Its bylaws no longer reflected their own ideology, and they resented being called upon to strike in solidarity with workers with whom they felt no common bond. Employees of the State Railway system in general comprised something of a privileged group in Chile during the 1920s. Legislation in 1911 and 1918 provided them with accident insurance, social security benefits, and a livable pension long before most workers enjoyed these benefits.[123] In 1917, all railway employees were granted the eight-hour workday by government decree, and in similar fashion gained large wage increases in March of 1921.[124] Contract employees enjoyed great job security through a seniority system. It is little wonder, therefore, that the railway concejos of the FOCh and the independent mutualist associations refused to join the general strike in support of coal miners in February, 1922. The Federación Ferroviaria voted to continue its adherence to the RILU, but it was an empty gesture, since the majority of organizations within the federation refused to alter their bylaws to reflect RILU principles.

During 1923, most of the anti-Communists within the FOCh were purged or left the organization. Enrique Bunster, leader of the Santiago Council Number 14 (commercial employees) was branded a "fascist" by *La Federación Obrera* and purged in August, 1923, to be followed by the Democratic politician Juan Pradenas Muñoz.[125] Syndicalist leader Enrique Díaz Vera was expelled by a vote of the delegates at the Chillán convention held in December, 1923. The original expulsion vote had been thirty-three for and twenty-four against, indicating considerable support for Díaz Vera within the FOCh. These figures were withheld from publication in *La Federación Obrera*, however, until a "new" vote showing "unanimous" support for his ouster could be produced.[126] In fact, the "unanimous" vote was never taken, since Díaz Vera's public criticisms of the PC were judged sufficiently incriminating "to decide upon his expulsion without the necessity of resorting to further bourgeois procedures."[127] Ex-Secretary General Carlos A. Martínez was expelled from the FOCh soon after Díaz Vera, eliminating the last of the "reformists."

The Chillán convention also voted to *incorporate* the FOCh rather than merely adhering to the RILU, and declared *La Federación Obrera* to be the organ of the PC as well as the FOCh. Despite resistance to these measures, all votes were reported to be unanimously in favor of further linkage with Communism.[128] The complete domination of the FOCh by the PC was reflected by the election of eight Communists to the nine-member Federal Executive Board of the FOCh.[129] Recabarren's "boring from within" tactics paid off. The FOCh, or what was left of it, had at last become the property of the Marxists.

Catholic-inspired mutual aid societies and trade unions won the support of perhaps several thousand urban workers during the 1920s, but had little effect on the overall nature of industrial relations in Chile. A Christian *Casa del Pueblo,* or Workers' Club, was founded in Santiago in 1917 to promote Catholic trade unionism and acquaint workers with what by 1918 was being called "Christian Democracy."[130] Catholic workers did participate in the November, 1918 demonstration held by the AOAN, but later withdrew their support and began to criticize the Anarchists and the FOCh for their aggressive tactics and anti-Christian ideologies.

A Chilean Federation of Labor was formed by Catholic trade unionists in early 1922, claiming as its object "social peace with the greatest possible well-being for all classes of society, especially the working class."[131] The appearance of Catholic federations at a time when urban labor unions suffered great setbacks at the hands of capital caused Anarchists and fochistas to brand them as "yellow," or employer-controlled. Catholic workers defended themselves by disclaiming any connection with employers or non-workers and by affixing the adjective "white" to the titles of many of their unions. By 1925, the Catholic societies of Santiago and perhaps other cities had formed two central organizations, the Confederación Sindical del Trabajo and the Confederación de Sindicatos Blancos.[132] Neither was a job-oriented organization, but rather a conglomeration of mutual aid societies intent on promoting Christian ideas. As an ideology, Christianity won far fewer converts in urban Chile than did Anarchism, Marxism, or the "laborist reformism" of the PD-Alessandri variety.

It is necessary to study the interunion relationships of urban labor organizations during the 1920s on two levels: the ideological and the practical. At times, conflict over ideology produced sufficient hostility between two labor groups to affect everyday union affairs or rank and file behavior, while on other occasions, it did not. Ideological strife with practical repercussions often reflected the economic situation of the workers involved, as in the case of the well-off railwaymen, who saw no reason to strike in sympathy with their union brothers during the coal strike of 1922. It is useful, therefore, to analyze the apparent cleavages in the labor movement from 1921 to 1924 from these two points of view.

As ideological lines became more strictly drawn between 1921 and 1924, union rivalries deepened considerably. Anarchists before 1921 frequently criticized the FOCh for what they considered its reformist mentality, lack of combativeness, and poor organization.[133] The appearance of the IWW in late 1919 introduced a new participant in the struggle for influence within the urban working class which had been going on between the FOCh and the Anarcho-Syndicalists. IWW raids on FOCh membership in Valparaíso, Talcahuano, and Antofagasta produced ill will, as did attempts by Wobbly organizers to set up a dual union among coal miners.[134] Influenced by the IWW example, the FOCh at its Rancagua convention in 1921 voted to eventually replace its federal (regional) councils with industrial councils grouped into six categories. The FOCh and the Wobblies remained rivals in several industries and individual plants during the 1920s, especially construction, urban transport, and the Hucke factory of Valparaíso.

By 1921, after the FOOC, FOI, and FOCh became more entrenched in their ideologies, the bulk of organized urban workers could be grouped into one of four camps: the Marxist FOCh; the industrial Syndicalist IWW; the independent Anarcho-Syndicalist FOOC, FOI, USP, and resistance societies; and the reformist-Democratic FOCh and mutual aid societies. Ideologically, the IWW was closer to the Anarcho-Syndicalists to begin with, and as the 1920s progressed, the Wobbly bylaws reflected a growing Anarchist influence. It is important to bear in mind, however, that Marxists such as C. A. Sepúlveda held leadership positions in Anarcho-Syndicalist organizations in the early 1920s and, likewise, noted Anarchists (M. J. Montenegro, Francisco Pezoa) remained in the FOCh. Attempts at dual-unionism and rivalries notwithstanding, the four groups showed considerable solidarity before 1924.

The antilabor campaign of employers initiated in July, 1921, prompted the IWW and the FOCh to sign a pact of "common defense" in September. [135] Under its terms, the only labor organizations in Chile which could claim unions in more than two cities agreed to undertake a massive propaganda campaign to recruit new workers to the union fold and to convince "free" (independent) labor organizations to affiliate with them. The Shoeworkers', Printers', and Students' Federations also signed the agreement, although none had any intention of being swallowed up by the FOCh or the IWW. [136] True to the terms of their agreement, FOCh coal miners briefly supported the IWW during the 1921 lockout/strike by walking off the job in solidarity. The Wobblies and the Anarcho-Syndicalists reciprocated during the general strike of February, 1922. May Day rallies in Santiago in 1922 and 1923 continued to be jointly planned and carried out by the IWW, FOCh, and Anarcho-Syndicalists. A series of coordinated rallies and marches to protest the Sacco and Vanzetti trial, the imprisonment of Wobblies in the United States, and police brutality at home also took place in 1922 and 1923. Representatives of the FOCh were allowed to join the Worker Committee for Social Action formed in May, 1922, by the Anarcho-Syndicalists and the IWW in Santiago. The main purpose of the Committee for Social Action was to organize and carry out rent strikes in Santiago. A similar organization, called the Committee against High Rents, functioned in Valparaíso.

Despite this evidence of practical solidarity, the IWW-FOCh pact did not have much effect in halting the employer counteroffensive, nor were any steps taken to unite the two sides. In accordance with RILU policy, the FOCh during 1922 and 1923 continuously urged the formation of a "united front" (*frente único*) with the IWW against capitalism. [137] Many Wobblies had second thoughts about the previous solidarity pact, however, and the growing influence of the PC in the FOCh convinced others that the IWW should stand alone. The FOCh in early 1922 hoped that the presence of the American Wobbly leader "Big Bill" Haywood in the Soviet Union would result in RILU membership for the U.S. and Chilean IWWs and, consequently, a certain frente único at home. [138] A letter to the Santiago IWW from Wobbly delegate George Williams at the Third International Conference of 1921 describing Communist plans to take over the IWW fortified the anti-RILU sentiment of most Chilean Wobblies. [139] The incipient Anarcho-Syndicalist international in Europe considered the Chilean IWW for membership as early as July, 1922, and in October, Rudolf Rocker invited Santiago to send a representative to join in the foundation of the IWMA in Berlin.[140] A delegate left Valparaíso for Europe in November but arrived too late to take part in the IWMA convention. The Chilean IWW immediately adhered to the new international nonetheless.[141]

The alignment of the IWW in the Anarcho-Syndicalist camp and its increasingly libertarian outlook doomed the frente único to failure. Instead, the FOCh on one hand, and the IWW, FOOC, FOI, and resistance societies on the other, grew farther apart. Rounds of name-calling and criticism ensued. Anarchists and Wobblies assailed the authoritarian nature of the Soviet regime, the mistreatment of Russian Anarchists by the Bolsheviks, and PC participation in the FOCh.[142] Under RILU influence, the FOCh in turn condemned the Russian Anarchists as "thieves, criminals, and bandits," and by early 1923 began to apply those labels to Chilean libertarians. The FOCh/Anarcho-Syndicalist split ran deeper in Vaparaíso than in Santiago. In March, 1923, a group of Anarchists in Valparaíso were verbally assaulted by Recabarren at a propaganda rally, after which they were set upon and badly beaten by the fochistas and Communists in attendance.[143] In June, *La Federación Obrera* accused the Wobblies of being "enemies of the revolution" and insinuated that they were police agents, a common charge hurled back and forth between both sides.[144] The IWW and the FOCh held separate May 1 rallies in Valparaíso in 1923, while in Santiago the events were still jointly planned. Wobblies in Valparaíso refused to deal with the FOCh provincial council during the April, 1924, port strike, while FOCh construction workers in Santiago joined their IWW counterparts in a massive strike effort.

Thus, by 1924, Communists, Wobblies, Anarcho-Syndicalists, Democrats, and Catholics within the urban labor movement had defined themselves ideologically. Unification of the urban labor movement became impossible after 1921, when Communist influence in the FOCh precluded any organizational links with the Anarcho-Syndicalists. Chilean libertarians could not bring themselves to participate in the electoral game, while the PC as early as June of 1923 began planning its campaign strategy for the 1924 congressional elections. The FOCh stood for everything the Anarcho-Syndicalists traditionally loathed: politics, centralized authority, and bossism. These deep ideological divisions within the working class greatly reduced the potential effectiveness of organized labor. External events after 1923 occasionally united the labor camps for brief periods, but the factions quickly reasserted themselves once again. As we shall see in chapter 8, most of the major social struggles of 1924–27, including the rent strikes, anti–labor legislation campaign, and general strikes, were weakened by Anarchist-Marxist rivalry.

There is much evidence to indicate that only a small percentage of union men, generally those in leadership positions, were convinced ideologues.

Many of the union rivalries, therefore, resulted from conflicts between ideas held by a very small group of people. Articles written in *Verba Roja* and *La Opinión* during the 1917–20 strike wave commented that workers joined unions not because of any ideological predisposition, but because job-oriented labor organizations provided them with concrete economic benefits.[145] Luis Heredia, secretary general of the FOOC in 1925 and the Unión Industrial del Cuero in 1926, claimed that the rank and file of those nominally Anarcho-Syndicalist organizations had little interest in ideology, did not read the working class press, and, aside from their pleasure in singing revolutionary songs, did not demonstrate any ideological commitment whatsoever.[146] They were, however, concerned with the well-being of their plant union and the federation because they perceived the practical value of solidarity and organization. Clotario Blest, a young public servant active in Catholic worker organizations in the 1920s, also admitted that rank and file unionists were attracted by the economic and social aspects of labor organizations.[147] Union leaders won rank and file respect not through ideological zeal, but by dedicated service to the union. PC member Carlos A. Sepúlveda, for example, was an active figure in the Anarcho-Syndicalist FOOC during the 1920s because he remained a shoeworker and continued to meet his union obligations.[148] Recabarren retained the admiration of many Anarchists for his undeniable dedication to the labor movement, and yet was criticized by those same people for his role in the PC.[149]

Ideologically committed workers formed the leadership cadre of the labor movement. PC members were a militant minority within the FOCh throughout the 1920s, moving the federation in whatever political direction they wished. Likewise, Anarchists in the IWW, "independent" unions, and later, the Workers' Federation of the Chilean Region (FORCh), controlled those organizations despite their reduced numbers. These were the men who published the working class press, crisscrossed the country on speaking tours, led the strikes, staffed the social studies centers, and dealt with bourgeois allies and enemies. IWW leader Luis A. Triviño remarked of this leadership stratum: "They are few, but good, solid, and dedicated. They are the yeast which any day now will cause the enormous mass to rise."[150]

Both Communists and Anarcho-Syndicalists bemoaned what they considered the near impossibility of implanting an ideological conviction in the mass of the urban working class.[151] Chilean workers, they claimed, could be easily mobilized by inflammatory words, and willingly responded to the dictates of union leaders, but their enthusiasm evaporated just as suddenly as it appeared. A demonstration, rally, or riot could be brought about with relative ease, but few workers expressed interest in long-term union activities.

Judging by the survival of most labor unions in the face of the employer counteroffensive of 1921-23, this evaluation appears too harsh. The great majority of union men and women may not have understood the teachings of Kropotkin or Marx, but they did perceive the potential benefits of organization. Ideologically sophisticated or not, Chilean workers by the thousands sacrificed and struggled to better their lives during the 1920s. Perhaps the most widespread working class movement since the AOAN rallies of 1918–19 was that of the tenant leagues in 1925. These organizations derived their strength from the spontaneity and combativeness of the urban mass. Elites in the past responded only to stimuli from the masses, often in the form of violence or rioting. The role of rank and file union members and the faceless urban crowd in shaping the industrial relations system of early twentieth-century Chile cannot be overlooked.

8

Labor Laws, Politics, and Repression, 1924-27

THE THREE-YEAR PERIOD between 1924 and February, 1927, was of great importance in the development of organized labor in Chile. During that brief span, urban workers and their unions faced rampant inflation, two military coups, labor legislation regulating virtually all aspects of industrial relations, several key elections, and the continued hostility of employers' associations. These factors deepened the cleavages within the ranks of organized labor which had been developing since 1921 and by 1927 would leave the labor movement splintered and ripe for destruction at the hands of Carlos Ibáñez.

As the economic power of the unions weakened, the political prestige of organized labor grew. Both Marxist and Anarchist-inspired labor federations established links with disgruntled, reform-oriented sectors of the urban middle class, resulting in greater legitimacy for their aspirations. In 1925, five Communists were elected to the Chamber of Deputies, and the party gained its first senator. Anxious to find a working class group which it could admit into the "political game" after the reformist military coup of January, 1925, elites briefly recognized the FOCh and hence the PC as spokesmen for the working class. However superficial its power and fleeting its "success," organized labor became a more legitimate entity within Chilean society.

Behind the facade of prestige thrown up by the Communist Party in 1925 lay a labor movement of weakened organizational resilience. The unions had begun to recover from the depression and employer counterattack of 1921 by late 1923. In 1924 and 1925, urban workers once again initiated a wave of strikes to counter the rise in the cost of living during those years. Employers put up stiff resistance to the union challenge, and with the help of the state, eventually slowed the strike movement. After the coup of January, 1925, urban workers seized the opportunity to press forward with a series of demands aimed at relieving their economic hardship. Anarchist-led tenant leagues in Santiago and Valparaíso extracted concessions from the new

211

military junta by threatening violence. Direct action tactics briefly thrust organized labor into the position of a power contender during the first months of 1925. Many working class leaders felt that the revolutionary moment had at last arrived.

Such was not the case. Instead, the tenant leagues were defused by legalizing them and dividing their influence among several factions. In like manner, the labor legislation passed by Congress in 1924 produced rifts in the urban labor movement. Repression in June of 1925 and economic recession the following year weakened labor's bargaining power *vis-à-vis* employers. Unable to relieve their economic plight through strikes, many workers turned to political action or to movements of a purely defensive nature, such as that which fought Law 4054. The solidarity of past years disappeared, as demonstrated by the failed general strikes of 1926 and 1927. The "popular front" with middle class *empleados* (white collar workers) and professionals quickly collapsed, leaving labor an easy victim for repression in 1927.

LABOR UNIONS AND STRIKES

The strength of the organized labor movement in terms both of membership and effectiveness rebounded during 1924 and early 1925. Increased industrial and mining production and higher employment provided the economic preconditions for labor's resurgence. Skyrocketing food and rent costs during those years further prodded urban workers into joining labor unions. Working class discontent erupted in a wave of strikes and popular protests which peaked during the first half of 1925.

The organizational base for labor's outburst of activity in 1924–25 had been laid during the postwar years. Most of the major labor unions and federations which coordinated the socioeconomic struggles of 1925 had been established between 1917 and 1921. The new wave of strikes and agitation did not, therefore, reflect the formation of a series of new labor organizations, but the strengthening of previously constituted unions. Nor did the alignment of the great majority of labor unions into one of two ideological camps, Anarcho-Syndicalist or Communist, change in any significant fashion between 1924 and 1927.

Of these two groups, the Anarcho-Syndicalists continued to be the stronger in both Santiago and Valparaíso. The Printers' Federation won yearly wage increases for its members in both cities from 1924 to 1926 and established local unions in Antofagasta, Curicó, Chillán, Talca, and Temuco.[1] While consolidating its position as spokesman for the majority of printing workers, the FOICh pressed for increased coordination between the various Anarcho-Syndicalist unions. Its major ally in this effort was the FOOC, which in April, 1925, changed its name to the Industrial Union of Leather Workers to

212

reflect the entry of several hundred tannery workers into the organization. The FOOC had declined steadily in membership from 1921 to 1923, but by May of 1925 contained the entire workforce of some twenty-five shoe factories and three tanneries in Santiago, plus the bulk of shoe workers in Valparaíso.[2] Other previously organized unions of Anarcho-Syndicalist persuasion were the resistance societies of the building trades, the Woodworkers' Federation, the Tailors' Federation, resistance societies of tinsmiths and gas fitters, and the Bakers' Union (USP). The latter group attempted unsuccessfully to link its two local federations in Santiago and Valparaíso with other bakers' unions and mutual aid societies throughout Chile.[3] Added to these veteran Anarcho-Syndicalist unions was a new organization, the Union of Metal Workers, first established by foundrymen in the drydocks of Valparaíso and later extended to metal workers in Santiago.[4]

By 1924, most of the Anarcho-Syndicalist federations had completely severed ties with the IWW and attempted to form their own regulating organization. Libertarian ideas made great headway among unions, causing most to reject what they considered the authoritarian and excessively centralized nature of the IWW. Despite conciliatory gestures by the Wobblies at their fourth convention in March, 1924, the Anarcho-Syndicalist unions of Santiago formed a Federation of Autonomous Resistance Organizations in May.[5] The Printers' and Shoeworkers' Federations played a major role in founding this new organization, which also included most of the independent Anarcho-Syndicalist unions and deserters from the IWW's Construction Department. A similar organization was established in Valparaíso the following year.

It was not until 1926, however, that Chilean Anarcho-Syndicalists established an organization which cut across both industrial and regional lines. Most of the previously mentioned federations and resistance societies of Valparaíso, Santiago, and Viña del Mar banded together in January of that year to form the kind of Anarcho-Syndicalist organization which had been established in countries such as Brazil, Argentina, and Uruguay decades before.[6] The Workers' Federation of the Chilean Region (FORCh), as the new organization was called, was a loosely knit confederation of local (city-wide) federations of resistance societies and industrial federations. The FORCh exercised almost no control over its member groups. The pact of adherence between the FORCh and the regional federation of Valparaíso explained why: "We desire autonomy and self-control for each institution and individual. We recognize that liberty is derived from autonomy and take that as the basis for future happiness."[7] The FORCh was, in essence, a coordinating body meant to serve as the most visible spokesman for the Anarcho-Syndicalist unions in Chile. Its policies reflected rather than shaped the activities of its members. Despite the fact that it fulfilled the long-

213

standing dream of many Chilean Anarchists to organize the myriad libertarian societies into a single federation, the FORCh appears to have provided little more than an increased sense of self-awareness to Chilean Anarcho-Syndicalists.

The Anarcho-Syndicalist movement of 1924–27 benefitted from experienced and dedicated leadership. Two important directors of the Federación de Obreros de Imprenta de Chile, Pedro N. Arratia and Julio Valiente, had been continuously active in union affairs since the 1905–7 strike wave. The majority of Anarchist stalwarts were, however, products of the 1912–14 organizational drive or joined their respective unions during the 1917–21 period. Chamorro, Augusto Pinto, Luis Armando Triviño, Moisés Oyarzún, and Pedro Ortúzar were the principal figures of the former group, while Juan Gandulfo, Luis Heredia, Amaro Castro, and Alberto Baloffet represented the latter. The Printers' and Shoeworkers' Federations continued to provide the Anarcho-Syndicalist movement with its most effective militants. As in the case of earlier leadership cadres, the Anarcho-Syndicalists of the 1920s performed union duties without pay, continued to work at their various trades alongside the rank and file, staffed the many social studies centers of Santiago and Valparaíso, and published a host of Anarchist and labor union newspapers.

The IWW, as noted in chapter 7, lost most of its membership in the nonmaritime trades to the Anarcho-Syndicalists and company unions by 1924. The disappearance of the IWW as an effective force further widened the ideological gap between the Anarcho-Syndicalists and the Communist-dominated FOCh by eliminating a middle ground position.

Although historians have normally treated the FOCh as the principal labor organization in Chile during the 1920s, it more closely resembled the appendage of a political party than a labor union. The federation did increase in membership in 1924 according to figures for dues payments, but it remained extremely weak in Santiago and Valparaíso.[8] In 1925, the FOCh claimed to have seven industrial councils in operation, but most of these were skeletal or imaginary organizations. The bulk of dues payments collected by the Executive Council came from the ever-loyal unions of transport and mining workers in the Provinces of Tarapacá, Antofagasta, Concepción, and Arauco.[9] Membership in Santiago centered around tram conductors and drivers, glass workers, some construction workers, a few teamsters, and scatterings of workers in food processing and manufacturing. Teamsters, textile workers, tram workers, food processors, tobacco workers, and construction workers were the mainstay of the FOCh in Valparaíso and Viña del Mar. In terms of membership, the FOCh was certainly outnumbered by the Anarcho-Syndicalists in Santiago and Valparaíso. Its federated unions rarely went on strike in

1924 or 1925, and appear to have maintained far less bargaining leverage than did their libertarian counterparts.

The reputation of the FOCh as Chile's most important labor organization during the 1920s rested on its political rather than economic performance. In their desire to scale the ladder of electoral politics, the Communist leaders of the FOCh attempted to form alliances with working and middle class groups for the purpose of common political action. Despite their mutual antagonism, the FOCh could count on the cooperation of the Anarcho-Syndicalists during most of their protest rallies and political strikes, events for which the FOCh alone tended to receive credit. In 1925, the FOCh/PC rode the waves of middle class discontent to elect several deputies and a senator. With a daily newspaper, visible leaders, a sizable treasury collected from the nitrate and coal zones, and the presence of the Executive Committee to bolster its image, the FOCh in Santiago appeared far more powerful than it really was.

Railroad workers vacillated between a mutualist and a labor union stance regarding job action. The Federación Ferroviaria had been rife with internal dissent at the time of its founding in 1922, and in 1924 split again into two rival groups, one composed mainly of shop (maestranza) workers in Santiago and San Bernardo, and the other of Valparaíso line and shop workers.[10] Engineers and firemen continued to favor their own mutual aid society, the Federación Santiago Watt, over membership in the Federación Ferroviaria, thus seriously limiting the effectiveness of railway workers during strikes.

Mutual aid societies emerged from their lethargic state in 1924 with the passage of the Obligatory Social Security Law (4054). By deducting a percentage of each worker's wage for social security benefits, the state and the employer under the terms of Law 4054 usurped a crucial function of the mutual aid societies and therefore undermined their *raison d'être*.[11] Fearing widespread losses in membership, the mutualists joined with their long-standing enemies, the Anarcho-Syndicalists, to conduct a vigorous campaign against the new law.

The strike wave of 1924–25 acquired tremendous proportions throughout Chile. More strikes occurred in Santiago and Valparaíso in 1925 than in any other year since 1919, totaling at least sixty-seven in number.[12] Since I did not include the years 1922–24 in my strike sample, I have no reliable figures for the number of strikes in Santiago and Valparaíso during that period. Table 8.1, however, indicates a rapid rise in the number of strikes in Chile as a whole between 1922 and 1925.

The same factors which appear to have caused the strike waves of 1905–7 and 1917–20 also fueled that of 1924–25. In all three cases, a period of increased strike activity had been preceded by several years of high unemployment and economic depression which greatly weakened the strength of

Table 8.1
Incidence of Strikes in Chile, 1922–25, and in the Municipalities of
Santiago and Valparaíso, 1925

Year	Chile Total (Labor Office)[a]	Chile Total (Barría-Barrera)[b]	Santiago-Valparaíso[c]
1922	19	29	—
1923	41	58	—
1924	86	52	—
1925	114	56	67

[a]Source: figures from the Oficina del Trabajo cited in U.S. Bureau of Labor Statistics, *Monthly Labor Review*, vol. 21, no. 1, July, 1925, p. 195. For 1924 and 1925, *BOT* 24, 1926, anexo 52 and following pages.

[b]Source: Manuel Barrera, "Perspectiva histórica de la huelga obrera en Chile," in *Cuadernos de la realidad nacional*, no. 9, September, 1971, p. 133.

[c]Source: See note 12.

organized labor. The recovery of the nitrate industry (1905, 1916, 1923) led to a gradual increase in strike activity. As the pace of economic recovery quickened, the rate of inflation increased dramatically and peaked at the same time as or slightly after the zenith of the strike wave. The cost of living rose by 9 percent between 1923 and 1924 and 13 percent the following year. (See graph 3.1.) Thus, the improved bargaining position enjoyed by workers due to reasonably high employment coupled with shrinking real wages as a result of inflation stimulated the strike wave of 1924–25.

The major economic strikes of the 1924–25 period took place in 1924. On March 4, merchant sailors in Valparaíso voted to strike the major shipping companies, demanding a 70 percent wage hike.[13] The original walkout involved both the IWW and its rival, the Federación de Gente de Mar, but the Wobblies quickly gained control of the strike. Shippers and contractors refused to consider the petition, and began at once to recruit strikebreakers from the Valparaíso area. They were greatly aided in this endeavor by the navy, which dispatched sailors from the fleet to serve as scabs and permitted steamers to leave port with undersized or female crews. On March 12, the strike spread to cargo handlers at the State Customshouse, lightermen, and metal workers in the drydocks. A week later, a crowd of strikers was fired on by police, leaving twenty wounded. Despite halfhearted attempts by the government to reach a settlement, the affair dragged on until the first week of April and then collapsed. Most of the 4,000 port workers who eventually joined the strike won no concessions whatsoever.[14]

Soon after the initiation of the maritime strike, FOCh tram conductors and drivers went out in Santiago. Their principal demand was that tram inspectors be allowed to join the union. Meetings between Alessandri, the strike committee, and the intendant of the province resulted in a most disadvantageous settlement for the workers. The tram company once again was allowed to cripple the union by firing a number of its militants and simultaneously by discharging those inspectors who favored association with the FOCh.[15]

The largest strike to take place in Santiago during 1924 involved some 10,000 construction workers. Several small strikes were already in progress on March 17, when a committee composed of building trades workers from the IWW, resistance societies, and the FOCh decided to petition many large-scale contractors for higher wages and better working conditions.[16] The association of contractors, architects, and engineers responded with an industry-wide lockout effective March 24. The IWW took charge of the strike and declared that a general walkout would be declared if the workers' petition was not met. In typical fashion, the contractors urged their workers to sign anti-union contracts and return to the job.

By the first week of April, some twenty-five architects and contractors of the approximately 150 involved in the lockout had signed the union contract, and it appeared that a complete victory would be forthcoming. The Contractor's Association voted to lift its lockout on April 5 and attempted to resume work under the old conditions. Claiming that a cache of dynamite had been hidden in the IWW hall, police raided the premises on April 12, but to their dismay, found nothing.

The strike slowly ground to a halt during the month of April. Perhaps as many as half of the workers involved, especially the more highly skilled craftsmen of the resistance societies, achieved their demands and left the strike. Many construction workers bolted the IWW soon afterward to join Anarcho-Syndicalist unions. This proved to be the last major strike led by the Wobblies in Chile.

Other unions had more luck with large-scale strikes in 1924. The Syndicalist-oriented Tailors' Federation won a battle for higher wages in May, and the ever-successful Printers' Federation forced employers to accept their union contract in July.[17] In November, however, a strike of some 5,000 railroad workers in the Central Zone collapsed after only a few days due to lack of coordination between the many different organizations involved.[18]

Analyzed collectively, the sixty-seven strikes which I recorded as having taken place in Valparaíso and Santiago in 1925 demonstrate the continuation of many patterns in industrial conflict established during the years 1917–21. Far more strikes (fifty-two) occurred in Santiago than in Valparaíso (fourteen), with one taking place in both cities. As in the past, more strikes (eighteen) were called by shoe workers than by any other group, although eleven took place in the recently organized metal industry, followed by seven in construction, six in wood and furniture, four in commerce, three in printing, and two in textiles. The percentage of strikes involving women (41) remained nearly constant with that of the 1917–21 period. The mean duration of strikes in 1925 was 15.4 days, only slightly greater than that of 1917–21 strikes.

In similar fashion to the 1917–21 strike wave, the great majority of strikes in 1925 were carried out by the Anarcho-Syndicalists rather than the FOCh. Members of an Anarcho-Syndicalist federation, such as the FOOC, FOICh, USP, etc., participated in twenty-three different strikes in 1925, while independent Anarcho-Syndicalist resistance societies struck twelve times, mutual aid societies eight, the FOCH seven times, and the IWW twice. Thus, libertarians directed four times as many strikes as the FOCh.

Workers appear to have struck mainly over bread-and-butter issues. Wages were a factor in 60 percent of the strikes for which I obtained complete information, followed by hours and the recognition of the union by employers (22 percent each), work rules (20 percent), and the rehiring of fired workers (19 percent).

As during the 1917–21 period, 95 percent of strikes in 1925 occurred in the private sector of the economy. Strikebreakers were introduced in some 37 percent of strikes, nearly the same percentage as in other years. A final settlement was reached through mediation by government officials in 34 percent of the strikes for which complete information was available, a figure nearly equal to those of 1918 and 1919, peak years of government intervention in labor disputes.

Only a few strikes involved more than 200 workers. The Valparaíso branch of the Printers' Federation forced employers to accept proposed changes in its annual, industry-wide contract in January. The following month, major strikes occurred in the Fábrica Nacional de Vidrios, the Lourdes textile factory of Santiago, and the Customshouse in Valparaíso. All three failed. A month-long strike of some 600 metal workers, mainly those employed by the Libertad foundry of Santiago, won hours and wage concessions in April. That same month, boilermakers and foundrymen of the Pearson foundry in Valparaíso struck successfully for higher wages. Tailors and tram workers in Santiago also gained concessions through strike action. Most other strikes were relatively unimportant affairs. The Shoeworkers' Federation employed its normal tactic of isolating a single factory for a job action and then striking another as soon as a settlement was reached. Despite the large number of strikes occurring in 1925, labor unions and unorganized workers alike focused their primary attention on several issues which could not be resolved by directly confronting employers.

Mass Mobilization, Co-optation, and Repression

On September 8, 1924, a military junta presided over by General Luis Altamirano forced Congress to pass a series of seven labor laws derived from legislation introduced by the Conservatives and Liberals in 1919 and 1921.

218

Immediately afterwards, Congress was dissolved and Alessandri abdicated in favor of military rule. James O. Morris, in his study of the labor laws, claims that the reasons for the military's interest in social legislation are not entirely clear. After taking into consideration developments in the industrial relations system of Chile between 1902 and 1924, the growth of independent labor unions, and the stipulations of the laws themselves, however, one can only assume that the military wished to achieve the same end as civilian elites, the emasculation of organized labor. Morris himself admits that "the major objective of the laws was to prolong authoritarianism and not to take genuine strides toward a pluralistic society through encouragement of free unions."[19] It is no wonder, therefore, that the military perceived such legislation as useful in halting the spread of radical labor unions.

We have already seen that the armed forces often played an active role in industrial conflict. They enforced martial law, operated trains, provided strikebreakers for civilian shipping companies, and used violence whenever events got out of hand. It is inconceivable that the middle and upper class officers who controlled the Chilean armed forces were pleased with the development of an independent labor movement led by Anarchists and Communists. In an essay entitled "The Army and the New Social Doctrines," which won a prize from the Club Militar de Chile in 1922, Captain David Bari expressed the fear that radical students, Anarchists, and Socialists were luring thousands of young Chilean workers into subversive organizations. In terms quite similar to those voiced by Alessandrist reformers, Bari proposed that the army take up the cause of the worker, since the Church, the government, and the "false aristocracy" all failed to do so.[20] His argument also resembled the paternalism of the Conservative Party and echoed the Labor Office's contention that the working class would become permanently radicalized if left in the hands of the existing labor unions. Ideas such as these may have attained widespread acceptance within the officer corps of the armed forces and hastened the forced passage of the labor laws.

Once put into effect, the seven labor laws would place the government in control of what had previously been a laissez-faire industrial relations system. Law 4053 regulated work contracts and child and female labor, superseding several laws which had never been put into practice.[21] One of the most unpopular pieces of legislation with labor proved to be Law 4054, which deducted 2 percent of a workman's wage each month for a social security fund. Law 4055, that of Workmen's Compensation, replaced the Work Accident Law of 1916. Labor disputes were regulated by Law 4056. Under its terms, all strike action became illegal unless the workers' previous contract had expired, a majority of two-thirds of the total union membership voted by secret ballot to go on strike, and a government-controlled Permanent Conciliation Board ruled that these conditions had been met. Unions not complying with these stipulations were subject to a fine of up to $500. The law implied that legal strikes could only be conducted by legal unions. Thus, Law 4056 threatened the ability of independent labor unions to function as economic entities.

Law 4057 set up a system of legal labor unions grouped into two categories: craft-based (*sindicatos profesionales*) and plant-based (*sindicatos industriales*). Plant unions were to be legally incorporated in establishments employing twenty-five or more workers. Once formed, all blue collar workers in the plant regardless of trade were required to join the union. Only one plant union per establishment was allowed. The law prohibited *sindicatos industriales* from federating with each other for purposes of collective bargaining. Union revenues were to be derived primarily from a profit sharing plan with employers, and all expenditures came under the strict control of the government. Law 4057 forbade the collection of strike funds and did not allow union officials to be paid on a full-time basis.

Although the Labor Union Law allowed *sindicatos profesionales* to form federations and bargain collectively, its terms, once applied, would have totally altered the nature of the organized labor movement. The most important labor unions and federations in Chile, including the FOICh, USP, Shoeworkers' Federation, FOCh, IWW, and many others, would be considered illegal and therefore outside the realm of collective bargaining. Law 4057 would eventually splinter the labor movement into isolated, impoverished, and employer-dominated legal unions of negligible effectiveness in defending the economic interests of their members.

Law 4058 regulated the establishment and operation of cooperatives. The White Collar Worker Law (*Ley de Empleados Particulares*), Number 4059, was also intended to weaken the potential power of the working class by separating it from white collar workers. It established a legal distinction between "workers" (obreros) and "employees" (empleados), the latter being "all persons irrespective of age or sex who are engaged in work which is of a more intellectual than physical nature."[22] White collar workers employed by the state were not allowed to form unions, nor were they covered by the terms of Law 4059.

By guaranteeing the white collar worker a series of benefits far more generous than those given to workers, the government hoped to forever prevent an alliance between empleados and obreros. Teachers, commercial employees, inspectors, and communications workers had on various occasions during the early 1920s expressed great dissatisfaction with their economic lot and had made overtures of coordinated action with labor.[23] Under the terms of Law 4059, however, white collar employees received yearly bonuses derived from profit sharing of up to 25 percent of their annual salary, a maximum forty-eight-hour week, a guaranteed written contract, sick pay, a retirement fund, two weeks' paid vacation per year, and a generous separation payment should they be discharged. Obreros received none of these benefits. A further stipulation requiring foreign companies to hire a minimum fixed percentage of Chilean empleados caused an outburst from the Foreign Chamber of Commerce in Santiago, and the law was temporarily shelved in 1924. Ironically, the joint campaign of workers and empleados to enforce Law 4059 formed one of the bases for the popular front action of 1925.

These seven laws, threatening as they might have been to the organized labor movement of 1924, were not to go into effect until the issuance of their regulatory acts a year or more hence. The urban labor unions were faced with a more pressing concern in September, 1924: the position they would take regarding the Military Junta itself. The armed forces by no means adopted an antilabor position; only days after assuming power, the Junta sent representatives to confer with leaders of the major labor unions in Santiago and solicit their support.[24] On October 1, the Junta delighted the Bakers' Union (USP) by declaring an end to night work in bakeries and personally wiring its congratulations to USP headquarters in Santiago.[25] The labor press remained open after the coup, and the Junta made no attempt to interfere with the free functioning of the unions.

Anarchists, with a long tradition of antimilitarism behind them, generally showed disfavor towards the military government. In a veiled threat, the IWW soon after the coup declared that it would oppose any movement in Chile which curtailed individual liberties.[26] *El Sembrador,* organ of the Iquique Anarchists, declared after the military takeover: "In Chile, we are on the verge of a cruel and ignominious dictatorship . . . we can expect nothing else from capitalist-bred militarism."[27] In October, the Anarchist-inspired Federation of Chilean Students called for a united front to overthrow the Junta.[28]

The FOCh and PC vacillated widely in their reactions to the coup. On September 9, an editorial in *Justicia* declared that military rule could not have any positive effect on the working class.[29] Two days later, *Justicia* changed its mind and expressed the hope that the Junta might improve the lot of the worker. Immediately afterward, Recabarren urged that "our present and future course of action should be to carry out the Program [the *Manifestación* promising social reform] of the Military Junta at whatever cost."[30] Party and Federation leaders ordered the FOCh councils to adopt a "wait and see" attitude toward the military government, a policy which remained in effect until the closing of the federation's newspaper *La Defensa* of Tocopilla in late October. *Justicia* on that occasion condemned the "odious repression" directed against organized labor by the Junta, and the FOCh joined the Anarcho-Syndicalists of Santiago in forming a Pro–Public Liberties Committee.[31] The editor of *La Defensa* was quickly released from prison,

221

and relations between the Junta and the FOCh might have improved had it not been for the government's decision to postpone the application of the White Collar Worker Law until April, 1925. Sensing a chance to at last form a popular front with other "progressive" elements of Chilean society, the PC approached the newly established Union of White Collar Workers of Chile with an offer of solidarity while continuing to agitate for "public liberties" alongside the Anarcho-Syndicalists. On January 18, 1925, the FOCh, PC, and UECh announced that they would call a general work stoppage in Santiago on February 3 if Law 4059 was not put into effect and the prisoners taken during the San Gregorio incident of 1921 not released.[32]

The strike proved unnecessary. On January 23, 1925, the Altamirano government was overthrown in a bloodless coup carried out by junior officers. The new military government pledged itself to fulfill the promises of social reform made by the previous regime and called for the return of constitutional rule with Alessandri as President.

Labor immediately agreed to support or at least cooperate with the new Junta. On January 24, the FOCh offered its "moral and material adhesion" to the junior officers, while the Anarcho-Syndicalists adopted a position of sympathetic neutrality.[33] Immediately after the coup of Janurary 23, the FOCh and the UECh cemented their relationship by forming a National Workers' Committee.[34] This organization served as a pressure group through which the PC and proAlessandri empleados could defend and at the same time influence the military government.

The junior officers' coup created a momentary power vacuum in Chile. Oligarchic politicians and their military allies were removed from power, but the golpistas maintained a very tenuous hold on the government. The new regime desperately needed popular support, especially that of organized labor and empleados, in order to avoid falling victim to a counter-coup by the navy or right-wing parties. Labor unions in Santiago and Valparaíso quickly perceived that they held trump cards and proceeded to play many of them. Organized labor, perhaps for the first time, found itself in a position of great political influence. Interunion rivalry and political differences prevented labor from fully exploiting its temporary role as a power broker, however.

During the first six weeks following the coup, the unions agitated in favor of several different causes and the FOCh strengthened its ties with the middle class elements. Anxious to retain the support of labor unions, the Junta responded to their every demand. On January 28, for example, the Comité Obrero Nacional petitioned for an Amnesty Law for political prisoners. Five days later, the Junta decreed such a law, and the workers imprisoned after the Puerto Natales incident of 1919 were released.[35] Under further pressure, the Junta dictated a series of "decree-laws" which raised the salaries of government workers, freed the prisoners taken at San Gregorio, reformed old laws regulating working class housing and the employment of pregnant women and mothers, released the Anarchist assassin Efraín Plaza Olmedo, and put Law 4059 (the White Collar Worker Law) into effect.[36] Labor's methods in procuring these reforms bordered on extortion, most commonly the threat of a disruptive rally or a general strike. Organized labor did, however, agree to the Junta's enforcement of a state of siege beginning March 3 as a means of dealing with subversion from the right.[37]

In the midst of this unstable political situation, a grass roots movement of great significance emerged among the workers of Valparaíso and Santiago, the tenant leagues. Anarchist labor unionists had formed previous ligas de arrendatarios in 1907 and 1914, and much tenant agitation accompanied the AOAN rallies and the social unrest of the early 1920s. In these cases, however, rent strikes appear to have been fomented by labor unions or other organized groups. The tenant league movement of 1925 was more spontaneous and certainly more widespread than those in the past.

Working class rent-payers in Chile had good reason to be dissatisfied. The conventillos of Santiago and Valparaíso had become increasingly crowded during the depression of 1921 and afterward (see table 3.1), and rents began to climb alarmingly in 1924. Labor Office surveys showed an average rent increase of 30.5 percent in Santiago during 1924.[38] With food prices also on the rise during 1924 and 1925, the urban working class found itself in desperate financial shape. The response of workers to this difficult situation was simple and illegal: to pay only 50 percent of their normal rents.

The "50 percent" movement first appeared in Valparaíso several days after the coup of January 23, 1925. By the twenty-seventh, a tenant league integrated by organized and unorganized workers alike had been formed.[39] On January 30, the league held a huge rally in the Centro of Valparaíso, during which the 30,000 demonstrators present pledged to pay only half of their rent beginning February 1.[40] Impressed by events in Valparaíso, workers in Santiago formed their own tenant league and placed an IWW militant at its head. The Santiago league held several massive rallies to publicly announce its intention of paying only 50 percent of normal rents and placing a moratorium on unpaid back rents. One such rally, held Sunday, February 8, drew 80,000 people, according to *La Nación*.[41]

The tenant leagues of both cities decided to coordinate their activities and press for a law which would legally recognize the lower rents they had begun paying on February 1. Accordingly, the leagues voted to declare a general strike in Valparaíso to take effect at midnight on February 12 should a rent law not be passed. The Military Junta huddled in conference during the early hours of February 13, and finally announced a decree-law at 6 A.M.[42] The strike went on as scheduled, however, since word of the settlement did not arrive in Valparaíso in time to halt it. Mounted army units and police clashed with the huge crowd assembled in the Centro of the city on the morning of the thirteenth, resulting in many injuries, but the strikers finally dispersed when they became aware of the law.

Although the Rent Law of February 13 temporarily calmed the crowd in Valparaíso, neither tenants nor landlords were satisfied with its stipulations. The law ordered that Housing Committees (Tribunales de Vivienda) composed of representatives of the government, municipality, and tenant league, should be constituted in each ward of major Chilean cities.[43] A Housing Committee had the power to declare any property to be "unsanitary" and lower the rent to one-half of its former value. Other clauses in the law regulated the repair and tax assessment of conventillos, but its principal features involved the Housing Committees and lowered rents for buildings officially judged unsanitary.

The tenant leagues contended that the law offered very little relief for the harried rent-payer. In the last week of February, 1925, leaders of the Valparaíso and Santiago leagues drafted a counter proposal calling for an end to rent payments for "unsanitary" housing and a 50 percent reduction of rents for all other dwellings.[44] It further called for the establishment of Housing Committees each composed of five representatives, one from the government, one from the municipality, and three from the tenant leagues. The leagues threatened to continue paying illegal rents of 50 percent across the board if their proposed law was not adopted.

Tenement owners reacted to the Housing Law by forming a League of Property Owners in both Santiago and Valparaíso.[45] They also formulated a revision of the law which called for higher minimum rents and representation of their organization on the Housing Committees. The League of Property Owners organized themselves along the same lines as the tenant leagues, with local officials in each ward and a city-wide council to speak for the entire membership. A bitter contest of strength therefore emerged between tenants and landlords.

In early March, the tenant league of Valparaíso split into two factions, the Liga de Arrendatarios and the Liga de Arrendatarios en Resistencia.[46] The former group consisted of those people who supported the Junta's Rent Law and wished to achieve legal status for their organization in order to participate in the Housing Committees. Leadership of this faction came mainly from the mutual aid societies. Anarchists directed the latter group, which adhered to the policy of seeking rent reductions for all tenants. On March 31, the government granted legal status to the mutualist league, probably in hopes of undercutting the direct action tactics of the Anarchists.

The enforcement decree of March 17 which activated the Rent Law clearly demonstrated the government's intention to use the Housing Committees to benefit property owners. It stipulated that each committee would consist of a government representative, a member of the League of Property Owners chosen from among the highest taxpayers in each ward, and a member of the tenant league who had never been arrested and had paid his rent on schedule during the past two years.[47] Since the government representative was normally a member of the middle class or a person of some economic means and the tenant league representative could not be a militant who had previously refused to pay his rent, the Housing Committees were certain to be landlord-controlled. Furthermore, only two parties constituted a quorum when conducting the business of the committees, leaving the door open for private sessions between the representatives of the government and the landlords.[48]

Despite its early criticism of the Rent Law, the Communist Party concluded that the legally established Housing Committees might provide a means of increasing its influence within the working class. On April 8, when the Anarchists in Santiago led a general strike in support of the universal rent reduction of 50 percent, the FOCh and the PC did not participate, and the crowd was smaller than could normally have been expected.[49] Three days later, the Communists set up a splinter "Federal Council of Tenants" to rival the Anarchist-led tenant league. The PC based its strategy on compliance with the terms of the Rent Law and winning rent reductions by having more tenements judged "unsanitary."

During the next few months, the Anarchists continued to wage a desperate struggle to force landlords to accept 50 percent of their normal rents. Many landlords did give in to pressure and agreed to the reduced rent, while others countered with evictions and blacklists of uncooperative tenants, and by cutting off water and electricity to conventillos whose tenants refused to pay the full rent.[50] Police units carried out some 2,000 evictions by August, 1925, often in the presence of hostile crowds of onlookers.[51] Landlords sidestepped those regulations of the Rent Law which they considered unfavorable by bribing housing inspectors and manipulating the Housing Committees.[52]

The Communists failed completely in their attempt to use the tenant league to increase the party's power base. *Justicia* admitted in a series of articles that tenant participation in the Housing Committees achieved no results and that the Rent Law had been a ploy by the government to defuse the rent strike movement. In August of 1925, the FOCh/PC called a rally in Santiago to urge the drafting of a new rent law, but by that time, the power of the tenant leagues (both Anarchist and Communist) had weakened greatly. The final blow against the tenant movement was struck by the Ministry of Justice in September when it shifted jurisdiction in matters involving housing from the hands of the Housing Committees to the completely unresponsive civil courts.[53] The Anarchist tenant league in Santiago continued to function until

225

early 1927, but it had very little further success in forcing lower rents on landlords.

Despite their eventual neutralization by internal division and unfavorable legislation, the tenant leagues of Valparaíso and Santiago affected the working people of those cities perhaps more profoundly than had any past movement. According to Labor Office statistics, rents fell sharply during 1925, due at least in part to the rent strikes of February–April.[54] More important, thousands of men and women who had never before participated in an organized, collective effort to better their lives gained such an experience in tenant leagues.[55] Chilean Anarchists correctly perceived the rent strikes as being revolutionary events, and fully realized that the rent laws of February and March were enacted by the Junta as stopgap measures. Until the "narcotic" of the rent laws eventually took hold and the tenant leagues of both Santiago and Valparaíso splintered into rival factions, Chilean elites experienced an uneasy few months.[56] For the Anarchists, the tenant league movement had been the first step toward a new social order in Chile. In the words of *Tribuna Libertaria* of Santiago:[57]

> This movement since its first moments had been essentially revolutionary. The tactics of direct action were preached by libertarians with highly successful results, because they managed to instill in the working classes the idea that if landlords would not accept the 50 percent lowering of rents, they should pay nothing at all. In libertarian terms, this is the same as taking possession of common property. It completes the first stage of what will become a social revolution.

As long as the Military Junta which came to power in January, 1925, remained weak and threatened by counter-revolution, it was forced to appease the angry Chilean working class with piecemeal reforms and temporary measures. Alessandri's return to Chile in March greatly strengthened the Junta's position by reducing the potential of a *golpe* from the right. Once constitutional government was re-established, Alessandri and his supporters in the military could turn their full attention to the social upheaval which had shaken the entire country during the first half of 1925.

Elite fear of social revolution had been steadily building since the January coup. According to the British minister, "alarm was universal" among elites in Santiago directly following the fall of Altamirano.[58] Strikes, general work stoppages, and the rise of the tenant leagues, not to mention the Junta's desperate moves to placate labor rather than taking the normal recourse of repression, exacerbated the tension. The gradual neutralization of the tenant leagues after April eased the situation somewhat, but the strike wave began to reach its peak in May and June. Walkouts in coal, nitrate, and copper mining put additional pressure on the government. Alessandri declared May 1, for the first time in Chilean history, to be a sanctioned holiday, in order to render it meaningless as a day of revolutionary protest.[59] Decree-laws and proclamations would not, however, end the large-scale strikes in the North and South. Nor would they calm the minds of worried elites who, like the British minister, feared that Chile was about to experience a social revolution.

In late May, Alessandri set the wheels of repression in motion. A battle fleet transporting the "Rancagua" regiment of the Tacna garrison was dispatched to Iquique to extinguish strikes and protests in the Province of Tarapacá. Soldiers raided and closed the Anarchist and Communist press in Iquique and moved out to the *pampa* as if on a full-scale campaign. Near the La Coruña nitrate camp, a "battle" took place on June 4 between nitrate workers armed with dynamite and troops of the line, including artillery units.[60] British diplomats estimated that from 600 to 800 workers were killed in the resulting massacre, while the army suffered no casualties.[61] Meanwhile, over 1,000 arrests were taking place throughout the Provinces of Tarapacá and Antofagasta. Official censorship of telegraph messages prevented news of the La Coruña killings from reaching Santiago and Valparaíso for several days. Right of assembly in the nitrate camps was quickly suspended, and a force of carabineros was sent to guard each oficina.

The "grave disorders" in the North rekindled fears among urban elites that subversive elements were once again at work. Anarchists and Communists under arrest in the North were branded as "Peruvian agents" *a la* 1920, and "patriotic leagues" of a notably anti-Anarchist nature began to reorganize themselves in the principal cities.[62] On June 10, Alessandri declared a state of siege in the coal mining zone to crush the strikes which had begun in May. Police agents stepped up their campaign of infiltrating and spying on the labor unions of Santiago and Valparaíso. Soon after the La Coruña massacre, military officials began censoring the working class press and continued to blot out whatever articles they found objectionable until censorship was lifted in November.[63]

Repression and the threat of further violence brought the strike wave of 1924–25 to an abrupt halt. Labor Office statistics show that while ninety-five strikes occurred in Chile during the first six months of 1925, only eighteen took place from July to December.[64] In Santiago and Valparaíso, fifty-nine strikes were initiated from January to June, 1925, and only eight thereafter.[65] Despite the fact that at least some of its members were among the nitrate workers killed at La Coruña, the FOCh did not respond to the massacre with an outburst of condemnation. Although it knew soon after June 4 that many had been killed, the FOCh delayed registering an official protest with Alessandri until the seventeenth.[66] Judging by the late appearance and remarkably

227

respectful tone of its statement, the FOCh did not wish to closely associate itself with the massacre. Many elements in the PC wanted to launch an immediate public protest, but the Federal Executive Council ruled out any such move.[67] Military censorship prevented a normal discussion of the affair in the PC/FOCh press, but from all appearances, Communist leaders did not wish to jeopardize their chance to participate in the drafting of Chile's new constitution or form an effective alliance with middle class elements for the upcoming presidential and parliamentary elections. Popular front tactics ruled out any behavior which could be judged "subversive" by more legitimate participants in the Chilean political game. The FOCh may, therefore, have shrunk from protest and further mass action until the elections were over. The Anarchists continued to press ahead with rent strikes and opened their campaign against Law 4054, although neither issue could make much headway once authoritarian rule had been re-established. As in the case of 1907 and 1920, a surge of popular unrest was effectively stifled by violence.

WORKING CLASS POLITICS

By several standards of measurement, the urban working class had "arrived" politically in 1925. Five Communists won election to the Chamber of Deputies and one (the party's first) to the Senate that year. For the first time, a prolabor candidate challenged the "traditional" parties in a presidential election and received 34,000 votes in Santiago and Valparaíso alone. Members of the PC were invited by Alessandri to assist in drawing up Chile's new constitution. These events all seem to indicate that the working class had at least achieved the status of a legitimate power contender in the political system.

Such "victories," however, were not brought about through any rapid growth of either the FOCh or the PC. In fact, both organizations seem to have experienced a decline in membership and effectiveness several months before the elections of 1925. The apparent rise of the PC as a political force instead took place as the result of popular front tactics in accordance with Comintern policy which united the FOCh with mutual aid societies and empleados. When this unofficial popular front disintegrated, the PC found itself with neither a political nor a labor base.

After failing in the early 1920s to establish a united front with the IWW and independent labor unions, the FOCh entered wholeheartedly into the electoral game. Despite occasional outbursts of revolutionary rhetoric, Communist Party leaders as early as June, 1923, mapped out a political strategy which they felt would eventually permit the PC to participate in a coalition government, much as the PD had previously done. When asked if the Communists would be willing to enter into an electoral agreement with other

228

parties before the congressonal elections of 1924, Recabarren unequivocally stated: "We will form pacts with any party, naturally giving preference under similar circumstances to those groups which include in their platforms the most advanced ideas concerning the moral and material improvement of the working classes."[68] The PC decided to put forward a candidate in every district which contained a Communist Party section and made an all-out effort to register as many people as possible to vote. True to Recabarren's words, the party entered into a pact with the Liberal Alliance, promising to support *aliancista* senatorial candidates in exchange for a pledge by the Alessandrists to suspend vote-buying in districts where the Communists ran a candidate.[69] In its desperation to win control of both the Chamber and Senate, the Liberal Alliance did not comply with the bargain, but instead employed the most fraudulent means at its disposal to steal votes from Communists and Conservatives alike.[70] As a result, the PC failed to re-elect its two active deputies and won only twenty municipal positions throughout the entire country.

The elections of 1924 did not sidetrack the PC from its goal of establishing a front organization to catapult the party into prominence. In December of 1924, the FOCh joined the UECh and several labor organizations in forming a United Committee of Wage Earners, which, immediately following the coup of January, 1925, became the National Workers' Committee. At the same time as it laid the foundation for a labor front, the PC approached the Democratic Party in hopes of establishing a political union.[71] When it became apparent that constitutional law would be restored, the PC quickened the pace of its activities. The National Worker's Committee staged demonstrations in support of the new military regime and the party attempted to extend its political influence. In March, 1925, a Constituent Assembly of Wage Earners and Intellectuals met in Santiago to adopt a common "labor" position regarding the new national constitution to be drafted. Communist leader Manuel Hidalgo was the principal moving force behind the Assembly, and 25 percent of all delegates present were members of the FOCh or the PC. Other participating groups included the Railroad Workers' Federation, UECh, FECh, Teachers' Association, and IWW. After much heated debate, mainly between the Communists and the Anarchists of the Teacher's Association and the IWW, the Assembly voted to recommend that Chile's new constitution establish a federal system of government, declare all land as "social property," and guarantee a host of socioeconomic reforms.[72] These recommendations were, of course, intended to be position statements rather than stipulations which had any chance of being adopted by those who would actually draft the new constitution.

As 1925 progressed, the PC increasingly subordinated the economic needs of FOCh members to the party's political goals. Legal, legitimate behavior was practiced at the expense of strikes against employers or landlords. The FOCh/PC picked up allies along the way, because the labor laws of 1924 and inflation had temporarily radicalized other segments of Chilean society. Empleados had become infuriated when the Altamirano government refused to put Law 4059 into practice. Mutualists, on the other hand, felt certain that Law 4054 (establishing obligatory social security insurance) would undercut their own existence and thus sought to prevent its enforcement. Teachers felt that they were oppressed by an oligarchic society which classified them as something "between a servant and a bureaucrat."[73] In 1912 and 1915, Santiago teachers had formed short-lived mutual aid societies, and in 1918 they called the first in a series of bitter strikes which would last into the 1920s.[74] The Asociación General de Profesores de Chile was founded in 1923 to unify the existing teachers' organizations and bring about educational reform. Leaders of the Teachers' Association in Santiago and Valparaíso maintained a distinctly Anarchist outlook during the 1920s, favoring direct rather than political action to win higher salaries and better working conditions. Many of these teacher-Anarchists had been former members of the FECh, where they received their first doses of libertarian philosophy. Included among them were Carlos Sepúlveda Leyton, César Godoy Urrutia, and Miguel Ruz González.[75] The Teachers' Association maintained close contact with the IWW and the Anarcho-Syndicalists, but demonstrated little sympathy for the FOCh or the PC.

Participants in the many front organizations and pressure groups of 1925 thus formed a motley crew of Anarchists, Communists, mutualists, intellectuals, teachers, and white collar empleados. Many were members of the Democratic or Radical Parties who turned politically leftward as a result of hard times and the unwillingness of their own parties to move toward reform. Their common bond was dissatisfaction with the current state of socioeconomic affairs, although some, like the Anarchists, sought total change, while others (the empleados, for instance), could be placated by specific reforms.

The arrival of Arturo Alessandri in Santiago on March 20, 1925, threatened to break up the PC's incipient electoral front before it could become effective. Most of the mutual aid societies of the Capital sent official delegations to the Central Train Station to welcome Alessandri back, but the FOCh and the Anarchists showed very little interest.[76] Alessandri had, after all, sided with employers during the lockouts of 1920–23 and was no longer considered an ally of the labor movement. The mutualist rank and file, however, flocked to the Station to catch a glimpse of *el León*, whose arrival produced "a delirious, frenetic acclamation; a real sense of madness among the lower classes."[77]As in early 1921, Alesssandri was immediately bombarded with appeals by workers from all parts of the country to personally intervene in their strikes and wage disputes. Within a few months, however, the initial enthusiasm of the mutualists over Alessandri's return gave way to anxiety as Law 4054 drew closer to enforcement, the traditional parties sought a compromise candidate for President, and the wave of repression commenced.

In April, the PC at last made its electoral pact with the Democrats, forming a "Republican Social Front" aimed at "the complete renovation of institutional forms which have become archaic and their replacement by others which more closely reflect modern times."[78] This alliance came about mainly as a result of the seemingly impossible union formed between Conservatives and Radicals for the upcoming congressional elections of November, 1925. The PC also undertook an all-out campaign to register voters for the elections. A new law passed in 1924, which reformed procedures for voter registration and decreased the possibilities of fraud, improved the PC's chances of electoral success.[79] Its dedication to politics caused the party to overlook the La Coruña massacre and steer the FOCh-controlled sectors of the tenant leagues into collaboration with the Housing Committees. Nothing was to stand in the way of political objectives.

The Constitutional Convention of July–August, 1925, was completely dominated by the will of Alessandri to strengthen the power of the executive at the expense of Congress. Communist representatives received an invitation to take part in the proceedings, perhaps to demonstrate that the resulting constitution was a document which truly represented all political opinions.[80] In statements directly contradicting its traditional position that the "Parliamentary Republic" maintained oligarchic rule, Hidalgo and the PC claimed that Alessandri's constitution would return Chile to the "despotic authoritarianism" of the pre-1891 era.[81] The sudden nostalgia of the PC for the parliamentary system reflected the party's optimism that gains in the November elections would allow it to enter a coalition government. The PC therefore urged its supporters to vote the "blue" ballot in the plebiscite of August 30, calling for a constitution which placed strict limitations on the power of the President and his ministers. Alessandri's constitutional proposals were overwhelmingly favored by those who voted in the plebiscite, but abstention was so high that the constitution of 1925 went into effect with the approval of only 43 percent of all registered voters.[82]

During the month of September, the PC strove to patch together an electoral front for both the presidential and congressional elections. In October, the Democrats broke their previous agreement with the Communists by adhering to the presidential campaign of Emiliano Figueroa, a compromise candidate supported by all the traditional parties. Alessandri once again abandoned the Presidency under military pressure. The sudden linkage of the "legitimate" political parties set the stage for a unique development in Chilean history, a presidential campaign waged entirely by forces having no support from traditional political groups.

A National Convention of Salary Earners formed by the PC, UECh, and mutualists met in Santiago on October 4, 1925, to nominate army physician and former Minister of Health and Social Welfare Dr. José Santos Salas for President. The former FOCh leader and recognized head of the mutual aid society movement in Santiago, Carlos A. Martínez, became director of the Salas campaign, with the Communist Carlos Contreras as vice-chairman. After two years of failure, the Communists had at last succeeded in forming a popular front, although not with any of the traditional parties. The PC regarded the Salas candidacy as a stage in the historical process, a further step towards the replacement of oligarchic rule in Chile with that of a reformist bourgeoisie. *Justicia* commented two weeks before the election, "the hour of Communism's triumph has not yet arrived," but seemed content with the success of the PC in joining forces with white collar workers, renegade Democrats and Radicals, and mutualists.[83]

Figueroa emerged the overwhelming winner in the election held October 24, with 169,638 votes to 71,717 for Salas. Considering his nontraditional base of power, however, Salas made a tremendous showing. He beat Figueroa in three working class wards of Santiago (Ultra Mapocho—4th; Quinta Normal—5th; and Matadero—10th) and lost in the urban zone of Santiago by only 640 votes—18,367 to 17,727.[84] Several factors caused the vote to be so close. The Santiago section of the PD rejected national party leadership two weeks before the election and openly supported Salas. Ironically, the popular front vote may have also benefitted from the support of Anarcho-Syndicalists who had previously boycotted all elections. Luis Heredia, at that time secretary general of the Shoeworkers' Federation and a leading figure in the Anarcho-Syndicalist movement, claimed that many libertarians in Santiago had been attracted by the "small-change candidate" (*el candidato de la chaucha*), as Salas was affectionately called by his supporters, and voted for him.[85] Anarchist influence within the still-functioning tenant leagues and Teachers' Association probably garnered votes from those organizations as well.

Anarchist participation in the election, the "popular" nature of the Salas campaign, and the increased socioeconomic awareness of the working class in Santiago and Valparaíso due to the tenant leagues, as well as the registration reforms of 1924, accounted for the large jump in political participation between 1920 and 1925. In the presidential election of 1920, for example, 16,551 people cast votes in the urban zone of Santiago, while 36,094 did so in 1925, a gain of 118 percent.[86] The number of votes cast in the Province of Santiago and in Valparaíso rose by nearly the same figure. The number of registered voters in the Department of Santiago climbed from 26,221 in 1921 to 38,275 in 1924 and then jumped to 55,086 in 1925.[87] These figures clearly demonstrate a great surge in electoral activity during the 1920s.

The PC claimed that the election had been stolen from Salas by fraud and called on the young officers who carried out the coup of January 23 to intervene again.[88] Two days after the election, the supporters of Salas called a forty-eight-hour general work stoppage in Santiago to protest the election results. The government responded by declaring a state of siege for fifteen days and moving extra military units into the Capital.

Shortly after the presidential election, the UECh, Railroad Workers' Federation, Teachers' Association, and assorted groups of white collar workers formed a new organization called the Republican Social Union of Wage Earners of Chile (*Unión Social Republicana de Asalariados de Chile*-USRACh) to continue their struggle in the congressional elections held in November. Among the USRACh leaders were C. A. Martínez of the mutual aid societies, Angel Mella, secretary general of the Railroad Workers' Federation, and Oscar Schnake, ex-FECh militant and IWW member. The USRACh quickly formed an electoral pact with the Democratic and Communist Parties to coordinate their efforts in the congressional elections. In areas where the PC and the empleados were thought to be exceptionally strong, the USRACh and PC ran two candidates for deputy, and in other areas, only a Communist or a USRACh member was put on the ballot.[89] By carefully picking the candidates from among themselves and pledging support (in an electoral system of multiple votes) to each other, the PC, USRACh, and PD hoped to avoid defeat by splitting the "popular" votes.

Popular front tactics once again bore fruit. The PC elected five deputies and its first senator, while the USRACh gained four deputies.[90] On no other occasion had more than two members of nontraditional political parties been elected to the Chamber of Deputies, and none had ever reached the Senate.

The victory of the PC appears to have been due mainly to its linkage with the USRACh organizations. Without large numbers of empleados casting votes for the Communists, it is certain that Hidalgo could not have been elected, nor probably would several of the deputies. The numerical strength of the PC at this time was less than 3,000 nationwide, centered in Iquique and Antofagasta.[91] Given the weakness of the FOCh in Santiago and Valparaíso and the constant quarrels between the Santiago section of the PC and the National Executive Committee, it would be fair to assume that the Communist deputies (Sepúlveda and Cruz) elected in Valparaíso and Santiago owed their victories to the USRACh. The PC may have been able to stand by itself in the North and in Concepción, but the central cities had traditionally proven to be infertile ground for Marxist politicians. Nor is it likely that PC gains in the congressional elections reflected larger party

233

membership or a sudden increase in the PC's popularity among urban workers. Judging from the ineffectiveness of both the PC and the FOCh in late 1925 and 1926, the electoral victory does not appear to have strengthened either organization.

While the presence of six Communists in Congress may have increased the party's prestige among elites and advanced its reputation as a legitimate participant in the political system, the popular front tactics which brought the electoral victory about undermined the PC's already tenuous linkage with the working class. The FOCh throughout Chile since 1924 had been little more than the labor wing of the PC. Its power in the urban center remained concentrated in the glass, textile, and food processing industries, but its most important concejo was that formed by tramway workers in Santiago. By controlling this crucial public service, the PC/FOCh could temporarily disrupt the city whenever it wished. A general work stoppage by the FOCh was, therefore, perceived as a significant event in the eyes of the citizenry and press of the Capital. The Anarcho-Syndicalists might shut down everything else in town, but the public did not feel the effects immediately except in the case of bakery strikes. For this and other reasons, such as its representation in Congress and influence in coal and nitrates, the FOCh appeared to be far stronger in Santiago than it really was.

Appearances were of little help to the federados themselves, however. The PC plan of action in 1924–25 did not call for a unionization drive to replenish the depleted ranks of the FOCh or expand into other industries, but to momentarily unite with the party those reformist elements which had earlier been purged from the FOCh. C. A. Martínez, groups of empleados, and the railway workers were actively courted for the popular front. The PC in essence attempted to politically reconstruct in 1925 what the FOCh of 1920 had built under the leadership of Martínez, Díaz Vera, and the reformists. The popular front of 1925, however, lacked the institutional base that the FOCh enjoyed in 1920 before infighting, government repression, and a series of lockouts caused the federation to splinter.

The concejos of the FOCh of 1925 do not appear to have been represented in the PC by members of their own organizations. Communist leaders, in fact, were generally workers who had long been detached from unions in their own trades. Recabarren, Cruz, Elías Lafertte, and Galvarino Gil (PC secretary general, 1924–25) were all printers by trade, and yet none could claim to represent a single printing worker in Chile.[92] The PC and FOCh did not recruit their top leaders from the labor unions, but from the ranks of politically oriented workers and middle class radicals. During the formation of the popular front in 1925, the PC invited the "worker, white collar employee, and intellectual" to join.[93] Some professionals, such as lawyers Carlos Contreras and Gregorio Guerra, became Communists after first participating in an empleado organization. Communist claims to speak for the working classes of Santiago and Valparaíso were therefore derived from the party's self-conception as the vanguard of the proletariat rather than from any basis in fact. The party's relationship with the labor unions is reflected in a statement made by PC deputy Ramón Sepúlveda Leal at an FOCh convention in late 1926: "I didn't come to submit to the will of labor leaders, but to take advantage of labor elements in favor of our cause."[94]

The PC in Santiago was further weakened by internal dissent, which normally pitted the National Executive Committee against the Santiago section. Just as the Santiago branch of the PD traditionally took a more radical, libertarian position than that of the national party, so did the PC fight a continuous battle with rebellious santiaguinos. In late 1924, a group of young worker-Communists in Santiago publicly challenged Recabarren's hegemony within the party, branding him a "Tsar" and accusing him of hypocritical behavior.[95] Recabarren still possessed enough authority to have the Santiago section purged, but the leader of the rebels was later reinstated after Recabarren's suicide in December, 1924. Immediately after the elections of November, 1925, the Executive Committee once again purged the Santiago section for its "indiscipline." In April, 1926, the Santiago section was completely dissolved by the national party, and in August, further purges eliminated long-standing leaders such as C. A. Sepúlveda and Julio Moya.

The popular front fell apart soon after its brief success. As early as January, 1926, *Justicia* began to condemn the USRACh as an organization formed by the "petty bourgeoisie and deserters from traditional parties."[96] Perhaps as a response to the Anarchist background of many of its leaders, such as Oscar Schnake and Ramón Alzamora, the USRACh in 1926 adopted a nonpolitical position and vigorously attacked the PC and the FOCh. The UECh and several mutualist groups continued to verbally support the PC/ FOCh in 1926 and early 1927, but effective coordinated action between these very dissimilar organizations proved impossible.

A directive of the Latin American Secretariat of the Comintern in November, 1926, that was sent to the Chilean PC listed three major flaws in the local party's development: (1) the fact that the party had not been organized into cells; (2) its low membership; and (3) the fact that "the proletarian base of the party is absolutely insufficient."[97] The sections of the party operated in near independence of each other, and PC congressmen refused to submit to the discipline of the National Executive Committee. The Comintern noted that the preoccupation with electoral politics at the expense of the labor base was a serious error, and urged a vigorous "bolshevization" of the party.

At the suggestion of the Comintern, the PC in late 1926 adopted the tactic of "boring from within" the recently created legal plant unions in order to establish a new base of power within the working class.[98] By doing so, the

Communists demonstrated their lack of support among workers in the independent unions. The failure of the PC to broaden its base of power in the working class resulted when the party sacrificed the well-being of the FOCh for greater representation in a Congress which after 1925 played no meaningful role in the political system.

THE END OF AN ERA

The steady decline in the effectiveness of the urban labor movement which commenced in the second half of 1925 continued unabated until the coup of Colonel Carlos Ibáñez in February, 1927. Economic recession, spurred as always by a crisis in the nitrate industry, was partly responsible for the weakening of most labor unions. Nitrate production began to fall in 1925, leaving several thousand workers without jobs. As demand for coal slackened, the principal mining companies began laying off their workers. Industrial production fell slightly in 1925 and continued to drop until 1928. By June, 1926, half of the nitrate oficinas in the North were no longer operating, and thousands of discharged workers once more made their way to Santiago at government expense.[99] The bargaining position of urban workers suffered from an expanding pool of the unemployed, and strike activity diminished considerably during 1926.

Repression by the armed forces further curtailed strike action in Chile during the latter half of 1925 and helped contribute to labor's decline in 1926. The fact that the attention of many labor unions became riveted on the abolition of Law 4054 rather than on strike activity indicates a general weakness of labor unions vis-à-vis employers. The eventual failure of the campaign against Law 4054 also demonstrated the organizational disarray and lack of solidarity of the urban labor movement.

The unions themselves realized that their power was steadily declining and attempted in vain to remedy the situation. Anarcho-Syndicalists in Santiago and Valparaíso admitted that disunity greatly limited the potential strength of their movement and called for the creation of a new organization to coordinate the activities of the many federations and resistance societies in existence. Yet, when the FORCh was finally created in early 1926, its founders refused to renounce their own institutional autonomy, thus rendering the federation useless as a unifying force. By November, 1926, IWW leaders noted that pessimism and inactivity among union men had reached "epidemic" proportions.[100] Luis Heredia of the Shoeworkers' Federation and FORCh bemoaned the fact that many Anarcho-Syndicalists had even begun to doubt the value of labor unions as a revolutionary vehicle, while the "infantile" battle between "federalists" and "industrialists" continued to debilitate the labor movement.[101]

The FOCh was in even worse shape than the Anarcho-Syndicalist unions.

Justicia complained in May, 1926, that the federation's financial and organizational situation had deteriorated considerably. For the first time in many years, *Justicia* was forced to print commercial advertisements at the expense of propaganda or news of the labor unions. Participation in the PC declined to the point that a mere twenty-four people at the Convention of January, 1927, voted to elect the crucial National Executive Committee, which ran both the FOCh and the party.[102]

Attempts at coordinated action between the various segments of the urban labor movement ended in failure. We have already seen that the tenant leagues of 1925 splintered into several factions soon after the Rent Law took effect. In this case, the willingness of the PC and the mutualists to accept the law allowed the government to eventually co-opt and defuse the rent strike movement. Interunion rivalry also sabotaged the last major attempt by organized labor in Santiago and Valparaíso to defend its economic interests: the campaign against Law 4054.

Most urban labor unions did not publicly express any immediate opinion concerning the seven labor laws passed by Congress in September, 1924. The Anarcho-Syndicalists had in the past condemned social legislation *per se*, but remained silent about the 1924 laws. The FOCh did not come to a decision regarding the laws until November, 1924, when a series of articles written by L. V. Cruz in *Justicia* urged the FOCh to adopt the RILU tactic of using social legislation to further revolutionary ends. Very little mention of the labor laws appeared in the working class press between September of 1924 and October, 1925, however. Most union effort was spent on tenant league affairs, strikes, and political activity. The laws themselves were not activated until their regulatory decrees were issued in late 1925 and early 1926, thereby delaying the practical effect they would have on the labor movement.

Of the seven labor laws of 1924, the Obligatory Social Security Law (Law 4054), drew the most criticism from the working class. Under its terms, all persons fifty-five years of age or younger earning a wage of less than $26.66 per day (all workers earned less than that amount) were required to pay 2 percent of their wages to a Social Security Fund. Employers contributed a sum amounting to 3 percent of each worker's wage into the Fund. Self-employed workers were required to pay 3-1/2 percent of their earnings to the Fund and were heavily fined for noncompliance. The Fund provided sickness and disability payments to contributors and a retirement stipend for those fifty-five years of age or older.

Labor chose to attack this law in particular because it adversely affected nearly all working people, while the trade union and collective bargaining laws threatened only the Anarcho-Syndicalists and Communists. Few workers or petty merchants could afford a deduction of 2 or 3-1/2 percent of their

237

income, especially at a time of high inflation. Neither did most workers live long enough to draw their retirement pension. Mutual aid society members feared that the state would usurp the function of their own organizations and that the funds they had already contributed towards their retirement and social security would be lost. In short, many workers tended to agree with the Anarchist definition of Law 4054 as "legal robbery."

The mutualists and Anarcho-Syndicalists began to criticize the law during the months of June and July, 1925. A National Mutualist Congress voted to urge Health and Social Welfare Minister José Santos Salas to revise Law 4054 to place the entire burden of payment on employers rather than workers. By early November, the Anarcho-Syndicalists in Valparaíso organized a Committee in Favor of the Abolition of Law 4054 to combat the law, and their comrades in Santiago quickly followed suit.[103] On November 29, another Mutualist Congress in Santiago voted to support the anti-4054 committee in its effort to abolish the law. The movement spread rapidly to other cities in the Center-South. Virtually all of the Anarcho-Syndicalist federations, resistance unions, and mutual aid societies had enlisted by early December. As far as the Anarchists were concerned, they had discovered another issue around which they could mount a campaign of direct action and mass mobilization. The tenant leagues had already been neutralized by the government, and many hoped that this new effort would bear richer fruit.

Preoccupied with their elections and generally less attentive to issues of economic importance within the working class, the Communists were the last to jump on the anti-4054 bandwagon. On December 10, 1925, the provincial council of the FOCh in Valparaíso voted to reject Laws 4054 and 4057 (the Labor Union Law) and reform 4053 (work contracts).[104] The Santiago section also expressed its willingness to support the anti-4054 committee.

Law 4054 took effect on January 22, 1926. Immediately afterward, the Anarchist-led anti-4054 committee began planning a general work stoppage in Santiago and Valparaíso to demand that the law be rescinded. Monday, February 22, was settled on as the day for the protest walkout. All working class organizations in Santiago, including the Anarcho-Syndicalist federations (printers, bakers, shoe, metal, and construction workers, and tailors), the FORCh, the mutual aid societies, and the provincial council of the FOCh, pledged their adherence.[105] The walkout would be the most impressive since the May 1 rallies of the early 1920s. Workers in Valparaíso eventually decided not to hold a similar event.

Interunion rivalry prevented the general work stoppage of February 20 from reaching its full potential. Fearful of participating in a movement directed by the Anarcho-Syndicalists, the Federal Executive Council of the FOCh on February 15 forbade its member organizations from taking part in the affair.[106] Its hypocritical reason for doing so was because the FOCh could not enter a movement of such magnitude unless it received the approval of all of its unions. Without consulting the locals, however, the Executive Council in the same breath ordered its own one-day protest rally against Law 4054 for March 8.

Under pressure from above, the Santiago concejos of the FOCh announced that they would not strike on February 20. The Anarchists were furious, but could not dissuade the Santiago fochistas from obeying their bosses. The walkout took place as planned, and the city was completely shut down except for the trams and busses, which were controlled by the FOCh.[107] When the law remained in effect, *Justicia* chided the Anarcho-Syndicalists for not producing any results with their work stoppage.

Having partly sabotaged the Anarcho-Syndicalist rally, the FOCh proceeded with its own protest work stoppage. Its campaign received the aid of the "respectable" press of Santiago (*La Nación, El Mercurio*), which printed in bold type the FOCh press releases announcing the protest.[108] Evidently, the adherence of the empleados to the FOCh walkout and the respectability of the PC, with its deputies and senator, had legitimized the affair. Besides, the FOCh was scheduled to present a petition in the proper fashion to "his most Excellent Señor President" Figueroa. As always, the fact that no trams were running on March 8 impressed the average onlooker, who had no idea if the city's factories and construction projects operated. The FOCh, of course, declared its walkout to have been a great success, despite the government's refusal to abolish Law 4054. One month after the FOCh-UECh work stoppage, the PC completely purged its Santiago section, perhaps because of the original intention of the provincial council of the FOCh to cooperate with the Anarcho-Syndicalists.

Labor union activity ground to a near-halt during most of 1926. The Anarcho-Syndicalists pressed ahead with the anti-4054 campaign, but could do nothing to prevent the law from slowly taking effect. In like fashion to 1921, the Communists organized unemployed nitrate workers in Santiago into a "various trades" council for purposes of street agitation. It was not until the anti-4054 work stoppages led by the Shoeworkers' Federation (UIC) in late 1926 that the urban labor unions showed much enthusiasm for action.

The UIC remained, along with the FOICh, the most powerful and prestigious of the Santiago labor unions. It still controlled several thousand workers in shoe factories and tanneries and formed other local unions in Valparaíso and Concepción.[109] In September of 1926, the UIC reached the conclusion that pressure against Law 4054 should be placed on employers rather than the government, and therefore declared that any shoe factory deducting the 2 percent from wages would be immediately struck. To demonstrate the seriousness of its warning, the UIC staged a half-day work stoppage on Septem-

239

ber 30, the day before the first deduction was to be made. Employers in the leather industry as well as most others in Santiago and Valparaíso voiced "strong opposition" to Law 4054, since it nominally cost them an additional 3 percent in wages and placed an extra clerical burden on their employees.[110] A Labor Office survey found that only 29 percent of manufacturing establishments in Chile which employed women complied with Law 4054 in April, 1926. In October, however, the shoe factories of Santiago intended to make the first 2 percent deduction, triggering an indefinite general strike by the UIC, which was seconded by the other Anarcho-Syndicalist unions and the mutualists. In an uncommon show of solidarity, the FOCh tram workers, this time with PC approval, declared a one-day walkout on October 5. The government eventually convinced the workers to call off their strike and join in forming a committee of worker, employer, and government representatives to reform the law. Labor's willingness to cancel its general walkout is a clear indication of its lack of strength.

The ill-fated general strike on January, 1927, proved to be the labor movement's last gasp. It was inspired by the first sign of serious discontent among railroad workers that had surfaced in several years. The State Railways had recently broken the terms of an earlier law by ordering their employees to work longer than eight hours per day. Railway workers were also dissatisfied with the operation of their retirement fund. In early January, 1927, the Confederación Ferroviaria, heir to the Federación Ferroviaria of earlier years, began seeking the support of other unions for a general strike to force the government into granting its demands.[111] A Central Strike Committee representing many sectors of the organized working class of Santiago decided to hold a national one-day work stoppage on January 17 and then allow any group wishing to continue the strike to do so. Each participating organization put forward its own particular demand for the government to meet. No petitions were to be sent to employers.

The general work stoppage of January 17 demonstrated the divisions, weakness, and lack of direction of the urban labor movement of 1925–27. No single issue was at stake, but rather a score of them. The anti-4054 committee demanded that the government abolish one law, while the empleados of the UECh urged that it fully enforce another (4059). The Bakers' Union hoped the strike would result in the application of the Night Work Law, the Teachers' Association wanted educational reform, the FOCh demanded full employment, etc. It was thought that a massive display of unity on the part of organized labor would bring these reforms about. The government, however, knew that such patchwork alliances had failed in the past and took the necessary steps to assure the failure of this one.

On January 15, two days before the strike, the government announced that it would soon meet all of the demands of the railway workers and warned

240

that sufficient numbers of strikebreakers were available to keep the trains running. The Unión Ferroviaria, a rival of the Confederación Ferroviaria, and the Federación Santiago Watt of engineers and firemen vowed not to participate in the strike. Fearing that the walkout would achieve no more practical effect than the 4054 strike in November of 1926, the FOCh teamsters and tram workers also decided to remain on the job. When the strike occurred on January 16, most trains, busses, and trams ran on schedule. Past experience had shown that no general strike in Santiago could have the appearance of success without the solidarity of the tram workers. In this case, the general work stoppage was in every sense a disaster because the factory and construction workers of the FORCh did not take part either. The IWW closed the port of San Antonio almost completely, but the work stoppage attracted little support in Valparaíso and other provincial capitals. To make certain that the failure of the walkout would be complete, police in Santiago and Valparaíso arrested scores of workers and disrupted their public rallies. Only a section of the railway workers stayed out after the first day, and eventually achieved the reforms which the government promised before the strike occurred.

The weak and divided urban labor movement of February, 1927, bore scant resemblance to the vigorous, combative unions of 1919–21. The FOCh was little more than a paper organization in Santiago and Valparaíso, unable to control the activities of the last of its powerful branches, the teamsters and tram workers. Anarcho-Syndicalists had failed to halt the application of Law 4054 and saw their once-active tenant leagues rendered helpless by government co-optation and internal dissent. Aggressive employers forced the bakers of the USP to accept night work despite a law to the contrary. Few unions retained much bargaining leverage *vis-à-vis* their bosses, perhaps only those of printers, shoeworkers, and the skilled building trades. Efforts to win benefits from the government through general strikes or political action failed. Eventually, the labor laws of 1924 would challenge the very existence of those labor unions which managed to retain their organizational identity despite the anti-union activities of employers and the state.

On February 23, 1927, Colonel Carlos Ibáñez del Campo decreed the end of the independent urban labor movement. A declaration was posted throughout the country which stated:[112]

> In view of the activities of limited groups of politicians and Communists, daily becoming more anarchistic, the government has abandoned the position of harmony which it was maintaining and will now exercise its authority without vacillation or irresolution. Henceforth, there will be in Chile neither Communism nor Anarchism.

Ibáñez meant what he said. Since the abdication of Alessandri in October,

1925, he had, with the armed forces behind him, maneuvered himself into a position of de facto control of the Figueroa government. Shortly before the declaration of February 23, Ibáñez assumed the position of Vice-President and Minister of the Interior, giving him control of police and carabineros as well as the army. To completely consolidate his power en route to establishing himself as a military dictator, he needed to remove the last vestiges of opposition which remained: the labor movement and a handful of unfriendly politicians.

Both groups fell easy victim to the *golpe* of February 23. At the same time that the declaration was made public, police raided the headquarters of the FORCh, IWW, FOCh, USP, FOICh, UIC, and other working class organizations.[113] Leading Anarchists and Communists were dragged from their homes in massive roundups designed to leave the working class leaderless. Arrested workers were held in military prisons, barracks, and warships as the purge continued. No other act of repression in the past matched the scope and effectiveness of the blow Ibáñez aimed at labor. Within weeks, all major labor leaders in Chile had been arrested, gone into hiding, or fled the country.[114] Labor unions collapsed or operated clandestinely until Ibáñez formed legal unions to take their place. PC leaders and congressmen joined the union men in prison, and in March, the party itself was declared illegal. For the first time, thousands of Chilean workers suffered imprisonment at the same time.[115]

Further raids netted additional labor union prisoners throughout 1927. Ibáñez shipped many of them off to the penal colony on Más Afuera Island of the Juan Fernández Group, some 360 miles west of Valparaíso.[116] Others were sent to newly established prison camps in the far south of Chile. For all practical purposes, Ibáñez encountered no resistance to his coup. The labor unions had been aware of the growing influence he exercised over the Figueroa government and predicted the eventual establishment of military rule, but when the blow was struck, they were helpless to prevent it. Although the coup immediately shut down the working class press, clandestine newspapers and handbills condemning the Ibáñez government frequently appeared in Chilean cities.[117] Argentine Anarchists welcomed their Chilean compañeros and provided them with the funds necessary to carry out anti-Ibáñez propaganda from Buenos Aires.[118]

It was not until the fall of Ibáñez in 1931, however, that labor could once again operate in the open. The *golpe* of February, 1927, effectively brought an end to the nonpolitical independent labor union movement in Chile. Although weakened by economic fluctuations, lockouts, repression, co-optation, and "social legislation," it had up to that time maintained its organizational integrity. The labor movement of the 1930s would travel a different road, that leading to domination by political parties.

Conclusion:
The Growth and Nature
of the Labor Movement

THE CHILEAN LABOR MOVEMENT of 1902-27 developed on a step-by-step basis. No single law, organization, individual, or event before 1924 had any crucial effect on its long-term growth. The rise and consolidation of the labor movement was linked to fluctuations in the nitrate economy. Labor unions generally were organized and expanded in times of prosperity, and disappeared or went into decline during major recessions and depressions. Before 1917, economic crisis resulted in the demise of many labor unions, but after that date, most key unions achieved sufficient organizational stability to weather even the most severe depression. The years 1902 to 1927 can be divided into four periods of expansion and decline in the size and effectiveness of the labor movement:

1902–May, 1907:	expansion
June, 1907–1909:	decline
1910–August, 1914:	expansion
Sept., 1914–1916:	decline
1917–August, 1921:	expansion
Sept., 1921–1923:	decline
1924–June, 1925:	expansion
July, 1925–1927:	decline

While the labor movement had periods of severe retrogression, in each case major unions were able to regroup their strength. The recovery of the labor movement and its further growth between 1917 and 1920 were spectacular. It is likely that labor unions in Santiago and Valparaíso contained more members in 1919-20 than at any other time before 1927, although union strength was also great in the years 1924-25.

Unions in the skilled manufacturing trades and in transportation enjoyed the greatest organizational stability and economic success between 1902 and 1927. Those industries which were first unionized in 1902-7 generally remained the center of labor union activity during the entire period. They included printing, baking, leather, wood, railroads, urban tramways, metallurgy, construction, marine transport, and garments. Unions in some industries (printing, furniture making, construction) prospered because of the high level of skill needed to perform the jobs involved. The relative prosperity and high level of competition in other industries (shoes, tanning, woodwork, metallurgy, garments) aided workers in establishing leverage in bargaining with their employers. Workers in industries of a public service nature or those crucial to the infrastructure of the Chilean economy (baking, tramways, railroads, marine transport) also enjoyed organizational stability.

The least effective or stable unions were formed by workers in the glass, textile, brewing, tobacco, food processing, and match industries. A number of factors inhibited the growth of unions, including the monopolistic nature of several of these industries, the high percentage of women and children employed, the low skills involved in production, and the availability of strikebreakers. Women proved willing and enthusiastic labor unionists when organized alongside men in the same industry, especially in the case of shoe factories, but were unable to sustain unions in establishments where they stood alone.

The nature of the Chilean economy in the early twentieth century effectively limited the growth potential of the urban labor movement. Boom/bust cycles in nitrate production were felt throughout other sectors of the national economy, resulting in periods of widespread unemployment. As shown in chapter 1, industrial production rose only slightly between 1913 and 1927, and few new jobs were created in manufacturing. The industrial base on which labor unions in Chile might have expanded therefore remained virtually fixed. When rapid expansion and higher productivity took place in an industry, such as in shoes from 1916 to 1920 and metallurgy in the 1920s, labor unions in those industries also prospered, but such developments were rare. Unions in the construction industry and in railway maintenance suffered whenever state revenues from the tax on nitrate exports fell and government spending was curtailed. The stagnation of the nitrate industry and only sluggish growth in manufacturing output from 1920 to 1927 prevented the organized labor movement from duplicating the kind of expansion that it achieved between 1917 and 1920.

Other factors inhibited the growth of the labor movement, perhaps the most important being the tenacious and unabated opposition of Chilean and foreign employers to labor organizations. Repression by the state often hampered the activities of unions and limited their potential for expansion. Because of the reluctance of members to pay their dues, labor unions found themselves in continuous poverty. Most unions required very low monthly dues payments and initiation fees because of the chronic difficulty workers faced in meeting basic expenses for food, shelter, and clothing. Rampant inflation assaulted the urban worker during much of the 1902–27 period, a factor which ironically stimulated labor union activity while at the same time it limited the ability of union members to pay their dues.

The Chilean labor movement from 1902 to 1927 was characterized by decentralization. Despite the efforts of Marxist historians and those who have drawn upon their work to portray it as a powerful, majority force among organized workers in Chile, the FOCh was a unified and national organization in name only. Its strength in the coal mining zone and in a few northern ports may have been considerable, but FOCh concejos in Valparaíso and Santiago exercised minimal influence as economic entities. In terms of membership, the FOCh by all indications contained only a small fraction of the numbers attributed to it by nearly all students of Chilean labor history. The Communist Party of Chile was also a weak organization whose base of power was confined to workers in Iquique, Antofagasta, and the coal zone. Because they lacked a sizable following in Santiago and Valparaíso, Chile's main centers of industry, population, commerce, and transportation, the FOCh and the PC must be viewed not as national institutions, but as regionally and industrially based organizations of significant yet limited influence.

Anarcho-Syndicalists dominated the most important and effective labor unions in Santiago and Valparaíso. The first "resistance societies," or job-related unions of an ideological character, were splinter groups from mutual aid societies. Most at first contained workers of only one craft or plant, but at the height of the resistance society movement in 1905–7, some (shoes, printing, furniture, baking) began to consolidate their position on an industrial basis. From 1917 onward, nearly all major unions in Santiago and Valparaíso came under the influence of Anarcho-Syndicalism, including those of printing, baking, construction, garment, marine transport, leather, and metal workers. The failure of the Anarcho-Syndicalists to form a national or even a regional organization from their many unions resulted in part from interunion rivalry but also from the natural aversion of most libertarians to centralized authority. While the IWW did briefly organize marine and construction workers in several cities on an industrial basis, industrial unionism normally did not cross municipal lines. The Shoeworkers' and Printers' Federations claimed adherents in cities other than Santiago and Valparaíso, but all member unions functioned in complete autonomy. Autonomous unions confined to workers of a single industry and city thus characterized the organized labor movement in Santiago and Valparaíso.

Urban workers were divided by ideology as well as organization in urban Chile, especially after 1921. Formal revolutionary ideology spread slowly from 1902 to approximately 1920, but afterwards gained widespread acceptance among most labor leaders. Anarcho-Syndicalism was the ideological tendency which achieved broadest appeal in Santiago and Valparaíso, mainly because it fitted the needs of most workers in those cities. The libertarian

245

insistence on direct economic action in winning higher wages appealed to mutual aid society members who no longer were satisfied with passive steps. The disdain which Anarcho-Syndicalists held for politics struck a responsive chord among workers, who perceived the futility of attempting socioeconomic reform through elections. The fact that Anarcho-Syndicalist union leaders were nearly all Chilean citizens and workers with no aspirations toward middle class status doubtless impressed urban workers. Their willingness to suffer unemployment, arrest, and imprisonment for the good of the union was well known. Finally, Chilean Anarchists seldom led the rank and file into fruitless general strikes whose aims were political rather than economic. Anarcho-Syndicalism in Chile had revolutionary ends, but it never ignored the basic economic needs of workers.

Catholic labor unions won little support from organized workers in Santiago and Valparaíso. The FOCh did make notable gains among textile, railway, tram, brewery, food processing, and glass workers in those cities between 1918 and 1921, but employer resistance, economic conditions, and ideological infighting left the FOCh concejos totally destroyed or weakened by 1922. Those within the FOCh who dreamed of forming a working class political party eventually won control of the organization in 1921, but the Communist federation which emerged from the radical-reformist struggle enjoyed far less power than its basically nonpolitical predecessor had. Independent Socialists attempted at times to make inroads within the working class, but failed to generate a popular following.

By 1925, the only important labor unions in Chile which had not officially declared themselves to be Anarcho-Syndicalist or Communist were those of railroad workers. The general strike of June, 1907, which resulted in pay at a fixed rate of exchange to the gold peso for shop workers, set the railwaymen on a path toward conservatism. Government officials eventually came to realize that the threat of revolutionary unionism among railway workers could be defused by further reforms. Soon after breaking the general railway strike of 1916 by force, the state extended a series of benefits far superior to those enjoyed by the mass of working people to all employees of the State Railways. Railway workers as a consequence did not engage in any major strike activity throughout the turbulent period of 1917–21. Job security guaranteed by a strict seniority system and an obligatory no-strike contract signed by engineers and firemen practically assured their loyalty to the state. These highly paid men formed their own mutual aid society and remained aloof from the activities of lower-ranked workers. Railway workers split from the FOCh at the time of its takeover by the Communists and went on to form a series of conservative federations in the middle 1920s.

While preferential treatment by the State Railway turned ferrocarrileros into conservatives between 1907 and 1918, most other unions were gradually radicalized. The appeal of Anarcho-Syndicalism to workers in Santiago and Valparaíso has already been mentioned, but these people would not have embraced a revolutionary ideology had they, like the railwaymen, been placated with reform legislation or wage concessions from employers. Instead, the urban worker operated as an individual in a system of industrial relations which pitted him against his employer in an unregulated contest of strength. No laws had any practical effect on his job conditions, work contract, form of pay, job security, hours of work, wages, or any aspect of his relationship with his boss. Women and children labored under essentially the same conditions as men, with no one to protect them from overwork and low wages. Periodic increases in unemployment plunged thousands of urban workers into a state of utter destitution, while inflation ate away at real wages in more prosperous times. Workers in Santiago and Valparaíso for the most part inhabited conventillos, whose high rents and unspeakable hygienic conditions were a further cause of misery.

Few workers could scale the ladder of social mobility and thus escape their dismal existence. Opportunities for economic advancement were reserved for those with higher education, either traditional or technical, but few working class children completed even the first years of elementary school.

Held in check by a lack of upward social mobility, Chilean workers could neither count on formal politics nor elitist philanthropy to better their lot. A few scraps of "social legislation" were tossed their way by Congress, generally as a result of violent mass protest, but the prospect of basic reform from above must have seemed remote to most workers. Countless petitions went unanswered, and many campaigns seeking specific reforms failed. Employers respected little more than force in their relationship with workers. The state rarely intervened except to repress. Mutual aid societies were incapable of standing up to employers or influencing the state to take legislative action on behalf of the working class. No significant political party adequately represented the needs of urban workers.

The acceptance of Anarcho-Syndicalist unions by workers in Santiago and Valparaíso is therefore understandable. Unions embued with revolutionary zeal and some good ideas for improving the here-and-now gained steady and lasting support during the entire period because the causes of working class unrest and alienation did not disappear between 1902 and 1927. The laissez-faire system of industrial relations remained in effect. As the militant resistance societies gained support after 1902, strikes often more closely resembled industrial warfare than labor disputes. Frequent repression by the state and die-hard resistance from employers won new converts to the Anarchist fold. By the early 1920s revolutionary ideology had become a permanent characteristic of the organized working class.

247

The radicalization of Chilean labor therefore resulted from the day-to-day struggle of unions to represent the economic needs of workers. During the early years, only a handful of people in each union may have been convinced Anarchists or social revolutionaries, but their numbers increased. The Bolshevik Revolution and contact with the Anarcho-Syndicalist and Communist Internationals of the 1920s stimulated the further growth of revolutionary unionism in Chile. It must be remembered, however, that foreign agitators played no significant part in the radicalization of the Chilean working class. Instead, the growth of ideologically oriented labor unions began when urban workers turned to the Anarchists as the only members of their own class or any other which offered them hope for a better future. Few workers may have cared if that future entailed a social revolution, as long as the road to utopia was paved with gold. Whether convinced ideologues or bread-and-butter materialists (or both), most Chilean union men stuck by their organizations and were not enticed by Catholic or reformist currents of thought.

UNIONS AND EMPLOYERS

The attitude of employers, both foreign and native, regarding labor unions stimulated the spread of revolutionary ideologies within the working class. With few exceptions, employers in Chile were overwhelmingly hostile to labor unions. Until 1902, employers had been able to deal with their workers on an individual basis, purchasing labor power at whatever price the worker would accept and exercising complete control over the performance of work. The resistance societies gave a momentary advantage to the worker by enhancing his bargaining position. Strikes generally proved necessary for winning wage increases during the 1902–8 period, since employers were not inclined to raise wages unless forced to do so. Many bosses refused to acknowledge the de facto existence of labor unions by recognizing union leaders as bargaining agents, although some were forced to. In times of economic hardship, however, employers quickly scrapped all previous agreements with their workers, fired union leaders, or locked out the entire workforce in order to rid themselves of unions.

Most employers maintained their "rugged individualism" until the strike wave of 1917–20. Unions before then lacked the organizational stability necessary to deal with bosses on a continuous basis. The threat of labor unionism appeared periodically in most establishments, but a single failed strike often resulted in the union's demise. Jealous of their managerial prerogatives, employers in Chile opposed the few social laws passed by Congress before 1924 and learned to sidestep their stipulations. Employers vigorously condemned the labor laws of 1924 and resisted their application, despite the fact that the laws were designed to hobble labor unions.

During labor's great resurgence in 1917–20, employers suddenly found themselves in a disadvantageous position. New unions in printing, shoes, baking, textiles, construction, and transportation proved far more difficult to handle than the resistance societies of the previous decade. Strike after successful strike forced the beleaguered employers to give up hitherto undreamed-of concessions, including the written recognition of unions as bargaining agents. Early attempts to counterattack with employer associations and lockouts, such as that of the Santiago shoe factory owners in 1918, ended in total failure.

By 1921, however, depression and government repression had seriously weakened the labor movement, and employers began to organize themselves more efficiently. Employer associations in Chile had once before (1907) appeared near the end of a strike wave, but dissolved themselves once the threat was eliminated. Like the new unions of the 1920s, employer associations headed by the national Asociación del Trabajo were intended to be permanent organizations. The lockouts of 1921–23 in many cases halted and rolled back union gains won during the previous years.

The hostility of employers to labor unions both fostered and preserved a system of industrial relations based on conflict rather than consensus. Bosses resisted union demands with what at times resembled fanaticism. Tram companies, bakery owners, and steamship companies were especially zealous in defending their perceived "rights" as employers. Tram workers, bakers, and marine workers consequently resorted to violence with greater frequency than did other workers during their strikes. Unwilling to accept government interference in strikes which held out even a faint possibility of being broken, employers prolonged many industrial conflicts when a conciliatory settlement could easily have been reached. The Valparaíso maritime strike of 1903 is an excellent example of employer intransigence leading to labor violence and bloodshed. Such events opened the eyes of increasing numbers of workers to the brutality directed against them by the state and their bosses. Political elites rather than employers were first to realize that the extra-legal industrial relations system in Chile had resulted in an independent, radicalized, and potentially dangerous labor movement.

INDUSTRIAL CONFLICT

The number of strikes which took place in Chile increased rapidly between 1902 and 1927. At the beginning of the period, labor walkouts were rare in Santiago and Valparaíso. Mutual aid societies, which constituted the only form of labor organization in those cities at the turn of the century, did not consider the strike a valid tactic for improving the economic lot of workers.

249

When resistance societies began drawing workers away from the mutualist movement after 1902, strikes became much more commonplace. Urban Chile experienced its first real "strike wave" between late 1905 and 1907.

Strikes in Chile were extra-legal in the sense that no legislation dealt with them. Workers therefore had no fear of their walkouts being declared illegal by the courts, but neither could they count on the right to picket or conduct strikes without state intervention. The unregulated nature of strikes before 1925 contributed to the radicalization of the labor movement by allowing many industrial conflicts to terminate in violence. The labor laws of 1924 established legal procedures to be followed before strikes could be initiated, but the laissez-faire system of industrial relations which governed labor conflicts prior to that time remained in effect until the Ibáñez coup of February, 1927.

The three great strike waves of the period studied (1905-7, 1917-21, 1924-25) all took place in times of inflation and reasonably full employment. They ended when economic crisis and government repression made successful strike action nearly impossible. General strikes normally occurred when a strike wave was in full swing, and their usual lack of success acted as a brake on further walkouts. The strike wave of 1905-7 culminated in the general strike of June, 1907. The unsuccessful general strike of September, 1919, greatly slowed the strike wave of 1918-19, while the massacre of nitrate workers at La Coruña in June, 1925, and repression elsewhere, brought the strike wave of 1924-25 to a halt.

A brief examination of the strike statistics gathered for the years 1902-8, 1917-21, and 1925 will shed more light on the nature of industrial conflict and labor unions in Chile. During these three periods, at least 380 strikes took place in the central cities. Of these 380, 285 occurred in Santiago, ninety-three in Valparaíso, and two in both cities. Table A. 1 (Appendix) demonstrates a seasonal imbalance in the occurrence of strikes. More strikes began in April (13.4 percent of the total) than any other month, followed by March (10.5 percent), June (10.8 percent), and May (10.5 percent). Only sixteen strikes, 4.2 percent of the total number, were initiated in September. Workers may have been more strike-prone during the autumn months (March-June) because food prices were normally lower due to the harvest, and the coming of winter promised higher expenses for clothing and fuel. September was the month of fewest strikes probably because workers did not wish to ruin their five-day celebration of Dieciocho by striking or spending the money they might have saved for the festivities. From this we can conclude that much forethought went into the preparation of strikes in urban Chile.

A breakdown of strikes by industry (table A.2) demonstrates a very high occurrence (31 percent of the total) of strikes in the shoe and leather industry.

The union tactic of isolating a single employer to be struck at one time caused this imbalance. Printers also showed themselves to be strike-prone (10 percent of the total), followed by textile, construction, and metal workers. Eleven percent of all strikes occurred among transport workers.

Some 60 percent of all strikes involved between fifty and 500 strikers (table A.3). Almost no strikes occurred in small-scale establishments, but strikes of less than ten workers would in any case have gone unnoticed by the press. Strikes in Valparaíso tended to involve many more workers than those in Santiago, reflecting the large-scale nature of most industries there, as well as the need for solidarity and coordinated action in maritime strikes. For example, a third of all strikes in Valparaíso involved 1,000 workers or more, while in Santiago, only 10 percent of all strikes reached similar proportions. As can be expected, transport strikes normally affected large numbers of workers, but a high percentage of strikes in baking and printing were also large-scale because the Printers' and Bakers' Federations struck on an industry-wide basis. (Table A.4.)

Strikes tended to be of increasingly long duration between 1902 and 1925, indicating that both workers and employers were willing and able to extend the length of strikes. This trend runs opposite to the tendency towards successively shorter strikes in early twentieth-century Europe.[1] The mean duration of strikes in Santiago and Valparaíso rose from eleven days in 1902–8 to fourteen in 1917–21 and fifteen in 1925. On the average, strikes in the metal industry were the longest (twenty-six days, mean), followed by textiles (twenty days) and shoes (nineteen days). (Table A.5.) Railroad, tram, and printing strikes on the average lasted a much shorter time. In the first two cases, early settlement resulted from rapid government intervention, while printing strikes ended quickly because employers normally capitulated to union demands after only brief resistance.

Statistics for the sex of striking workers demonstrate two major changes over time. (Table A.6.) The number of strikes involving both men and women jumped from 18 percent of the total in 1902–8 to 37 percent in 1917–21 and 1925. The larger percentages reflect the success of shoe and textile factory workers in organizing unions which integrated both sexes. Women rarely formed their own labor unions or went on strike by themselves, but combined with men, they played an important role in labor disputes after 1917. The reduction in the number of strikes involving children from 20 percent of the total in 1902–8 to 2 percent in 1917–21 bears witness to the success of many labor unions (in printing and metallurgy, especially) in virtually eliminating child labor from their industries. The decline of children as a percentage of the total workforce was, however, slight in comparison to the number of strikes involving child workers. Throughout the period, all-male strikes accounted for at least half of the total number.

251

The great majority of strikes in Chile during the 1902–27 period were undertaken by organized workers. Table A.7 demonstrates that at least 82 percent of all strikes began with a conflict involving workers who had organized their union before walking off the job. In a number of cases, workers formed their unions after declaring a strike, so that nearly 90 percent of all strikes ended with workers in an unionized state (table A.8). On the average, and with very little change over time, 80 percent of all striking groups presented their employers with a grievance petition before going on strike (table A.9). It can be fairly stated, therefore, that the great majority of strikes in Santiago and Valparaíso during the entire period were planned rather than spontaneous affairs.

Anarcho-Syndicalists were involved in at least two-thirds of all strikes taking place in Santiago and Valparaíso during each of the three periods studied. Table A.10 shows that the resistance societies (of Anarchist orientation) led 67 percent of all strikes during 1902–8, while in 1917–21, the various Anarcho-Syndicalist groups (the Anarchist federations, resistance societies, and IWW) participated in 72 percent of the total. At the peak of its strength between 1917 and 1921, the FOCh participated in forty-six different strikes, while the combined Anarcho-Syndicalist groups took part in 148, more than three times as many. In 1925, the Anarcho-Syndicalist dominance was even greater —thirty-seven strikes to seven for the FOCh. These figures add further evidence to support my conclusions regarding the weakness of the FOCh vis-à-vis the Anarcho-Syndicalists in Santiago and Valparaíso.

The great majority of strikes during the entire period were directed against private employers (table A.11). Frequent railroad worker strikes between 1902 and 1908 accounted for the higher (12) percentage of strikes against the state in that period. After the railway unions received special benefits in 1911, 1917, and 1918, the number of strikes against state enterprises fell to between 2 and 3 percent of the total in 1917–21 and 1925, while the percentage of strikes against private employers rose even higher.

Figures for the primary response of employers to strikes reinforce the conclusion that bosses in Santiago and Valparaíso maintained a continuously strong resistance to labor unions and were unwilling to compromise with their workers. Table A.12 reveals that the great majority of employers immediately and entirely rejected the grievance petitions presented them by workers during all three periods, although this response was proportionately higher in 1925. In very few cases (none in 1925) did employers offer an immediate compromise solution. The relatively higher, but numerically low compromise figure for 1917–21 reflects the favorable bargaining position enjoyed by most workers during those years. The continued opposition of employers to labor unions and the economic demands of workers played a critical role in the radicalization of the organized labor movement between 1902 and 1927.

Employers recruited blacklegs in slightly more than one-third of all strikes, with almost no variation during the three periods (table A.13). The use of strikebreakers did, however, vary greatly from industry to industry. As table A.14 indicates, bakery owners recruited strikebreakers during nearly all (88 percent) of the strikes affecting their industry, followed by the tram companies (71 percent) and employers in the marine transport industry (58.3 percent). The state supplied blacklegs to both private employers and government agencies in 25 percent of cases in which strikebreakers were used. Employers in most instances did not introduce scab labor in their establishments until the strike was two weeks old. Table A.15 shows that the occurrence of blackleg labor rose quickly between the second and fourth week of the strike and that those strikes which lasted from thirty-one to sixty days were in three-fourths of all cases marked by the presence of strikebreakers.

A token force of police was by law ordered to the scene of each strike, but additional contingents of police, carabineros, or members of the armed forces became involved in 40 percent of strikes for which there is complete information (table A.16). This figure can be compared to the lower percentage (25) of strikes in which government intervention took the form of nonforceful mediation or arbitration. The state therefore showed itself considerably more inclined to use force than its good offices in settling strikes.

One-fourth of all strikes resulted in some form of violence between 1902 and 1925, with a slightly higher occurrence of violent strikes in Valparaíso than in Santiago (table A.17). On only three occasions, however, was anyone killed as the result of strike-related violence. Those industries most prone to industrial violence were baking, State Railroad shops, and tramways. In the case of bakers and tram workers, the frequent use of blackleg labor to break their strikes may have triggered violence, although the appearance of strikebreakers does not have any statistical association with the outbreak of violence in most other industries. (See table A.18.) The resistance societies were at first inclined to use aggressive tactics in their strikes, accounting in part for the high incidence of violence in tram and railroad maestranza strikes. The occurrence of violence in strikes remained near the 25 percent level during each of the three chronological periods studied, further indication that the laissez-faire industrial relations system changed very little over time.

One factor which does appear to have been closely associated with the outbreak of violence during strikes is the duration of the strike. Table A.19 clearly demonstrates that the longer a strike lasted, the greater was the chance for the violence to erupt. The unwillingness of employers to conciliate or compromise during many strikes had much to do, therefore, with the strikes' extension and the subsequent outbreak of violence.

As noted in chapter 6, the percentage of strikes settled by mediation and arbitration rose from only 13 percent of the total during the 1902–8 period to 34 percent in 1925 (table A.20). The willingness of the FOCh to engage in mediation and the frequent invocation of the Yáñez Decree in 1918 and 1919 were the main causes of this rise. Only five cases of strikes ending in binding arbitration occurred during the entire period. An industry-by-industry breakdown demonstrates that the ideology of the union involved and the nature of work in the struck industry greatly influenced the settlement of strikes (table A.21). We see, for example, that workers in the skilled trades who were normally Anarcho-Syndicalists, such as printers, construction tradesmen, wood-workers, and metal workers, seldom allowed their strikes to be mediated or arbitrated. In semiskilled and unskilled industries organized by the Anarcho-Syndicalists (shoemaking, tanning, baking), strikes also had lower than average rates of mediation and arbitration. The only Anarcho-Syndicalist groups which consistently allowed their strikes to be settled through mediation were those of the marine transport workers, probably because the government pressed them and their employers to come to terms quickly to avoid the serious economic effects caused by an extended shipping strike. Most of the strikes settled by mediation involved workers in industries organized by the FOCh, including tramways, glass, food processing, textiles, and communications.

Remarkably, and to a certain extent inexplicably, strikes by workers in Santiago and Valparaíso were highly successful. Table A.22 demonstrates that on the average, more than twice as many strikes ended in total success for workers than in total failure. When the power of the FOCh peaked between 1917 and 1921, the percentage of strikes ending in compromise rose substantially, reflecting the increased occurrence of mediated settlements. Bearing in mind the high success rate indicated in table A.23, it would be fair to say that the urban unions compiled an excellent record in the strikes they undertook.

The fact, however, that almost all strikes analyzed in this study took place in times of reasonably full employment and rapid inflation had much to do with producing settlements favorable to workers. Strike waves broke out when employers were most able to pay higher wages and unions most determined to win benefits. Workers counted on large wage gains in prosperous times to offset inflation and help them weather the periods of unemployment which normally followed. Stagnant or shrinking wages (both in money and real terms) in 1914–16 and 1921–23 gave workers greater incentive to hold out for generous settlements during the strike waves of 1917–20 and 1924–25. Urban workers therefore went on strike mainly when prospects for success were greatest, resulting in a high percentage of favorable settlements. One must take into account real wage losses suffered during less prosperous times before declaring the organized labor movement to be of great effectiveness.

Many factors were associated with the final outcome of strikes. Table A.23 demonstrates a high success rate among printers (63 percent of their total strike settlements), construction workers (59 percent), and metal workers (55 percent), all of whom were highly skilled or organized industrially with workers having high skills. Tram drivers and conductors, marine transport workers, and textile factory workers, all semiskilled or unskilled, had the highest rates of failure. A breakdown of final results according to the union which led the strike demonstrates that the Anarcho-Syndicalists won more favorable settlements than the FOCh. By combining the scores for complete success of the three types of Anarcho-Syndicalist unions (resistance societies, Anarchist federations, the IWW) in table A.24 and comparing them to the FOCh's record, we see that the Anarcho-Syndicalists were completely successful in 48 percent of their strikes while the FOCh figure was only 16 percent. One reason for the smaller success of the Federación Obrera is found in the manner in which the final settlements of its strikes came about. Table A.25 demonstrates that mediated and arbitrated settlements were less favorable to workers than those brought about by direct conciliation with employers, the normal bargaining tactic of the Anarcho-Syndicalists.

Violence appears in most cases to have worked against a successful settlement for labor, although on several occasions, such as the maritime strike of 1903 in Valparaíso, turmoil and bloodshed brought about a more favorable arrangement than would otherwise have been expected. Table A.26 shows that those strikes marked by violence had failure rates of 46.5 percent as compared to 13.5 percent for violence-free strikes. Conversely, violent strikes succeeded totally in 21 percent of cases as compared to 39 percent for nonviolent strikes. Workers may have become violent when it appeared that their strikes were doomed to failure, thus partially causing the correlation between violence and failure.

The use of strikebreakers appears to have influenced the outcome of many strikes. Table A.27 shows that 34 percent of strikes in which scabs were introduced ended in total failure, as opposed to only 7 percent of strikes free of scab labor. Some 45 percent of blackleg-free strikes ended in total success, compared with only 17 percent of strikes involving scabs.

Unlike the largely successful industrial strikes which took place during the strike wave of 1905–7, 1917–21, and 1925, general strikes between 1902 and 1927 normally failed to achieve their objectives. The first general strike to affect both Santiago and Valparaíso, that of May–June, 1907, won benefits only for the railway workers. General strikes in Valparaíso in 1917 and 1921 resulted in total failure, as did that of September, 1919, in Santiago. During the 1920s, most general strikes were intended to win specific benefits from the state rather than put pressure on private employers. Only when the political leverage of organized labor became enhanced by the instability of government, such as after the military coup of January, 1925, could the unions win any favorable concessions through general strikes and work stoppages. Labor's last attempt at a hybrid political-economic general strike in January, 1927, ended in total defeat.

General strikes failed because the state succeeded in breaking up union solidarity either through naked repression or by co-opting key unions. Governing elites used any and all means at their disposal to settle general strikes as quickly as possible. Concessions, false promises of future arbitration, empty legislation, military strikebreakers, and martial law were all employed at one time or another to enervate general strike movements. The decentralized nature of the organized labor movement shielded it from total repression, but at the same time made coordinated activity more difficult. Even when unions in various industries struck with ostensibly a common purpose in mind, their solidarity could be broken, especially after 1920, when ideological rivalry weakened interunion cohesion. In no case did any general strike between 1902 and 1927 have subversive ends, such as the overthrow of the government.

ORGANIZED LABOR AND THE STATE

The state played a major role in fomenting the spread of revolutionary ideology within the Chilean labor movement of 1902–27. Government participated in the extra-legal system of industrial relations in such a way as to serve the interests of foreign and native employers. The series of weak and unimaginative politicians who ruled Chile during the first two decades of the twentieth century normally held the same laissez-faire views as employers concerning the role of the state in the economy. For that reason, state intervention in labor affairs until 1917 was mainly limited to repressing strikes and disturbances which threatened to upset the social or economic status quo. Because of its overwhelming dependence on nitrate exports, the state did not hesitate to take action whenever a strike seriously disrupted the production and transport of that mineral. Employers in many instances forced the state to take a more actively hostile position with organized labor than it would perhaps have wished to by creating crisis situations during strikes, which could be resolved only by the intervention of the armed forces. The state therefore became identified, along with capital, as the enemy of organized labor, and as labor's hostility towards employers deepened, so did its alienation from the state.

It was not until the so-called "social question" reached alarming urgency that political elites in Chile began to consider formal means for controlling the labor movement. Until 1919, stopgap measures, such as short-term repression or superficial reforms aimed at temporarily allaying a particular grievance, normally held urban workers in check. The paltry "social legislation" passed by Congress or executive decree during this time came more as the result of pressure from below than the philanthropic urge of politicians.

Labor's resurgence in 1917 and the strike wave of 1918–19 caused deep concern among elites. The massive rallies of the AOAN prompted Congress to pass a residence law in November, 1918, and grant state of siege powers to the President two months later. More far-sighted members of the Conservative Party introduced a series of labor laws in Congress in June, 1919, a time of great social unrest. The Conservative legislation had as its goal the destruction of free labor unions and their replacement by employer-dominated plant unions. For the first time, a sector within the Chilean elite recognized the growing alienation and potential power of the organized labor movement, and sought to control it through a legal system of industrial relations. The Alessandri Liberals presented further legislation to Congress in 1921, but political rivalry prevented either proposal from becoming law until the military coup of September, 1924. The two major political forces within the elite, as well as the military, therefore recognized the need to dismantle independent labor unions and subject the working class to a formal system of industrial relations. Employers, however, could not perceive the benefits of either the Conservative or Liberal laws and opposed their passage before 1924 and their subsequent enforcement. Most labor unions also fought the laws of 1924 in an effort to preseve their independence.

Labor legislation appeared in Chile at too late a date to eradicate Anarchist and Marxist ideology. Between 1917 and 1924, organized labor had grown enormously and fought a desperate struggle to maintain its strength in the face of determined opposition from employers and the state. The influence of the Bolshevik Revolution and the Anarcho-Syndicalist and Communist Internationals on Chilean workers was significant. Continuous bouts with inflation and unemployment hardened the ideological lines of many workers. Had the government passed its labor laws in 1917 rather than 1924 and had employers been willing to abide by their terms, the spread of revolutionary ideology within the working class might have been slowed. Given the attitude of most politicians and employers regarding labor unions and the role of government in the economy, however, only the fear of widespread social unrest could have prompted the formulation and passage of such legislation.

Elites eventually turned to legislation as a means of dominating the unions because the nature of Chile's political system and the composition of the working class greatly limited the capacity of the state to repress organized labor. Executive officials from the President of the Republic to local police chiefs used force to break strikes and quell civil disturbances, but always as a stopgap solution. Despite the infiltration of labor organizations by police agents, the arrest of union leaders, and other acts of harassment, the government did not attempt to permanently dissolve unions. The repression ordered by President Sanfuentes in July, 1920, was the most determined effort of any regime before 1927 to suppress major labor unions by force, but they regained their former effectiveness within six months.

Chilean Presidents during the time of the Parliamentary Republic exercised limited powers and could not make far-reaching decisions without the cooperation of Congress. The host of political parties and their unstable congressional alliances paid little attention to the working class unless social upheaval threatened. In those instances, legislation calling for short-term repression, such as the granting of state of siege powers to the President or increasing the size of the armed forces, were the normal responses. Even when major political parties clearly perceived the growing stability and leftist orientation of the labor movement, rivalry prevented them from enacting laws to prevent the continued independence of labor.

Other factors limited the government's repressive capabilities. Chile's independent judiciary system would not automatically convict and imprison union leaders arrested by police. Because the urban labor movement was highly decentralized and had no single leader, the government could not easily "decapitate" the unions by arresting a few people, nor could it bring labor into line by co-opting a handful of individuals. Labor newspapers were protected by freedom of the press guarantees. An excessive use of force, especially in urban areas where violence was more visible, often embarrassed and politically weakened governing coalitions. Political parties both in and out of government could exploit public opinion regarding the "social question" to their own benefit.

The overwhelming preponderance of Chilean citizens in the labor movement posed another barrier to potential repression by the state. The Ley de Residencia reflected the misconception of elites that "foreign subversives" were responsible for the increased number of strikes and protest demonstrations. Only a handful of people were ever deported. Nor could the Chilean government pit native workers against foreigners by means of preferential treatment or appeals to xenophobia.

Boom and bust cycles in the nitrate industry inhibited the steady growth of organized labor in Chile and therefore reduced the need for state intervention to repress unions. Most of the resistance societies in Santiago and Valparaíso disappeared when the financial panic of 1907 led to widespread unemployment in 1908. When employers laid off workers, union organizers and militants were the first to go. The labor brotherhoods and resistance societies of the North were also nearly all eliminated by the middle of 1908. Organized labor partially rebuilt its strength when the economy recovered, but those gains were erased by the depression of 1914. The spectacular growth of the labor movement after 1917 resulted in sufficient organizational resiliency to allow most unions to weather the depression of 1921. When organized labor surged forward again in 1924, it became clear to elites that fluctuations in the economy would no longer result in the demise of important unions.

Chilean workers remained isolated from the mainstream of national politics throughout the first quarter of the twentieth century. No major political party took up the cause of the working class, although all managed to secure the votes of some workers by the cohecho, or system of vote buying and selling. Attempts to form a genuine labor party failed, either due to the political apathy of workers or the fraudulent electoral tactics of elite parties which limited the possibilities of labor party success. The few Democrats elected to Congress before 1916, when that party became a "legitimate" participant in the political game upon receiving a ministerial post, and the Communist Party in the 1920s, accomplished nothing to concretely benefit the working class. Indeed, formal politics was a fruitless pursuit from the working class point of view at least until 1925.

Arturo Alessandri was the first candidate of a major party to win the widespread support of the working class. Much of this "support" was, as in the past, purchased, but the large crowds won over to Alessandri's side during the campaign of 1920 did aid in securing his selection as President. While a number of labor unions unofficially backed Alessandri, few continued to support him after the maritime strike/lockout of August, 1921. His strategy of using the revamped Oficina del Trabajo to lure workers away from the Anarcho-Syndicalist and Communist camps failed completely because Congress would not cooperate by passing legislation and employers resisted interference by the Labor Office in what they considered their private affairs.

Not until 1925 did urban workers show any interest in electoral politics. The registration reforms of 1924, rampant inflation, government repression, the radicalization of empleados, and the fielding of a compromise candidate by the elite parties all had a role in bringing about a record vote in the presidential election of 1925. Labor's apparent political power, as reflected by the election of several Communists to Congress, was, however, illusory, since it resulted from the ephemeral alliance between the PC and white collar workers.

In sum, the state made little effort to change the industrial relations system prevalent in Chile between 1902 and 1924. By allowing the unregulated conflict between employers and organized workers to continue for more than twenty years, by intervening in favor of the former whenever labor's bargaining position improved or when strikes disrupted the economy, and by failing to integrate workers into national politics by providing them with an institutional means of political expression, the state fostered the rise of independent, revolutionary labor unions.

THE LEGACY OF THE LABOR MOVEMENT

The period between 1902 and 1927 was crucial in the development of organized labor in Chile. From a handful of short-lived resistance societies at the turn of the century, the labor movement grew to significant size and importance during the 1920s. A series of authoritarian labor laws and systematic repression during the regime of Carlos Ibáñez failed to weaken the attachment of Chilean workers to revolutionary ideology which had developed during this period. Traditional political parties had by 1927 lost their opportunity to attract working class support. Nor could the state hope to politically control the labor movement, despite its success in limiting the economic capabilities of unions.

Much of the credit for the growth and survival of revolutionary ideology within the urban working class must be given to the Anarcho-Syndicalists. It was they who first began organizing labor unions at the turn of the century and they who initiated the resurgence of the labor movement in 1917. Anarcho-Syndicalist successes aided the organization drive of the FOCh in 1919. By refusing to allow intellectuals or politicians to play a major role in the affairs of their unions, the Anarcho-Syndicalists strengthened the independence and working class character of the Chilean labor movement. The decentralization of authority within the Anarcho-Syndicalist camp made repression by the state more difficult.

Most important for future political developments in Chile, the survival of an active Anarcho-Syndicalist movement in Santiago and Valparaíso during the 1920s kept alive anti-authoritarian, anti-Communist, and revolutionary spirit in the working class at a time when libertarians elsewhere in Latin America were losing ground to the Communist Party or reformism. The formation in Chile of Latin America's only important Socialist Party in 1933 was facilitated and in part brought about by members of the Anarcho-Syndicalist movement of the 1920s. Appendix 2 clearly indicates that many Anarchists helped form or eventually joined the Socialist Party. It is entirely likely that the party's ability to attract organized workers to its ranks during the 1930s was due to the work of ex-Anarchists. Six of the twelve members of the Central Directory of the Socialist Party in October, 1933, were former Anarchists (Alzamora, Bianchi, Piña, Pinto, Schnake, and Soto) who converted to revolutionary politics after the fall of Ibáñez.[2] Schnake served as the party's secretary general during its first years of life.

Anarcho-Syndicalist unions reappeared after 1931, but failed to achieve as much influence within the labor movement as they enjoyed during the 1920s. Nevertheless, the Anarchist movement played a crucial role in the development of labor unions in Chile. It instilled in Chilean workers a much deeper sense of class identity than they had ever before possessed. Anarchists taught several generations of workers to view labor unions as a means of bettering their lives as well as a vehicle for protest against oppression. Consequently, any improvements in the well-being or organizational capacity of the Chilean working class before 1927 were brought about by workers themselves. No well-meaning elites, reformist politicians, or intellectuals, with the possible exception of the university students of the FECh, aided workers in their struggle. This was not to be the case in the decades to follow, when most labor unions became the property of political parties. Linkage with the PC and Socialist Party left organized labor with no alternative but to rise and fall with the fortunes of the left.

Reference Material

Appendix 1

Table A.1
Initiation of Strikes, by Month and Period
(N = 380)

Month	1902–8	1917–21	1925	Month Total	Percentage of all Strikes
January	3	22	2	27	7.1
February	5	13	11	29	7.6
March	6	21	17	44	11.6
April	18	21	12	51	13.4
May	8	20	12	40	10.5
June	8	28	5	41	10.8
July	6	18	1	25	6.6
August	8	20	0	28	7.3
September	2	14	0	16	4.2
October	6	18	0	24	6.3
November	8	16	1	25	6.6
December	6	17	6	29	7.6
unknown	0	1	0	1	.4
TOTAL	84	229	67	380	100.0

265

Table A.2
Initiation of Strikes, by Industry and Period
(N = 380)

Industry	1902–8	1917–21	1925	Total	Percentage of All Strikes
tramways	6	7	1	14	3.7
railroad shops	5	2	0	7	1.8
marine transport	5	10	1	16	4.2
land transport	2	2	1	5	1.4
printing	17	19	3	39	10.3
shoes and leather	15	84	18	117	30.8
baking	4	5	0	9	2.4
brewing	2	2	0	4	1.0
metallurgy	4	8	11	23	6.0
construction	1	17	7	25	6.6
textiles	4	18	2	24	6.3
wood and furniture	1	12	6	19	5.0
other	18	43	17	78	20.5
TOTAL	84	229	67	380	100.0

Table A.3
Size and Location of Strikes, 1902–25
(N = 205)

Maximum Number of Strikers	Santiago	Valparaíso	Total	Percentage of All Strikes
10 or less	2	1	3	1.5
11–50	25	3	28	13.7
51–100	41	4	46[a]	22.4
101–200	29	8	37	18.0
201–500	36	5	41	20.0
501–1,000	13	5	18	8.8
1,001–5,000	16	9	26[a]	12.7
more than 5,000	2	4	6	2.9
TOTAL KNOWN	164	39	205	100.0
UNKNOWN	121	54	175	
TOTAL	285	93	380	

[a]Includes one strike affecting both Santiago and Valparaíso.

Table A.4
Size of Strikes and Industries Affected, 1902–25
(N = 205)

Industry	Maximum Number of Strikers						
	1–10	11–50	51–500	501–1,000	1,001–5,000	More Than 5,000	Total
tramways	0	0	3	5	3	0	11
railroad shop	0	0	1	0	3	0	4
marine transport	0	0	5	2	4	0	11
teamsters	0	1	1	0	0	0	2
printing	1	4	7	3	4	0	19
shoes	1	10	48	2	2	0	63
baking	0	0	0	2	4	0	6
brewing	0	1	1	0	1	0	3
metallurgy	1	4	7	1	1	0	14
construction	0	1	7	0	0	0	8
textile	0	0	16	1	0	0	17
wood and furniture	0	3	3	1	1	0	8
other	0	4	25	1	3	6[a]	39
TOTAL	3	28	124	18	26	6	205
PERCENTAGE OF ALL STRIKES	1.5	13.6	60.5	8.8	12.7	2.9	100.0

[a]Six general strikes which involved workers of many different industries.

Table A.5
Duration of Strikes, by Industry, 1902–25
(N = 232)

Industry	Strikes	Strikes for Which Duration Is Known	Mean Duration (Days)	Minimum Duration (Days)	Maximum Duration (Days)
metallurgy	23	11	25.8	3	120
textiles	24	13	19.5	1	60
shoes and leather	117	55	19.4	1	128
construction	25	13	16.8	3	43
baking	9	7	14.6	2	26
land transport (teamsters)	5	3	14.0	6	20
brewing	4	4	12.8	1	45
marine transport	16	14	12.7	3	33
wood and furniture	19	8	9.6	1	25
printing	39	26	8.8	1	35
railway shops	7	6	6.8	1	31
tramways	14	14	6.0	1	14
other	78	58	7.8	1	53
TOTAL/MEAN	380	232	13.4		

Table A.6
Sex and Maturity of Strikers, by Period
(N = 371)

Characteristics of Strikers	Number of Strikes and Percentage of Total by Period							
	1902–8	Percentage	1917–21	Percentage	1925	Percentage	Total	Percentage
men only	47	(55.9)	113	(50.9)	36	(55.4)	196	(52.8)
women only	3	(3.6)	11	(4.9)	2	(3.1)	16	(4.3)
men and women	15	(17.9)	84	(37.8)	24	(36.9)	123	(33.2)
men and children[a]	17	(20.2)	5	(2.3)	2	(3.1)	24	(6.5)
men, women, and children	2	(2.4)	9	(4.1)	1	(1.5)	12	(3.2)
TOTAL	84	(100.0)	222	(100.0)	65	(100.0)	371	(100.0)

[a] *Children*—under sixteen years of age.

Table A.7
Level of Worker Organization at the Beginnings of Strikes, by Period
(N = 356)

Organizational Level	Number of Strikes and Percentage of Total by Period							
	1902–8	Percentage	1917–21	Percentage	1925	Percentage	Total	Percentage
workers organized	67	(85.9)	191	(88.0)	50	(82.0)	308	(86.5)
workers unorganized	11	(14.1)	26	(12.0)	11	(18.0)	48	(13.5)
TOTAL	78	(100.0)	217	(100.0)	61	(100.0)	356	(100.0)
UNKNOWN	6		12		6		24	

Table A.8
Level of Worker Organization at the Ends of Strikes, by Period
(N = 356)

| Organizational Level | Number of Strikes and Percentage of Total by Period | | | | | | | |
	1902–8	Percentage	1917–21	Percentage	1925	Percentage	Total	Percentage
workers organized	69	(87.3)	200	(92.6)	54	(88.5)	323	(90.7)
workers unorganized	10	(12.7)	16	(7.4)	7	(11.5)	33	(9.3)
TOTAL	79	(100.0)	216	(100.0)	61	(100.0)	356	(100.0)
UNKNOWN	5		13		6		24	

Table A.9
Presentation of Grievance Petitions to Employers before Strikes, by Period
(N = 298)

| Procedure before Striking | Number of Strikes and Percentage of Total by Period | | | | | | | |
	1902–8	Percentage	1917–21	Percentage	1925	Percentage	Total	Percentage
petition presented	67	(84.8)	129	(79.1)	48	(85.7)	244	(81.8)
no petition presented	12	(15.2)	34	(20.9)	8	(14.3)	54	(18.2)
TOTAL	79	(100.0)	163	(100.0)	56	(100.0)	298	(100.0)
UNKNOWN	5		66		11		82	

Table A.10

Categories of Labor Organization Taking Part in Strikes

(N = 331)

Labor Organization[a]	Number of Strikes and Percentage of Total by Period							
	1902–8	Percentage	1917–21	Percentage	1925	Percentage	Total	Percentage
resistance society	50	(67.5)	25	(12.2)	12	(22.6)	87	(26.3)
mancomunal	7	(9.5)	0	(00.0)	0	(00.0)	7	(2.1)
mutual aid society	17	(23.0)	8	(3.9)	8	(15.1)	33	(10.0)
Anarcho-Syndicalist federation	0	(00.0)	110	(53.9)	23	(43.4)	133	(40.1)
Federación Obrera de Chile *concejo*	0	(00.0)	46	(22.6)	7	(13.2)	53	(16.0)
IWW	0	(00.0)	13	(6.4)	2	(3.8)	15	(4.5)
other	0	(00.0)	2	(1.0)	1	(1.9)	3	(1.0)
TOTAL	74	(100.0)	204	(100.0)	53	(100.0)	331	(100.0)
UNKNOWN	25		39		19		83	
							414[b]	

[a] *Resistance societies* in this study are labor unions using the words *de resistencia* or *en resistencia* in their titles and which are not affiliated with the mancomunales of 1905–8 or Anarcho-Syndicalist federations. *Mancomunal* signifies any labor organization affiliated with the mancomunales of Valparaíso and Santiago between 1905 and 1908. *Anarcho-Syndicalist federates* are organizations of Anarcho-Syndicalist orientation, normally encompassing a single industry. The Shoeworkers' Federations (FZA, FOOC, UIC), Printers' Federation (FOICh), Bakers' Federation (USP and others), Federación de Sastres, Woodworkers' Federation (Elaboradores en Madera), Tanners' Federation, and members of the Federación de Organizaciones Autónomas are all included in this category.

[b] The total is greater than 380 because several organizations at times participated in the same strike.

Table A.11
Categories of Employer Involved in Strikes
(N = 380)

| Employer | Number of Strikes | | | | | | | | | |
	1902–8	Percentage	1917–21	Percentage	1925	Percentage	Total	Percentage
private company	69	(82.1)	218	(94.7)	64	(95.5)	351	(92.3)
municipality	5	(5.9)	4	(1.7)	1	(1.5)	10	(2.6)
Republic of Chile	7	(8.3)	5	(2.0)	2	(3.0)	14	(3.7)
private company and Chile	3	(3.7)	0	(0.0)	0	(0.0)	3	(0.8)
municipality and Chile	0	(0.0)	1	(0.8)	0	(0.0)	1	(0.3)
all three	0	(0.0)	1	(0.8)	0	(0.0)	1	(0.3)
TOTAL	84	(100.0)	229	(100.0)	67	(100.0)	380	(100.0)

271

Table A.12
Initial Responses[a] of Employers to Strikes
(N = 273)

Employer Response	1902–8	Percentage	1917–21	Percentage	1925	Percentage	Total	Percentage
			Number of Strikes and Percentage of Total by Period					
capitulates to workers' demands	6	(7.5)	5	(3.3)	2	(5.1)	13	(4.8)
refuses demands entirely	50	(62.5)	96	(62.3)	31	(79.5)	177	(64.8)
offers a compromise proposition to workers	8	(10.0)	24	(15.6)	0	(00.0)	32	(11.7)
declares a lockout	6	(7.5)	6	(3.9)	3	(7.7)	15	(5.5)
does nothing	10	(12.5)	15	(9.7)	2	(5.1)	27	(9.9)
agrees to have strike mediated	0	(00.0)	6	(3.9)	1	(2.6)	7	(2.6)
agrees to accept binding arbitration	0	(00.0)	2	(1.3)	0	(00.0)	2	(0.7)
TOTAL	80	(100.0)	154	(100.0)	39	(100.0)	273	(100.0)
UNKNOWN	4		75		28		107	
							380	

[a]Responses occurring within twenty-four hours after strikes were called.

Table A.13
Employers' Use of Strikebreakers
(N = 246)

Employer Strategy	Number of Strikes and Percentage of Total by Period							
	1902–8	Percentage	1917–21	Percentage	1925	Percentage	Total	Percentage
strikebreakers used	24	(36.4)	52	(37.1)	15	(37.5)	91	(37.0)
strikebreakers not used	42	(63.6)	88	(62.9)	25	(62.5)	155	(63.0)
TOTAL	66	(100.0)	140	(100.0)	40	(100.0)	246	(100.0)
UNKNOWN	18		89		27		134	
							380	

Table A.14
Employers' Use of Strikebreakers, by Industry, 1902–25
(N = 246)

Industry	Strike-breakers Used	Percentage	Strike-breakers Not Used	Percentage	Total
baking	7	(87.5)	1	(12.5)	8
tramways	10	(71.4)	4	(28.6)	14
marine transport	7	(58.3)	5	(41.7)	12
wood and furniture	5	(50.0)	5	(50.0)	10
land transport (teamsters)	2	(50.0)	2	(50.0)	4
construction	6	(42.9)	8	(57.1)	14
textiles	6	(33.3)	12	(66.7)	18
shoes and leather	16	(29.1)	39	(70.9)	55
printing	7	(28.0)	18	(72.0)	25
brewing	1	(25.0)	3	(75.0)	4
metallurgy	2	(16.7)	10	(83.3)	12
railroad shops	1	(20.0)	4	(80.0)	5
other	21	(32.8)	43	(67.2)	64
TOTAL	91		154		245
UNKNOWN					135
					380

Table A.15
Duration of Strikes and Employers' Use of Strikebreakers, 1902–25
(N = 211)

Duration (Days)	Strike-breakers Used	Percentage	Strike-breakers Not Used	Percentage	Total
1 or less	2	(7.4)	25	(92.6)	27
2–5	14	(23.3)	46	(76.7)	60
6–14	23	(31.5)	50	(68.5)	73
15–30	13	(48.1)	14	(51.9)	27
31–60	14	(73.7)	5	(26.3)	19
61 or more	2	(40.0)	3	(60.0)	5
TOTAL/PERCENTAGE	68	(32.2)	143	(67.8)	211
UNKNOWN					169
					380

Table A.16
Strike Intervention by Police or Armed Forces[a]
(N = 254)

Year(s)	Intervention	Percentage	No Intervention	Percentage	Total
1902–8	32	(45.7)	38	(54.3)	70
1917–21	52	(35.6)	94	(64.4)	146
1925	16	(42.1)	22	(57.9)	38
TOTAL/PERCENTAGE	100	(39.3)	154	(60.7)	254
UNKNOWN					126
					380

[a]*Intervention*—the presence of extraordinary numbers of police or troops to control a strike, serve as strikebreakers, or forcefully end a strike.

Table A.17
Frequency of Strike-Related Violence, by City, 1902–25
(N = 248)

City	Violent Strikes	Percentage	Nonviolent Strikes	Percentage	Total
Santiago	39	(22.3)	136	(77.7)	175
Valparaíso	22	(31.0)	49	(69.0)	71
both	1		1		2
TOTAL/PERCENTAGE	62	(25.0)	186	(75.0)	248
UNKNOWN					132
					380

Violence is defined as the occurrence of a physical battle between police/armed forces and workers; the wounding of workers, police, strikebreakers, employers, or bystanders in a strike-related incident; the destruction of property in a strike-related incident; the arrest of workers as the result of a strike; or the death of anyone in a strike related incident. *Nonviolent strikes* are those for which sufficient information was available to determine that no such incidents occurred.

Table A.18
Use of Strikebreakers and Outbreak of Violence in Strikes, by Industry, 1902–25
(N = 248)

	Percentage of Strikes in Which:	
Industry	Strikebreakers Were Used	Violence Occurred
baking	87.5	62.5
tramways	71.4	50.0
marine transport	58.3	30.8
land transport (teamsters)	50.0	25.0
wood and furniture	50.0	18.2
construction	42.9	16.7
textiles	33.3	33.3
shoes and leather	29.1	22.5
printing	28.0	3.9
brewing	25.0	25.0
metallurgy	16.7	16.7
railroad shops	16.7	60.0
other	32.8	23.8

Table A.19
Duration of Strikes and Outbreak of Violence, 1902–25
(N = 217)

Duration (Days)	Violent Strikes	Percentage	Nonviolent Strikes	Percentage	Total
1 or less	5	(19.2)	21	(80.8)	26
2–5	7	(11.1)	56	(88.9)	63
6–14	15	(19.5)	62	(80.5)	77
15–30	7	(26.9)	19	(73.1)	26
31–60	7	(36.8)	12	(63.2)	19
61+	3	(50.0)	3	(50.0)	6
TOTAL	44		173		217
UNKNOWN					163
					380

276

Table A.20
Means of Settlement of Strikes, by Period
(N = 224)

Percentage	Strike Broken, Workers Return	Percentage	Conciliation[a]	Percentage	Arbitration Mediation[b]	Percentage	Total
1902–8	13	(18.9)	47	(68.1)	9	(13.0)	69
1917–21	14	(11.4)	70	(56.9)	39	(31.7)	123
1925	4	(12.5)	17	(53.1)	11	(34.4)	32
TOTAL/ PERCENTAGE	31	(13.8)	134	(59.8)	59	(26.4)	224
UNKNOWN							156
							380

[a]*Conciliation*—settlement through collective bargaining between employers and worker representatives without any outside interference.

[b]*Mediation*—settlement through the intervention of a third party, normally a government official. All settlements arrived at through the successful invocation of the Yáñez Decree are classified as mediated. The third party normally helped bring employers and workers to the bargaining table, although in many cases the mediator played little or no role in the actual bargaining process. *Arbitration*—the decison of employers and workers to allow a third party to make the strike settlement for them and to agree to respect the terms of the settlement. All instances of arbitration were binding.

Table A.21
Means of Settlement of Strikes, by Industry, 1902–25
(N = 224)

Industry	Strike Broken, Workers Return	Percentage	Conciliation	Percentage	Arbitration Mediation	Percentage	Total
printing	2	(7.7)	24	(92.3)	0	(0.0)	26
construction	0	(0.0)	10	(90.9)	1	(9.1)	11
wood and furniture	0	(0.0)	8	(80.0)	2	(20.0)	10
shoes and leather	4	(7.7)	39	(75.0)	9	(17.3)	52
transport/teamsters	0	(0.0)	3	(75.0)	1	(25.0)	4
brewing	1	(25.0)	3	(75.0)	0	(0.0)	4
baking	0	(0.0)	4	(66.7)	2	(33.3)	6
metallurgy	1	(9.1)	7	(63.6)	3	(27.3)	11
tobacco	0	(0.0)	5	(55.5)	4	(44.5)	9
textile	2	(14.3)	6	(42.8)	6	(42.8)	14
food processing	1	(12.5)	3	(37.5)	4	(50.0)	8
railroad shops	2	(33.3)	2	(33.3)	2	(33.3)	6
tramways	3	(25.0)	2	(16.7)	7	(58.3)	12
communications	1	(16.7)	1	(16.7)	4	(66.6)	6
glass	3	(42.9)	1	(14.3)	3	(42.9)	7
marine transport	5	(33.3)	2	(13.3)	8	(53.4)	15
other	6	(26.0)	14	(60.9)	3	(13.1)	23
TOTAL/PERCENTAGE	31	(13.8)	134	(59.9)	59	(26.3)	224
UNKNOWN							156
							380

Table A.22
Outcome of Strikes from the Workers' Point of View, by Period
(N = 231)

Period	Total Failure	Percentage	Compromise	Percentage	Total Success	Percentage	Total
1902–8	15	(21.4)	22	(31.5)	33	(47.1)	70
1917–21	23	(17.7)	65	(50.0)	42	(32.3)	130
1925	6	(19.3)	11	(35.5)	14	(45.2)	31
TOTAL/PERCENTAGE	44	(19.0)	98	(42.4)	89	(38.6)	231
UNKNOWN							149
							380

Table A.23

Outcome of Strikes from the Workers' Point of View, by Industry, 1902–25

(N = 231)

Industry	Total Failure	Percentage	Compromise	Percentage	Total Success	Percentage	Total
tramways	7	(53.8)	4	(30.8)	2	(15.4)	13
railroad shops	2	(33.3)	0	(0.0)	4	(66.7)	6
marine transport	5	(38.5)	5	(38.5)	3	(23.0)	13
land transport (teamsters)	0	(0.0)	2	(50.0)	2	(50.0)	4
printing	2	(7.4)	8	(29.6)	17	(63.0)	27
shoes and leather	5	(9.3)	23	(42.6)	26	(48.1)	54
baking	0	(0.0)	4	(66.7)	2	(33.3)	6
brewing	1	(25.0)	2	(50.0)	1	(25.0)	4
metallurgy	1	(9.1)	4	(36.4)	6	(54.5)	11
construction	0	(0.0)	5	(41.7)	7	(58.3)	12
textile	4	(28.6)	8	(57.1)	2	(14.3)	14
wood and furniture	0	(0.0)	6	(54.5)	5	(45.5)	11
other	17	(30.4)	27	(48.2)	12	(21.4)	56
TOTAL/PERCENTAGE	44	(19.0)	98	(42.4)	89	(38.6)	231
UNKNOWN							149
							380

Table A.24

Outcome of Strikes from the Workers' Point of View,
by Type of Labor Organization Involved, 1902–25
(N = 182)

Labor Organization	Total Failure	Percentage	Compromise	Percentage	Total Success	Percentage	Total
resistance society	8	(14.3)	21	(37.5)	27	(48.2)	56
mancomunal	2	(66.7)	1	(33.3)	0	(0.0)	3
mutual aid society	3	(21.4)	6	(42.9)	5	(35.7)	14
Anarcho-Syndicalist federation	5	(8.3)	26	(43.3)	29	(48.4)	60
FOCh	9	(23.7)	23	(60.5)	6	(15.8)	38
IWW	2	(25.0)	2	(25.0)	4	(50.0)	8
other	0	(0.0)	2	(66.7)	1	(33.3)	3
TOTAL/PERCENTAGE	29	(15.9)	81	(44.5)	72	(39.6)	182

Table A.25

Outcome of Strikes from the Workers' Point of View,
by Means of Settlement, 1902–25

(N = 186)

Means of Settlement	Total Failure	Percentage	Compromise	Percentage	Total Success	Percentage	Total	Percentage
conciliation between employers and workers	5	(3.8)	50	(38.1)	76	(58.1)	131	
mediation and arbitration	6	(10.9)	43	(78.2)	6	(10.9)	55	
TOTAL/PERCENTAGE	11	(5.9)	93	(50.0)	82	(44.1)	186	
UNKNOWN							194	
							380	

Table A.26

Outcome of Strikes from the Workers' Point of View
and Outbreak of Violence during Strikes, 1902–25

(N = 213)

Violent/Nonviolent Strikes	Total Failure	Percentage	Compromise	Percentage	Total Success	Percentage	Total	Percentage
violent strikes	20	(46.5)	14	(32.6)	9	(20.9)	43	
nonviolent strikes	23	(13.5)	80	(47.1)	67	(39.4)	170	
TOTAL/PERCENTAGE	43	(20.2)	94	(44.1)	76	(35.7)	213	
UNKNOWN							167	
							380	

Table A.27
Employers' use of Strikebreakers and Outcome of Strikes
from the Workers' Point of View, 1902–25 ⁻
(N = 211)

Final Result of Strike	Strike-breakers Used	Percentage	Strike-breakers Not Used	Percentage	Total	Percentage
failure	29	(41.4)	14	(9.9)	43	(20.4)
compromise	29	(41.4)	64	(45.4)	93	(44.1)
success	12	(17.2)	63	(44.7)	75	(35.5)
TOTAL	70	(100.0)	131	(100.0)	211	(100.0)
UNKNOWN					169	
					380	

Appendix 2

Name	Anarcho-Syndicalist Connection	Socialist Party Role
Alzamora, Ramón	Leader, Anarchist social studies center, "Rebeldía," Antofagasta, early 1920s.	Founding member, 1933. Member, Central Directive Committee, 1934.
Baloffet, Alberto	Member, Santiago IWW, 1920-27. Director, IWW Ateneo, 1926.	Member, Comité Político, 1934.
Bianchi Gundián, Arturo	Writer for IWW organ *Acción Directa* while in exile in Buenos Aires, 1928.	Member, Partido Socialista Marxista, 1933. Member, Central Directive Committee, 1933.
Caro, Carlos	Writer for the Anarchist paper *La Batalla*, 1914. Frequent contributor to the Anarchist press. Member, Anarchist sector of the FECh, 1920s.	Member, Acción Revolucionaria Socialista, 1933. Founding member, PS, 1933.
Castro, Amaro	Secretary general, IWW, 1922. Member, IWW, Santiago, 1920-27.	Delegate to PS General Congress, 1934. PS Deputy, 1937.
Godoy Urrutia, César	Teacher, convinced Anarchist, 1925-31. Member, Anarchist FORA, Buenos Aires, 1927-30. Present at International Syndicalist Conference in Spain, 1931.	Founding member, 1933. PS deputy, 1937.
González Rojas, Eugenio	Writer for *Verba Roja*, 1919-22. Leader, Anarchist section of the FECh, 1920s.	Member, Acción Revolucionaria Socialista. Founding member, PS, 1933.

285

Name	Anarcho-Syndicalist Connection	Socialist Party Role
Lagarrigue, Alfredo	Member of the Anarchist section of the FECh, 1920s. A well-known positivist.	Founding member, 1933.
López, Gerardo	Anarchist collaborator, 1920s. Contributed funds to *Acción Directa*.	Member, Partido Socialista Marxista. Founding member, PS, 1933.
López, Pablo	Member, Anarchist Bakers' Union (USP), 1920s. Delegate to Congress of Autonomous Organizations, 1925.	Member, Central Directive Committee, 1939.
Ortiz de Zárate, Julio	Painter; member of the Anarchist sector of the FECh, 1920s.	Member Nueva Acción Pública, 1932.
Pinto, Augusto	Member, Federación de Zapateros, 1917–27. Member, IWW, 1920–27. Director of IWW Ateneo in Santiago.	Member, Acción Revolucionaria Socialista, 1933. Founding member, PS.
Piña, Benjamín	Member, IWW, 1920–27. Member, IWW Governing Council, 1924. Director of *Acción Directa*, 1926.	Member, Acción Revolucionaria Socialista, 1933. Founding member, PS,
Schnake, Oscar	Member, IWW, 1920–22. Contributor to *Verba Roja*, 1924. Leader, Anarchist sector of the FECh, 1920s.	Member, Acción Revolucionaria Socialista, 1933. Founding member, PS, 1933. Secretary general of the PS in the 1930s.
Soto, Zarcarías	Member, IWW, 1926. Sent by IWW on a propaganda tour of Ecuador, 1926.	Founding member, PS, 1933.
Uribe, David	Member, Printers' Federation, 1920s. Secretary, 1920. Leader, social studies center *La Verdad*, Santiago, 1921.	Member, Partido Socialista Marxista, 1933. Founding member, PS, 1933.
Valiente, Julio E.	Publisher of *Numen*, 1920. Member, Printers' Federation, 1902–27. Contributor to *Verba Roja*.	Member, Acción Revolucionaria Socialista, 1933.

Source Abbreviations

ADGT	*Archivo de la Dirección General del Trabajo*, Santiago
AE	*Anuario Estadístico*, Santiago
ANCh	Archivo Nacional Santiago
BOT	*Boletín de la Oficina del Trabajo*, Santiago
BSOFOFA	*Boletín de la Sociedad de Fomento Fabril*, Santiago
ELDI	*El Diario Ilustrado*, Santiago
ELH	*El Heraldo*, Valparaíso
ELMS	*El Mercurio*, Santiago
ELMV	*El Mercurio*, Valparaíso
IISG	Internationaal Instituut voor Social Geschiedenis, Amsterdam
LaFOCh	*La Federación Obrera*, Santiago
LaN	*La Nación*, Santiago
LaOp	*La Opinión*, Santiago
LaRef	*La Reforma*, Santiago
LaU	*La Unión*, Valparaíso
PROFO	Public Record Office, Foreign Office, London.
SE	*Síntesis Estadística*, Santiago
USNA	United States National Archives, Washington
VR	*Verba Roja*, Santiago

Notes

INTRODUCTION

1 This orthodox view of Chilean labor history was formulated by official Communist and Socialist Party historians Hernán Ramírez Necochea and Julio César Jobet, respectively. Ramírez mentioned twentieth-century events briefly in *Historia del movimiento obrero en Chile, siglo XIX* (Santiago, 1956), and in his later book, *Origen y formación del partido comunista de Chile* (Santiago, 1965), stated the view in its purest form, mercilessly ridiculing all labor organizations not contributing to the development of the Communist Party. Jobet, in *Luis Emilio Recabarren* (Santiago, 1955), was noticeably (and understandably) kinder to the Anarcho-Syndicalists, but nonetheless pictured the labor movement as being the product of Recabarren's efforts. Jorge Barría Serón, in *Los movimientos sociales de principios del siglo, 1900–1910* (Santiago, 1953), worked closely with Jobet, and eventually reached similar conclusions concerrning the FOCh and Recabarren in a later book, *Los movimientos sociales en Chile desde 1910 hasta 1926* (Santiago, 1960). Luis Vitale's *Historia del movimiento obrero* (Santiago, 1962) follows the orthodox view closely. A later study by Michael Monteón, "The Nitrate Miners and the Origins of the Chilean Left, 1880–1925" (Ph.D. thesis, Harvard University, 1974), echoes earlier claims that nitrate workers, the POS, the FOCh, and Recabarren were the driving forces behind the Chilean labor movement. Those who have studied other aspects or periods of Chilean history have used Jobet, Vitale, Ramírez, Barría, and other secondary sources in support of the theory that nitrate workers and the FOCh were absolutely predominant. These include: James O. Morris, *Elites, Intellectuals, and Consensus* (Ithaca, N.Y., 1966); James Petras, *Politics and Social Forces in Chilean Development* (Berkeley and London, 1972); Alan Angell, *Politics and the Labour Movement in Chile* (London, 1972); and Arthur Lawrence Stickell, "Migration and Mining: Labor in Northern Chile in the Nitrate Era, 1880–1930" (Ph.D. thesis, Indiana University, 1979). Finally, the orthodox view has been propagated by authors of recent histories of Latin American labor movements, especially Hobart A. Spaulding, Jr., *Organized Labor in Latin America: Historical Case Studies of Workers in Dependent Societies* (New York, 1977), and Julio Godio, *Historia del movimiento obrero latinoamericano*, vol. 1 (México, 1980).

2 Paul W. Drake, *Socialism and Populism in Chile, 1932–52* (Urbana, Chicago, and London, 1978).

3 For Argentina, see Richard Yoast, "The Development of Argentine Anarchism: A Socio-Idelogical Analysis" (Ph.D. thesis, University of Wisconsin–Madison, 1975). For Brazil, see Sheldon Maram, "Anarchism, Immigrants, and the Brazilian Labor Movement" (Ph.D. thesis, University of California–Santa Barbara, 1975). Also Sheldon Maram, "Urban Labor and Social Change in the 1920s," *Luso-Brazilian Review* 16:2 (Winter, 1979): 101–16; and "Labor and the Left in Brazil, 1890–1921," *Hispanic American Historical Review* 57:2 (May, 1977): 254–72. For a more detailed comparison of Argentina, Chile, and Brazil, see: Thomas E. Skidmore, "Workers and Soldiers: Urban Labor Movements and Elite Responses in Twentieth-Century Latin America," in Virginia Bernhard, ed, *Elites, Masses, and Modernization in Latin America, 1850–1930* (Austin and London, 1979).

4 For good discussions of the development of Anarchist ideology and its major tenets, see James Joll, *The Anarchists* (New York, 1966) and George Woodcock, *Anarchism* (London, 1963).

CHAPTER 1: URBANIZATION AND INDUSTRIALIZATION

1 Chile, *Censo de 1930,* vol. 1, p. 13.

2 Ibid., p. 50.

3 Calculated from population figures, *ibid.*, pp. 40–42, 45.

4 Instituto de Higiene de Santiago, *Boletín de higiene i demografía,* "Resumen anual de 1902," Santiago, año 6, no. 12, December, 1903, p. 185. For 1910 see ibid., 1910, vol 1.

5 Chile, *Censo de 1920,* p. xxvii.

6 Carl Solberg, *Immigration and Nationalism, Argentina and Chile, 1890–1914* (Austin and London, 1970), p. 35.

7 Ibid.,p. 46.

8 Arnold J. Bauer, *Chilean Rural Society from the Spanish Conquest to 1930* (Cambridge, England, and New York, 1975), pp. 148–60; Brian Loveman, *Struggle in the Countryside—Politics and Rural Labor in Chile, 1919–1973* (Bloomington, 1976), p. 29.

9 Bauer, *Chilean Rural Society,* pp. 159–60; Stickell, "Migration and Mining," chapter 3.

10 Claudio Véliz, *Historia de la marina mercante de Chile* (Santiago, 1961), Appendix 2, pp. 376–77.

11 Marcelo Carmagnani, *Sviluppo industriale e sottosviluppo economico: il caso cileno, 1860–1920* (Turin, 1971), Appendix 9, pp. 181–83.

12 USNA, microfilm series M487, roll 15, Report of Consul McMillan, "Chilean Port Improvement Works," August 26, 1924.

13 Carlos Peña, *Santiago de siglo en siglo* (Santiago, 1944), pp. 276,280.

14 Ibid., pp. 288, 291.

15 Ibid., p. 291. Sociedad de Fomento Fabril, *Boletín* (hereafter *BSOFOFA*), April

1901, p. 118; Prefectura de Policía de Santiago, *Guía de informaciones policiales* (Santiago, 1909), pp. 160–62.

16 René León Echaíz, *Nuñohue: Historia de Nuñoa, Providencia, Las Condes, y La Reina* (Santiago, 1972), p. 182.

17 Chile, *Alcantarillado de Santiago* (Santiago, 1904), vol. 1, p. 3; vol. 2, pp. 13–57. The map on page 57 demonstrates quite clearly that the city had no intention of paving working class neighborhoods in 1903.

18 *AE*, 1915, vol. 2, p. 136.

19 Juan de Dios Ugarte, *Valparaíso, 1536–1910* (Valparaíso, 1910), p. 69.

20 Ibid., pp. 69–72.

21 Ibid., pp. 23–50.

22 Ibid. Ugarte evaluates each cerro according to its population in 1910, but one can almost assume from a modern-day walking tour of Valparaíso that the housing situation of 1910 changed very little in years to come.

23 William Henry Kirsch, "The Industrialization of Chile, 1880–1930" (Ph.D. dissertation, University of Florida, 1973); Carmagnani, *Sviluppo;* Oscar Muñoz, *Crecimiento industrial de Chile, 1914–65* (Santiago, 1968); Mario Ballesteros and Tom E. Davis, "The Growth of Output and Employment in Basic Sectors of the Chilean Economy, 1908–1957," *Economic Development and Cultural Change* 2 (January, 1963): 152–76.

24 Kirsch, "Industrialization," p. 13.

25 Ibid., pp. 18, 19.

26 Ibid., pp. 25–28.

27 Carmagnani, *Sviluppo*, p. 15.

28 Kirsch, "Industrialization," p. 49.

29 Ibid., pp. 194–233. Stickell, "Migration and Mining," pp. 340–41.

30 Kirsch, "Industrialization," p. 89. The only notable change between 1917 and 1927 occurred in the metal industry, which more than doubled its output percentage.

31 For 1910 see: *BOT* 3, 1911, p. 107; *BOT* 21, 1923, p. 120; *AE*, 1925, vol. 9, p. 3.

32 See Kirsch, "Industrialization," table 1.5, p. 260, for 1910 figures. For 1925 see *AE*, 1925, vol. 9, p. 3.

33 *AE*, 1925, vol. 9, p. 3. A comparison of 1910 and 1925 figures shows a rapid capitalization of the tobacco industry as mechanized producers and, later, the monopolistic Compañía Chilena de Tabacos dominated the industry.

34 Kirsch, Industrialization," p. 262. His figures come from *AE*, 1914–25.

35 Ibid., pp. 28, 154.

36 *AE*, 1925, vol. 9, p. 4.

37 Ibid.

38 Ibid.

39 The SOFOFA, in its 1905 municipal survey of Santiago industries, presented the problem in a slightly different light: "It is worthwhile noting that many industrialists have refused to provide information, some out of ignorance, but many others from indolence." *BSOFOFA*, September, 1906, p. 347.

40 All the studies understate the size of the industrial establishment in both cities, especially in the case of the 1905 municipal census. It is likely that all figures refer almost entirely to the urban areas of Santiago and Valparaíso-Viña, in spite of the classifications of "province," "department," and "municipality." Furthermore, by the 1920s, the Municipality of Santiago was the only city of any consequence within the department, since San Bernardo, Melipilla, and San Antonio were all located in other sectors. The figures for employment in Valparaíso between 1895 and 1910 are difficult to believe, given the fact that the number of establishments rose substantially during those years. The studies do not include workers engaged in nonfactory employment. For 1895 see: Aurelio Montenegro, *Estudio general de la industria fabril de Chile* (Santiago, 1947), p. 66. For 1905M: *BSOFOFA*, September, 1906, pp. 347–50. For 1906D: Adolfo Ortúzar, *Chile of To-Day* (New York, 1907), pp. 348–51. For 1906P: SOFOFA, *Resumenes generales de la estadística industrial* (Santiago, 1908), p. 10. For 1910P: *BOT* 3, 1911, p. 106. For 1912P: *BOT* 8, 1914, pp. 284–85. For 1925P: *AE*, 1925, vol. 9, p. 4.

41 Perhaps the only reliable way of determining the size, distribution, and composition of the urban workforce is to use census materials. The SOFOFA and government industrial surveys indicate trends in the distribution of workers among the various factories in Santiago and Valparaíso, but they do not mention nonmanufacturing labor. National censuses recorded the task a worker performed and, by doing so, normally revealed the industry in which he worked. Unfortunately, the censuses are not comparable over time, since the occupational categories into which census takers grouped workers changed between 1907 and 1920.

42 Ortúzar, *Chile of To-Day*, pp. 348–51.

43 *BOT* 3, 1911, p. 106; *AE*, 1925, vol. 9, p. 25.

44 Chile, *Censo de 1920*, pp. 459–67.

45 See: SOFOFA, *Estadística industrial de la Provincia de Santiago* (Santiago, 1906), pp. 70–81; Zig-Zag, *Directorio de Santiago* (Santiago, 1913), p. 28.

CHAPTER 2: WORK IN THE CITIES

1 For nitrates see Stickell, "Migration and Mining," p. 70. Also ADGT, *Servicio de Colocación,* 1914–15.

2 *ELMS*, April 4, 1915, p. 17.

3 *ELMV*, articles and editorials from July 22 to August 16, 1917.

4 The redondilla was first established in Antofagasta and later went into effect in Iquique, Coronel, and Talcahuano.

5 ADGT, *Crisis salitreras,* 1919, "Reglamento de las faenas marítimas del puerto de Iquique."

6 ADGT, *1921 varios,* "Reglamento del fallo arbitral, 12 abril, 1921." Also Peter DeShazo, "The Industrial Workers of the World in Chile, 1917–1927" (M.A. thesis, University of Wisconsin–Madison, 1973), pp. 53–60.

7 For the reaction of British shippers to the redondilla, see: PROFO 371/7204, Legation to Foreign Office, December 7, 1921, and enclosed clippings; PROFO

371/4455, "Memorandum in Regard to Present Strike at Iquique," July 24, 1920; DeShazo, "The IWW," pp. 57–58.

8 *LaOp, May 4, 1917, p. 2.*

9 *La Federación de Obreros de Imprenta,* November 3, 1918, p. 1; *LaOp,* August 21, 1919, p. 4.

10 *LaN,* April 7, 1921; *El Obrero Panadero,* September 1, 1924, p. 1; *LaFOCh,* May 30, 1923, p. 2; ADGT, *Inspección regional, Valparaíso,* 1921, vol. 1, contract between the USP and bakery owners, July 7, 1921.

11 Miranda interview.

12 Asamblea Tipográfica, *Boletín de la Asamblea Tipográfica* 14, July 10, 1902.

13 For worker concern over mechanization, see: *La Unión Gráfica,* August 15, 1918, p. 1. For the 1925 FOICh-printers' contract see: *Justicia,* January 19, 1925, p. 1.

14 *La Federación de Obreros de Imprenta,* November 30, 1918, pp. 1–4.

15 *Ibid.,* pp. 1–4; *Justicia,* January 19, 1925, p. 1.

16 *BSOFOFA,* November, 1917, p. 707.

17 Pepay interview.

18 Heredia and Pepay interviews. For an excellent visual account of shoe production in Santiago factories see *LaN,* October 12, 1924, p. 13, the Sureda Factory.

19 The following discussion of skills in the building trades is based on interviews with Félix López and readings of labor contracts.

20 *BSOFOFA,* October, 1913, p. 965.

21 USNA, M487, roll 15, Report of Consul McMillan, "Chilean Port Improvement Works," August 26, 1924; Véliz, *Historia de la Marina Mercante,* pp. 287, 312.

22 This conclusion is evident from a general reading of strike demands for the years 1902–8, 1917–21, and 1925 as analyzed in later chapters.

23 See, for example, the statistics for the Province of Santiago in 1921 as compiled by the Labor Office in *BOT* 18, 1922, pp. 175–99. Earlier statistics often named a day rate for workers who were paid by the piece rate by having their employers calculate their daily earnings when responding to Labor Office and SOFOFA questionnaries.

24 Payment in fichas helped trigger strikes in the North, including the ill-fated movement of December, 1907, which led to the massacre at the Escuela Santa María de Iquique. Fichas were not totally eradicated in Chile until the 1920s, in spite of laws outlawing them. See Marcelo Segall, "Biografía social de la ficha salario," *Mapocho* 2:2 (1964): 98–130. Also Stickell, "Migration and Mining," chapter 8.

25 For a comparison of manufacturing wages in all Chilean provinces for 1909 and 1910, see *BOT* 3, 1911, p. 113. For nitrates, see Stickell, "Migration and Mining," p. 264.

26 Stickell calculates a 20 percent difference between real wages for nitrate workers and those employed in manufacturing in the urban center in 1909 and 1910. Stickell, "Migration and Mining," p. 270

27 *BOT* 1, 1911, pp. 91, 95, 96.

28 See, for example, the pay scale in the unionized Antonio Ferrer factory in December, 1917, as given in ADGT, *Formularios de huelgas,* 1918, December 12, 1917 report on A. Ferrer & Co. strike. The female assemblers in the shoe industry had their wages tied to those of the men in collective bargaining, resulting in rates that were far higher than those paid to women in other industries.

29 Statistics on wages paid to manufacturing workers were compiled by the SOFOFA before 1910 and by the Oficina del Trabajo afterward. In both cases, employers provided the statistics, which were solicited either by letter or in person by police or Labor Office functionaries. The samples surveyed were often too small to be of much statistical significance. On other occasions, information from only one or two establishments represented trends for the entire industry. Neither is it clear that employers did not claim in the SOFOFA and OT surveys to pay higher wages than they actually paid, a tactic they frequently used to influence public opinion during strikes. Other statistics are available from the archive of the Labor Office. The most reliable of all sources are the actual contract agreements between employers and workers, which were often published in the daily and labor press after a wage settlement or strike. The four classifications of pay rates listed were derived from a scrutiny of all these sources. Some of these figures are to be found in ADGT, *Estadística del trabajo,* 1906, police reports on wages in Santiago; *Estadística del trabajo,* 1907, "Salarios medios, 1907" and "Salarios jornales, 1905"; *BOT* 1, 1911, pp. 90–99; *BOT* 10, 1915, pp. 35–43; *BOT* 12, 1919, pp. 122–35; *BOT* 24, 1926, p. 141, anexo 51.

30 *ELMV,* April 21, 1903, p. 4; *LaU* April 22, 1903, p. 4; ADGT, *Estudios y trabajos,* 1917, p. 51.

31 See, for example, *BOT* 21, 1923, p. 64.

32 *BOT* 1915, pp. 43–47; ADGT, *Estudios y trabajos,* 1918, State Railway wages, 1905–17, p. 8; *LaU,* March 17, 1918, p. 17; *LaU,* March 26, 1918, p. 7.; *LaOp,* February 7, 1919, p. 7; Barría, *Los movimientos de 1910 hasta 1926,* p. 222.

33 *LaN,* April 23, 1918, p. 12. These are the base salaries. Workers received a fixed bonus rate slightly higher than base pay if they worked thirteen of each fifteen days. Valparaíso salaries remained constant between 1913 and 1919.

34 *La Federación de Obreros de Imprenta,* November 3, 1918, p. 4.

35 *BOT* 24, 1926, anexo 51.

36 Ibid.

37 *LaU,* January 3, 1923, p. 1; *LaFOCh,* May 30, 1923, p. 2; *LaFOCh,* September 13, 1923, p. 4. *LaN,* March 18–April 14, 1924, for construction strike.

38 Strike records show that Valparaíso printers and metal workers and Santiago foundrymen, truck and cart builders, tailors, woodworkers, tram workers, and shoe factory personnel all won significant wage increases. Labor Office statistics for the metal industry also show widespread pay raises. *BOT* 24, 1926, anexo 51.

39 *BSOFOFA,* September, 1906, "Estadística de las industrias del territorio municipal de Santiago en 1905," pp. 362–64.

40 *BOT* 1, 1911, pp. 90–99; *BOT* 18, 1922, pp. 176–99.

41 *La Lei,* March 15, 1902, p. 2.

42 *BSOFOFA,* February, 1909, p. 75. Figures for work accidents reported to the OT and categorized according to the day of occurrence show the lowest rate (7.2 percent) for Sunday and the highest (12.7 percent) for Wednesday.

43 ADGT, *Estudios y trabajos,* 1917, pp. 273, 345.

44 *El Obrero Panadero,* January 1, 1925, p. 3.

45 Despite widespread protest by the USP in Santiago and Valparaíso and the sympathy of the Labor Office in favor of strict application, the law went totally unobserved. ADGT, *Communicaciones recibidas,* 1926, Valparaíso labor inspector to DGT, 28 May, 1926; Jefe de Inspección, Santiago, to DGT, December 18, 1926; *El Obrero Panadero,* January 1, 1926, p. 1.

46 *BOT* 7, 1915, p. 250.

47 In July, 1919, President Sanfuentes urged Congress to enact a law establishing the eight-hour day and a minimum wage for all businesses employing five or more workers. This proposal came at a time of intense agitation by the Workers' Assembly on National Nutrition (AOAN). *LaN,* July 24, 1919, p. 9.

48 *El Obrero Gráfico,* July 9, 1926, p. 1; *LaU,* January 16, 1925, p. 12.

49 *BSOFOFA,* October, 1913, pp. 973, 979, 983, 1,088; January, 1916, p. 8. PROFO 371/206, Monthly Summary, Santiago Legation, December 10, 1906; *ELDI,* June 9, 1907, p. 1; *LaOp,* February 6, 1918, p. 1; *Valparaíso Gráfico,* August 15, 1918, p. 1; Heredia interview.

50 *BOT* 22, 1924, p. 169.

51 Prefectura de Policía de Santiago, *Boletín de la policía de Santiago,* crime statistics in volumes for 1900–1909.

52 *BSOFOFA,* June, 1926, p. 364.

53 *La Lei,* April 1, 1903, p. 1; *LaOp,* July 4, 1918, p. 1; *BOT* 18, 1922, p. 274; *BOT* 22, 1924, p. 188.

54 *La Evolución* 7, July, 1917, p. 3; *El Obrero Panadero,* April 1, 1925, p. 1.

55 López interview. From the first baking strike in 1903 to that of 1921, bakers built a reputation for violent, aggressive behavior during strikes.

56 *BOT* 18, 1922, p. 274.

57 This was especially true of the large shoe companies, textile factories, and printing shops in both Valparaíso and Santiago. See: *BOT* 18, 1922, p. 274; *BOT* 1, 1911, "Condiciones del trabajo y vida obrera en Valparaíso."

58 *BOT* 18, 1922, p. 274.

59 *BOT* 21, 1923, pp. 89–91.

60 *BOT* 18, 1922, p. 274.

61 *BOT* 6, 1913, p. 70.

62 *BOT* 6, 1913, pp. 36, 60; *BOT* 10, 1915, p. 120; *BOT* 12, 1919, pp. 74–80; *BOT* 22, 1924, pp. 224–25.

63 *BSOFOFA,* February, 1917, p. 69.

64 *BSOFOFA,* January, 1925, p. 11. Employers claimed that early morning drinking caused many work accidents. In 1910, more accidents occurred among

workers in Santiago of less than sixteen years of age than among those in the 30–35 age bracket. *BOT* 6, 1913, p. 64. According to *La Lei*, January 19, 1906, p. 1, the children's ward of Santiago's main hospital, San Juan de Dios, was constantly filled with the mutilated victims of industrial accidents.

65 Miranda interview.

66 *ELMV*, October 28, 1913, p. 3; *BSOFOFA*, July, 1903, p. 217.

67 *BSOFOFA*, January, 1903, p. 3; July, 1903, p. 217.

68 ADGT, *Lei y reglamento sobre accidentes del trabajo*, Law 3.170, 1917.

69 *ELMS*, May 28, 1919, p. 16; *BOT* 18, 1922, p. 274.

70 The Valparaíso bakers' union retained the services of a lawyer to expedite claims involving accident insurance indemnities, but it is very doubtful that many other working class groups went to such effort or expense. *LaU*, May 5, 1918, p. 17.

71 *BOT* 21, 1923, p. 162. This figure demonstrates rather high compliance with the Work Accident Law compared with the response to other legislation.

72 ADGT, *Comunicaciones recibidas*, 1926, Report of Valparaíso police, May 15, 1926.

73 For a description of early labor legislation which claims that their roots lay in sentiments of noblesse oblige of Chilean elites, see: Pedro Felipe Iñíguez Irrará zaval, *Notas sobre el desarrollo del pensamiento social en Chile, 1901–1906* (Santiago, 1968).

74 For the history of the formation and intent of these bills, see: James O. Morris, *Elites, Intellectuals and Consensus* (Ithaca, 1966), pp. 144–244.

75 ADGT, *Comunicaciones recibidas*, 1926, report of Weber to Ministro de Previ sión Social, May 31, 1926, and December, 1926; ibid., Jefe, Inspección del Trabajo, Santiago, to DGT, December 18, 1926; *BOT* 24, 1926, pp. 97, 142.

76 In 1932, there were only 55,000 workers in legal unions. Morris, *Elites*, p. 252.

77 The unions had established widespread use of the eight-hour day by the early 1920s, and even after the 1924 law went into effect (1925), it is likely that workers who did not then enjoy the eight-hour day obtained it through collective bargaining rather than through application of the law. A 1902 decree established a 100-kilo maximum load to be hand-carried by marine workers. This decree was not applied in 1903, and it was not until 1920 that the IWW in Valparaíso effectively limited the load to eighty kilos from what had previously been more than 100. In 1923, Congress declared eighty kilos to be the legal maximum. Jorge Errázuriz Tagle and Guillermo Eyzaguirre, *Monografía de una familia obrera de Santiago* (Santiago, 1903), p. 91; Barría, *Los movimientos, 1900–1910*, p. 55; *Claridad*, January 10, 1921, p. 1; *BOT* 21, 1923, p. 199.

78 *La Lei*, April 5, 1902, p. 2; *La Ajitación* (S), April 19, 1902, p. 2.

79 This sum was lowered in 1907 and later abolished. *LaRef*, April 13, 1907, p. 1.

80 *BSOFOFA*, July, 1903, p. 217.

81 In 1904, the Chilean consul in San Luis, Argentina, noted an exodus of Chilean workers across the Andes seeking employment in Argentina. *BSOFOFA*, April, 1904, p. 121. Carl Solberg also claims that many Chilean workers emigrated

between 1880 and 1914 as a result of higher wages paid elsewhere. Solberg, *Immigration and Nationalism*, pp. 45–46. Also PROFO 881/9189, "Chile, Annual Report, 1907," p. 8.

82 Solberg, *Immigration and Nationalism*, pp. 28–32; *El Chileno*, November 17, 1906, p. 2; *ELDI*, November 14, 1906, p. 1.

83 For the results of the poll and a very interesting view of labor in Chile from the point of view of employers, see: *BSOFOFA*, October, 1913, pp. 973–83; November, 1913, pp. 1084–90.

84 See ibid., October, 1913, pp. 973–74, 978–79, 983; November, 1913, pp. 1,084, 1,086, 1,088, 1,090.

85 Ibid. This argument was, sadly, echoed by many working class organizations.

86 *La Lei*, March 28, 1903, p. 1.

87 This was admitted by labor and employer alike. See *El Chileno*, February 11, 1906, p. 1. ADGT, *Estadística del trabajo*, 1906, nos. 117, 169, and letter of the Municipality of San Miguel, November 26, 1906.

88 Leo S. Rowe, *The Early Effects of the European War upon the Finance, Commerce and Industry of Chile* (Washington, 1918), p. 47; *Luz y Vida* 59, August, 1913, p. 4; *Luz y Vida* 62, November, 1913, p. 1.

89 Rowe, *Early Effects*, pp. 51, 65; *ELMS*, April 4, 1915, p. 17; Stickell, "Migration and Mining," p. 102.

90 *BOT* 9, 1914, p. 63. *ELMS*, April 4, 1915, p. 17.

91 *BOT* 9, 1914, p. 63. The figures claimed that 4,142 workers of approximately 14,400 workers engaged in manufacturing were unemployed.

92 *La Batalla*, September 1, 1914, p. 1.

93 *ELMS*, April 4, 1915, p. 17.

94 Ibid. Stickell, "Migration and Mining," p. 115.

95 PROFO 371/1924, letters of the Amelia, Aguas Blancas, and Tarapacá-Tocopilla Nitrate Companies to the Foreign Office; Santiago Nitrate Company to the Foreign Office, August 14, 1914.

96 *La Batalla* 41, October, 1914, p. 3.

97 PROFO 371/3677, Board of Trade, Industries, and Manufactures to the Foreign Office, September 4, 1919.

98 PROFO 371/3677, Report of British Legation to Foreign Office, January 17, 1919. ADGT, *Notas eviadas*, Primer Semestre, 1919, Report 405, April 23, 1919; *Notas enviadas*, Primer Semestre, 1919, Report 405, April 23, 1919; *Notas enviadas*, 1919, vol. 2, dispatch 587, July 19, 1919.

99 ADGT, *Notas enviadas*, 1919, vol. 2, dispatch 587, July 19, 1919.

100 *LaOp*, February 7, 1919, p. 1; *ELMS*, August 28, 1919, p. 19.

101 ADGT, *Comunicaciones enviadas*, 1921, pp. 18–19; Jorge Baraona Puelma, *El paro forzoso* (Santiago, 1924), p. 165.

102 PROFO 371/5553, Legation to Foreign Office, July 7, 1921; USNA, M487, roll 4, "General Conditions Prevailing in Chile, May 27–June 10, 1921." *LaN*, September 11, 1921, p. 14.

103 For a description of life in the albergues, see: *LaN,* June 10, 1921, p. 11; August 24, 1921, p. 11; September 11, 1921, p. 14; November 17, 1921, p. 1.

104 *LaN,* November 17, 1921, p. 1.

105 ADGT, *Inspección regional Valparaíso,* 1922, vol. 2, Memorandum, Jefe, Inspección del Trabajo, Valparaíso, May, 1922, p. 6.

106 ADGT, *Comunicaciones recibidas,* November, 1926, Report of DGT Director Weber, no date.

107 Stickell claims that unemployed nitrate workers often preferred to remain idle rather than work at low-paying jobs. "Migration and Mining," pp. 121–24.

108 See Iñíguez, *Notas;* and Morris, *Elites.*

109 Kirsch, "Industrialization," pp. 154, 202.

110 For the Bakers' Union's opinion of foreign bosses, see: *El Obrero Panadero,* July 1, 1925, p. 3.

111 Tram smashing was a favorite pastime of Chilean workers, who were often joined in the destruction by young members of the "aristocracy." A number of tram riots took place following the first in 1888 in Santiago, usually as the result of increased fares. See: *ELMV,* November 24–December 10, 1914; *LaU,* March 11–21, 1920.

112 For a good sampling of employer opinions of Chilean workers, see: *BSOFOFA,* October, 1913, p. 965; November, 1913, p. 1,007.

113 Solberg, *Immigration and Nationalism,* pp. 157–60.

114 PROFO 371/1309, General Manager, Chilean Electric Tramway Company, to FO, September 2, 1919.

115 Ibid., Annual Report of the Legation, 1911, p. 19; 371/5558, Legation to FO, June 13, 1921; 371/7204, McLeod Report, February 3, 1922; 371/5556, Consul Antofagasta to Legation, May 10, 1921.

116 For examples, see: *ELMS,* July 22, 1906, p. 9; *LaOp,* February 12, 1918, p. 1; August 15, 1917, p. 2; February 6, 1918, p. 1; February 10, 1918, p. 1.

117 *El Chileno,* May 4, 1907, p. 1.

118 *LaOp,* December 17, 1917, p. 1.

119 ADGT, *Comunicaciones enviadas,* 1920, p. 10.

120 *LaN,* November 4, 1919, p. 11; November 8, 1919, p. 12. ADGT, *Inspección regional, Valparaíso,* 1921, vol. 1, Report of September 23, 1921.

121 PROFO 16/344, Telegram from Valparaíso Consulate, June 3, 1903; 371/17, Cable, General Manager to the Antofagasta and Bolivia Railway Company, February 7, 1906; 371/17, Voerwerk and Company to British Legation, February 8, 1906; 371/3679, Chilean Electric Tramway and Light Company to Foreign Office, September 2, 1919.

122 *LaN,* October 21, 1921, p. 15.

123 Ibid.; *LaFOCh,* February 11, 1922, p. 1; Asociación del Trabajo, *Boletín 3,* July 30, 1925, p. 2; no. 11, April 30, 1926, p. 1.

124 Morris, *Elites,* p. 202; Asociación del Trabajo, *Boletín 8,* January 30, 1926, p. 10.

125 Asociación del Trabajo, *Boletín 12, April 30, 1926.*

126 Eric J. Hobsbawm, *Labouring Men: Studies in the History of Labour* (London, 1964), p. 273.

CHAPTER 3: THE CONDITION OF THE URBAN WORKING CLASS

1 See Peter N. Stearns, "National Character and European Labor History," in Peter Stearns and Daniel Walkowitz, eds., *Workers in the Industrial Revolution* (New Brunswick, N.J., 1974) pp. 16–21.

2 Chile, *Censo de 1920*, 44; *Censo de 1930*, p. 105.

3 Interviews with Blest, Heredia, López, Schweitzer.

4 Most of the conventillo addresses were taken from Santiago newspapers, especially for the 1917–19 period and 1925.

5 Ugarte, *Valparaíso*, pp. 23, 50.

6 Instituto de Higiene de Chile, *Higiene pública en Chile* (Santiago, 1908), p. 68. The High Council on Worker Housing claimed that 1,251 conventillos existed in Santiago in 1908 with a total population of 72,000 residents. Given the general lack of efficiency of the High Council and the widespread agreement that conventillos were the typical form of working class dwellings, these figures appear too low.

7 OT, *Las habitaciones obreras en Chile* (Santiago, 1911), p. 55; Chile, *Censo de 1907*, p. 423.

8 *AE*, 1915, vol. 2, p. 180; *BOT* 12, 1919, p. 12.

9 It is difficult to accurately estimate the total conventillo population, mainly due to shifts in the population density per conventillo as calculated by the OT. For example, OT statistics for 1916 give 41.7 as the average population per conventillo studied, for an extrapolated total population of 84,175 (given 2,022 conventillos.) The 1924 figure is 78.58 per conventillo, which indicates either a total conventillo population of around 157,000 or far greater crowding. *BOT* 12, 1919, p. 10; *BOT* 24, 1925, anexo 45.

10 James R. Scobie, *Buenos Aires: Plaza to Suburb, 1870–1910* (New York, 1974), p. 147.

11 ADGT, *Estadística del trabajo*, 1907, "Precios de habitaciones obreras."

12. The best description of a typical conventillo is found in the thesis of R. Osvaldo Marín, *Las habitaciones para obreros* (Santiago, 1903). Other sources which describe individual Santiago conventillos or give general accounts of working class housing are: *La Lei*, February 11, 1904, p. 2; Julio Pérez Canto, *Las habitaciones para obreros* (Santiago, 1898), pp. 214–15; *LaN*, March 12, 1917, p. 8; USNA, M487, roll 21, Report of Collier, June 5, 1921; López and Heredia interviews.

13 Pérez, *Las habitaciones*, p. 214.

14 *LaRef*, October 15, 1907, p. 1.

15 One need only trace the history of the great rent strike movements to draw this conclusion. Muckraking articles about conventillos frequently found their way into elitist dailes such as *El Mercurio*, *La Lei*, and *La Nación*, as well as the reformist *La Opinión*. U.S. ambassadors, university students, and important politicians all made periodic appearances in working class districts to tour conventillos, especially if housing legislation was being discussed by Congress.

16 For tax assesments in Santiago, see: Alberto Prado Martínez, *Anuario Prado Martínez 1903* (Santiago, 1903), pp. 652–708.

17 Marín, *Las habitaciones*, p. 10; Pérez, *Las habitaciones*, p. 215.
18 *LaOp*, January 18, 1917, p. 1; November 7, 1918, p. 6.
19 Chile, Concejo Superior de Higiene Pública, *Memorias y actas*, 1902, vol. 11, pp. 63-64.
20 Heredia interview. Also interview and walking tour with Félix López. Both men grew up in conventillos. Good examples of pre-1927 conventillos and cités still exist in Santiago along Romero and Erasmo Escala between Chacabuco and Libertad.
21 For 1911 figures, see OT, *Las habitaciones*, pp. 51, 56-58.
22 Ibid., p. 59.
23 A 1914 figure showed Iquique workers as spending 7.4 percent of their total income on housing as opposed to the 14-16 percent figures recorded for Santiago and Valparaíso, indicating that the figure of 12.47 percent would probably be higher if only Valparaíso and Santiago were taken into account. *BOT* 2, 1911, p. 21; *BOT* 18, 1922, pp. 90-91; *BOT* 24, 1926, anexo 50. ADGT, *Formularios de monografías*, 1912.
24 *VR* 14, July, 1919, p. 4.
25 For the texts and descriptions of these laws see: Policía de Santiago, *Boletín* 7, January, 1902, p. 92; Héctor Holley, *Las huelgas* (Santiago, 1905), pp. 156-58; OT, *Las habitaciones*, p. 30.
26 OT, *Las habitaciones*, p. 38.
27 *BOT* 12, 1919, p. 25.
28 *BSOFOFA*, March, 1904, p. 83.
29 *LaOp*, June 2, 1920, p. 4.
30 *ELMS*, October 4, 1919, p. 15.
31 ADGT, *Formularios de monografías*, 1912. *BOT* 2, 1911, p. 21; no. 18, 1922, pp. 90-91; no. 24, 1926, anexo 50. The range in percentage of income spent on food was 29.6 to 90.4.
32 López interview.
33 *BOT* 18, 1922, p. 25.
34 Errázuriz and Eyzaguirre, *Monografía*, p. 25.
35 *BOT* 18, 1922, p. 85. For bread and potato costs, see the yearly *BOT.*
36 López interview; *BOT* 24, 1926, p. 79.
37 PROFO 371/206, Rennie Report, September 9, 1907. *LaOp*, January 19, 1917, p. 5; August 27, 1918, p. 1. Arnold Bauer, in his study of rural Chile, claimed that agricultural workers ate very little meat during the late nineteenth and early twentieth centuries. Bauer, *Chilean Rural Society*, p. 74.
38 Errázuriz and Eyzaguirre, *Monografía*, p. 25.
39 1902 figures are from the Sunday commercial page of *La Lei*. Figures for 1925 are from the commercial section "frutos del país" in *ELMS*. Both sets of prices are quotes from wholesalers in La Vega, Santiago's principal market.
40 The "weighted" price index is meant to take working class consumption patterns into consideration in determining the rise in cost of living. In combining the detailed 1903 Errázuriz-Eyzaguirre study with per capita consumption figures for 1913-19 issued by the OT, I decided to weight the value of each food article

as a percentage of its total physical weight in the working class diet. The following numbers were assigned to the various food items, denoting their relative importance: bread (15), potatoes (13), meat (4), beans (3), sugar (3), corn (2), rice (1), coffee (.25). People obviously ate more of one item and less of another in the face of price fluctuations. The weights given above are intended to reflect the near balance between bread and potatoes which appears to have been achieved by 1919. The overwhelming importance of these two items in the working class diet did not change during the period.

41 USNA, M487, roll 29, Report of Consul Thompson, October 10, 1922.

42 See, for example, *La Comuna,* August 23, 1919, p. 3; *VR,* first issue of November, 1918, p. 1; *LaOp,* November 8, 1918, p. 3; *BSOFOFA,* July, 1919, p. 464.

43 *LaOp,* November 23, 1918, p. 1.

44 *BOT* 2, 1911, "Precios medios de los artículos de consumo."

45 López interview.

46 Policía de Santiago, *Boletín,* June, 1918, p. 228.

47 *Justicia,* July 16, 1925, p. 1.

48 *BOT* 2, 1911, p. 21; *BOT* 18, 1922, pp. 90–91.

49 Heredia interview.

50 *La Lei* Sunday commercial page; *ELMS* "frutos del país" Sunday section.

51 BSOFOFA 2, February, 1924, pp. 99–102.

52 *BOT* 22, 1924, p. 207.

53 Nicolás Sánchez Albornoz, *The Population of Latin America—A History* (Berkeley, 1974), p. 171.

54 The Instituto de Higiene de Santiago, in its *Boletín de higiene i demografía,* año 6, no. 12, December, 1903, p. 185, año 7, 1906, Resumen, p. vi, and vol. 8, Resumen of 1905, p. 306, claimed mortality coefficients of 31.0 and 31.5 in 1902 and 1903 and 36.1 in 1905. The 1929 figures for Santiago and Chile are from *SE,* 1929, p. 2.

55 *La Lei,* November 5, 1902, pp. 1–2; December 11, 1902, p. 1.

56 *SE,* 1929, p. 4.

57 Ibid., p. 5.

58 USNA, M487, roll 14, Deichman Report, December 5, 1921.

59 Chile, Junta Central de Vacuna, *Memoria,* 1906, p. 1. *La Lei,* August 19, 1905, p. 3; May 10, 1906, p. 1. In 1903, one student of the public health problem estimated that only 10 percent of the population in Chile was vaccinated against smallpox. Vaccination in Chile was not obligatory during the 1902–27 period, although the government at times ordered the inoculation of people in threatened areas. As late as 1921, many labor unions, including the FOCh and the Anarcho-Syndicalists, opposed mandatory vaccination as an affront to personal dignity. See also Juan Miquel, *De la vacuna obligatoria* (Santiago, 1903), p. 21.

60 Concejo de Higiene de Valparaíso, *Archivo,* first semester, 1900, p. 240; *LaN,* September 24, 1921, p. 9; PROFO 371/7206, Annual Report, 1921, p. 28.

61 USNA, M487, roll 51, enclosure from *ELMV,* July 7, 1905.

62 Policía de Santiago, *Boletín,* October, 1906, p. 109.

63 *LaOp,* November 22, 1917, p. 1; Concejo de Higiene de Valparaíso, *Archivo,* 1899, and first semester, 1900, p. 222; *La Lei,* July 8, 1903, p. 2.

64 As late as 1916 in Santiago, only 10,065 individual domiciles had plumbing which met municipal standards. See *AE,* 1915, vol. 2, p. 137.

65 Carlos Anabalón Sanderson, *El problema sanitario* (Santiago, 1917), pp. 14–28; PROFO 371/1309, Annual Report, 1912, p. 20.

66 For a description of the curanderos and their effect on the working class, see: *LaOp,* January 3, 1920, p. 1; *LaU,* July 1, 1920, p. 71; *La Lei,* July 7, 1903, p. 3.

67 Municipalidad de Santiago, *Boletín municipal de estadística,* First Semester, 1908, p. 18.

68 Ibid., p. 18. Policía de Santiago, *Boletín,* November 1917, p. 371.

69 Policía de Santiago, *Boletín,* September, 1911, p. 262; Liga Chilena de Higiene Social, *Memorias,* 1920–21, pp. 18–88.

70 Municipalidad de Santiago, *Boletín municipal,* first semester, 1908, p. 17; *AE,* 1926, vol. 2, pp. 50–56.

71 *LaN,* December 21, 1920, p. 3.

72 *El Deber* 22, January 1, 1908, p. 1; *El Surco,* November, 1924, p. 1; *El Sembrador,* November 20, 1926, p. 2.

73 Concejo de Higiene de Valparaíso, *Archivos,* p. 256; Alejandro Miqueles, *Recopilación policial* (Santiago, 1917), p. 612; Policía de Santiago, *Boletín* 14, April 30, 1903, p. 152.

74 *LaOp,* August 21, 1919, p. 4; *La Lei,* March 17, 1908, p. 1. These are unique articles for their detailed account of the underworld connections of white slavery in Chile, a problem which received widespread attention in the press.

75 Concejo de Higiene de Valparaíso, *Archivos,* p. 256; Liga de Higiene Social, *Memorias,* 1920–21, p. 199.

76 Chile, *Censo de 1920,* pp. 247–48.

77 Instituto de Higiene de Santiago, *Boletín de higiene,* año 8, 1906, p. vi.

78 López and Heredia interviews. In his study of early twentieth-century German workers, people far more educated than their Chilean counterparts, Moritz Bromme found that they were unaware of any methods of birth control aside from coitus interruptus. Cited in Stearns, ed., *Workers in the Industrial Revolution,* p. 19.

79 Sánchez Albornoz, *The Population,* p. 200.

80 Instituto de Higiene de Santiago, *Boletín de higiene,* año 7, resumen 1903, p. vi; ibid., vol. 8, resumen 1905, p. 306; *SE,* 1929, p. 4. The actual rates were 346 in 1903, 331 in 1905, and less than 233 (the provincial figure) for 1929.

81 Luis Calvo Mackenna, *Encuesta sobre la mortalidad infantil en Chile* (Santiago, 1930), p. 6.

82 For discussions of the cause of infant mortality from various sources, see: Calvo Mackenna, *Encuesta,* pp. 29–66; Anabalón, *El problema,* pp. 44–46; *La Campaña* 9, November, 1900, p. 1; *ELMS,* January 13, 1919, p. 12; *LaFOCh,* March 24, 1924, p. 1.

83 *LaN,* April 6, 1917, p. 8; *LaU,* April 17, 1918, p. 10; *LaU,* July 5, 1920, p. 5.

84 Chile, *Censo de 1930,* vol. 2, p. 434.

85 Ibid.

86 Jorge González von Marees, *El problema obrero en Chile* (Santiago, 1923), p. 58.

87 Amanda Labarca Huberson, *Historia de la enseñanza en Chile* (Santiago, 1939), pp. 216, 280.

88 Ibid., p. 279; González von Marees, *El problema*, p. 58.

89 *La Gran Federación Obrera de Chile* 40, November 1, 1911; *LaOp,* March 31, 1919, pp. 1, 8.

90 *AE,* 1926, vol. 5, pp. 18-19.

91 Labarca, *Historia,* p. 280.

92 *AE,* 1926, vol. 5, p. 1.

93 Concejo Superior de Higiene Pública, *Memorias y actas,* 1903, vol. 12, pp. 31-33.

94 For an excellent description, see Díaz, *Recopilación,* pp. 78-104.

95 *BSOFOFA,* January, 1922, pp. 8-9.

96 Bauer, *Chilean Rural Society,* p. 29; Loveman, *Struggle in the Countryside,* p. 175.

97 López and Heredia interviews. For accounts of the lack of religiosity of the working class, see: Javier Díaz Lira, *Observaciones sobre la cuestión social en Chile* (Santiago, 1904), p. 11; Charles M. Pepper, *Panama to Patagonia* (Chicago, 1906), p. 208. *BSOFOFA,* July, 1903, p. 241.

98 For a good discussion of the Conservative Party's beliefs regarding the "social question," see: Iñíguez, *Notas;* and Díaz Lira, *Observaciones,* p. 11.

99 Iñíguez, *Notas,* p. 44; *El Proletario* (Tocopilla) 34, December 24, 1904, p. 2; *La Ajitación* (Estación Dolores), July 9, 1905, p. 4.

100 For an account of the Viernes Santo riot and the career of Pope Julio, see: *ELDI,* April 23, 1905, p. 1; *ELMS,* April 22, 1905 p. 5; *El Ferrocarril,* April 22, 1905, p. 1. Fernando Pinto Lagarrigue, *Crónica política del siglo XX* (Santiago, 1970), p. 34.

101 *La Gran Federación Obrera de Chile,* August 1, 1911, p. 2; October 5, 1912, p. 2.

102 *LaFOCh,* October 15, 1923, p. 2; December 11, 1921, p. 3. *La Batalla* 11, June, 1913, p. 4.

103 López interview; Pepper, *Panama to Patagonia,* p. 213.

104 Municipalidad de Santiago, *Boletín municipal,* 1908, p. 60; *BSOFOFA,* February 1, 1910, p. 94.

105 Prices fell to less than fifty cents for cheaper seats in many theatres. See also *Justicia,* July 3, 1925, p. 4; July 6, 1925, p. 5; March 15, 1925, p. 6. *LaN,* June 17, 1925, p. 9.

106 César E. Zilleruelo, *El alcoholismo en Chile* (Santiago, 1909), p. 67. Zilleruelo estimated the national average for per capita consumption to be greater than seven liters and placed the figure for the Province of Tarapacá at ten. Antonio Cárdenas Soto, in *El alcoholismo en Chile* (Santiago, 1909), p. 15, estimated average per capita consumption throughout Chile to be fifteen liters.

107 USNA, M487, roll 15, Report of U.S. Economic Consul in Valparaíso to the Consul General, January 4, 1921.

108 Zilleruelo, *El alcoholismo*, p. 67.
109 See map of legal bars in Santiago in *ELDI*, November 28, 1906, p.1.
110 López interview; *BSOFOFA*, January, 1925, p. 11.
111 López interview. This statement still holds true today.
112 *LaOp*, March 3, 1917, p. 3; *La Gran Federación Obrera de Chile*, January 20, 1912, p. 2; López interview.
113 *BSOFOFA*, September, 1913, pp. 979, 983, 1,087. Bauer's study of rural labor notes that hacendados of the Central Valley blamed alcohol for the scarcity of labor at harvest time. Bauer, *Chilean Rural Society*, p. 147. Also *ELDI*, June 9, 1913.
114 Countless articles in the working class press hammered forth this theme. Every labor group from Anarchist to Catholic named alcoholism as a major working class problem.
115 Miqueles, *Recopilación*, p. 451.
116 Zilleruelo, *El alcoholismo*, pp. 61–63; Hernán Correa, *El alcoholismo y la lei* (Santiago, 1910), pp. 38–41.
117 Zilleruelo, *El alcoholismo*, p. 92; *AE*, 1902, vol. 4, p. 123.
118 Policía de Santiago, *Boletín*, 1903–10.
119 Fluctuations in the number of people arrested and jailed did occur, but due to incomplete information, poor categorization of statistics by the Central Office of Statistics, and discrepancies between the figures given by the Santiago police and the Ministry of Justice, it is impossible to draw any conclusions from these statistical variations. The police periodically enforced the Ley de Alcoholes with greater and lesser zeal, further complicating the problem.
120 Zilleruelo, *El alcoholismo*, p. 95.
121 Policía de Santiago, *Boletín*, February, 1920, pp. 72–74.
122 *LaN*, March 5, 1918, pp. 13–15.
123 *La Gran Federación Obrera de Chile*, February 1, 1912, p. 1.
124 It is difficult to separate drunks from criminals in most of these cases. See *AE*, 1913, col. 4., p. 57; 1919, vol. 4, p. 35; 1925, vol. 4, p. 35. Ministerio de Justicia, *Estadística carcelaria*, 1908, p. 13; Policía de Santiago, *Boletín*, March, 1905, p. 206.
125 *AE*, 1925, vol. 4, p. 77.
126 Colchagua, Arauco, Antofagasta, and Cautín were the most murder-prone provinces. See: Ministerio de Justicia, *Estadística carcelaria*, 1908, p. 25; Policía de Santiago, *Boletín*, 1904–08.
127 Policía de Santiago, *Boletín*, December, 1909, p. 621.
128 Ibid., March, 1907, p. 191; *AE*, 1914, vol. 4, pp. 82–83, 101.
129 Policía de Santiago, *Boletín*, 1901–09. Few workers could afford a handgun, but many sources mention the frequent and skillful use of knives by the working class.
130 Ibid., April, 1907, p. 251.
131 López and Heredia interviews; Policía de Santiago, *Boletín*, February, 1917, p. 73.
132 Of the eighty-nine families surveyed in the 1911–25 OT monographs, fifty-six

finished the stipulated period with a budgetary deficit. Many of the remaining families may have also gone into debt, since the expenditures measured included only food, shelter, clothing, and heating costs.

133 *LaFOCh,* November 23, 1922, p. 1.

134 In 1915, foreigners owned 171 of the 271 pawnshops registered in Chile. Of the 171, Spaniards owned 131, and they controlled four-fifths of the total capital held by all 271. Foreign-owned pawnshops dominated in the Santiago-Valparaíso urban areas. See *SE,* 1915, p. 83.

135 *ELMS,* January 19, 1919, p. 19. The husband and wife in the Errázuriz and Eyzaguirre monograph had nearly half of their clothes in hock during the year they were under observation.

136 See figures for 1917 and 1918 in *LaN,* January 17, 1918, p. 1, and *LaOp,* January 20, 1919, p. 3.

137 *AE,* 1913 and 1924, vol. 10, "Comercio interior, casas de préstamo."

138 Ibid., 1919, 1921, 1922, 1923, 1925, 1927.

139 For descriptions of the functioning and regulation of pawnshops, see: José Cervantes Cortínez, *Breve estudio sobre las casas de préstamos* (Santiago, 1903), pp. 11–22; *BSOFOFA,* December, 1909, p. 595; *LaOp,* May 5, 1919, p. 4; *LaOp,* January 20, 1919, p. 3; *LaOp,* October 22, 1919, p. 1; *LaN,* July 24, 1919, p. 9; *LaN,* March 25, 1920, p. 10; *ELMS,* September 7, 1919, p. 19.

140 Stickell, "Migration and Mining," p. iii.

141 In 1925 the average wage in the nitrate fields was higher than that paid to unionized construction laborers, including helpers in the skilled trades, tram car drivers, and printers in the non-"master" categories. Nitrate workers on the average made double the salaries of unskilled and even semiskilled factory laborers. All other comparisons are based on information presented in Stickell, "Migration and Mining."

CHAPTER 4: THE RISE OF LABOR UNIONS

1 Marcelo Segall, *Las luchas de clase en las primeras décadas de la República de Chile* (Santiago, 1962), pp. 39–42.

2 Oscar Parrao, "La mutualidad en Chile," in *BOT* 21, 1923, pp. 13–25.

3 Ibid., pp. 13–14. Parrao did not include the eighty all-female societies operating in 1922, which had an estimated membership of 18,000.

4 ADGT, *Estadística de la Asociación Obrera,* 1910, pp. 24, 30, 57.

5 Segall, *Las luchas,* pp. 8, 33–42.

6 Ibid., pp. 33–37; Jobet, *Luis Emilio Recabarren,* p. 83.

7 Marcelo Segall, "En Amerique Latine, development du movement ouvier et prosciption," in "1871: Jalons pour une histoire de la Commune de Paris," *International Review of Social History* 17 (1972): 325–69.

8 Max Nettlau, the Anarchist historian and bibliographer, cites correspondence of the Argentine Socialist José Ingenieros as mentioning the formation of the Chilean branches of the AIT by members of the Workers' Federation of Uruguay. Cited in Segall, "En Amerique Latine," p. 348.

9 Max Nettlau, "Contribución a la bibliografía anarquista de la América Latina hasta 1914," in *Certamen Internacional* of *La Protesta* (Buenos Aires), 1927, p. 8; Ramírez, *Historia del movimiento obrero*, pp. 146–47.

10 Osvaldo López, *Diccionario biográfico obrero: libro precursor* (Concepción, 1910). Also, ibid., vol. 2 (Santiago, 1912).

11 Ramírez, *Historia del movimiento obrero*, pp. 227–54: Jobet, *Luis Emilio Recabarren*, pp. 91–100.

12 *El Perseguido*, December 7, 1890, p. 1; April 5, 1891, p. 3; July 5, 1891, p. 1.

13 Ibid., October 23, 1892, p. 3.

14 *El Oprimido*, May 16, 1893; September 18, 1893.

15 Alejandro Escobar y Carvallo, "Inquietudes políticas y gremiales a comienzos del siglo," *Occidente* 120 (October, 1959): 8.

16 *La Protesta Humana*, June 12, 1898, p. 3; *La Tromba*, March, 1901, p. 3.

17 *El Perseguido* 82, May 31, 1895, p. 4. The Spanish edition of *The Conquest of Bread* arrived in Chile by way of Argentina.

18 *El Rebelde* (Buenos Aires) 58, March 10, 1901, p. 3.

19 *El Rebelde* (S) 1, November 20, 1898; no. 2, May 1, 1899, p. 1.

20 A survery of the holdings of the European Anarchist press at the IISG produces very few references to Chile before 1903. No mention is made in *Tierra y Libertad* (Madrid) before 1903, one article in *El Corsario* (La Coruña) in 1896, nothing in *Freedom* (London) between 1886 and 1899, nothing in *Les Temps Nouveaux* (Paris) between 1895 and 1898. Notably, all of these papers frequently mentioned Cuba, Mexico, Brazil, Argentina, and Uruguay, mainly through personal correspondence with European immigrants.

21 Diego Abad de Santillán, "La Protesta, su historia, sus diversas bases, y su significación en el movimiento anarquista en América del Sur" in the *Certamen Internacional* of *La Protesta* (Buenos Aires), 1927, pp. 35–39. *La Protesta Humana* 119, April 20, 1901, p. 4; no. 121, May 5, 1901, p. 3.

22 On July 16, 1925, three gunmen "with marked Spanish accents" robbed $50,000 from a branch of the Banco de Chile in Santiago. They were Durruti, Ascaso, and Jover, currently hiding out in Latin America after a crime spree in Europe. A few days earlier, they botched a holdup at the Club Hípico racetrack and missed a chance for a good haul at the Central Train Station on July 18 when an employee lost his keys to the strongbox containing the State Railway payroll. After this failure, the trio crossed the Andes into Argentina, where they robbed the "Caballitos" metro station and killed a guard on November 17. Schweitzer interview (he defended the driver of the getaway car). *LaN*, July 17, 1925, p. 1; July 19, p. 25; Abel Paz, *Durruti, the People Armed* (Montreal, 1976), p. 78.

23 *La Ajitación* (S), February 14, 1902, p. 1; *El Siglo XX*, May 18, 1901, p. 1; *La Rebelión*, November, 1901, p. 1.

24 Jobet, *Luis Emilio Recabarren*, p. 103; Barría, *Los movimientos, 1900–10*, p. 92.

25 Baldomero Lillo, Pablo Burchard, Augusto D'Halmar, Mariano LaTorre, Julio Ortiz de Zárate, and Fernando Santiván participated in the "Tolstoyanist" colony of the Calle Pío Nono in Santiago's Ultra Mapocho district. See Fernando Santiván, *Memorias de un tolstoyano* (Santiago, 1955).

26 Manuel Barrera, in "Perspectiva histórica de la huelga obrera en Chile," *Cuadernos de la Realidad Nacional* 9 (September, 1971): 125, has added up the strikes mentioned by Ramírez in *Historia del movimiento,* Marcelo Segall in *El desarrollo del capitalismo en Chile* (Santiago, 1953), and Marcia de Ortiz and Ivan Ljubetic in *Estudio sobre el origen y desarrollo del proletariado en Chile durante el siglo XX* (Santiago, 1954), and arrives at the figure of seventy-five strikes. Since none of the authors indicate how they went about gathering their information, it is difficult to evaluate the accuracy of the figure.

27 Floreal Recabarren Rojas, *Historia del proletriado de Tarapacá y Antofagasta, 1884–1913* (Santiago, 1954), pp. 227–32.

28 *ELMS,* March 28–April 4, 1902, p. 1; Luis Miranda Sepúlveda, "Reseña histórica de la FOEICh," *Boletín de la FOEICh, Edición especial del centenario de la Federación de Obreros y Empleados de Imprenta de Chile* (Santiago, 1972), p. 3; Asamblea Tipográfica, *Boletín,* June 9–16, 1902.

29 *El Martillo,* January 26, 1902, p. 3; February 10, 1902, pp. 1–2.

30 *ELMS,* March 28–April 3, 1902, p. 1.

31 The sailors returned to the mutual aid style organization that they had before the strike. The union's Anarchist leader, Ignacio Mora, left Valparaíso to begin a career as an agitator in the nitrate zone.

32 *Jerminal!* March 25, 1904, p. 1.

33 *La Luz,* first fortnight, March, 1902, p. 1; no. 11, April, 1902, p. 3. *La Lei,* May 8, 1902, p. 3.

34 Barría, *Los movimientos, 1900–10,* p. 79.

35 Recabarren Rojas, *Historia del proletariado,* p. 198; Barría, *Los movimientos, 1900–1910,* pp. 99–100.

36 Recabarren Rojas, *Historia del proletariado,* pp. 197–98.

37 Most of the mancomunales expressed a social democratic line befitting the left wing of the PD. Articles by Anarchist writers did appear in the brotherhood press, but those selected for publication were normally of a vague or utopian nature. The goal of the brotherhoods as outlined in the 1904 program of the Combination of the Chilean Mancomunales was to "achieve the economic, social, and intellectual betterment of the worker." *El Trabajo* (Iquique), October 4, 1905, p. 1. See also: *El Marítimo* (Antofagasta), *El Trabajo* (Coquimbo), and *El Deber* (Chañaral).

38 See chapter 3, section on food prices.

39 *El Carpintero* 2, February, 1905; *El Alba* 2, September, 1905, p. 1.

40 *El Alba,* March 1, 1906, p. 4; no. 10, March, 1906, p. 3; no. 13, May 1, 1906, p. 1.

41 *La Lei,* May 2, 1906, p. 2. May 1 had first been observed in Santiago and Valparaíso during the late 1890s and normally involved indoor meetings or brief parades staged by the Anarchists. It was not until 1905 that May 1 demonstrations began to attract much attention in the daily press. Mainly due to the efforts of the Anarchists, May 1 grew to the stage of a de facto working class holiday in 1907, although it did not become an official holiday in Chile until 1925. The

attendance at May 1 rallies provides an excellent indication of the strength of organized labor.

42 *El Trabajo* (Coquimbo), May 11, 1907, p. 2.

43 *LaRef* October 9, 1906 p. 4.

44 *ELMV,* May 19, 1906, p. 7; *El Chileno,* July 1906, p. 2; *ELH* June 12, 1907, p. 4.

45 *La Lei,* March 27, 1907, p. 2; *El Trabajo* (Coquimbo), May 11, 1907, p. 3.

46 *LaRef,* July 24, 1906, p. 1.

47 The following conclusions were derived from biographical information obtained by a careful reading of the working class press during the 1902–27 period, as well as secondary works. No single source apart from the López *Diccionario biográfico obrero* dicusses the lives of working class leaders, and his study generally includes only those union leaders who were also members of the PD. Information concerning labor union men is available from their obituaries in the labor press, although there is no way of finding out when most of them died. The biographical material presented in this study, therefore, came from more than a hundred different sources and was pieced together bit by bit.

48 *LaRef,* October 27, 1906, p. 1; November 3, 1906, p. 1.

49 *Luz y Vida* 34, July, 1911, gives his obituary.

50 *La Lei,* January 26, 1906, p. 1.

51 Barría, Recabarren, and I all obtained information regarding strikes by scanning newspapers on a day-to-day basis. Recabarren totaled up the number he had identified per year but made no attempt to systematically evaluate them. Barría did not count the number of strikes, either by year or in total, nor did he evaluate the strikes on a statistical basis. In some cases he did not identify the establishment where workers were on strike or go into detail as to why they had struck. He rarely mentioned anything about the organization of the workers, the outcome of the strike, the response of employers and government, etc. For strikes during the years 1906–8, it appears that his only source of information was *La Reforma.*

Barrera based his analysis of strikes during the 1900–10 period entirely on Barría's book. His totals probably included all the work stoppages and protest strikes (including May 1 strikes) listed by Barría, although he doesn't say.

The purpose of my research was to gather data regarding strikes which could be analyzed statistically and therefore provide both a broad and detailed view of the nature of strikes in Chile at given periods of time between 1902 and 1927. Because my research time and resources were limited, I confined my study of strikes to the years 1902–8, 1917–21, and 1925. These years witnessed the heaviest strike activity and the most dynamic periods of unionization in the history of Chile. I defined a "strike" as the abandonment of work by members of the working class for periods of time which had not been predetermined before the strike began and for reasons not involving politics. For example, a work stoppage to protest the arrest of workers would not be considered a strike. Nor would a predetermined one- or two-day walkout for any reason be considered a strike. I do not count May 1 as a strike in my analysis, nor could the failure to work during a period of public disorder, such as the October, 1905, riot in Santiago, be a strike unless workers presented grievance petitions to their employers.

A strike had to be individually carried out in order to be considered a single strike, in this analysis. If, for example, the Shoeworkers' Federation decided to stop work in four different shoe factories on a given day, I measured those four walkouts as one strike. Likewise, the general strikes which occurred from time to time were counted as a single strike rather than many strikes.

The process involved in identifying and tracing the development of each strike was painstaking and often led to a dead end. I normally used a daily newspaper with few pages or specific columns dedicated to news about labor as a "scanner" to identify a strike. As the strike developed and I failed to find all the required information in the paper, I consulted another and then others if necessary. Many strikes simply disappeared without a trace from the pages of all available newspapers. In other cases, information was obtained for the strike's settlement, but no news of its beginning could be found. For these reasons, the number of strikes recorded each year must be regarded as the *minimum* number which occurred. The number of unknown examples within each of the thirty-one variables I tabulated also fluctuated with the information available.

I used the Radical Party daily *La Lei* as my Santiago "scanner" and then turned to *El Mercurio, El Diario Ilustrado,* and *El Chileno* for further reference for the years 1902–8. *La Reforma* and the labor press were also of great value in filling out the strike forms. *El Heraldo* proved an easily readable paper for scanning the Valparaíso labor scene, with *El Mercurio* and *La Unión* providing the details. I was often able to check information provided by workers against employers' accounts of the strikes. Newspapers frequently published the written agreements between both parties after collective bargaining produced a solution.

I am confident that the sample of strikes as analyzed in this and the following chapters faithfully represents trends in the nature and occurrence of strikes during the period. More attention was paid by the daily press to strikes in transportation than to those in manufacturing because of the nature and size of the operations involved, but I do not believe that the sample is greatly skewed in favor of large-scale strikes.

52 *La Lei,* March 9–15, 1902, p. 2.

53 *La Lei,* March 14, 1902, p. 2. The reason for this early hatred of *El Mercurio* is not entirely clear. After the killing of seven workers by *El Mercurio's* employees in Valparaíso on May 12, 1903, the newpaper's unpopularity became overwhelming.

54 For an account of the strike, see: *La Lei,* January 30, 1902, p. 1; March 6, 1902, p. 1. *La Ajitación* (S), April 19, 1902, p. 1; *ELMS,* March 29–April 3, 1902, p. 1.

55 See: Asamblea Tipográfica, *Boletín,* June 9–16, 1902.

56 For a more complete account of the strike, see Peter DeShazo, "The Valparaíso Maritime Strike of 1903 and the Development of a Revolutionary Labor Movement in Chile," *Journal of Latin American Studies* 2 (May, 1979): 145–68.

57 *ELMS*, July 26-August 23, 1903, pp. 5-6; *ELMV*, August 8-29, 1903, pp. 5-6.
58 Food prices from *La Lei*, Sunday commercial section. Strikes from my survey.
59 *La Lei*, October 4-7, 1905, p. 2.
60 *LaRef*, June 23-July 2, 1906.
61 *ELMS*, July 22, 1906, p. 9.
62 *El Chileno*, July 26, 1906, p. 2.
63 *ELMS*, July 22, 1906 p. 9; *La Lei*, August 4, 1906, p. 4; *ELH*,December 26, 1906, p. 4; *ELH*, January 7, 1907, p. 1; *LaRef*, March 22, 1907, p. 4.
64 *El Trabajo* (Coquimbo), March 23, 1907, p. 2.
65 *LaRef*, February 25-March 4, 1907.
66 *ELH*, March 12, 1907, p. 1.
67 *La Lei*, May 2, 1907, p. 2; *LaRef*, May 3, 1907, p. 2.
68 Except where otherwise stated, this account of the strike is derived from issues of *La Lei, LaRef, ELDI, ELH,*and *El Trabajo* (Coquimbo), May 28-June 12, 1907.
69 *LaRef*, June 7, 1907, p. 1.
70 *La Lei*, June 8, 1907, p. 1.
71 *La Lei*, June 11, 1907, p. 1; *LaRef*, June 12, 1907, p. 1.
72 *ELDI*, June 8, 1907, p. 1.
73 *La Lei*, June 8, 1907, p. 1; *ELH*, June 10, 1907, p. 1.
74 *LaRef*, June 12, 1907, p. 1; *ELDI*, June 8, 1907, p. 1.
75 *ELH*, June 17, 1907, p. 5; June 20, 1907, p. 5.
76 *La Lei*, June 12, 1907, p. 1.
77 *El Trabajo* (Coquimbo), July 6, 1907, p. 2; July 13, 1907, p. 1.
78 Ibid., July 6, 1907, p. 2.
79 Floreal Recabarren, in *Historia del proletariado*, notes that workers carried out their strikes in more orderly fashion during the first decade of the twentieth century, but lists mainly failures as the result. Michael Monteón's study of nitrate and northern workers barely mentions labor organizations or strikes at all for this period. See Monteón, "The Nitrate Miners."
80 For 1902, see *La Patria*, February 13, 1902; and *La Ajitación* (S) February 14, 1902, p. 7. For 1904, see USNA, M487, roll 51, "Report of Strikes in Tocopilla," October 27, 1904. For 1905, see: *La Ajitación* (Estación Dolores), July 9, 1905, p. 1. For 1906, see: *El Industrial*, February 15, 1906. For 1907, see: *La Patria*, December 16-29, 1907.
81 Recabarren Rojas, *Historia del proletariado*, pp. 199-201; *La Ajitación* (Estación Dolores), March-August, 1905.
82 Barría, *Los movimientos, 1900-10*, p. 170.
83 *La Lei*, September 13, 1907, p. 2.
84 *LaRef*, January 22, 1908, p. 1.
85 Ibid., May 12, 1908, p. 1.
86 *El Chileno*, June 28, 1908, p. 1.
87 Miranda, "Reseña histórica," p. 3.
88 Segall, *Las luchas*, p. 8.
89 *La Comuna* (S) March, 1896; *La Unión Obrera*, April 26, 1896.

90 Paul S. Reinsh, "Parliamentary Government in Chile," *American Political Science Review,* (November, 1909): 522.

91 USNA, M487, roll 3, Henry B. Fletcher to Secretary of State, March 16, 1912.

92 Samuel Ortíz, *Vicios electorales* (Santiago, 1909), pp. 1–16.

93 *El Proletario* (Tocopilla), October 7, 1905, p. 2.

94 *La Democracia,* October 7, 1905, pp. 1, 4; October 15, p. 2; October 22, pp. 1, 3.

95 *El Ferrocarril,* March 6, 1906 p. 1; March 7, 1906, p. 1.

96 *La Democracia,* October 29, 1905, p. 2.

97 Ibid., p. 2.

98 Chile, Congreso Nacional, Cámara de Diputados, *Sesiones ordinarias,* October 28, 1905, p. 75.

99 *LaRef,* January 15, 1907, p. 1.

100 Ibid., October 4, 1907, p. 1.

101 The number of males over twenty-one years of age in the Department of Santiago was approximately 100,000 in 1912, judging from the size of that population group in the Censuses of 1907 and 1920. With an estimated literacy of 73 percent (69 in 1907, 77 in 1920), some 73,000 people in the Department of Santiago were eligible to vote. For the figure for 1912, see *AE,* 1912, vol. 3, p. 7.

102 *AE,* Censo Electoral, 1921, p. 88.

103 For examples, see: *El Oprimido* (S) second fortnight, May, 1906, p. 1; *Jerminal!* September 2, 1904, pp. 1, 2.

104 Policía de Santiago, *Boletín,* July 15, 1901, p. 63.

105 *La Lei,* December 13, 1902, p. 1.

106 Díaz Lira, *Observanciones,* p. 5; Carlos Roberto Gonzáles, *Las huelgas* (Santiago, 1908), p. 3.

107 *ELDI,* May 15, 1903, p. 1.

108 PROFO 471/17, report dated December 28, 1905, entitled "Chile's Present Economic and Political Situation."

109 *La Democracia,* October 7, 1905, p. 1; October 15, 1905, p. 2.

110 The following account of events leading up to, during, and proceeding the October 22, 1905 rally is, unless otherwise noted, derived from: *El Chileno, ELDI, ELMS,* and ANCh, Ministry of the Interior, *Policías, notas, y decretos,* October, 1905 vol. 2970. See also Gonzalo Izquierdo, "Octubre de 1905. Un episodio en la historia chilena," *Historia* 13 (1976): 55–96.

111 ANCh, Ministry of the Interior, *Policías, notas, y decretos,* October, 1905, vol. 2970, Report of Chief of Police, Santiago, October 23, 1905.

112 Ibid., p. 20.

113 *ELMS,* October 24, 1905, p. 6; *El Chileno,* October 24, 1905, p. 1; Benjamín Vicuña Subercaseaux, *El socialismo revolucionario y la cuestión social en Europa y en Chile* (Santiago: 1908), pp. 9, 73.

114 Adapted from information gathered by Gonzalo Izquierdo and later used in Izquierdo, "Octubre de 1905."

115 ANCh, Ministry of the Interior, *Policías, notas, y decretos,* October, 1905, vol. 2970, Report of Chief of Police, Santiago, October 25, 1905.

116 Alejandro Escobar y Carvallo, "La ajitación social en Santiago, Antofagasta, y Iquique," *Occidente* 121 (November–December, 1959): 5–7.
117 See, for example: ELDI, April 23, 1905, p. 1; *La Lei,* March 1, 1908, p. 1; Policía de Santiago, *Boletín* 89, November, 1909, p. 529; Vicuña Subercaseaux, *El socialismo revolucionario,* p. 120.
118 *ELMS,* May 2, 1907, p. 1.
119 Policía de Santiago, *Boletín,* January, 1914, p. 31. The following summary of police tactics in strikes is derived from this article. A careful study of labor disputes shows that these tactics were in fact employed.
120 Alberto Polloni Roldán, *Las fuerzas armadas de Chile en la vida nacional* (Santiago, 1972), p. 257; *LaU,* March 18, 1921 p. 1.
121 *LaRef,* January 19, 1907, p. 2; PROFO 881/9549, "Chile, Annual Report, 1908" p. 5.

CHAPTER 5: DECLINE, RECOVERY, AND DEPRESSION

1 Barría, *Los movimientos, 1900–1910,* p. 111.
2 The Labor Office obtained these figures by sending questionnaires regarding size, dues, bylaws, and legal status to the leaders of every known working class organization in Chile in May 1909. The intendant of each province was also requested by the office to provide similar information. In 1909, only 60 percent of the organizations receiving questionnaires completed and returned them. In both 1909 and 1912, the Labor Office estimated the total number of organizations and their membership from the returned questionnaires and from its knowledge of those unions which failed to respond.

The figures given are mere approximations of the actual number of organizations and their members. Most of the groups surveyed were mutual aid societies. Resistance societies, because of their Anarchist orientation, normally did not reply to Labor Office surveys. Other groups included in the surveys were neither labor unions nor mutual aid groups, but sporting and music clubs. Some workers may have been counted two or more times if they held dual membership. Others surveyed were commercial employees. Since both the 1909 and 1912 surveys were carried out under the same circumstances, there is no reason to believe one to be more accurate than the other.
3 *La Batalla* 27, February, 1914, p. 4.
4 Recabarren Rojas, *Historia del proletariado,* pp. 199–200.
5 Jobet, *Luis Emilio Recabarren,* p. 133; *La Gran Federación Obrera de Chile* 2, November 1, 1910, p. 2.
6 *La Gran Federación Obrera de Chile* 2, November 1, 1910, p. 2.
7 The FOCh even refused to support the general strike in Valparaíso in 1913. *La Gran Federación Obrera de Chile* 12, February 10, 1911, p. 1; no. 41, November 10, 1911, p. 3.
8 Ibid., no. 21, May 5, 1911, p. 1; no. 45, November 20, 1911, p. 1.
9 Ibid., no. 10, January 20, 1911, p. 1; *BOT* 7, 1913, p. 655.
10 *LaOp,* May 21, 1917, p. 2.
11 *La Gran Federación Obrera de Chile* 12, February 10, 1911, pp. 1, 3.

12 *Mar y Tierra* 1, March 12, 1911, pp. 1–4.

13 López, *Diccionario biográfico, libro precursor,* p. 2.

14 ADGT, *Estadística de la Asociación Obrera,* 1910, pp. 24–30.

15 *La Batalla* 18, November, 1913, p. 1.

16 Ibid., no. 26, February, 1914, pp. 1, 2.

17 *El Productor* 10, October, 1912, p. 4; no. 14, February, 1913, p. 1; *La Batalla,* second fortnight, February, 1914, p. 1.

18 *La Verdad* 2, May, 1909, pp. 18, 19.

19 *La Tribuna Libre,* May 8, 1910, p. 18; *La Gran Federación Obrera de Chile* 21, May 5, 1911, p. 2; *El Productor* 52, May, 1912, p. 1; *La Batalla* 8, May, 1913, p. 1; no. 32, May, 1914, pp. 1, 3; *LaU,* May 2, 1913, pp. 1, 7.

20 For the activities of resistance societies in the North between 1909 and 1914, see *Luz y Vida.*

21 For rising wages, real wages, employment, and production in the nitrate industry from 1909 to 1914, see Stickell, "Migration and Mining," pp. 309–10, 312, 340. Only sixteen strikes occurred in the Provinces of Tarapacá and Antofagasta from 1908 to 1912, according to the best study available. Recabarren Rojas, *Historia del proletariado,* p. 227. Monteón mentions no important strikes or labor organizations in his discussion of nitrate miners for the entire 1908–16 period. Monteón, "The Nitrate Miners," pp. 187–215. For accounts of the difficulties involved in organizing nitrate workers, see *Luz y Vida* 13–69, July, 1909–November, 1914.

22 *Luz y Vida* 35, August, 1911, p. 1.

23 *La Batalla* 39, September, 1914, p. 1; no. 40, September, 1914, p. 4.

24 Ibid., no. 42, October 3, 1914, pp. 1, 2.

25 Unlike Recabarren, who, from at least 1905, received a sizable stipend from labor organizations. See *El Trabajo* (Tocopilla) 44, April 2, 1905, p. 2: no. 53, June 4, 1905.

26 Osvaldo Arias Escobedo, *La prensa obrera en Chile* (Santiago, 1970), p. 54. For their articles and poems, see *La Batalla,* 1912–15.

27 See note 51, chapter 4, above. The fact that two sets of figures are so askew in most years limits their credibility considerably.

28 *BOT* 7, 1913, pp. 200–217.

29 For the course of the strike, see *LaU,* June 12–19, 1912, p. 6.

30 For the course of the strike, see *ELMV,* October 17, 1913, p. 13; October 18, p. 11; October 31, p. 11. Also *La Batalla,* nos. 19, 20, 21, November–December, 1913.

31 *ELMV,* November 1, 1913, p. 12.

32 *ELMS,* February 16, 1916, p. 6.

33 Ibid., February 17, 1916, p. 12.

34 For the course of the strike, see *ELMS,* March 3, 1916, p. 12; March 6, p. 11; March 8, p. 11; March 15, p. 12; March 16, p. 13; March 18, p. 13.

35 *La Gran Federación Obrera de Chile* 50, February 10, 1912, p. 1.

36 Díaz received a mere 398 votes in his bid for deputy Recabarren Rojas, *Historia del proletariado,* p. 204.

37 *La Gran Federación Obrera de Chile,* March 10, 1912, p. 1.
38 *La Batalla* 13, August, 1913, p. 3.
39 Ibid., no. 57, May, 1915, p. 2.
40 Oscar Venegas Cabello, *La Dirección General del Trabajo* (Santiago, 1942), p. 15.
41 Ibid., 113 –14.
42 Policía de Santiago, *Boletín,* November, 1909, p. 529.
43 *Luz y Vida* 25, August, 1910, p. 2.
44 José Tomás Guzmán Bezanilla, *El anarquismo y la lei* (Santiago, 1913), p. 18; *El Productor* 6, June 1, 1912, p. 2; *ELMS* and *ELDI,* December 22-24, 1911.
45 *Luz y Vida* 40, January, 1912, p. 1; PROFO 371/1060, Monthly Report of Santiago Minister, December 31, 1911.
46 López interview.
47 Guzmán, *El anarquismo y la lei,* p. 20.
48 *LaN,* June 6, 1918, p. 12.
49 *LaN,* February 26, 1925, p. 5; April 30, 1925, p. 19.
50 *La Batalla* 48, January, 1915, p. 1.
51 *ELMV,* November 24, 1914, p. 7; November 29, 1914, pp. 3, 7.
52 *La Batalla* 47, December, 1914, p. 3; *ELMV,* December 2, 1914, p. 7.
53 *ELMS,* December 15, 1914, p. 3; *ELDI,* December 15, 1914, p. 1; *La Batalla* 48, January, 1915, p. 1.

CHAPTER 6: ORGANIZATIONAL SUCCESSES

1 Kirsch, "Industrialization," pp. 49, 271; Stickell, "Migration and Mining," pp. 340-41.
2 *LaOp,* October 3, 1917, p. 3; April 21, 1919, p. 4.
3 *LaOp,* January 8, 1918, p. 2.
4 *LaOp,* June 29, 1917, p. 2; July 14, 1917, p. 2.
5 *LaOp,* December 14, 1917, p. 2.
6 For an account of the course of the strike, see *LaN,* January 28, 1918, p. 8; *LaOp,* February 2, 1918, p. 5. Heredia interview.
7 *LaOp,* April 3, 1919, p. 4; August 21, 1918, p. 4.
8 Heredia interview.
9 *LaOp,* January 21, 1920, p. 4.
10 Ibid. I will refer to the FZA, FOOC, and the UIC of 1924-27 as the "Shoeworkers' Federation," since the basic composition of the 1918 FZA remained the same despite two changes in name.
11 Heredia interview.
12 *LaOp,* June 23, 1917, p. 2; November 16, 1917, p. 1. *ELMS,* January 13, 1919, p. 16.
13 *LaU,* March 5, 1918, p. 10.
14 *La Unión Gráfica,* September, 1918, p. 1.
15 *LaOp,* November 26, 1917, p. 2; August 3, 1918, p. 2.
16 *LaOp,* May 19, 1919, p. 4.

17 See *LaOp,* July 23–25, 1917; August 4–15, 1917; November 26–30, 1917; and December 10–26, 1917, for information on the strikes of Santiago and Valparaíso construction workers.

18 *LaN,* April 18, 1917, p. 8; *ELMV,* April 19, 1917, p. 3.

19 *ELMV,* July 21–August 16, 1917; *Mar y Tierra* 11, July, 1917, p. 2; no. 12, July, 1917; special edition, July 30, 1917.

20 DeShazo, "The IWW," pp. 20–21.

21 *LaOp,* February 6, 1918, p. 2; November 5, 1918, p. 4.

22 *La Evolución,* nos. 1 (March, 1917) through 8 (August, 1917); *LaOp,* November 5, 1918, p. 4.

23 *LaOp,* July 30, 1918, p. 2; May 10, 1919, p. 4.

24 *La Unión Gráfica,* September 15, 1918; Miranda, "Reseña histórica," pp. 3–4.

25 *LaOp,* December 20, 1918, p. 1.

26 *La Federación de Obreros de Imprenta,* February 15, 1919, p. 3.

27 *Valparaíso Gráfico,* January 15, 1919, p. 1; February 15, 1919, p. 1.

28 *LaOp,* May 21, 1917, p. 2.

29 *LaOp,* January 2, 1919, p. 2.

30 *La Comuna* (Viña), January 7, 1920, p. 3. The Valparaíso councils were organized by railroad shop workers, tobacco workers, carpenters, tram conductors and drivers, painters, customs workers, railroad firemen, and metal workers.

31 *LaOp,* January 27, 1919, p. 1.

32 This information comes from my investigations of strikes for the year 1919.

33 *ELMS,* January 11, 1919, p. 20. The FOCh systematically overstated its membership figures, at time carrying its claims to absurd extremes.

34 DeShazo, "The IWW," pp. 18–22. Scholars have overlooked efforts by the IWW to establish foreign chapters. IWW national administrations were founded in Great Britain, South Africa, Australia, New Zealand, Mexico, Ecuador, and Canada as well as Chile. Robert Halstead and Peter DeShazo, "Los Wobblies del Sur: The Industrial Workers of the World in Chile and Mexico" (unpublished paper prepared in 1974).

35 DeShazo, "The IWW," pp. 42–43.

36 Heredia interview. Participation in union affairs was extremely high among members of the FZA and its successors. As many as 3,500–4,000 members attended the general union meetings in 1918–19 out of a total membership of no more than 4,500, a remarkable turnout by the standards of other unions. *LaOp,* July 31, 1918, p. 2; October 21, 1919, p. 4.

37 The quotation is taken from the minutes of the 1919 convention as reproduced in *La Comuna* (Viña), January 15, 1920, p. 1.

38 Ibid., December 13, 1919, p. 1.

39 *LaN,* August 6, 1920, p. 1.

40 *El Socialista,* October 18, 1919, p. 7.

41 *Numen,* October 18, 1919, p. 7. *Numen* attacked the Bolsheviks as early as October, 1919, but the anti-USSR campaign did not reach full swing until 1921. The first anti-Soviet article in the IWW's organ *Acción Directa* appeared in January, 1922.

42 *La Comuna* (Viña), February 19, 1920, p. 1; *La Voz del Mar,* May 1, 1920, p. 1.

43 Martínez, Díaz Vera, and Carlos A. Sepúlveda, all of whom were eventually purged from the FOCh, appear to have been among the most popular labor leaders in Santiago and Valparaíso. Recabarren enjoyed great personal prestige among urban workers, but his lieutenants in those cities did not.

44 *LaOp,* April 25, 1917, p. 1; *LaN,* April 8, 1912, p. 12; José Santos González Vera, "Los estudiantes del año veinte," *Babel*[7] (1945): 36; Frank Bonilla and Myron Glazer, *Student Politics in Chile* (New York, 1970), pp. 31–34. See also *Claridad,* 1920–24.

45 Gandulfo was one of the few professionals to lead a working class organization (the IWW); and, unlike many of the "Generation of 1920," he remained an Anarchist throughout the 1920s. He died in an automobile accident in 1932. Schweitzer interview. Also Daniel Schweitzer, "Juan Gandulfo," *Babel* 7 (1945): 15–30.

46 *LaOp,* May 1 and 2, 1917, pp. 1–2; May 2, 1918, p. 2. *LaU,* May 2, 1918, p. 10.

47 *LaN,* May 2, 1919, p. 10; *VR,* May 15, 1919, p. 5, and enclosed flyer printed by *Numen; LaU,* May 2, 1920, p. 2.

48 *LaU,* April 12, 1917, p. 8; *LaOp,* April 30, 1917, p. 1.

49 See graph 3.1, above.

50 *AE,* 1916–18, vol. 11, "Comercio exterior," pp. 159–61, 168–72, 190–93.

51 *LaOp,* October 7, 1918, p. 4.

52 *ELMS,* November 21, 1918, p. 20; November 22, 1918, p 15.

53 *ELMS,* November 21, 1918, p. 20.

54 *ELMS,* November 23, 1918, p. 7. *LaOp,* November 23, 1918, p. 1; November 28, 1919, p. 3; February 6, 1919, p. 1.

55 *LaOp,* December 2, 1919, p. 1.

56 *LaOp,* December 13, 1919, p. 1.

57 *ELMS,* November 27, 1918, p. 19; November 28, p. 21.

58 *LaOp,* January 14, 1919, p. 8.

59 *ELMS,* January 28, 1919, p. 13.

60 *ELMS,* February 1, 1919, p. 3; *LaN,* February 4, 1919, p. 9.

61 *ELDI,* February 3, 1919, p. 3; *ELMS,* February 2, 1919, p. 3. The press had since the November 1918 rally increasingly labeled the AOAN a subversive organization.

62 *LaOp,* February 8, 1919, p. 1.

63 *ELMS,* March 10, 1919, p. 12; March 13, p. 13.

64 *ELMS,* August 30, 1919, p. 3.

65 *VR,* first fortnight, September, 1919, p. 1.

66 *Numen,* December 13, 1919, p. 1.

67 *LaOp,* February 10, 1920, p. 3.

68 *SE,* 1920, p. 148; 1921, p. 148.

69 These are my personal estimates, given the information available. FOCh and other union memberships in the 1920s can be more accurately determined.

70 I carried out my statistical investigation of strikes for the years 1917–21 in much the same manner as I did for the earlier period and analyzed the same variables. *La Opinión* of Santiago, certainly the most prolabor of the Capital's daily newspapers, served as my "scanner" and most valuable source. Because no such paper existed in Valparaíso, I feel that I probably missed some of the strikes that took place in that city. For additional information about strikes in Santiago, I turned to *La Nación, El Mercurio,* and *El Diario Ilustrado,* generally in that order. Most of my information for Valparaíso was first found by scanning *La Opinión* and then using *El Mercurio* and *La Unión* of Valparaíso. *Verba Roja* and *La Comuna* proved to be the most useful working class newspapers. Strikes taking place in Viña del Mar are listed throughout as Valparaíso strikes.

71 *ELMV,* August 9, 1917, p. 9; August 15, p. 10; August 16, p. 10. *Mar y Tierra* 11–12, July, 1917; no. 13, July 30, 1917.

72 *La Federación de Obreros de Imprenta* 8–11, November 2–30, 1918.

73 *LaOp,* August 4, 1919, p. 1.

74 Miranda, "Reseña histórica," p. 5.

75 *LaOp,* December 17, 1917, p. 1.

76 Ibid.

77 Articles in daily newspapers announcing the end of strikes often included the terms of the final settlement without describing how the settlement was reached; hence the large number of unknowns in table 6.4. Most of the unknown factors pertained to smaller strikes, which received less attention in the press.

78 ADGT, *Communicaciones enviadas,* 1920, no. 245, May 5, 1920.

79 *ELMS,* January 13, 1919, p. 16; *LaOp,* January 16, 1919, p. 4.

80 *LaOp,* January 20 and 31, February 1, 1918, p. 2.; January 21, 1920, p. 4.

81 *ELMS,* May 30, 1919, p. 8.

82 *LaOp,* September 3, 1919, p. 8.

83 For an account of the strike, see *ELMS,* September 2, 1919, p. 18; September 3, 1919, p. 20; September 4, 1919, p. 1; *LaN,* September 4, 1919, p. 10; September 5, 1919, p. 9; *LaOp,* September 5, 1919, p. 1; September 6, p. 1.

84 *VR,* first fortnight, September, 1919, p. 4.

85 *ELMS,* September 5, 1919, p. 3.

86 *LaN,* September 5, 1919, p. 3; *ELDI,* September 4, 1919, p. 3.

87 *LaOp,* September 8, 1919, p. 1; *ELMS,* September 7, 1919, p. 18.

88 *LaOp,* September 20, 1919, p. 1.

89 *ELMS,* October 12, 1919, p. 21.

90 Peter DeShazo, "Urban Workers and Labor Unions in Chile, 1902–1927" (Ph.D. thesis, University of Wisconsin–Madison, 1977), Table 6.5, p. 363.

91 Ibid., tables 6.6, 6.7, pp. 364–65.

92 Jobet, *Luis Emilio Recabarren,* p. 144; Morris, *Elites,* p. 107; Ramírez, *Origen y formación,* p. 116.

93 Drake, *Socialism and Populism,* p. 53.

94 Frederick Pike, *Chile and the United States, 1880–1962* (Notre Dame, 1962), p. 171. Paul Drake underlines the fact that the conservative National Union adopted

a platform very similar to that of Alessandri. Drake, *Socialism and Populism,* p. 48.

95 *VR,* first fortnight, March, 1920, p. 4; *LaOp,* July 13, 1920, p. 4.

96 *LaOp,* May 27, 1920, p. 3; June 2, 1920, p. 3.

97 The first three endorsed Barros for president, while *El Mercurio* maintained a position of hostile "neutrality" toward Alessandri. *LaOp,* May 28, 1920, p. 3; May 22, p. 3; *ELMS,* June 22, 1920, p. 9.

98 *ELMS,* June 26, 1920, p. 12.

99 *El Socialista,* May 11, 1920, p. 1.

100 *ELMS,* May 2, 1920, p. 25.

101 *ELMS,* June 23, 1920, p. 11.

102 Manuel Rivas Vicuña, *Historia política y parlamentaria de Chile* (Santiago, 1964), vol. 2, p. 191.

103 *ELMS,* February 5, 1920, p. 17.

104 *El Socialista,* March 11, 1920, p. 1; May 30, p. 2; June 3, p. 1. *LaOp,* June 5, 1920, p. 8.

105 *LaU,* June 20, 1920, p. 3; *ELMS,* June 18, 1920, p. 3; June 26, pp. 12, 15. *LaN,* June 8, 1920, p. 11; June 10, p. 1; June 26, p. 7.

106 Rivas Vicuña claimed that the Alliance drew on virtually limitless financial resources for its campaign and probably bought more votes than the Unión. Rivas Vicuña, *Historia política y parlamentaria,* vol. 2, p. 196. Alessandrists reportedly paid thirty pesos (about three days' wages) per vote in Antofagasta. *El Socialista,* June 27, 1920, p. 1; June 29, p. 1.

107 *AE,* "Censo Electoral," 1921, pp. 106–7; ibid., "Elecciones ordinarias, 1912," 1914, vol. 3, p. 7.

108 The voting for President was indirect. Each party put forward a slate of candidates bound either to Alessandri or to Barros. *AE,* "Censo Electoral," 1921, pp. 88, 89.

109 *El Socialista,* July 7, 1920, p. 1.

110 *AE,* "Censo Electoral," 1921, pp. 106–7.

111 Rivas Vicuña claimed that the Alessandrists had actually begun to arm themselves in the event that their leader was denied the Presidency. His insistence on assuming office "at whatever cost," coupled with popular unrest, certainly influenced the decision to name him President. Rivas Vicuña, *Historia política y parlamentaria,* vol. 2, p. 211. Paul Drake also shares this interpretation. Drake, *Socialism and Populism,* p. 53.

CHAPTER 7: DEPRESSION AND DECLINE

1 *LaU,* April 16, 1918, p. 1. *LaN,* August 26, 1918, p. 1; June 2, 1919, p. 1; June 19, 1919, p. 1.

2 *ELMS,* August 24, 1918, p. 9. Included among these IWWs was Tom Barker the English organizer and propagandist who later spread the IWW creed to Argentina, where he organized two branches of the Marine Transport Workers in Buenos Aires and Rosario. See E. C. Fry, *Tom Barker and the IWW* (Canberra, 1965), pp. 25–36.

3 See *ELMV,* November 27, 1919, p. 3; *ELMS,* July 27, 1920, p. 5.

4 *VR* 3, December, 1918, p. 1.

5 *LaOp,* January 17, 24, 27, 1919, p. 1.

6 *Numen* 21, September 6, 1919, p. 1.

7 *LaOp,* August 30, 1919, pp. 1, 8.

8 *LaOp,* March 23, 1920, p. 1.

9 *LaN,* April 2, 1920, p. 9; April 14, p. 13. *LaOp,* March 31, 1920, pp. 1, 8; April 6, 1920, p. 1.

10 *LaU,* April 22, 1920, p. 1.

11 *LaOp,* July 14, 1920, p. 8.

12 *LaU,* July 14, 1920, p. 8.

13 *LaU,* May 25, 1920, p. 6; June 21, p. 5.

14 Policía de Santiago, *Boletín,* May, 1920, p. 177.

15 USNA, M487, roll 3, Shea Telegram, July 1, 1920. No warships were sent.

16 Frederick Nunn, *Chilean Politics, 1921-1931* (Albuquerque, 1970), p. 23; Francisco Frías Valenzuela, *Historia de Chile* (Santiago, 1949), vol. 4, p. 237.

17 Intendencia de Valparaíso, Archivo, *Llegadas, policía, Mayo-Septiembre, 1920,* Sección de Investigaciones to Chief of Police, July 8, 1920; July 12, 1920; Prefect to Intendant, July 14, 1920.

18 Ibid., *Salidas, Ministerio del Interior, 1920,* Intendant to Minister of the Interior, July 19, 1920.

19 The entire affair came to light during an appeals trial in 1921. Caballero was judged innocent of any wrongdoing in framing the IWW, however, because the appeals court ruled that the dynamite had no bearing on the case against the IWW! *LaU,* November 26, 1921, p. 6.

20 *LaU,* July 22, 1920, p. 7.

21 *ELDI,* July 23, 1920, p. 1.

22 *ELDI,* August 3, 1920, p. 11.

23 *LaN,* July 27, 1920, p. 10.

24 *LaN,* July 27, 1920, p. 3; August 6, pp. 1, 12. *LaU,* August 6, 1920, p. 1.

25 *LaU,* October 20, 1920, p. 1.

26 Rivas Vicuña, *Historia política y parlamentaria,* vol. 2, p. 209.

27 Rivas Vicuña claims that in August, Alessandri agreed to sign a list of "guarantees" to respect the parliamentary and electoral systems, while at the same time promising to settle conflicts between labor and capital in order to appear more palatable to the Tribunal of Honor. Rivas Vicuña, *Historia política y parlamentaria,* vol. 2, p. 241.

28 *LaN,* November 3, 1920, p. 12.

29 See: *LaU,* January 12, 1921, p. 9; January 15, p. 7; January 16, p. 12; January 19, p. 10; January 23, p. 16; January 24, p. 8; January 25, p. 6.

30 *ELMS,* January 23, 1921, p. 17; ADGT, *Inspección Regional, Valparaíso,* 1921, vol. 1, "Federación de Gente de Mar, Poder," January 24, 1921; *LaU,* January 25, 1921, p. 6.

31 *LaN,* January 29, 1921, p. 11; *LaU,* January 25, 1921, p. 6.

32 *LaU,* February 16, 1921, p. 16.

33 See *LaN,* March 9, 1921, p. 8; March 22, p. 10; March 31, p. 13.

34 PROFO 371/5556, Legation to Foreign Office, February 14, 1921. British diplomats claimed that Alessandri had ordered the troops not to fire at the San Gregorio workers in spite of the fact that they had earlier killed an English employee of the nitrate company. After the conflict, however, Alessandri visited the barracks of the troops involved in the affair to reassure the generals that he did not favor workers over the armed forces. PROFO 371/5555, Santiago Legation to FO, March 27, 1921.

35 *LaN,* February 12, 1921, p. 12; February 18, p. 1; April 18, p. 9.

36 *LaU,* March 7, 1921, p. 1.

37 *AE,* "Censo Electoral," 1921, pp. 21, 85.

38 Ibid., p. 21.

39 *LaU,* May 29, 1921, p. 7.

40 *LaN,* June 23, 1921, p. 11.

41 PROFO 371/5555, Vaughn to Foreign Office, July 13, 1921; Santiago Legation to Foreign Office, May 27, 1921.

42 *La Comuna* (Viña), February 19, 1921, p. 1; PROFO 371/5556, Legation to FO, May 27, 1921.

43 *LaN,* July 18, 1921, p. 11.

44 For the conduct of the strike, see *LaU,* June 2, 921, p. 8; June 5, p. 13; June 7, p. 7; June 10, p. 6; June 18, p. 5; June 23, p. 5.

45 *LaN,* June 22, 1921, p. 11.

46 *LaU,* June 13, 1921, p. 8.

47 *LaU,* June 28, 1921, p. 5; June 29, p. 7; June 30, p. 5; July 2, p. 6; July 4, p. 1.

48 *LaU,* June 29, 1921, p. 7.

49 ADGT, *Inspección Regional, Valparaíso,* 1921, vol. 1, "Convenio de Julio 7, 1921," agreement of the USP and bakery owners, July 7, 1921; *LaU,* July 8, 1921, p. 1.

50 *LaN,* July 16, 1921, p. 10; July 18, p. 11; July 19, p. 12; July 20, p. 11; July 23, p. 10.

51 ADGT, *Inspección regional, Valparaíso,* 1921, vol. 1, Report 162, May 13, 1921; Report 186, May 23, 1921; Report 195, May 24, 1921.

52 With about 6,000 members in July, 1921, the IWW was the largest union in the city. Barría, *Los movimientos de 1910 hasta 1926,* pp. 175-76; ADGT, *Inspección regional, Valparaíso,* 1921, vol. 2, updated report on the IWW Second Convention and strength in the marine transport industry.

53 Intendencia de Valparaíso, Archivo, *Salidas varias Enero–Mayo, 1921,* Asociación General de Comerciantes to Intendant, May 23, 1921; vol. 1, letter of Kosmos Line to Labor Office, June 16, 1921; vol. 2, Comité de Defensa del Gremio de Donkeros to Asociación de Comerciantes, May 18, 1921; Gremio de Lancheros to Asociación de Comerciantes, April 26, 1921.

54 The Labor Office especially feared IWW inroads in the boss-ridden and corrupt Federación de Gente de Mar union. ADGT, *1921 varios,* no. 589, Poblete Troncoso to Minister of the Interior, June 6, 1921; *ADGT, Inspección regional,*

Valparaíso, 1921, vol. 1, Report 162, May 13, 1921.

55 ADGT, *Inspección regional, Valparaíso,* 1921, vol. 1, Convenio de Julio 7, 1921.

56 This account of the lockout and general strike is derived from *LaU,* August 18–September 13, 1921; *ELMV,* same dates; USNA, M487, roll 5, Monthly Report, August 20–September 20, 1921; *Solidaridad* (Chicago), April 7, 1923, p. 2; *The South Pacific Mail,* August 25, 1921–September 29, 1921.

57 *LaU,* August 31, 1921, p. 6.

58 ADGT, *Inspección regional, Valparaíso,* 1921, vol. 1, Report of September 23, 1921.

59 *ELMV,* September 10, 1921, pp. 1, 7; *LaU,* September 10, 1921, p. 6.

60 *LaU,* September 13, 1921, p. 7.

61 *ELMV,* September 21, 1921, p. 3; September 22, 1921, p. 7.

62 *LaU,* October 25, 1921, p. 6.

63 *Solidaridad* (Chicago), April 7, 1923, p. 3.

64 *LaN,* October 21, 1921, p. 15.

65 ADGT, *Inspección Concepción, comunicaciones recibidas,* 1922, no. 57, January 3, 1922.

66 *LaFOCh,* January 24, 1922, p. 3; January 20, p. 2; February 4, p. 1.

67 *LaN,* February 10, 1922, p. 3.

68 *LaN,* February 10, 1922, p. 3; *ELMS,* February 11, 1922, p. 13.

69 *LaFOCh,* February 11, 1922, p. 3.

70 ADGT, *Inspección Concepción, comunicaciones recibidas,* 1922, no. 23, March 24, 1922; *LaFOCh,* March 21, 1922, p. 3.

71 ADGT, *Inspección Concepción, comunicaciones recibidas,* 1922, no. 23, March 24, 1922.

72 *LaFOCh,* March 7, 1922, p. 3; May 22, 1922, p. 3; July 13, 1923, p. 4.

73 Ibid., December 6, 1922, p. 4; January 31, 1923, p. 1.

74 DeShazo, "The IWW," pp. 81–83.

75 *LaFOCh,* May 13, 1923, p. 3; May 17, 1923, p. 1.

76 *LaN,* October 12, 1921, p. 8.

77 *LaFOCh,* November 24, 1921, p. 7; *LaN,* November 24, 1921, p. 9.

78 *LaFOCh,* March 17, 1923, p. 2.

79 One has only to read the original questionnaires and the results to clearly see that the Oficina del Trabajo did not know even the number of labor unions, legal or not, which existed in Chile. See ADGT, *Formularios de sociedades obreras,* 1921.

80 Moisés Poblete Troncoso, *La organización sindical de Chile y otros estudios sociales* (Santiago, 1926), anexo 5.

81 *LaN,* March 15, 1924, p. 4. For instance, the FOCh claimed 17,000 coal miners as members, more than the total number employed in the industry. Poblete passed these ridiculous figures along to *La Nación.*

82 *ELMS,* January 11, 1919, p. 20; PROFO 3713679, Chilean Electric Tramway Company to Foreign Office, September 2, 1919. These figures, when broken down by industry, appear to be inflated.

83 *LaFOCh*, January 1, 1924, p. 1.
84 Ibid., December 27, 1923, p. 1.
85 *LaOp*, July 17, 1919, p. 4.
86 *LaFOCh*, December 30, 1921, p. 1.
87 Ibid., October 10, 1922, p. 2.
88 Ibid., August 1, 1923, p. 1.
89 Ibid., January 1, 1924, p. 1.
90 *Justicia*, April 19, 1926, p. 4.
91 Monteón, "The Nitrate Miners," p. 284; Angell, *Politics and the Labour Movement*, p. 37. For the size of the workforce, see Stickell, "Migration and Mining," pp. 340–41.
92 Even this figure may be generous. The FOCh almost always received its highest contributions of dues from the same towns, but the concejos rarely sent their donations every month. Therefore, the payment records in *Justicia* and *LaFOCh* may include contributions for two or even three months, indicating still lower membership. These towns and their maximum contributions over a three-year period were: Province of Tarapacá: Arica (200), Alto de San Antonio (1,500), Iquique (500), Buenaventura (500), Huará (600); Province of Antofagasta: Gatico (500), Pampa Unión (1,500), El Toco (2,500), Aguas Blancas (150), Tocopilla (200), Antofagasta (1,250). Total: 9,400. Figures from *LaFOCh*, January 1, 1924, p. 1; March 17, 1924, p. 2; *Justicia*, August 22, 1924, p. 3; March 18, 1925, p. 2; March 20, 1925, p. 1; April 19, 1926, p. 4.
93 *LaFOCh*, January 1, 1924, p. 1.
94 Many factors indicate a stronger IWW than FOCh presence among workers in Iquique. The pages of the important Anarcho-Syndicalist paper *El Sembrador*, published in Iquique from 1922 to 1924, show much IWW activity in the port while indicating that the Anarchists had been unable to rival the FOCh on the pampa. The fact that the IWW could hold out against the shipping companies in Iquique for eight-two days despite arrests and the closing of its press by the armed forces indicates considerable strength. Contributions from the FOCh concejos in Iquique to the Executive Council of the Federation were very small.
95 Since we as yet lack a serious study of labor unions and strikes in the North after 1913, it is difficult to compare the level of strike activity in the North with that of the urban center with complete certainty. Barrera, using Barría's research, claims 231 strikes in the Great North from 1911 to 1925, a figure which can be compared to the 296 strikes I counted in Santiago and Valparaíso for a six-year period only (1917–21, 1925). Barrera, however, may be counting May 1 demonstrations, work stoppages, and protest rallies as strikes. Barrera, "Perspectiva histórica," chart 5, p. 134. Labor Office figures, however understated, show no strike activity on the nitrate pampa from 1916 to mid-1919, increased but not widespread strikes in 1920, and much lower levels in 1921. It is very hard to imagine workers carrying out much strike activity during the depression years of 1919–21. *BOT* 12, 1919, ppl 62–69; no. 18, 1922, pp. 263–73. Monteón mentions no major northern strikes between 1921 and 1925. Monteón, "The Nitrate Miners," pp. 331–55. The FOCh and Anarcho-Syndicalist press of San-

tiago and Valparaíso made almost no mention of strikes in the North except port strikes during the 1917–24 period. The San Gregorio affair was the only exception. Notably, they did mention the strikes in the coal zone in great detail. See: *Acción Directa, Mar y Tierra, Verba Roja, LaFOCh,* and *Justicia.*

96 Labor in the coal mining zone has yet to be studied. An excellent source of information is the ADGT reports, especially *Inspección Concepción, comunicaciones recibidas, 1922.*

97 ADGT, *Inspección regional, Valparaíso,* 1921, vol. 2, report on IWW Convention.

98 *LaOp,* October 31, 1918, p. 8; Heredia interviews. Luis Heredia claimed in one interview that the Shoeworkers' Federations of 1917–27 organized "the entire personnel of a shoe factory or nobody."

99 *LaFOCh,* November 13, 1921, p. 1.

100 *LaN,* May 2, 1925, p. 17; *Solidaridad* (S) 6, May, 1926, p. 1.

101 The Census of 1920 listed only 2,662 printing workers in Santiago. *La Federación de Obreros de Imprenta* 20–21, February 15, 1919, p. 3.

102 The fact that more than half of all the printers in the industry paid dues to the FOI in 1925 was by Chilean standards surprising, indicating strength on the part of the union as well as the ability of members to pay. *El Obrero Gráfico,* July 9, 1926, p. 3.

103 *La Voz del Mar,* January 15, 1925, p. 2.

104 *Claridad* 9, December 11, 1920; Intendencia de Valparaíso, Archivo, *Llegadas, Policía, Mayo–Septiembre, 1920,* Sección de Investigaciones to Chief of Police, July 12, 1920.

105 *LaN,* November 7, 1920, p. 23.

106 Secretariat, International Working Men's Association, *IWMA News Service* (Berlin), May 4, 1928, p. 5; *Solidaridad* (Chicago), March 10, 1923, p. 3.

107 Some 1,127 persons joined the IWW in Valparaíso in 1924. *La Voz del Mar,* March 24, 1925. See also *The Marine Worker,* 1924–25.

108 This figure may also be overstated. ADGT, *1925 varios, no.* 87, Report of June 18, 1925.

109 The Anarcho-Syndicalists placed great emphasis on "free" or "spontaneous" contributions from workers when the need arose, but at the same time attempted to coax more money out of the rank and file to support propaganda and union activities. The FOCh newspapers were consistently in better financial shape than those of the Anarcho-Syndicalists. The bulk of the FOCh's financial support came from workers in the coal and nitrate zones, but money was also occasionally raised from commercial advertising in the Federation newspapers.

110 *LaN,* August 6, 1921, p. 12; August 11, 1921, p. 9. *LaFOCh,* November 19, 1922, p. 2. The FOCh claimed that the police knew of his whereabouts all along.

111 For example, see: *LaOp,* November 6, 1916, p. 1; February 6, 1918, p. 2; *LaN,* August 11, 1921, p. 9; *LaFOCh,* June 2, 1924, p. 4; *Solidaridad* 6, May 1, 1926, p. 1.

112 Federación de Obreros de Imprenta de Chile, *Estatutos* (Valparaíso, 1921), p. 5; Miranda, "Reseña histórica," pp. 8–9.

113 *LaFOCh,* November 14, 1921, p. 1.

114 *El Obrero Panadero,* September 1, 1924, p. 4; March 1, 1925, p. 1. The term "Communist" once again reflects no link with the PC but refers to libertarian Communism. See also *LaN,* July 6, 1921, p. 5; July 10, p. 14.

115 The Chilean IWW, like its North American counterpart, visualized future society based on industrial departments to which each person, according to his job, would belong. See DeShazo, "The IWW," pp. 92–96.

116 IISG, Diego Abad de Santillán Archive, Notes from the Second IWMA Congress, Berlin, 1925; Minutes of the Third IWW Convention, March 16–18, 1924, pp. 3–6.

117 In May, 1919, the workers at the State Railway shops in San Bernardo (Concejo La Cisterna) quit the FOCh to form a company mutual aid society. In August, 1920, Enrique Cornejo and his dissatisfied railroad shop workers (Concejo No. 1, Santiago) were purged by the Federal Executive Council. *LaOp,* May 19, 1919, p. 4. *LaN,* August 6, 1920, p. 12; August 8, p. 22; August 9, p. 12; August 14, p. 13.

118 *LaFOCh,* December 29–31, 1921.

119 Morris, *Elites,* pp. 108–9.

120 *LaFOCh,* January 1, 1922, p. 3.

121 Ibid., March 24, 1922, p. 4.

122 Ibid., August 8, 9, 1924, p. 1.

123 ADGT, *Estudios y trabajos,* 1918, State Railway Retirement Law of September 1, 1911; U.S. Bureau of Labor Statistics, *Monthly Labor Review,* vol. 9, no. 12, August, 1919, pp. 536–39.

124 *LaOp,* December 31, 1917, p. 1; *LaN,* March 30, 1921, p. 11.

125 *LaFOCh,* August 5, 1923, p. 2; August 13, p. 2; August 24, p. 2.

126 Ibid., January 1, 1924, pp. 1–4.

127 Ibid.

128 Ibid., January 3, 1924, p. 1.

129 These were C. A. Sepúlveda, Roberto Salinas, Pedro J. González, Teresa Flores, Elías Lafertte, Luis Víctor Cruz, Juan Flores Tapia, and Onofre García. The affiliation of the ninth member, Abdón Neira, is unknown.

130 *El Sindicalista* 1, June, 1918, p. 1; no. 5, October, 1918, p. 1; no. 6, November, 1918, p. 1.

131 *La Federación Chilena del Trabajo* 1, April 19, 1922, p. 1.

132 *El Sindicalista* 36, December 6, 1925, p. 1.

133 *VR* 13, first fortnight, of July, 1919, p. 6; *Mar y Tierra,* April 17, 1920, p. 4.

134 *Mar y Tierra,* April 17, 1920, p. 2; May 1, 1920, p. 3; *Acción Directa* 9, January 1, 1922, p. 4.

135 *LaFOCh,* September 13, 1921, p. 3.

136 Ibid., October 7, 1921, p. 3; October 8, p. 3.

137 Ibid., January 1, 1922, p. 3; May 21, p. 1; August 18, p. 1; February 28, 1923, p. 1.

138 Ibid., January 1, 1922, p. 3.

139 *Acción Directa* 10, February, 1922.

140 Conference Syndicaliste Internacionale (Berlin, June 16–18, 1922), *Bulletín Internacionale*, June 16, 1922, pp. 34–35; *Acción Directa* 18, November, 1922, p. 1.

141 The Argentine FORA and the CGT of Mexico were the two other Latin American labor organizations to join the IMWA. The U.S. IWW never did.

142 *Claridad* 74, October 21, 1922, p. 1; *Acción Directa* 9, January, 1922, p. 4; no. 16, September, 1922, p. 1.

143 *LaFOCh*, March 26, 1923, p. 3. Monteón claims that Recabarren developed a deep dislike for Anarchists from his first trip to Argentina in 1906–8. Monteón, "The Nitrate Miners," p. 193.

144 *LaFOCh*, June 29, 1923, p. 3.

145 *LaOp*, October 19, 1917, p. 2; *VR*, first fortnight, January, 1920, p. 1.

146 Heredia interviews.

147 Clotario Blest interviews.

148 Heredia interviews.

149 *Acción Directa* 12, June, 1922. The IWW, FOI, and many other Anarcho-Syndicalist labor organizations officially participated in Recabarren's funeral in December, 1924.

150 *Claridad* 94, June 30, 1923.

151 For excellent examples, see: *Acción Directa* 9, January, 1922; and *LaFOCh*, August 25, 1921, p. 1.

CHAPTER 8: LABOR LAWS, POLITICS, AND REPRESSION

1 *El Obrero Gráfico* 28, December, 1926, p. 1.

2 *LaN*, March 29, 1925, p. 25; May 1, p. 15; May 2, p. 17. *ELMV*, March 25, 1925, p. 16.

3 *El Obrero Panadero*, November 1, 1924, p. 5.

4 *El Obrero Metalúrgico*, August, 1924–May, 1926.

5 *Autonomía y Solidaridad* 1, May 1, 1924, pp. 3, 4.

6 *El Sembrador*, Supplement, no. 10, May 22, 1926, p. 2; *Tribuna Libertaria*, February 22, 1926, p. 2; Barría, *Los movimientos de 1910 hasta 1926*, p. 183.

7 *El Sembrador*, Supplement, no. 10, May 22, 1926, p. 2.

8 *Justicia*, May 31, 1925, p. 4.

9 *Justicia*, August 22, 1924, p. 3; March 18, 1925, p. 3; March 20, 1925, p. 3.

10 *LaN*, February 5, 1925, p. 8.

11 *BOT* 24, 1926, p. 161.

12 Derived in the same manner as the studies of earilier strikes, 1902–8, 1917–21. My principal sources were *La Nación* and *Justicia* for Santiago and *La Unión* and *El Mercurio* for Valparaíso, as well as the working class press.

13 Unless otherwise stated, the account of this strike is derived from *LaU*, March 5–April 4, 1924.

14 *LaFOCh*, April 8, 1924, p. 3.

15 *LaN*, March 7–14, 1924.

16 For an account of the conduct of this strike, see *LaN*, March 18–April 14, 1924. Also *Autonomía y Solidaridad* 2, June 12, 1924, p. 3; *Acción Directa*, May 1, 1924, p. 7; *LaFOCh*, April 4, 1924, p. 3; April 9, p. 2; May 15, p. 4.

17 *LaFOCh,* May 20, 1924, p. 4; July 19, p. 4; *Autonomía y Solidaridad,* July 25, 1924, p. 1.

18 The motives for the strike are unclear. *Justicia,* November 21, 1924, claims that wages were an issue at stake, while *LaN,* November 21, 1924, p. 10, states that the transfer of key union leaders from one zone to another triggered the strike.

19 Morris, *Elites,* p. 239.

20 David Bari Menezes, *El ejército ante las nuevas doctrinas sociales* (Santiago 1922), pp. 14–15.

21 For the text of the laws in English, see: U.S. Bureau of Labor Statistics, *Monthly Labor Review,* vol. 12, no. 1, January, 1926, p. 20.

22 See Ibid., vol. 12, no. 6, June, 1926, p. 156.

23 This is especially true of public school teachers in Santiago, who normally attended IWW and FOCh conventions, maintained close links with the Student Federation, and struck for higher pay on several occassions.

24 *Tribuna Libertaria* 18, second fortnight, September, 1924, p. 1; *Justicia,* September 10, 1924, p. 3.

25 *El Obrero Panadero,* November 1, 1924, p. 3.

26 *Acción Directa,* Supplement of September 11, 1924.

27 *El Sembrador 108, September 27, 1924, p. 8.*

28 Claridad 126, October, 1924, p. 1.

29 *Justicia,* September 9, 1924, p. 1.

30 Ibid., September 13, 1924, p. 1.

31 Ibid., October 28, 1924, p. 1.

32 Ibid., January 19, 1925, p. 1. These prisoners were taken by the armed forces following the killing of an English employee of the San Gregorio nitrate office by workers.

33 *Justicia,* January 25, 1925, p. 1; *La Voz del Mar* 10, January 31, 1925, p. 2.

34 *LaN,* January 27, 1925, p. 6; *Justicia,* January 29, 1925, p. 3.

35 *Justicia,* January 29, 1925, p. 3; *LaN,* February 4, 1925, p. 14.

36 *LaN,* February 11, 1925, p. 9; February 13, p. 14; March 6, p. 7; March 10, p. 5. *Justicia,* February 17, 1925, p. 1.

37 *LaN,* March 3, 1925, p. 1.

38 *BOT* 24, 1926, anexo 46.

39 *Justicia,* January 27, 1925, p. 2.

40 *LaU,* January 29, 1925, p. 16; January 31, p. 4.

41 *LaN,* February 9, 1925, p. 8.

42 *LaU,* February 12, 1925, p. 1; February 14, p. 1. *LaN,* February 9, 1925, p. 8; February 11, p. 9; February 14, p. 8.

43 For the text of the decree-law, see *LaN,* February 24, 1925, p. 8.

44 *LaN,* February 25, 1925, p. 7.

45 *El Sembrador* 123, February 14, 1925, p. 11; *LaN,* February 21, 1925, p. 8.

46 *Justicia,* March 5, 1925, p. 3; *LaU,* March 28, 1925, p. 5.

47 *LaN,* March 17, 1925, p. 5.

48 *Justicia,* March 28, 1925, p. 5.

49 *ELMS,* April 9, 1925, p. 19; *LaN,* April 11, 1925, p. 14; *Justicia,* April 11, 1925, p. 5. This was also due to the fact that the Alessandri government declared the day a holiday for many government workers as a means of undermining the general strike.

50 *Justicia,* March 21, 1925, p. 3; June 4, p. 6; August 15, p. 2. *LaN,* March 17, 1925, p. 8.

51 Heredia interviews; *Justicia,* August 15, 1925, p. 2. *El Arrendatario* 1, May 16, 1925, p. 3.

52 *Justicia,* May 31, 1925, p. 1.

53 Ibid., September 11, 1925, p. 1.

54 *BOT* 24, 1926, anexo 46.

55 The total size of tenant league membership is unknown, although it appears to have been massive. In May, 1925, the Anarchist Tenant League in Santiago claimed to have 12,000 tenants registered with their organization in the 5th Ward (Ultra Mapocho) alone. *El Arrendatario,* May 30, 1925, p. 4.

56 Ibid., May 23, 1925, p. 3.

57 *Tribuna Libertaira* 20, March, 1925, p. 1.

58 PROFO 371/11126, Annual Report of Santiago Legation, 1925.

59 *LaU,* May 1, 1925, p. 1.

60 Quotation of the British Minister in PROFO 371/11126, Annual Report, 1925. For accounts of the La Coruña massacre, see: Guillermo Kaempffer Villagrán, *Así sucedió* (Santiago, 1962), pp. 247–58; Arnold Roller, "White Terror in Liberal Chile," *The Nation* 121:314–5 (October 14, 1925): 415.

61 PROFO 371/11126, Chile, Annual Report, 1925.

62 *LaN,* June 16, 1925, p. 13; *ELMS,* June 14, 1925, p. 27; *LaU,* June 22, 1925.

63 *La Voz del Mar,* July 17, 1925, p. 3; November 10, 1925, p. 1.

64 *BOT* 24, 1926, anexo 72.

65 Obtained from a month-by-month breakdown of the strikes I recorded as having taken place in Santiago and Valparaíso.

66 *Justicia,* June 18, 1925, p. 1.

67 Ibid., June 19, 1925, p. 1.

68 *LaFOCh,* June 1, 1923, p. 1.

69 Ibid., March 7, 1924, p. 1.

70 *ELMS,* March 3, 1924, p. 10; *ELDI,* March 2, 1924, p. 5; *LaFOCh,* March 4, 1924, p. 1.

71 *Justicia,* December 18, 1924, p. 1.

72 *LaN,* March 10, 1925, p. 8; March 12, p. 5.

73 Labarca, *Historia,* p. 223.

74 For the history of teachers' associations in Chile, see Labarca, *Historia;* and *LaN,* December 29, 1923, p. 9.

75 The newspaper of the Asociación General de Profesores, *Nuevos Rumbos,* is filled with articles by Anarchist writers such as Bakunin, Flores Magón, Angel Samblancat, Rafael Barrett, Malatesta, etc. See *Nuevos Rumbos,* November, 1923–July, 1925.

76 *LaN,* March 21, 1925, p. 1; *Justicia,* March 20, 1925, p. 1.

77 *LaN*, March 21, 1925, p. 1.

78 *LaN*, April 25, 1925, p. 5.

79 *LaN*, June 14, 1925, p. 15. Due either to the new law or increased interest in the upcoming constitutional plebiscite and campaigns, the number of registered votes in the Department of Santiago rose from 38,275 in 1924 to 55,086 in June, 1925.

80 Ricardo Donoso, *Alessandri, agitador y demoleador* (Mexico, 1952), pp. 417–18.

81 *Justicia*, August 4, 1925, p. 1; August 7, p. 1.

82 *LaN*, September 2, 1925, p. 3. According to *La Nacion's* figures, of the 296,259 registered voters, only 137,337 actually cast ballots, 128,381 of them for Alessandri's proposal.

83 *Justicia*, October 13, 1925, p. 1.

84 Police figures breaking down the vote by *comuna* in *LaN*, October 16, 1925, p. 10.

85 Heredia interviews. Salas himself claimed that working class groups of every persuasion pledged their support for his campaign. *LaN*, October 24, 1925, p. 4. There is a further indication of the role of the Anarchists in fattening the Salas vote in the dissimilarities between the presidential and congressional elections of 1925. While Salas gained 28.4 percent of total votes for President, the FOCh and USRACh won only 22 percent in the congressional election, and for the first time in decades, voter turnout was lower for a congressional than a presidential election. Notably, the Anarchists chose not to vote in the congressional election of 1925, lowering the "leftist" percentage and total voter turnout. Drake, *Socialism and Populism*, pp. 58–59.

86 1920 figures from *AE*, "Censo Electoral," 1921, p. 107. 1925 figure from *LaN*, October 25, 1925, p. 13.

87 *AE*, "Censo Electoral," 1921, p. 7; *LaN*, June 14, 1925, p. 15.

88 *Justicia*, October 27, 1925, p. 1; *LaN*, October 26, 1925, p. 10. Some Anarcho-Syndicalist unions, including the Printers' Federation, adhered to the strike, which was a truly interorganizational affair.

89 *Justicia*, November 8, 1925, p. 1; November 14, p. 1. Elías Lafertte, *Vida de un comunista* (Santiago, 1957), p. 183.

90 The Communists were: Reyes, Cruz, Barra, Quevedo, and Sepúlveda Leal. *ELMS*, November 24, 1925, p. 1. Ramírez, in *Origen y formación*, claims only two deputies for the USRACh and seven for the PC.

91 I was not able to find any "official" figures for PC membership, perhaps because the party did not wish to admit its small size. Ramírez, in *Origen y formación*, p. 182, claims the PC had 2,000 members in 1923. In March, 1925, 1,710 members paid their dues, 915 of them from the two northernmost provinces, seventy-five from Viña del Mar, 100 from Santiago, and none from Valparaíso. *Justicia*, April 12, 1925, p. 6. Editorials in *Justicia* frequently bemoaned the fact that the PC was unable to attract adherents.

92 Lafertte and Gil had been members of the Anarcho-Syndicalist Printers' Federation until becoming irrevocably linked with the PC. See Lafertte, *Vida de un comunista*, p. 156.

93 *Justicia,* April 17, 1925, p. 5.

94 Ibid., January 7, 1927, p. 3.

95 *Justicia,* October 17, 1924, p. 5; December 3, p. 3. Ramírez blames Manuel Hidalgo for the rebellious, uncooperative behavior of the Santiago section and for the failure of the party to become a truly Bolshevik organization during the 1920s. Ramírez, *Origen y formación,* pp. 196-205.

96 *Justicia,* January 1, 1926, p. 1.

97 Stephen Clissold, ed., *Soviet Relations with Latin America, 1918-68* (London and New York, 1970), p. 119.

98 *Justicia,* January 7, 1927, p. 1; January 10, p. 3.

99 ADGT, *Comunicaciones recibidas,* 1926, June, letter of the Asociación de Productores de Salitre to the DGT, June 20, 1926; November, 1926, report of DGT Inspector Weber, undated.

100 *Acción Directa* 44, November, 1926, p. 1.

101 *VR* 62, February, 1927, p. 4.

102 *Justicia,* January 15, 1927, p. 4.

103 Comité Pro-Abolición de la Ley 4054, *Boletín* 2, December 13, 1925.

104 *Justicia,* December 11, 1925, p. 3.

105 *LaN,* February 20, 1925, p. 3.

106 *LaN,* February 21, 1925, p. 26.

107 *LaN,* February 23, 1925, p. 14.

108 *LaN,* March 7, 1925, p. 28. In its release, the FOCh claimed to represent the working class of Santiago, calling itself "a powerful syndicalist organization."

109 *Solidaridad* 6, May 1, 1926, p. 1; *Justicia,* October 17, 1926, p. 1. The FOICh also had provincial branches (Valparaíso, Temuco, Chillán), as did the Bakers' Union. The IWW had established local unions of some significance in San Antonio, Talca, and Concepción.

110 ADGT, *Comunicaciones recibidas, Mayo, 1926,* Report of Inspección Feminina, April 1-May 25, 1926.

111 For an account of the strike, see: *Justicia,* January 9, 1927, p. 2. *ELMS,* January 12, 1927, p. 11; January 15, p. 9; January 17, p. 3; January 18, p. 8. *Acción Directa* 47, January 18, 1927, p. 8.

112 USNA, M487, roll 7, telegram from Ambassador Collier to Secretary of State, February 24, 1927. Contains quotation of the Ibáñez declaration.

113 DeShazo, "The IWW," pp. 137-42.

114 Because the raids took place in summertime, small groups of workers were able to flee to Argentina on foot. Luis Heredia was among them. Heredia interviews.

115 I was not able to find any precise figures for the number of arrested workers. The IWW claimed that as of July, 1927, 300 of their members had been imprisoned, indicating that the total for the rest of the labor organizations would be many thousands. *Solidaridad* (Chicago), September 17, 1927, p. 4.

116 DeShazo, "The IWW," pp. 137-42.

117 Heredia interviews. See, for instance, *Rebelión* 1, July, 1928.

118 Santillán interview. See also *Acción Directa* (Buenos Aires) 50, February, 1928.

CONCLUSION

1 Peter N. Stearns, "Measuring the Evolution of Strike Movements," *International Review of Social History* 19:1 (1974): 1–24.

2 As listed in Julio César Jobet, *El Partido Socialista de Chile* (Santiago, 1971), vol. 1, p. 86.

Note on Sources

Newspapers and the records of the General Labor Bureau (DGT) and the Labor Office were the most valuable sources consulted in researching this study. The periodicals collection in the basement of the Biblioteca Nacional in Santiago is absolutely first-rate, well organized, and easy to use. It contains a very large number of catalogued titles of both daily and labor newspapers. For the latter, the study by Osvaldo Arias, *La prensa obrera en Chile*, is a useful research tool but does not mention all of the labor papers in the collection. The International Instituut voor Sociale Geschiedenis in Amsterdam also holds some Chilean labor newspapers, especially those published by Anarcho-Syndicalists from 1900 to 1940 and some organs of the mancomunales of the northern ports from 1902 to 1910. There is surprisingly little overlap between the two collections. The holdings of the IISG are far smaller than the Biblioteca Nacional.

The Archives of the Dirección General del Trabajo contain Labor Office and DGT studies, reports, and inspections carried out from 1906 on. A great deal more material is available for the 1919–27 period than for the earlier years. All volumes are bound and catalogued by year and theme. DGT records are most useful for studying working conditions, food prices, labor contracts, worker housing, migration patterns, and the application of social legislation. Reports on labor unions and strikes are of little statistical use but do give an interesting subjective point of view. Some of the regional studies, such as the 1921 inspection in Valparaíso and the 1922 volumes on the coal zone, are especially complete and valuable sources of information.

The Archivo Nacional de Chile in Santiago's Biblioteca Nacional is a seldom-used but excellent source for studying workers. Because the volumes for the twentieth century were uncatalogued when consulted in 1975, some potentially useful resources may have been overlooked. Police records in the Ministry of Interior volumes and reports from the provincial intendants are the most useful in studying labor unions, riots, major demonstrations, and strikes. During times of cable and newspaper censorship, reporting between the intendants and the Ministry of the Interior was done in code, and the Archivo Nacional volumes often contain both the coded and decoded messages.

Police records for Valparaíso are found not in Santiago but in a very pleasant and well-kept library in the Intendencia of Valparaíso. The Court of Appeals of Valparaíso also has a small library with bound volumes but, alas, the individual *juzgado* cases of more than fifty years lie in an immense dusty pile in the basement of the building.

Consular and embassy reports by British and American diplomats in Chile frequently mention workers, strikes, and labor unions. The Public Record Office volumes in London also contain many letters to the Foreign Office from private companies operating in Chile. Between them, the British and Americans had diplomats in Concepción, Valparaíso, Santiago, Iquique, and Antofagasta during most of the 1902–27 period.

Chilean government statistics are most readily available in the library of the Instituto Nacional de Estadísticas, and the Biblioteca Nacional houses most of the publications of the municipalities of Santiago and Valparaíso, including published police bulletins and reports.

Bibliography

INTERVIEWS

CLOTARIO BLEST. Government worker. Active in the Catholic (White) labor movement in Santiago during the 1920s. Member of the Central Unica de Trabajadores, 1956–73, and at one time its Secretary General. Currently resides in Santiago. Interviewed in Santiago in March and July, 1975.

LUIS HERIDIA. Shoeworker, writer. Machinist at the Sureda shoe factory as a youth in 1912. Member, Federación de Zapateros y Aparadoras, 1917–20. Shop steward, Federación de Obreros y Obreras en Calzado, 1920–21. Secretary General, Unión Industrial del Cuero, 1925–26. Writer, editor for *Solidaridad* and *Tribuna Libertaria*. Imprisoned by Ibáñez in 1928–31. Secretary General, Confederación General del Trabajo, 1936. Currently resides in Santiago. Interviewed in Santiago in March, July, and August, 1975.

FÉLIX LÓPEZ CÁCERES. Master electrician. Member of the IWW Construction Department, Santiago, 1922–27. Escaped to Argentina during the Ibáñez purge, 1927. Leader of the CGT Construction Section, Santiago, 1933–36. Sent by the CGT to Spain, where he fought under the command of Cipriano Mera, 1937. Currently resides in Santiago. Interviewed in Santiago in May and July, 1975.

LUIS MIRANDA SEPÚLVEDA. Master typesetter. Began work as an apprentice printer in the 1920s. Joined the Federación de Obreros de Imprenta de Chile in 1926. Member of the FOICh, 1926–73. Treasurer, 1942. Secretary General, 1947. Member of the CGT during the 1930s. President, Unión de Tipógrafos, 1956, 1965–73. Currently resides in Santiago. Interviewed in Santiago in June, 1975.

AUGUSTÍN PEPAY. Master shoemaker. Owner of "Calzados Pepay," Santiago. Father a shoemaker and bootery owner who employed members of the Federación de Zapateros, 1905–8. Interviewed in Santiago in March, 1975.

DIEGO ABAD DE SANTILLÁN. Writer, intellectual. Member of the anarchist FORA in Argentina during the 1920s. Writer for *La Protesta,* Buenos Aires. Repatriated to Spain in 1930. Member of the Spanish CNT and FAI, 1930–39. A leading figure in the Anarcho-Syndicalist movement in Catalonia during the Spanish Civil War, 1936–39. Author of several books on Argentine and Spanish labor movements. Currently resides in Buenos Aires. Interviewed in Buenos Aires in December, 1974.

333

DANIEL SCHWEITZER. Lawyer. Emigrated to Chile from Argentina at age eleven. Member of the Student Federation (FECh), 1918–22. President, 1921. Defended arrested workers on many occasions, 1920–27. Lawyer for both the FOCh and the FOICh. Deported to Argentina by Altamirano, 1924. Defended the La Coruña prisoners, 1925. Known to be one of the most effective lawyers in defending labor union leaders and arrested workers. Currently resides in Santiago. Interviewed in Santiago in February, 1975.

ARCHIVES

Amsterdam. International Instituut voor Sociale Geschiedenis. Diego Abad de Santillán Archive.

Amsterdam. Internationaal Instituut voor Sociale Geschiedenis. Max Nettlau Archive, section "Libertare Drucke."

London. Public Record Office. Foreign Office. Decimal groups 16, 371.

Santiago. Archivo de la Dirección General del Trabajo. 1907–27.

Santiago. Archivo Nacional de Chile. Records of Ministerio del Interior.

Valparaíso. Archivo de la Intendencia de Valparaíso. Correspondence of the Intendant, Minister of the Interior, and Chief of Police.

Valparaíso. Archivo Judicial, Corte de Apelaciones de Valparaíso.

Washington, D.C. National Archives. Department of State. Microfilm series M-487, "Chile, Internal Affairs, 1910–1929."

Washington, D.C. National Archives. Department of State. Microfilm series M-10, "U.S. Ministers in Chile to Department of State, 1823–1905."

GOVERNMENT AND MUNICIPAL PUBLICATIONS

Concejo de Higiene de Valparaíso. *Archivos del Concejo de Higiene de Valparaíso, primer semestre, 1900, segundo semestre de 1900 a 1903.* 2 vols. Valparaíso: 1907.

Instituto de Higiene de Chile. *Higiene pública en Chile.* Santiago: 1908.

Instituto de Higiene de Santiago. *Boletín de higiene i demografía.* Santiago: 1902–10.

Municipalidad de Santiago. *Boletín municipal de estadística de la ciudad de Santiago.* Santiago: 1908.

Municipalidad de Valparaíso. *Boletín municipal.* Valparaíso: 1903.

Prefectura de Policía de Santiago. *Boletín de la policía de Santiago.* Santiago: 1900–24.

Prefectura de Policía de Santiago. *Guía de informaciones policiales.* Santiago: 1909.

República de Chile. Congreso Nacional. Cámara de Diputados. *Sesiones Ordinarias.* Santiago: 1903, 1905, 1919.

República de Chile. Dirección General de Estadística. *Censo de población de la República de Chile, 1920.* Santiago: 1925.

República de Chile. Dirección General de Estadística, Comisión Central del Censo. *Resultados del X Censo de la población efectuado el 27 de noviembre de 1930.* 2 vols. Santiago: 1931.

República de Chile. Junta Central de Vacuna. *Memoria, 1906*. Santiago: 1907.

República de Chile. Ministerio de Industria y Obras Públicas. *Alcantarillado de Santiago*. 2 vols. Santiago: 1904.

República de Chile. Ministerio de Justicia. *Estadística carcelaria, 1908*. Santiago: 1910.

República de Chile. Ministerio de Justicia. *Estadística criminal, 1900*. Santiago: 1901.

República de Chile. Oficina Central de Estadística. *Anuario estadístico de la Republica de Chile*. Santiago: 1910–27.

República de Chile. Oficina Central de Estadística. *Censo electoral, 1921*. Santiago: 1921.

República de Chile. Oficina Central de Estadística. *Síntesis Estadística*. Santiago: 1915–27.

República de Chile. Oficina Central de Estadística. *Síntesis estadística de la República de Chile, 1904*. Santiago: 1906.

República de Chile. Oficina del Trabajo. *Boletín de la Oficina del Trabajo* (after 1925 called *Boletín de la Dirección General del Trabajo*). Santiago: 1911–27.

República de Chile. Oficina del Trabajo. *Estadística de la asociación obrera*. Santiago: 1910.

República de Chile. Oficina del Trabajo. *Las habitaciones obreras en Chile*. Santiago: 1911.

U.S. Bureau of Labor Statistics. *Monthly Labor Review*. Washington: 1917–27.

PERIODICALS

Associations

Asamblea Tipográfica. *Boletín de la Asamblea Tipográfica*. Santiago: 1903.
Asociación del Trabajo. *Boletín de la Asociación del Trabajo*. Santiago: 1925–26.
Comité Pro-Abolición de la Ley 4054. *Boletín*. Santiago: 1925.
Conference Syndicaliste Internacionale, Berlin. *Bulletín Internacionale*. Berlin: 1922.
International Working Mens' Association. *IWMA News Service*. Berlin: 1928.
International Working Mens' Association. *Servicio de Prensa*. Berlin: 1923–24.
Liga Chilena de Higiene Social. *Memorias*, Santiago: 1921, 1922.
Sociedad de Fomento Fabril. *Boletín de la Sociedad de Fomento Fabril*. Santiago: 1902–27.

Daily and Political Newspapers

(S = Santiago, V = Valparaíso, with years consulted)

The Chilean Times (V). 1903.
El Chileno (S). 1902–8.
La Comuna (S). 1896.
La Democracia (S). 1905.
El Diario Ilustrado (S). 1902–27.
El Ferrocarril (S). 1905–6.
El Heraldo (V). 1902–8.

La Lei (S). 1902–9.
El Mercurio (S). 1902–27.
El Mercurio (V). 1902–27.
La Nación (S). 1912–27.
La Opinión(S). 1917–20.
The Record (V). 1903.
La Reforma (S). 1906–8.
El Socialista (Antofagasta). 1919–20.
The South Pacific Mail (V). 1920–21.
La Unión (V). 1902–27.
La Unión Obrera (S). 1896.

Labor Union Newspapers

Acción Directa (S). 1920–27.
La Ajitación (Estación Dolores, Tarapacá). 1905.
La Ajitación (S). 1901–3.
El Alba (S). 1905–6.
El Arrendatario (S). 1925.
Autonomía y Solidaridad (S). 1924.
La Batalla (S). 1912–15.
La Campaña (S). 1900–1901.
La Campaña Nueva (V). 1924.
Claridad (S). 1920–24.
La Comuna (Viña del Mar). 1919–21.
El Corsario (La Coruña, Spain). 1891–96.
El Deber (Chañaral). 1907–8.
La Evolución (V). 1917.
El Faro (S). 1902–3.
La Federación Chilena del Trabajo (S). 1922.
La Federación Obrera (S). 1921–24. ꞌ
La Federación de Obreros de Imprenta (S). 1918–19.
Freedom (London). 1886–99.
La Gran Federación Obrera de Chile (S). 1910–13.
La Imprenta (S). 1902–3.
Industrial Solidarity (Chicago and Cleveland). 1918–30.
Jerminal! (S). 1904.
Justicia (S). 1924–27.
La Luz (S). 1901–3.
Luz y Vida (Antofagasta). 1909–14.
Mar y Tierra (V). 1911, 1913, 1917, 1920–21.
The Marine Worker (New York). 1923–24.
El Marítimo (Antofagasta). 1905–6.
El Martillo (V). 1902.
Nueva Era (V). 1925.
Nuevos Rumbos (S). 1923–25.

Numen (V, S). 1918–19.
El Obrero Gráfico (V). 1926–27.
El Obrero Metalúrgico (V). 1924–26.
El Obrero Panadero (S). 1924–27.
El Oprimido (S). 1893.
El Oprimido (S). 1906.
El Perseguido (Buenos Aires). 1890–95.
El Productor (S). 1912–13.
El Proletario (Tocopilla). 1904–5.
La Protesta (Buenos Aires). 1927.
La Protesta (S). 1908–12.,
La Protesta Humana (Buenos Aires). 1897–1903.
El Rebelde (S). 1898–99.
Rebelión (S). 1928.
La Rebelión (S). 1901.
El Sembrador (Iquique, V). 1924–27.
El Siglo XX (S). 1901.
El Sindicalista (S). 1918–25.
Solidaridad (Chicago). 1919–27.
Solidaridad (S). 1925–26.
El Surco (Iquique). 1924–25.
Les Temps Nouveaux (Paris). 1895–98.
Tierra y Libertad (Madrid). 1897–1903.
El Trabajo (Coquimbo). 1906–8.
El Trabajo (Iquique). 1903–6.
Tribuna Libertaria (S). 1923–26.
La Tribuna Libre (S). 1910.
La Tromba (S). 1898.
La Unión Gráfica (S). 1916–19.
Valparaíso Gráfico (V). 1918–19.
Verba Roja (S). 1918–27.
La Verdad (S). 1909.
La Voz del Mar (V). 1920, 1924–26.

ARTICLES, BOOKS, AND DISSERTATIONS

Alvarez Andrews, Oscar. *Historia del desarrollo industrial de Chile*. Santiago: 1936.
Anabalón Sanderson, Carlos. *El problema sanitario*. Santiago: 1917.
Angell, Alan. *Politics and the Labour Movement in Chile*. London: 1972.
Arias Escobedo, Osvaldo. *La prensa obrera en Chile*. Santiago: 1970.
Ballesteros, Mario, and Tom E. Davis. "The Growth of Output and Employment in Basic Sectors of the Chilean Economy, 1908-1957," *Economic Development and Cultural Change* 2 (January, 1963):152-76.
Baraona Puelma, Jorge. *El paro forzoso*. Santiago: 1924.
Bari Menezes, David. *El ejército ante las nuevas doctrinas sociales*. Santiago: 1922.

Barrera, Manuel. "Perspectiva histórica de la huelga obrera en Chile," *Cuadernos de la Realidad Nacional* 9 (September, 1971):119-155.

Barría Serón, Jorge. *Los movimientos sociales de principios del siglo, 1900-1910*. Santiago: 1953.

Barría Serón, Jorge. *Los movimientos sociales en Chile desde 1910 hasta 1926*. Santiago: 1960.

Barría, Jorge, Julio César Jobet, and Luis Vitale, *Obras selectas de Luis Emilio Recabarren*. Santiago: 1972.

Bauer, Arnold J. *Chilean Rural Society from the Spanish Conquest to 1930*. Cambridge (England) and New York: 1975.

Bonilla, Frank, and Myron Glazer. *Student Politics in Chile*. New York: 1970.

Calvo MacKenna, Luis. *Encuesta sobre la mortalidad infantil en Chile*. Santiago: 1930.

Cárdenas Soto, Antonio. *El alcoholismo en Chile*. Santiago: 1909.

Carmagnani, Marcelo. *Sviluppo industriale e sottosviluppo economico: il caso cileno, 1860-1920*. Turin: 1971.

Cervantes Cortínez, José Augustín. *Breve estudio sobre las casas de préstamos*. Santiago: 1903.

Clissold, Stephen, ed. *Soviet Relations with Latin America, 1918-68*. London, New York, and Toronto: 1970.

Correa, Hernán. *El alcoholismo y la lei*. Santiago: 1910.

DeShazo, Peter. "The Industrial Workers of the World in Chile, 1917-1927," M.A. thesis, University of Wisconsin-Madison, 1973.

DeShazo, Peter. "Urban Workers and Labor Unions in Chile, 1902-1927." Ph.D. thesis, University of Wisconsin-Madison, 1977.

DeShazo, Peter. "The Valparaíso Maritime Strike of 1903 and the Development of a Revolutionary Labor Movement in Chile," *Journal of Latin American Studies* 2:1 (May, 1979):145-68.

Díaz, Eloísa. *Recopilación de informes del médico-inspector de escuelas públicas de Santiago*. Santiago: 1905.

Díaz Lira, Javier. *Observaciones sobre la cuestión social en Chile*. Santiago: 1904.

Donoso, Ricardo. *Alessandri, agitador y demoleador*. Mexico City: 1952.

Drake, Paul W. *Socialism and Populism in Chile, 1932-1952* Urbana, Chicago, and London: 1978.

Errázuriz Tagle, Jorge, and Guillermo Eyzaguirre. *Monografía de una familia obrera de Santiago*. Santiago: 1903.

Escobar y Carvallo, Alejandro. "La ajitación social en Santiago, Antofagasta, y Iquique," *Occidente* 121 (November-December, 1959):5-13

Escobar y Carvallo, Alejandro. "Inquietudes políticas y gremiales a comienzos del siglo," *Occidente* 120 (October, 1959):5-16.

Espinoza, Enrique. *Geografía descriptiva de la República de Chile*. Santiago: 1897.

Federación de Obreros de Imprenta de Chile. *Estatutos*. Valparaíso: 1921.

Frías Valenzuela, Francisco. *Historia de Chile*. 4 vols. Santiago: 1949.

Fry, E. C. *Tom Barker and the IWW*. Canberra: 1965.

Godio, Julio. *Historia del movimiento obrero latinoamericano*. Vol 1. Mexico City: 1980.

González, Carlos Roberto. *Las huelgas*. Santiago: 1908.

González von Marees, Jorge. *El problema obrero en Chile*. Santiago: 1923.

González Vera, José Santos. "Los estudiantes del año veinte," *Babel* (1945).

Guzmán Bezanilla, José Tomás. *El anarquismo y la lei*. Santiago: 1913.

Halstead, Robert, and Peter DeShazo. "Los Wobblies del Sur: The Industrial Workers of the World in Chile and Mexico," Unpublished paper, 1974.

Hobsbawm, Eric J. *Labouring Men: Studies in the History of Labour*. London: 1964.

Holley, Héctor. *Las huelgas*. Santiago: 1905.

Iñíguez Irrarázaval, Pedro Felipe. *Notas sobre el desarrollo del pensamiento social en Chile, 1901-1906*. Santiago: 1968.

Izquierdo, Gonzalo. "Octubre de 1905. Un episodio en la historia chilena," *Historia* 13 (1976):55-96.

Jobet, Julio César. *Luis Emilio Recabarren*. Santiago: 1955.

Jobet, Julio César. *El partido socialista de Chile*. 2 vols. Santiago: 1971.

Joll, James. *The Anarchists*. New York: 1966.

Kaempffer Villagrán, Guillermo. *Así sucedió*. Santiago: 1962.

Kirsch, William Henry. "The Industrialization of Chile, 1880-1930," Ph.D. dissertation, University of Florida, 1973.

Labarca Huberson, Amanda. *Historia de la enseñanza en Chile*. Santiago: 1939.

Lafertte, Elías. *Vida de un comunista*. Santiago: 1957.

Lagos Valenzuela, Tulio. *Bosquejo histórico del movimiento obrero en Chile*. Santiago: 1941.

León Echaíz, René. *Nuñohue: Historia de Nuñoa, Providencia, Las Condes, y La Reina*. Santiago: 1972.

López, Osvaldo. *Diccionario biográfico obrero: libro precursor*. Concepción: 1910.

López, Osvaldo. *Diccionario biográfico obrero*. Vol. 2. Santiago: 1912.

Loveman, Brian. *Struggle in the Countryside—Politics and Rural Labor in Chile, 1919-1973*. Bloomington:1976.

Maram, Sheldon. "Anarchism, Immigrants, and the Brazilian Labor Movement." Ph.D. thesis, University of California–Santa Barbara, 1975.

Maram, Sheldon. "Anarcho-syndicalism in Brazil," *Proceedings of the Pacific Coast Council in Latin American Studies*, Vol. 4, 1975.

Maram, Sheldon. "Labor and the Left in Brazil, 1890-1921: A Movement Aborted," *Hispanic American Historical Review* 57:2 (May, 1977):254-72.

Marín R., Osvaldo. *Las habitaciones para obreros*. Santiago: 1903.

Miquel R., Juan I. *De la vacuna obligatoria*. Santiago: 1903.

Miqueles, Alejandro. *Recopilación policial*. Santiago: 1917.

Miranda Sepúlveda, Luis. "Reseña histórica de la FOEICh," *Boletín de la FOEICh, Edición especial del centenario de la Federación de Obreros y Empleados de Imprenta de Chile*. Santiago: 1972.

Montenegro, Aurelio. *Estudio general de la industria fabril de Chile*. Santiago: 1947.

Monteón, Michael. "The Nitrate Miners and the Origins of the Chilean Left, 1880-1925." Ph.D. thesis, Harvard University, 1974.

Morris, James O. *Elites, Intellectuals, and Consensus*. Ithaca, N.Y.: 1966.

Muñoz, Oscar. *Crecimiento industrial de Chile, 1914–1965*. Santiago: 1968.

Nettlau, Max. "Contribución a la bibliografía anarquista de la América Latina hasta 1914," *Certamen Internacional* of *La Protesta*. Buenos Aires: 1927.

La nueva guía y plano de Santiago. Santiago: 1910.

Nunn, Frederick. *Chilean Politics, 1921–1931*. Albuquerque: 1970.

Ortíz, Samuel. *Vicios electorales*. Santiago: 1909.

Ortúzar, Adolfo. *Chile of To-Day*. New York: 1907.

Paz, Abel. *Durruti, the People Armed*. Montreal: 1976.

Peña Otaegui, Carlos. *Santiago de siglo en siglo*. Santiago: 1944.

Pepper, Charles M. *Panama to Patagonia*. Chicago: 1906.

Pérez Canto, Julio. *Las habitaciones para obreros*. Santiago: 1898.

Petras, James. *Politics and Social Forces in Chilean Development*. Berkeley, Los Angeles, and London: 1972.

Pike, Frederick. *Chile and the United States, 1880–1962*. Notre Dame: 1962.

Pinto Lagarrigue, Fernando. *Crónica política del siglo XX: desde Errázuriz Echaúrren hasta Alessandri*. Santiago: 1970.

Poblete Troncoso, Moisés. *La organización sindical en Chile y otros estudios sociales*. Santiago: 1926.

Polloni Roldán, Alberto. *Las fuerzas armadas de Chile en la vida nacional*. Santiago: 1972.

Prado Martínez, Alberto. *Anuario Prado Martínez*. Santiago: 1903.

Ramírez Necochea, Hernán. *Historia del movimiento obrero en Chile, siglo XIX*. Santiago: 1956.

Ramírez Necochea, Hernán. *Origen y formación del partido comunista de Chile*. Santiago: 1965.

Recabarren Rojas, Floreal. *Historia del proletariado de Tarapacá y Antofagasta, 1884–1913*. Santiago: 1954.

Reinsh, Paul S. "Parliamentary Government in Chile," *American Political Science Review* 3 (November, 1909):507–38.

Rivas Vicuña, Manuel. *Historia política y parlamentaria de Chile*. 3 vols. Santiago: 1964.

Rojas, Manuel. *Lanchas en la bahía*. Santiago: 1932.

Roller, Arnold. "White Terror in Liberal Chile," *The Nation* 121:3145 (October, 1925):415.

Rowe, Leo S. *The Early Effects of the European War upon the Finance, Commerce, and Industry of Chile*. Washington: 1918.

Ruíz, Ramón Eduardo. *Labor and the Ambivalent Revolutionaries: Mexico, 1911–1923*. Baltimore: 1976.

Sánchez Albornoz, Nicolás. *The Population of Latin America—A History*. Berkeley: 1974.

Santillán, Diego Abad de. "La Protesta, su historia, sus diversas bases, y su significación en el movimiento anarquista en América del Sur," *Certamen Internacional* of *La Protesta*. Buenos Aires: 1927.

Santiván, Fernando. *Memorias de un tolstoyano*. Santiago: 1955.

Schweitzer, Daniel. "Juan Gandulfo," *Babel* 7 (1945):15–30.

Scobie, James R. *Buenos Aires: Plaza to Suburb, 1870–1910.* New York: 1974.

Segall, Marcelo. "En Amerique Latine, development du movement ouvier et proscription," in "1871: Jalons pour une histoire de la Commune de Paris." *International Review of Social History* 17 (1972): 325–69.

Segall, Marcelo. "Biografía social de la ficha salaria," *Mapocho* 2:2 (1964):98–130.

Segall, Marcelo. *El desarrollo del capitalismo en Chile.* Santiago: 1953.

Segall, Marcelo. *Las luchas de clase en las primeras décadas de la república de Chile.* Santiago: 1962.

Shorter, Edward, and Charles Tilly. *Strikes in France, 1830–1968.* Cambridge, England: 1974.

Skidmore, Thomas E. "Workers and Soldiers: Urban Labor Movements and Elite Responses in Twentieth-Century Latin America," In Virginia Bernhard, ed., *Elites, Masses, and Modernization in Latin America, 1850–1930.* Austin and London: 1979.

Sociedad de Fomento Fabril. *Estadística industrial de la Provincia de Santiago.* Santiago: 1906.

Sociedad de Fomento Fabril. *Resúmenes generales de la estadística industrial.* Santiago: 1908.

Solberg, Carl. *Immigration and Nationalism, Argentina and Chile, 1890–1914.* Austin and London: 1970.

Spaulding, Hobart A., Jr. *Organized Labor in Latin America. Historical Case Studies of Workers in Dependent Societies,* New York: 1977.

Stearns, Peter N. " Measuring the Evolution of Strike Movements," *International Review of Social History* 19:1 (1974):1–24.

Stearns, Peter N. "National Character and European Labor History" In Peter N. Stearns and Daniel J. Walkowitz, eds., *Workers in the Industrial Revolution.* New Brunswick, N.J.: 1974.

Stickell, Arthur Lawrence. "Migration and Mining: Labor in Northern Chile in the Nitrate Era, 1880–1930," Ph.D. thesis, Indiana University, 1979.

Tilly, Charles. "Collective Violence in European Perspective," In Hugh Graham and Ted Gurr, eds., *The History of Violence in America.* New York: 1969.

Ugarte, Juan de Dios. *Valparaíso, 1536–1910.* Valparaíso: 1910.

Véliz, Claudio. *Historia de la Marina Mercante de Chile.* Santiago: 1961.

Venegas Cabello, Oscar. *La Dirección General del Trabajo.* Santiago: 1942.

Vicuña Fuentes, Carlos. *En las prisiones políticas de Chile.* Santiago: 1932.

Vicuña Fuentes, Carlos. *La tiranía en Chile.* 2 vols. Santiago: 1938.

Vicuña Subercaseaux, Benjamín. *El socialismo revolucionario y la cuestión social en Europa y en Chile.* Santiago: 1908.

Vitale, Luis. *Historia del movimiento obrero.* Santiago:1962.

Woodcock, George. *Anarchism.* London: 1963.

Yoast, Richard. "The Development of Argentine Anarchism: A Socio-Ideological Analysis," Ph.D. thesis, University of Wisconsin–Madison, 1975.

Zig-Zag. *Directorio de Santiago.* Santiago: 1913.

Zilleruelo, César E. *El alcoholismo en Chile i su relación con la criminalidad y la locura.* Santiago: 1909.

Index

350

COMPOSED BY LANDMANN ASSOCIATES INC., MADISON, WISCONSIN
MANUFACTURED BY CUSHING MALLOY, INC., ANN ARBOR, MICHIGAN
TEXT IS SET IN TIMES ROMAN, DISPLAY LINES IN WEISS

Library of Congress Cataloging in Publication Data
DeShazo, Peter, 1947–
Urban workers and labor unions in Chile, 1902–1927.
Bibliography: pp. 333–341.
Includes index.
1. Labor and laboring classes—Chile—History.
2. Trade-unions—Chile—History. I. Title.
HD8296.D46 1983   331.88′0983   82-70557
ISBN 0-299-09220-8